Protocols and Applications for the Industrial Internet of Things

Cristian González García
University of Oviedo, Spain

Vicente García-Díaz
University of Oviedo, Spain

B. Cristina Pelayo García-Bustelo
University of Oviedo, Spain

Juan Manuel Cueva Lovelle
University of Oviedo, Spain

A volume in the Advances in Business Information Systems and Analytics (ABISA) Book Series

IGI Global
DISSEMINATOR OF KNOWLEDGE

Published in the United States of America by
IGI Global
Business Science Reference (an imprint of IGI Global)
701 E. Chocolate Avenue
Hershey PA, USA 17033
Tel: 717-533-8845
Fax: 717-533-8661
E-mail: cust@igi-global.com
Web site: http://www.igi-global.com

Library of Congress Cataloging-in-Publication Data

Names: Gonzalez Garcia, Cristian, 1985- editor. | Garc?ia D?iaz, Vicente, 1981- editor. | Pelayo Garc?ia-Bustelo, Begona Cristina, 1971- editor. | Cueva Lovelle, Juan Manuel, editor.
Title: Protocols and applications for the industrial internet of things / Cristian Gonzalez Garcia, Vicente Garcia-Diaz, B. Cristina Pelayo Garcia-Bustelo, and Juan Manuel Cueva Lovelle, editors.
Description: Hershey, PA : Business Science Reference, [2018] | Includes bibliographical references.
Identifiers: LCCN 2017022432| ISBN 9781522538059 (hardcover) | ISBN 9781522538066 (ebook)
Subjects: LCSH: Internet of things--Industrial applications--Handbooks, manuals, etc. | Information resources management--Handbooks, manuals, etc..
Classification: LCC TK5105.8857 .P76 2018 | DDC 004.67/8--dc23 LC record available at https://lccn.loc.gov/2017022432

This book is published in the IGI Global book series Advances in Business Information Systems and Analytics (ABISA) (ISSN: 2327-3275; eISSN: 2327-3283)

British Cataloguing in Publication Data
A Cataloguing in Publication record for this book is available from the British Library.

All work contributed to this book is new, previously-unpublished material.
The views expressed in this book are those of the authors, but not necessarily of the publisher.

For electronic access to this publication, please contact: eresources@igi-global.com.

Advances in Business Information Systems and Analytics (ABISA) Book Series

ISSN:2327-3275
EISSN:2327-3283

Editor-in-Chief: Madjid Tavana, La Salle University, USA

MISSION

The successful development and management of information systems and business analytics is crucial to the success of an organization. New technological developments and methods for data analysis have allowed organizations to not only improve their processes and allow for greater productivity, but have also provided businesses with a venue through which to cut costs, plan for the future, and maintain competitive advantage in the information age.

The **Advances in Business Information Systems and Analytics (ABISA) Book Series** aims to present diverse and timely research in the development, deployment, and management of business information systems and business analytics for continued organizational development and improved business value.

COVERAGE

- Business Intelligence
- Information Logistics
- Data Analytics
- Algorithms
- Data Management
- Geo-BIS
- Statistics
- Legal information systems
- Performance Metrics
- Data Governance

IGI Global is currently accepting manuscripts for publication within this series. To submit a proposal for a volume in this series, please contact our Acquisition Editors at Acquisitions@igi-global.com or visit: http://www.igi-global.com/publish/.

The Advances in Business Information Systems and Analytics (ABISA) Book Series (ISSN 2327-3275) is published by IGI Global, 701 E. Chocolate Avenue, Hershey, PA 17033-1240, USA, www.igi-global.com. This series is composed of titles available for purchase individually; each title is edited to be contextually exclusive from any other title within the series. For pricing and ordering information please visit http://www.igi-global.com/book-series/advances-business-information-systems-analytics/37155. Postmaster: Send all address changes to above address.

Titles in this Series

For a list of additional titles in this series, please visit:
https://www.igi-global.com/book-series/advances-business-information-systems-analytics/37155

Value Sharing for Sustainable and Inclusive evelopment
Mario Risso (Niccolò Cusano University, Italy) and Silvia Testarmata (Niccolò Cusano University, Italy)
Business Science Reference • ©2018 • 398pp • H/C (ISBN: 9781522531470) • US $245.00

Supporting Innovation Through National R&D Programs Emerging Research...
Amiram Porath (Independent Researcher, Israel)
Business Science Reference • ©2018 • 158pp • H/C (ISBN: 9781522536529) • US $145.00

Always-On Enterprise Information Systems for Modern Organizations
Nijaz Bajgoric (University of Sarajevo, Bosnia and Herzegovina)
Business Science Reference • ©2018 • 257pp • H/C (ISBN: 9781522537045) • US $215.00

Knowledge Integration Strategies for Entrepreneurship and Sustainability
Neeta Baporikar (Namibia University of Science and Technology, Namibia & University of Pune, India)
Business Science Reference • ©2018 • 413pp • H/C (ISBN: 9781522551157) • US $265.00

Business Architectures for Risk Assessment and Strategic Planning Emerging Research...
James McKee (Wollongong University, Australia)
Business Science Reference • ©2018 • 118pp • H/C (ISBN: 9781522533924) • US $155.00

Handbook of Research on Emergent Applications of Optimization Algorithms
Pandian Vasant (Universiti Teknologi Petronas, Malaysia) Sirma Zeynep Alparslan-Gok (Suleyman Demirel University, Turkey) and Gerhard-Wilhelm Weber (Middle East Technical University, Turkey)
Business Science Reference • ©2018 • 812pp • H/C (ISBN: 9781522529903) • US $445.00

Cloud Computing Technologies for Green Enterprises
Kashif Munir (University of Hafr Al-Batin, Saudi Arabia)
Business Science Reference • ©2018 • 424pp • H/C (ISBN: 9781522530381) • US $215.00

For an entire list of titles in this series, please visit:
https://www.igi-global.com/book-series/advances-business-information-systems-analytics/37155

IGI Global
DISSEMINATOR OF KNOWLEDGE

701 East Chocolate Avenue, Hershey, PA 17033, USA
Tel: 717-533-8845 x100 • Fax: 717-533-8661
E-Mail: cust@igi-global.com • www.igi-global.com

Editorial Advisory Board

Table of Contents

Detailed Table of Contents

actors in vertical manufacturing cells that are horizontally coupled in end-to-end manufacturing processes. The HORSE system supports advanced dynamic actor allocation to work cells, direct robot control and human actor instruction, closed-loop local event processing, and near-real-time global event processing. The system handles abstract process definitions and status information on the one hand and directly interfaces to industrial sensors and actuators on the other hand, making it a system with a strong cyber-physical character. The physical side of the system is deployed in an internet-of-things context, where the things are the industrial robots controlled by the HORSE system, the sensors feeding data to the system, and the products being manufactured in the industrial process managed by the system. The system will be deployed in real-world, industrial pilot scenarios in a European Horizon 2020 project.

The industrial IoT marching towards the digital twin and the broad spectrum of applications need the specialized low power protocols for communication and data transfer. This chapter provides a comprehensive discussion on the challenges, opportunities, use cases, platforms, and protocols for the deployment of low power protocols in the context of IoT applications. Moreover, discussion extends to the various custom techniques for energy saving in the communication of sensors to hardware, hardware to Cloud, and deferred data pushing in edge computing. The traditional wireless data transfer and communication protocols are suitable in case of the hardware platforms connected with seamless power supply. However, there is need of low power protocols 6LoWPAN, LoRaWAN, Sub 1, ZigBee, BLE, NFC, and other telecommunication protocols across several IoT applications. The SBCs and micro-controllers are not always equipped with these protocol-enabled hardware. This chapter addresses the suitable hardware and combination with low energy options as per the budget, range, and specifications.

This chapter focuses on the comprehensive contents of various applications and principles related to Bluetooth low energy (BLE). The internet of things (IoT) applications like indoor localization, proximity detection problem by using Bluetooth low energy, and enhancing the sales in the commercial market by using BLE have the same database requirement and common implementation idea. The real-world applications are complex and require intensive computation. These computations should take less time, cost, and battery power. The chapter mainly focuses on the usage of BLE beacons for indoor localization. The motive behind the study of BLE devices is that it is supported by mobile smart devices that augment its application exponentially.

The major drawback of the industrial internet of things is the lack of interoperability across the plethora of IoT platforms. Cross-platform services often require the development of complex software components for protocol translation, device discovery, and thing lifecycle management. As a result, these systems are too expensive and hard to develop. The W3C Consortium launched the Web of Things Working Group to develop the standards for open interoperability in the internet of things. This chapter presents the web of things specifications for systems architecture and communication protocols and how they can be applied in industrial domains, building the industrial web of things. Finally, this chapter shows that this industrial web of things is built upon a network of systems and devices linked with universal open standards such as enterprise systems, which are nowadays communicated through the conventional "web of pages," as a key player in the Industry 4.0 revolution.

The future internet is expected to be an internet of things (IoT) that makes a huge increase in its capability to collect, investigate, and distribute data that can be turned into information or knowledge. The changeover to IPv6, having a common set of standards and developing energy sources for millions of minute sensors, are the challenges of IoT. The environment can be made smart and self-aware by the direct communication between more and more devices that are part of the IoT. The low power lossy networks (LLNs) that consist of more tiny sensors and low power devices are the elements of the IoT. The TCP/IP reference model is used for the internet connectivity, which is not exactly suited for the network that uses smart objects. There is a need to connect the local network that has the smart objects to the internet. The Internet Engineering Task Force (IETF) has come out with the standardized protocols like 6LoWPAN, RPL, COAP, etc. This chapter provides the various protocols used in the internet of things network with their specifications, benefits, and limitations.

New paradigms such as pervasive computing, cloud computing, and the internet of things (IoT) are transforming the software industry and the business world. Organizations need to redesign their models and processes to be sustainable. Smartphones are at the core of these paradigms, letting us locate and easily interact with the world around us. Frequently, the development of mobile software requires of the adaption of valuable and tested non-mobile software. Most challenges in this kind of software modernization are related to the diversity of platforms on the smartphones market and to the need of systematic and reusable processes with a high degree of automation that reduce time, cost, and risks. This chapter proposes a modernization framework based on model-driven engineering (MDE). It allows integrating legacy code with the native behaviors of the different mobile platform through cross-platform languages. Realizations of the framework for the migration of C/C++ or Java code to mobile platforms through the Haxe multiplatform language are described.

IoT, big data, and artificial intelligence are currently three of the most relevant and trending pieces for innovation and predictive analysis in healthcare. Many healthcare organizations are already working on developing their own home-centric data collection networks and intelligent big data analytics systems based on machine-learning principles. The benefit of using IoT, big data, and artificial intelligence for community and population health is better health outcomes for the population and communities. The new generation of machine-learning algorithms can use large standardized data sets generated in healthcare to improve the effectiveness of public health interventions. A lot of these data come from sensors, devices,

Preface

In the last years, we have lived a revolution in the world because, nowadays objects that can be considered intelligent or Smart Objects like sensors and actuators, together with their integration with the Internet of Things (IoT) is creating a new world that is trying to interconnect all the objects among themselves. This has given the opportunity of leveraging the whole collected information by the sensors, using this information in the Cloud, maybe through a personal server or by using some third-party Cloud service. In this Cloud, we could make the required computation to expand the possibilities of computation and storage of smart objects. In addition, we can use this Cloud to interconnect the objects, using different protocols and types of messages.

The classic and indefatigable example about the Internet of Things is the smart fridge. This fridge, in a near future, will call our smartphone when we are in the supermarket to notify us about what we have to buy. Or even, if we move forward in the future, our own servant robot will do this type of task while it talks and socialises with its friends, who will maybe be other smart electrical appliances that will stay in our house providing other services to us, like a tea pot, the TV, our car, or who knows what.

The Internet of Things is the interconnection of heterogeneous and ubiquitous objects among themselves. Currently, many people have things to make possible an IoT network. People have in their daily life many objects with Internet connection like smartphones, tablets, Smart TVs, micro-controllers, Smart Tags, computers, laptops, cars, sensors and actuators. With these things, people have heterogeneous objects because these are of different types and at the same time, they have ubiquitous objects because these objects are installed in different places and some of them can be moved around the world. If we think about this, we could already think that we are already living in the Internet of Things era.

However, the Internet of Things is a very big field with five subfields that are very important, such as Smart Homes to improve our daily life, the Industrial Internet of Things to create safer and easier jobs, Smart Towns to recover the livability and traditions, Smart Cities to improve the citizens' life, and Smart Earth to protect our world.

With the IoT, we can create an enormous network to interconnect objects and facilitate our daily life. Some examples of IoT applications are the next:

- To improve the life of the people with Smart Homes with the use of a Smart Fridge to help, for instance, ill people.
- To facilitate the garden maintenance with the use of Smart Objects and automations.
- To improve the tracking of deliveries, objects' situation in the supply chain, to improve the factory's production, or the security in industries.
- To improve the security of monuments, protecting the heritage and culture of towns, and their livability.
- To improve Smart Cities by helping citizens in their daily life, for instance, to park, avoid traffic jams, automate traffic lights, change the public transport in real time and so on.
- To prevent natural disasters, to automate actions in farms, or to obtain data about the ecosystem in order to protect the fauna and flora according to certain situations, which is known as Smart Earth.

This book will show the information about the different protocols that people can use to interconnect the different objects that build the Internet of Things. These objects can send us information about almost anything in any environment. However, one of the most important is the industry.

The Internet of Things was born in the industry, from the hand of Kevin Ashton, years ago. Notwithstanding, companies continue developing their systems every day to improve the efficiency of their machines and vehicles, save money, and create a better, easy, and safer job for the workers.

Here, they have to interconnect objects, which have a lack of standards and many different protocols of different levels with a lot of differences in the range, type of messages, energy consumption and many other parameters to be taken into account. Then, which one is the best? That depends on what we want to do and create. Then, it is here where this book could help everyone to solve their doubts, as it contains information about different protocols and different use cases that show possible applications for the Industrial Internet of Things.

The mission of this book is to bring researchers, practitioners, and students to one of the most promising fields in computer science, helping all of them to understand the current state of the art on the Industrial Internet of Things as well as the protocols that are used and different example applications. In addition, it will also explain what the future will bring. The objectives include:

- Bringing together the most relevant research on the Industrial Internet of Things.
- Updating the scientific literature on the Industrial Internet of Things.
- Identifying and addressing the complexities encountered in the application of the Industrial Internet of Things engineering technologies. Specifically, in how to interconnect and send data and how to manage huge quantities of data.
- Identifying the most important issues to be addressed by scientists in the coming years.

The target audience of this book will be composed of professionals and researchers working in the field of the Industrial Internet of Things in various disciplines. Moreover, the book will also be a reference for researchers, professionals, and students in computer science and related fields. It will provide a much-needed reference on the state of the art of the protocols that can be used to send data in the IoT. It will also include different examples of this field in the industry, different techniques that supports how to manage such data, different case studies in the industry, and the simplification and facilities to create these applications. On the other hand, it will provide foundations to professionals, researchers, and academics on the underlying theory and current applications for its use in the future advancement of the existing body of knowledge. This combination of theory, applications, and successful stories will provide the reader with an important and detailed view of the recent developments in the field and lay the background for future research.

This book will contain different topics about the most important areas and challenges in the Internet of Things. In the book, you will be able to read about the different protocols that are used in the Internet of Things and different IoT applications in the industry, also known as Industrial Internet of Things.

For instance, it is very important to understand the different options that we have to interconnect the applications using different protocols due to the differences that each protocol represents in different terms: range, energy, message types, security and so on. Using these protocols, we can send and manage the data that is obtained from different Smart Objects, maybe using a secure protocol or messages when the data is sent through insecure protocols.

In this book, readers can find different examples where these protocols have been used, information about them and the characteristics of each protocol, together with comparisons among them. Furthermore, the book contains some examples about how to manage the enormous data that is created in the IoT using Big Data and Machine Learning, how to prepare applications, and the IoT ecosystem with devices like the Raspberry Pi, examples of the use of protocols in Smart Cities, and facilities to create applications for the Industrial Internet of Things.

In the first chapter, we can read a state of the art about advanced visualisation systems in industrial environments written by Manuel Pérez-Cota, Miguel R. González-Castro, and María Díaz Rodríguez, entitled 'Advanced Visualization Systems in Industrial Environments: Accessible Information in Any Factory Place'. In this chapter, they talk about the displays that we can found in industry to obtain information about the industrial process.

The second chapter contains information about the HORSE system, which integrates human and robots in a manufacturing process and will be deployed in real world as a part of a European Horizon 2020 project. The chapter is entitled 'Developing a Cyber-Physical System for Hybrid Manufacturing in an Internet-of-Things Context' and the authors are Paul Grefen, Irene Vanderfeesten, and Georgios Boultadakis.

'Low Power Communication Protocols for IoT-Enabled Applications' is the title of the third chapter, which has been written by Manoj Himmatrao Devare. This chapter provides a discussion on the challenges, opportunities, use cases, platforms and protocols for the deployment of low power protocols for IoT applications.

Chapter 4 is 'Bluetooth Low-Energy-Based Applications: The State of Art' and presents a state of the art about IoT applications that use the Bluetooth Low Energy protocol. It was written by Smita Sanjay Ambarkar and Rakhi Dattatraya Akhare.

The next chapter, number five, was written by six members of the CTIC technology centre of Spain: Ángel Retamar, Daniel Ibaseta, Andrés G. Mangas, Iván Gallego, Irene Alonso Canella and Lucía Fernández. This chapter is about how the Web of Things could solve the problems of the Industrial Internet of Things using a standard from the W3C. Thus, they present the specification of that standard and how it should be applied in industry. The title is 'An Introduction to IWoT: How the Web of Things Helps Solve Industry 4.0 Challenges'.

In 'Communication Protocols for the Internet of Things', which is the Chapter 6, written by S. Umamaheswari, we can read a state of the art about the different communication protocols that we can find in the Internet of Things: their specification, benefits, and limitations.

Chapter 7 is 'A Framework for Modernising Non-Mobile Software: A Model-Driven Engineering Approach' by Liliana Maria Favre. In this chapter, the author presents a framework based on Model-Driven Engineering to develop software for mobile devices in an easier way.

Fernando Enrique Lopez Martinez and Edward Rolando Núñez-Valdez are the authors of 'Big Data and Machine Learning: A Way to Improve Outcomes in Population Health Management', the eighth chapter. They have focused this chapter in a case study about the Healthcare system that uses the Internet of Things, Big Data, and Artificial Intelligence to improve the effectiveness of public health interventions in Cartagena, Colombia.

Another case study is presented in Chapter 9, 'Smart City Based on MQTT Using Wireless Sensors'. In this chapter, the authors, Monika Bharatbhai Patel, Chintan Bhatt, Hamed Vahdat-Nejad, Hardik B. Patel, have explained the use of the MQTT protocol in a Smart City observing information of a remote area using wireless sensors.

Manoj Himmatrao Devare has written Chapter 10, which is entitled 'Preparation of Raspberry Pi for IoT-Enabled Applications'. It provides a guide to prepare a Raspberry Pi for the use of this microcomputer in an IoT environment, and to help people in this arduous task, a state of the art of their uses and a comparison between different protocols.

Finally, Chapter 11 is 'IoT and Big Data in Public Health: A Case Study in Colombia' by Fernando Enrique Lopez Martinez, Maria Claudia Bonfante, Ingrid Gonzalez, and Ruby Elena Muñoz Baldiris. This chapter shows a case study about the use of the Internet of Things and Big Data to try to control the blood pressure in patients with hypertension, the needed software, and the recommendations that people have to know about the use of this kind of software.

As a conclusion, we think that the book can be used to learn the new challenges related to the Industrial Internet of Things and the protocols that can be used to interconnect the different heterogeneous and ubiquitous objects in the Internet of Things. Moreover, chapters provide enough literature on a range of different topics such as the current state of the art and different case studies about the healthcare in Colombia, the use of protocols and a Raspberry Pi in the Internet of Things, and a case study about Smart Cities. Besides, we can see the new research lines in which we will work in the coming years regarding the Internet of Things.

Acknowledgment

We want to thank all the authors that have sent a chapter to this book, who have given their best effort in writing good chapters and correcting them, and to all the reviewers who have done a great job reading and suggesting improvements for each chapter.

Chapter 1
Advanced Visualization Systems in Industrial Environments:
Accessible Information in Any Factory Place

Manuel Pérez-Cota
University of Vigo, Spain

Miguel R. González-Castro
University of Vigo, Spain

María Díaz Rodríguez
University of Vigo, Spain

ABSTRACT

Today's advanced visualization systems will revolutionize the way information is perceived in industrial environments. This will help the different industrial workers to interact more efficiently with the machines, equipment, and systems installed in the industrial plant. The display devices will provide operators with all the information they need to perform their work more efficiently, as well as inform them of all the hazards and safety in their environment. Also, screen operators, thanks to the use of a single 2.5D/3D screen, will possess exhaustive knowledge of the state of the industrial process. This increases the amount on quantity and quality of information that is offered to the operator and it avoids the superfluous navigation between operation screens. This chapter explores advanced visualization systems in industrial environments.

DOI: 10.4018/978-1-5225-3805-9.ch001

INTRODUCTION

Industrial visualization systems have evolved because new computer display devices are being developed. The first industrial display systems were introduced with the birth of the DCS (Distributed Control System). This was and is a control equipment used principally in the continuous process industry (steel, cement, paper, etc.). This type of industry is characterized because it has a critical production process, in which any failure or stop can create very dangerous situations, both for the environment and for people. 40% of these faults are attributable to errors or failures of operation (McMahon, 2015), which implies that the efficiency of the operators becomes a critical element of this industry. This transforms the information offered to the operator in a fundamental area of improvement and any innovation that helps in the development of his/her work will generate an increase in the safety of the industrial process.

This paper takes a tour through the various types of industrial display systems. This journey begins with the primitive screens of the first DCS, a summary of the current industrial visualization systems, it continues with the imminent possibilities that will result from adapting of the new technologies of computer visualization to the industrial systems, watching them as Internet of Things, that are them at the end.

The first section of this document details the historical evolution of the DCS operating screens. The following section describes the state-of-the-art of current DCS operation screens. The next section examines the uses of Monocular AR (Augmented Reality) glasses in industrial environments. Next, different functions are analysed that can be done by the use of systems with binocular Augmented Reality glasses, when applied to the different industrial areas. The antepenultimate section explores the uses of virtual reality in today's industrial world. The penultimate section examines some innovative industrial management applications in 2.5D/3D environments. This type of interface increases the quantity and quality of information that is perceived by the operator; as it displays on a single 2.5D/3D graphic display the contents of a set of old 2D DCS operator displays. The last section describes the experiences of the operators who tested this interface.

EVOLUTION OF DCS OPERATOR SCREENS

DCS are devices that manage several thousands of analogic and digital signals; and also, have a distributed architecture, which increases considerably their reliability and availability. However, its essential feature is the intensive interaction with the operator, since he/she is the one who has to do the key decisions about the operation of the process under his/her control.

The first DCS marketed in 1975 by Honeywell and called TDC 2000. The operator interface, Figure 1, of the DCS of this time based on a CRT (Cathode Ray Tube), which allowed a very elementary representation of the data of the industrial process. The monitor was connected directly to the DCS or was connected via a serial communication port. This operator display showed the information in textual format and through bar diagrams, which limited the amount of process data that could be viewed. Also, the format was very unintuitive and forced the operator to do an effort to interpret the numerical values he/she perceived. Finally, the operator had a keypad and/or keyboard to send commands to the DCS.

The 1980s began with the birth of the IBM PC in 1981, which became a turning point in the world of computing, as it promoted the universalization of computers at a reasonable cost. This led to the generalization of the mouse or the increased performance in microprocessors, memories, peripherals and graphics cards. This resulted in the appearance of DCS screens that included elementary diagrams of the process chart, which grouped in a hierarchical structure to facilitate the visualization

Figure 1. DCS Console at the end of 70s

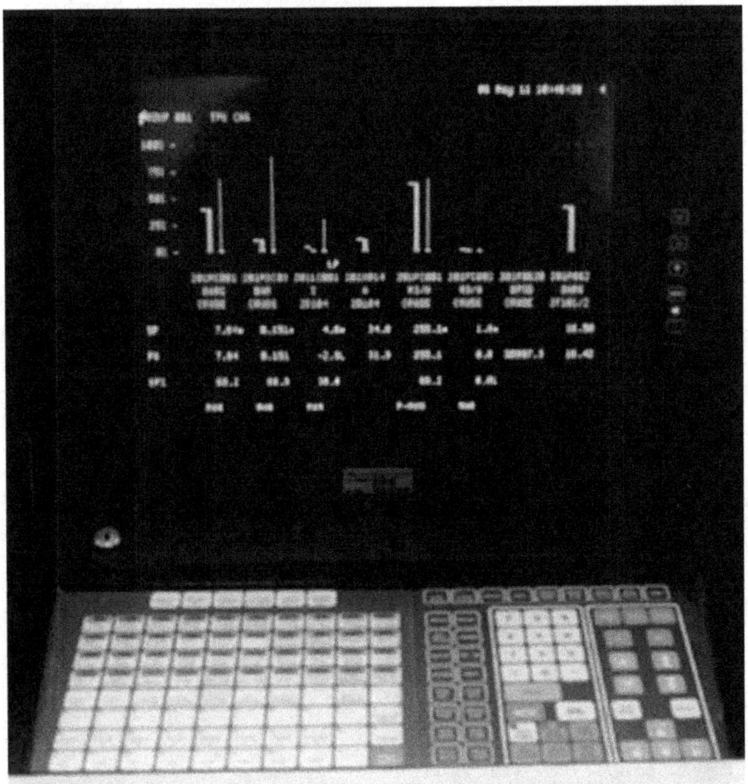

of the different stages of the industrial process, "Figure 2". However, the screens still had too much information in numerical format, which the operator had to decipher and understand in order to have an exact situation awareness of the process. The operator's command input interface transformed into the keyboard and mouse.

The 1990s began with the commercialization of the "Windows 3.0" operating environment in 1990, as well as the launch of the "Windows NT 3.1" operating system in 1993. Also in this decade the use of LAN and multimedia systems got popular. All these advances resulted in the use of personal computers or workstations as DCS operator consoles. This led to the appearance of complex graphic figures, which allowed the state of the industrial process to be shown through textual, numerical and graphic information. This graphic information used colours, levels, animations, etc., which was complemented by the use of pop-up windows that informed in more detail of the selected component. Likewise, the graphic O. S. allowed operators to display several process screens (windows) on the same monitor. The industrial process of these screens was a quasi-copy of the flowcharts used in the piping and instrumentation planes. The use of high-speed data networks provided greater transfer of information between the operator and the DCS. All this allowed the operator to increase the ability to understand the instantaneous state of the industrial process; since the visual information is easier to assimilate than the numeric or textual one. Finally, it should be noticed that this graphic representation format remains almost unchanged until now.

Figure 2. DCS console, final 80s decade

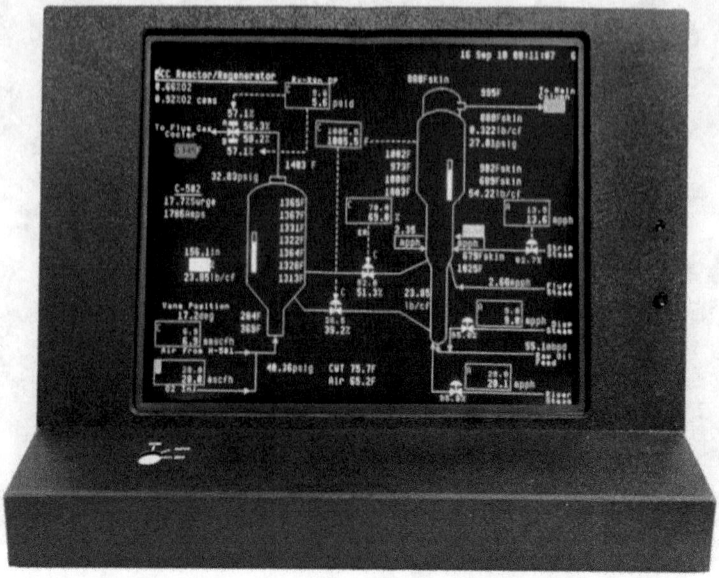

ACTUAL INDUSTRIAL VISUALIZATION SYSTEMS

The optimum operator interface must provide an accurate and thorough "situational awareness" in all industrial process conditions (normal, abnormal and emergency). Therefore, the best DCS screen designs are the ones that optimize the quantity and quality of information of the industrial process, which must be assimilated by the operator, in order to have an optimal knowledge of the situation of the process and thus, be able to make the best decision (Reising, 2010) (Errington, 2005). For this reason, institutions such as the ASM (Abnormal Situation Management Consortium) have developed guidelines or recommendations with best practices, which can be applied in the design of the operator's screens (ASM, 2017). These guides or recommendations were created to be applied only on 2D screens.

The DCS operator interfaces that are currently marketed have 2D monitors and, in addition, the screens contain diagrams or process diagrams in 2D format (Honeywell, 2006)(Siemens, 2017)(Emerson, 2017)(ABB, 2017)(Pérez Cota, 2011). This implies that if you want to have different views of the process, it is imperative to create new screens. The DCS alarms are indicated on the operation screen, with a change in the colour of the component that generates it and, also, they are listed in a table sorted by priorities and/or areas, which is accessible from different places on the screens. Likewise, the appearance of an alarm causes the emission of an audible signal, composed by several tones. All operation screens show the status of the components using a colour code; but some facilitate access to programming manuals, instrument manuals (valve, motor, etc.), block logic programs, electrical diagrams, piping diagrams or link to other management applications (Maximo, SAP ...). The typical input interface of the DCS is the keyboard and the mouse, although in some cases a touch screen as an advanced device is used. This is because it supports configurations predefined by the user, which facilitate the execution of complex tasks.

DCS screen operators typically manage up to fifty operation screens, with several thousand associated I/O signals; so there may be I/O screens or signals that are not accessed by them, for several work shifts or until an alarm is triggered. This forces to create summary screens with the most critical information of the process and/or forces the operator to navigate through all the existing screens in the DCS.

ABB and Umea's Interactive Institute have developed a prototype of a business management tool which facilitates tracking of any KPI (Key Process Indicator) (Breibvold, 2010). This management tool has a touch screen monitor, which displays the building of the production plant and/or industrial equipment in a 2.5D environment. The touch screen facilitates the rotation, movement and/or zoom of the scene. An overview of the plant only shows high-level KPIs; but a view of a section of the factory presents KPIs specifically related to that area, which may not be visible at

Figure 3. DCS Screen from beginning of 2000 decade

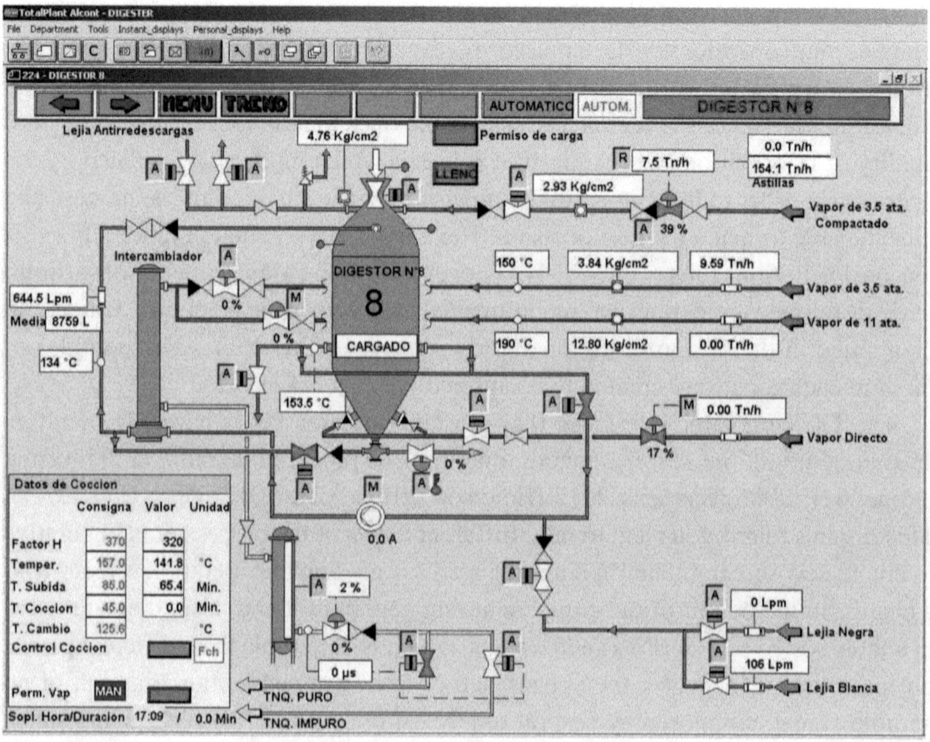

the top level. The data (KPI, multivariate, historical ...) are shown in a rectangular box containing the data name, its numerical value and a colour bar indicator with variable length. The application designed to convert the graphic display into a tool that would replace the classic projection screen, or portfolio. Thus, virtual drawings and annotations can be inserted, which remain fixed to the element and not to a physical position of the screen.

The Siemens Comos-Walkinside application facilitates management and engineering tasks throughout the lifecycle of an industrial plant (Siemens, 2017). This tool keeps all the technical documentation of the industrial plant up to date from the project phase to the operation phase, including detailed engineering, the execution project, the process design, etc. Likewise, the 3D visualization of the equipment of the industrial plant favours the work of learning and maintenance. This 3D environment is complemented with tabular and textual information in 2D.

ABB software and the Siemens Comos-Walkinside software were not intended to become a DCS operator interface, as they do not allow interaction with industrial devices to examine or modify their status.

Some entities performed various works on the use of advanced visualization systems in business, commercial and recreational activities. Thus, M.R. Kickeey described the nine activities (GPS, video-recording, transportation, construction, health, travel, education, safety and advertising), where Google Glasses could have a great impact ([Dickey, 2015). The educational field is one of the areas where more is being innovated in the use of advanced systems of visualization. Thus, the Glassist prototype was created to facilitate the work of teachers, by displaying in a Google Glass the data of the profile of the student, which is recognized by the use of facial recognition algorithms (Silva, 2014). Likewise, I. Malý developed a prototype that using a AR glasses show relevant information to operator over the robot he/she is watching (Malý, 2016). Then, tele-operation and tele-inspection tasks allow the use of Google Glass, so that the operator sends orders to the drone that was controlling and receive the images sent by the camera of that drone (Teixeira, 2014).

AUGMENTED REALITY MONOCULAR GLASSES

The ARM-G (Augmented Reality Monocular Glasses) are a display device, that it allows the user to visualize, on a frame of the lens, an artificial image that is superimposed over his/her field of view. The most known representative of this kind of devices are the Google Glass (Google, 2017). Its development focused on facilitating users to interact with their smartphones without using their hands, as well as accept commands or verbal commands. Likewise, the commands can be transmitted by pressing on the pin for those cases in which the operator/user can not communicate easily by voice commands. This device incorporates a multitude of technologies, such as a gyroscope, a video camera, ambient light sensors, proximity sensors and a bone induction system for sound transmission. It also allows communication via Wi-Fi and Bluetooth.

The ARM-G must be adapted to the user's language, so that it recognizes the verbal commands of the user; however, they are currently only available for the English language. The autonomy of ARM-G depends on the battery they use. These have an internal battery available, which is located on the back of the pin and allows a range of only a few hours. However, if you want to increase the autonomy of use they can be connected to an external battery that can be placed in the pocket of the user.

The use of the ARM-G by users is not an added annoyance for users, since a large number of people use or have used glasses on a regular or occasional basis. It is important to remember, that 60% of Spaniards wear graduated glasses daily (Cámara de Ópticos, 2013).

This technology, which was developed for personal use, was expanding in the field of surgery; as it facilitated the retransmission of interventions from advanced

Figure 4. Google Glass

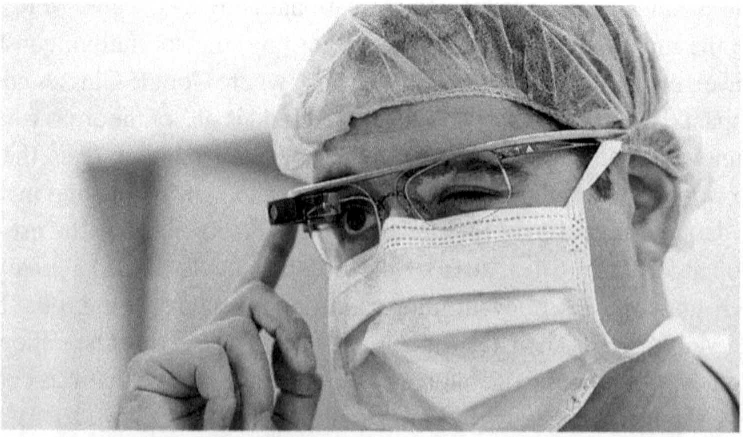

surgery to medical that are far. Likewise, these devices could have a huge numberless expansion when their use in industrial environments will be generalized.

The great advantage of using ARM-G in industrial environments is that it allows easy access to information without the use of hands; since it obeys commands verbally given. This allows industrial workers to remain focused on the task they were doing with their hands; while an enormous amount of information is superimposed over a box of part of his/her visual field. This box must have a cold colour background, so that there is an adequate contrast between the letters and/or graphics with the background. In addition, a bone induction system for sound generation allows Google Glass to be used in conjunction with sound protection systems, which are used in environments with high ambient noise.

Figure 5. Google Glass working scheme

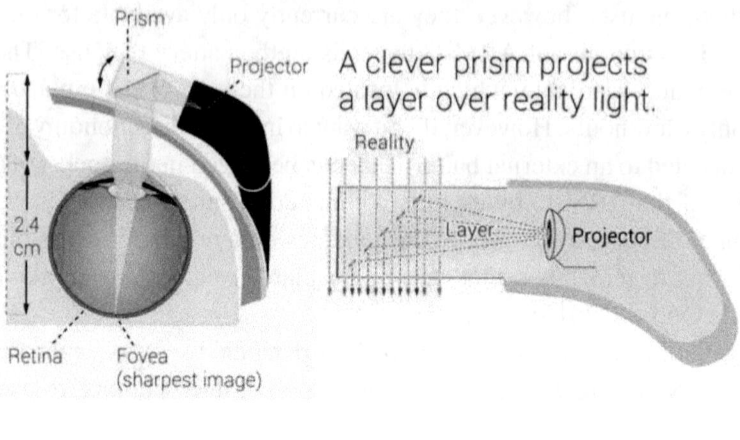

The use of these devices can be a great ally in preventing accidents or reducing errors. This is a consequence of the unnecessary obligation to turn the head or move one of the hands to pay attention to the information that is being received or to change the page of the manual that is being read. For example, in certain high-risk jobs, this loss of momentary attention to the task that he/she was developing, because of turning his head to hear some instruction or dropping a tool that was being held, can cause a work accident or a serious error in the task that was being done.

The use of visualization systems similar to ARM-G will allow any operator to have at their disposition an enormous amount of information, which is accessible immediately. This allows the operator to perform any task while simultaneously he/she is consulting the information he/she needs to perform the work he/she is doing. Likewise, this facilitates an optimization in the quality of work that he/she is doing, because if having all the information needed, it will eliminate fortuitous forgetting that could cause defects/errors in the quality of the work done.

Finally, these display devices substantially reduce the time spent in collecting information prior to the task being performed during the task. Pre-job information searches are kept to a minimum, as the operator knows that he/she carries all the information he/she needs, as it has been digitized in the factory databases and it is all available for use. However, the great improvement in the time spent in the execution of a task is due to the elimination of the time resulting from the detentions that are carried out in a task, for have not all the information that is needed and this requires a loss of time. This loss of time is not only compelled by the search for the information that is needed, but also due to the interval of time that the operator needs to return to focus on the task he/she was doing before the interruption, due to the search for information he/she had to perform.

"Vuzix Blade 3000" (Figure 6) is another example of ARM-G on whose right lens a 2D image is displayed, which can only be seen from the inside, since from the

Figure 6. Vuzix Blade 3000

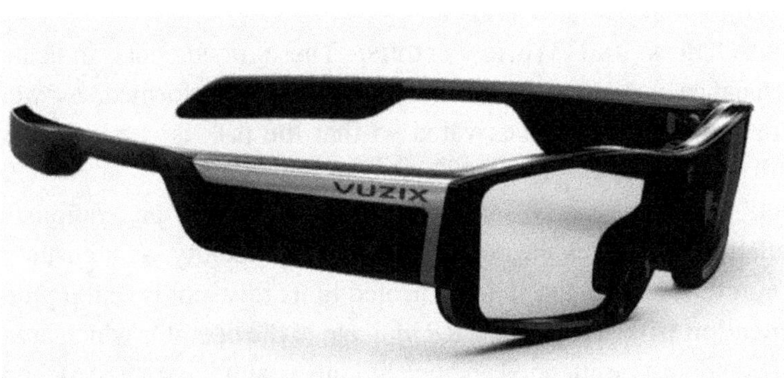

outside only several reflections are perceived (Vuzix, 2017). This functionality is achieved thanks to a tiny projector embedded in the right side of the glasses, which feeds the screen located inside the right lens. They also include an integrated GPS, directional sensors, an accelerometer, vibrating haptics, microphone and video camera.

Next, the different types of information that can be visualized with ARM-G are shown:

- **Manuals of the Productive Process:** These documents contains the exhaustive technical information of all industrial processes that exist in the company. This information is usually consulted for the complex technical calculations on which the production process of a large industry is based. Operators or managers need to promptly access this information to help them solve complex and unusual breakdowns.
- **Operation Manuals:** Operators of the production process will have access to the operational procedures that indicate what actions need to be performed to properly manage the stage of the process they are managing.
- **Disassembly of Equipment:** This documentation contains schemas that show the parts and/or parts in which a complex device is decomposed. This information is critical for maintenance technicians to perform proper repairing.
- **Electrical or Mechanical Plans at Various Scales:** These plans contain general information of the entire factory and/or details of each of the sections of the industrial plant.
- **Factory Floor Maps:** The smart glasses screen can show the operator the priority paths to move inside a factory. This will allow him/her to avoid closed ways as well as unsafe or dangerous ways.
- **Real-Time Operation Screens:** Operation screens show the status of an installation or equipment. The lens frame shows the contents of an operation screen, as this information makes it easier for the operator to perform a job more safely. This allows him/her to check the status of the equipment before proceeding to repair or overhaul.
- **Work Orders and Work Permits:** These documents indicate to the maintenance personnel the tasks that must be performed, as well as the assurances that must be activated so that the task is carried out with full security guarantees.
- **Check List:** The list of tasks of maintenance of an equipment or an installation, facilitates the commissioning of a facility; as it ensures that the operator followed all the steps indicated in its repair or revision procedure.
- **Connection with ERP:** The ERP indicate to the operator which are the work orders that must be attended and he/she can consult the state of the warehouse.

This allows he/she to know if the material, which he/she needs for repair, is in store or even make an order request for the Purchasing Department to take steps to acquire it.

- **Dangerous Areas:** The operator receives information from hazardous locations/places; as well as indicating the type, duration, origin and possible consequences of that danger.
- **Information in Noisy Environments:** Signaling or visualization of alarms in very noisy environments. The fact that the information can always be present in the field of view of the operator, prevents the user from needing to feel a vibration or to hear an alarm signal.
- **Emergency Information:** The user/operator receives information about the location and the ways that must follow to go to the emergency exits. This prevents users from having to consult documentation on paper or looking at symbols or signs indicating the outputs; because in environments with a lot of smoke or without visibility it is very confusing to determine which is the correct way to the exit.
- **Retransmission of Works:** The operator can retransmit in video the works that are being done, without having to carry any uncomfortable or annoying device. This allows him/her to record him/her task to analyze it at another time or to collect advice and indications from experts that a group of experts to analyze the task he/she is doing. This last task is of great help in repairing complex equipment in which the long distance experts can not move to check the fault in-situ.
- **Video Surveillance:** Real-time video showing the status of a restricted area or even images of security cameras to security personnel.
- **Locations of Equipment/Merchandise in the Warehouse:** This allows guiding the operator through the map of the warehouse, to direct it to the exact location of the material he/she is looking for.
- Reading of bar-codes or labels for identification of equipment, materials, or products.
- **OCR Tools:** The use of OCR tools facilitates the capture of texts that the operator is visualizing. Also, the captured text can be translated and displayed on the screen to the operator. This process is usually critical in repair tasks, where the equipment manuals are not translated into the operator's language.
- **Meetings:** One of the most important tasks of any industrial officer is reporting at meetings. This task is improved if the user has the most relevant information on the screen of his smart glasses. This helps to make a more fluid presentation in which the critical data are within reach a slight rotation of the eye.

In Spain the legislation of Prevention of Industrial Risks in the industry requires the use of Personal Protective Equipment (PPE), which are adapted to the hazardous that is being done (Figure 7). These PPE's may be made up of specific protections for some parts of the body or complete suits that fully protect the worker. Next, we will analyze the various benefits and damages that are derived from the use of ARM-G, depending on the PPE's that an industrial worker should use for each job:

- **Full Protective Suit:** Jobs that require the use of workers' comprehensive protective clothing are often used for tasks performed in hostile environments (chemical, nuclear, high temperatures, paint, mines, fire…). In these environments, the use of information on paper or shown on a tablet is completely inadequate; because paper or electronic devices would degrade very quickly if they were not properly protected. Likewise, the protective equipment, worn by the operator, drastically limits his/her field of vision; So it is very difficult to visualize any information that he/she has to hold with his/her hands, whether it is represented on paper or on an electronic screen. ARM-G is an excellent option for the operator to receive information, since the protective suit he/she wears, protects both him/her and the glasses he/she carries. In addition, the user has no obstruction in his/her visual field

Figure 7. Personal protective equipment (PPE)

that prevents him/her from accessing the information he/she needs to consult, since the glasses are located inside his/her protective suit.

- **Hearing Protectors:** The works, which run in very noisy environments, require the use of hearing protectors; but this makes it difficult to establish verbal communications. Thus, the exchange of information between operators deteriorates or even disappears. The use of smart glasses would allow the transmission of indications in text format, to be represented on the device's screen. He/she could even hear the messages transmitted verbally thanks to the bone induction system. Orders to ARM-G should be transmitted verbally through a microphone very close to the mouth or by the touch of a device similar to the one located on the temples of the glasses.
- **Special Protective Goggles:** The welding or cutting tasks require the operator to wear special glasses. The use of Google Glass together with the welding glasses depends on the design of the latter, since ARM-G must be protected by goggles, to prevent deterioration. Their joint use allows the operator to receive information regarding the task, while performing the welding. This action is not feasible without the ARM-G, because the opacity of the welding crystals prevent the operator can read or perceive any other type of visual information.
- **No Protection Required:** The works, which do not require any protection, allow the operator to carry the ARM-G without any difficulty.

The ARM-G are susceptible to be used for special applications, with some small adaptation in the peripherals that currently have installed. The installation of an infrared camera or a thermal camera facilitates the capture of a radio spectrum different from the scene that is captured. Infrared cameras can be of various types depending on whether they capture the near, middle or far infrared. Capturing infrared spectrum images allows viewing of night scenes or viewing scenes with a lot of smoke or intense fog. Night scenes are captured with the infrared camera and are projected onto the ARM-G lens, allowing the user to observe the actual image and the infrared image on the screen. The capture of images with null illumination or in smoke environments has a wide use in the industrial environments, because it improves the vision of the operator who works in conditions of extreme visibility.

Thermal cameras are used to capture the thermal radio-electric spectrum and are used to reveal the temperature of the objects being displayed or to differentiate objects according to their thermal structure. This represents an enormous help in industrial environments, because at the same time that an operator observes a scene with different materials, he/she can also classify them according to their internal structure (metal, wood, plastic, etc.). The operator also observes on the screen the temperature of the objects in front of him/her, in order to avoid touching any that has an extreme temperature and can cause some damage.

Finally, it must be indicated that there are devices that they allow to generate ARM-G without glasses. These devices usually are intelligent mobile phones, with their cameras, they capture the real image and next they show it fused with an artificial image, Figure 8. This will be a specific case of an ARM-G, because both eyes capture the image at the same time, and because the image has a 2D format this is the way the brain interprets it.

AUGMENTED REALITY

The ARB-G (Augmented Reality Binocular Glasses) are a visualization device that permits the user to visualize over both sides of glasses an artificial image that it is superimposed on his/her field of view (FOV). The ARB-G are devices that really offer a full sensation of augmented reality, because they add virtual information to the whole field of view of the user. Then these devices add virtual information to the physical information that is been viewed in that moment. Technological devices of augmented reality facilitate the superposition of computer data on the real scene that the user is perceiving. The enlarged image is composed simultaneously of a real and an artificial image. The latter is added to the original image to improve the interpretation of the real scene that the user is perceiving.

Figure 8. Augmented-reality apps for smartphones

Augmented reality devices can be grouped into two large families, depending on the method used to perceive the actual image. A group of devices superimpose an artificial image onto the lenses, through which the user perceives the actual image. However, the other group capture the actual image with an embedded camera within a (Head Mounted Display) HDM helmet and next it is fused with the artificial image, Figure 9. This aggregated image is shown on the HDM screen that it is in front of the user's eyes and gives a FOV of 37º.

The ARB-G devices are suitable for superimposing information relative to the image that the user is perceiving, without having to rotate the eyes of the point to which they are focusing. This allows the information to flow naturally to the user and does not require an additional effort to understand the information perceived.

Microsoft has created glasses called "HoloLens" (Figure 10), which blend augmented reality and 3D imaging (Microsoft, 2017). These glasses have translucent lenses on which holograms or 3D images are projected (visualized) and give the user the feeling that they are really inside the real scene that he/she is also perceiving. The visualization of the holograms gives the user a sensation of volume in the figures that he/she perceives and this increases the conviction that these artificial figures are a part of the real scene. Likewise, these glasses have an internal support of circular form that facilitate that the weight of the set is distributed evenly on the head and not on the nose and the ears. They have also several microphones, cameras, speakers with surround sound and Wi-Fi connection.

Figure 9. Virtual reality apps for smartphones

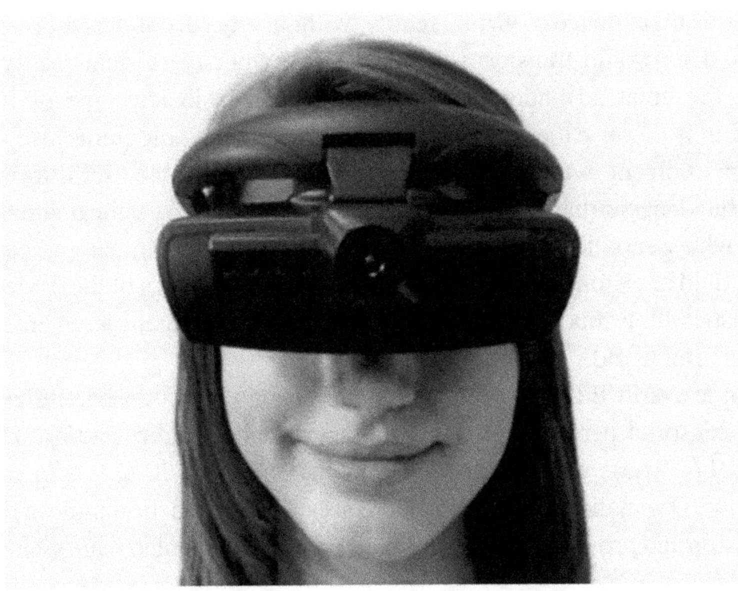

Figure 10. Augmented Reality created by the Microsoft HoloLens

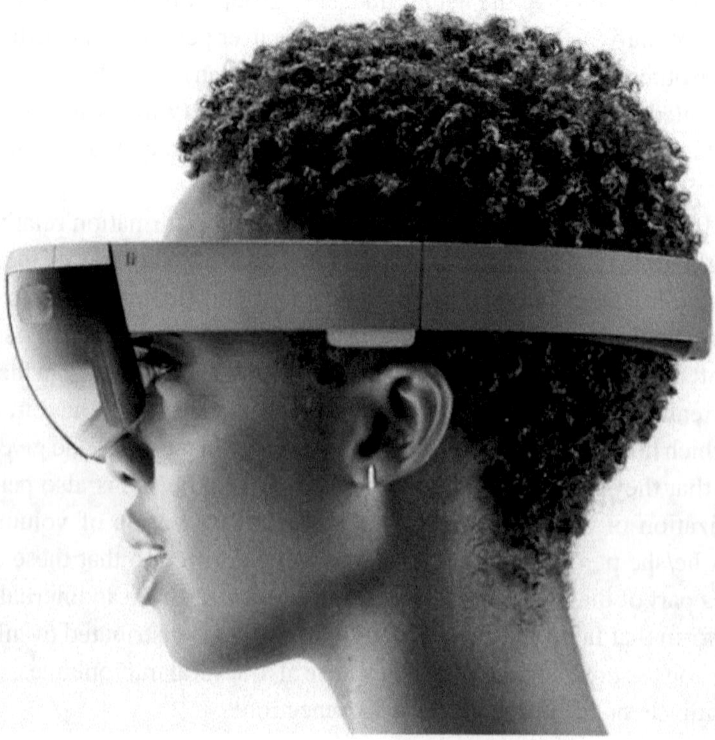

Visualizations of the HoloLens glasses can be carried to the extreme of only containing a single image of virtual reality, without any part of the real scene being perceived. This would transform them into an immersive virtual reality device. However, the great advantage of using these glasses in any type of industrial environment is because the user, in addition to seeing the holograms also observes the real environment of the scene in which he/she is. Thus, the user is aware of the innumerable dangers that exist around him/her. Likewise, in critical situations, an operator, who wears these glasses and wears a protective suit, can re-acquire his/her entire field of vision with a simple disconnection/shutdown of the device. These characteristics allow this device to be very suitable for introducing augmented reality to the industrial world.

"Epson Moverio BT-300" (Figure 11) are glasses with transparent lenses that allow the sensorial perception of an almost augmented reality and/or 3D images (Epson, 2017). These glasses have dual screens of 1280x720 pixels, in each lens, which allow 3D visualization. Also, the screens are centred in the middle of the user's field of vision and provide a 23° FOV. Therefore, the augmented reality sensation in

Figure 11. Epson Moverio BT-300

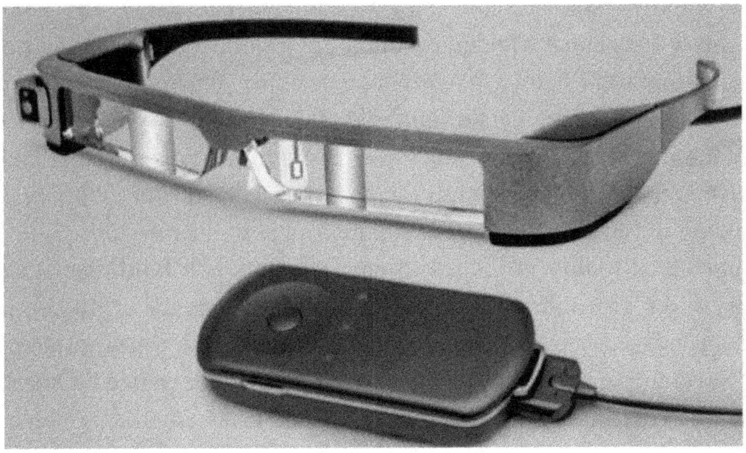

3D is limited, since the FOV of humans is 180º. Likewise, these glasses also have headphones, video camera, gyroscope, microphone, GPS, accelerometer, Wi-Fi

The "Meta 2" glasses (Figure 12) allow the visualization of 3D images, with a FOV of 90º (Metavision, 2017). This is achieved by the use of 2560 x 1440 pixels projectors located at the top and the images emitting images on the glasses. It also has an integrated camera, speakers and position sensors.

Figure 12. Meta 2

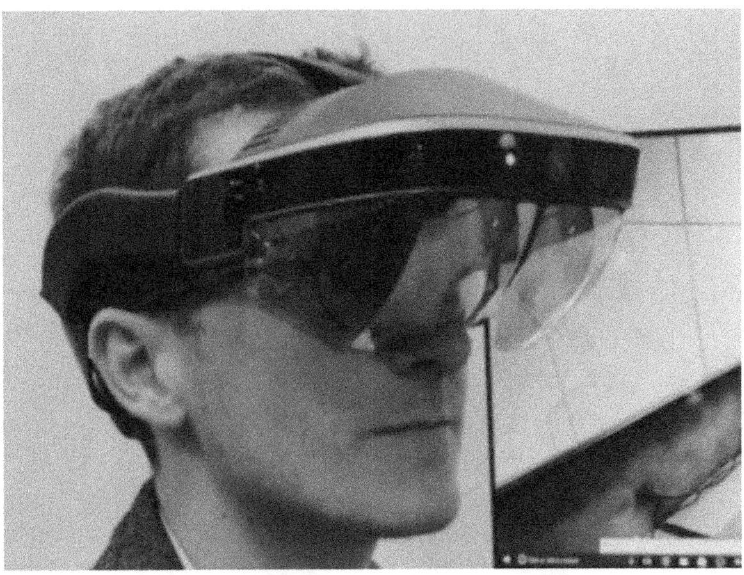

"C-Thru Smoke Diving Helmet" (Figure 13) is a helmet prototype, which helps firefighters improve their vision in smoky areas (Omerth, 2017). This helmet has a thermal camera that captures the image of the environment, and once it is processed, it is projected onto the helmet glasses/screens. This information is composed of alphanumeric data and geometric figures that delimit the edges of objects. Also, the helmet has a technology that suppresses background noise, so that the fireman can perceive more clearly the sounds (screams) of a person, structural weaknesses of the building in flames or any other sound critical to his mission.

The augmented reality in industrial environments is a field that is still at the dawn of its development. However, augmented reality devices will have a strong development in the very near future. At present, the first prototypes are already being designed, but their use in industrial plants will soon be universalized (Omerth, 2017) (Daqri, 2017). The following is a summary of the tasks where augmented reality will facilitate and improve the quality and safety of the work being performed by the operators:

- Showing hidden structures behind or inside a wall, equipment or bulky structure. For example, this allows the user to know which is the ideal place to drill a wall, without fear of drilling a pipe that exists inside.

Figure 13. C-Thru Smoke Diving Helmet

- Disclosing the values of the physical quantities of the equipment or components that are being perceived by the user. Thus, he/she can visualize the flow rate (m3/h, l/min) of a pipe, the current (Amperes) or voltage (Volts) of an electric line, etc.
- Including information about the objects in the scene that the user is watching. This allows the operator to indicate what he/she is perceiving on the scene. Thus, he/she can add arrows to the scene that point to the device, along with a text box that contains the component name or any other important information for the user. For example, it would be possible to know the name of the fluid (water, steam, oil, diesel, ...) circulating inside a pipe.
- Identifying keys or buttons on a keyboard, keypad or any other user interface. The scene could include arrows that point to each key or button, to inform the user of the function performed by each element of the user interface.
- Tracing, on the scene being watched by the user the route that he/she must follow to go from a source to a destination. This is similar to one of the features provided for Google Glass. However, augmented reality glasses indicate by arrows on the scene, which is the way the operator should follow. While, Google Glass show a plane on the lens and it is the path that must be followed from the source to the destination.
- Indicating what data the operator must complete in a document. The augmented reality device must recognize and identify the document being viewed; warn of the text that should be written in each of the blank spaces or clarify the meaning of each of the boxes that must be marked.
- To warn the danger of a device or installation through a colour code, so the operator intuitively perceives the risk that exists in their environment. For example, the red colour may be superimposed on hazardous equipment or the yellow colour on medium risk equipment.
- Superimposing infrared or thermal images to the actual scene the user is viewing. This allows, in environments with a lot of smoke, the user observes an infrared image about the reality that is perceived by him/her. This option is similar to another that is available for Google Glass, but in them, the image is displayed exclusively in a quadrant. However, augmented reality enables the infrared or thermal scene to overlap over the entire real scene. This allows us to intuitively reveal a reality that remained hidden from the operator.

The augmented reality allows the data superimposed on a real scene to complement and help to understand the image shown, since it improves the visual information of the scene that is perceived. Thus, the user next to the visual image also perceives an interpretation of reality, which is due to the written information that appears on the screen.

Likewise, if the information is not strictly complementary with the actual scene being perceived, it should not be shown or superimposed over the entire surface of the lens. For example, it would be inappropriate to superimpose a spreadsheet or chart over a real scene, where a pipeline distribution is being observed. This type of information causes a lot of confusion for the user, since texts or graphics become unintelligible in some areas, as well as blurring the details of the actual scene. This information is best suited to be shown in the Google Glass box.

Much of the information, shown on augmented reality devices, can be adapted to be displayed on Google Glass; since in its projection frame can be shown the real scene together with an artificial image superimposed. However, very little information specially adapted for Google Glass can be viewed on augmented reality devices.

Augmented reality glasses, which instead of lenses have LCD screens, are not suitable for use in all industrial environments. This is because the operator must remove the glasses he carries, to recover the entire visual field of the real scene; since the LCD screens only show a portion of the existing reality. In addition, this action would be impossible to carry out if the operator was inside a protective suit. Likewise, the fortuitous shutdown of this device would blind the operator, in an environment that could be dangerous to his/her physical integrity. Therefore, these glasses should only be used in closed environments, where there are no risks or hazards near of the industrial operator.

INMERSIVE VIRTUAL REALITY

Virtual reality is a visual and sensorial environment, where artificial scenes or objects, which are generated by computer technology, acquire real appearance and the user has the sensation of being immersed in this virtual world. This implies that the user's senses are sensing artificially created sensations, but the user interprets them as if they are real. This causes the user to feel that he/she is in a virtual world to which he/she is transported by his/her own senses.

At the very least, virtual reality equipment must have a helmet that generates 3D images. Also, gloves that capture hand movement, omnidirectional platforms (Cyberith Virtualizer, Virtuix Omni), etc. can be added. The virtual reality gloves capture the hands movement and transfer it to the virtual world in which the user is immersed. Omni-directional platforms detect user movement without actually moving from location. There are brands, as Samsung (2017), that facilitates positioning the mobile phone within an adapted HMD, in order that each screen zone shows to each eye their correspondent 2D image, once fused inside the brain the user perceives a 3D image.

Figure 14. Virtual Reality lab equipment. Courtesy of ESA

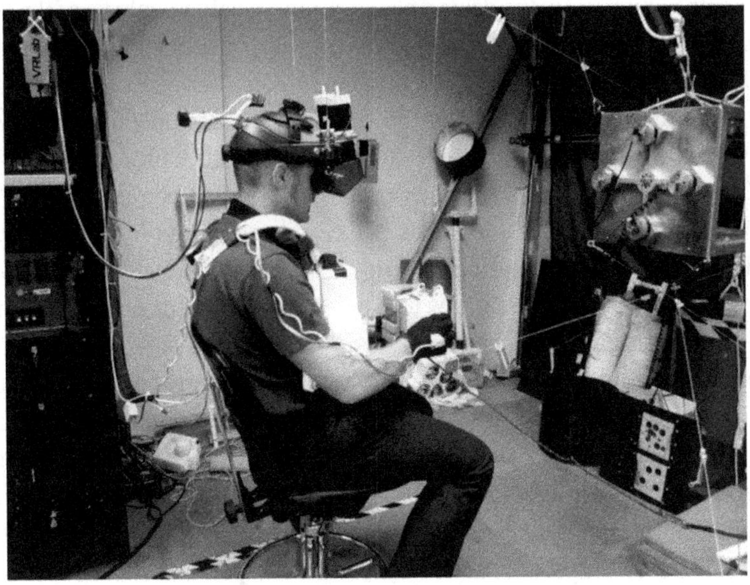

Next, the different types of information that can be visualized with the virtual reality systems are shown:

- Review of industrial structures. Visualization of industrial constructions or structures (beams, columns, tanks, etc.) while they are being designed allows for the early detection of problems that were not initially foreseen. For example, this makes it easier to see if there is any difficulty walking around the new structure. Likewise, it can be detected if it presents an anomaly that was not foreseen initially.
- Analysis of problems when repairing an industrial equipment. Thus, he/she can examine the tasks that should be performed by an operator, to repair a device in the least possible time. This task is very critical if the operator does not physically know the equipment to be repaired; because with it reduces the time of repair and increase their physical security. For example, the repair of critical equipment such as a nuclear reactor, a boiler or a turbine must be carried out in the shortest time possible, while ensuring the minimum occupational risk of the operator. These immersive devices facilitate the operator's knowledge of the installations; allow to test the different methods of repair, to optimize the task; and check the dangers of certain actions taken during such repair.

- Design of new products. The preview of the new industrial and/or consumer products, which are in the design phase, allows a better analysis of the technical characteristics that they must meet; since they can easily be observed from other approaches. Likewise, the designer can decompose each product in the parts that form it, to verify the difficulties that can arise in the stage of assembly. Likewise, it is possible to analyze the difficulties that will exist in the moment of making a repair or replacement of some piece of the product. For example, engineers can check if a car is accessible for repairs or how to facilitate the tasks that are performed in the repair shops.
- Showing the industrial facilities to the new operators, indicating how to reach the different areas of the factory. It also indicates the location of the different equipment or machines in the factory and how to get there. Likewise, it can be shown to some operators as it will be the future industrial plant in which they are going to work. Thus, when these users reach their new plant they will know it completely and can start working from the first day, minimizing their adaptation time to the new working environment.
- Training of process technicians. Virtual reality equipment allows process technicians to test the essential manoeuvers that must be performed on critical or complex industrial equipment. Some equipment or industrial machinery has such an extremely high cost that it is important to train technicians in how to perform certain tasks in the minimum time and with the highest quality. For example, the connection of a turbine, the heating of a boiler, etc.
- Actual views with superimposed operation data. The overlapping of real data of the industrial process to the actual images of the machines or instruments, allows the process operators to know the state of the industrial plant and even get to operate it. Thus, an operator can open/close valves, start/stop motors, etc. This operation is suitable for industrial equipment that is in the virtual surroundings of the place where the operator is located. If the actual equipment he/she had to deal with were far apart from one another, the operator would have to travel a virtual path to go from one to the other industrial device, which must operate. These operator paths, although virtual, are critical to the real time that this invests in that virtual displacement. This would be inadmissible in critical situations, where the operator's speed to activate/deactivate suitable equipment is critical to solving this problematic condition. Also, the visualization of the actual images of the process make it difficult for the operator to have a complete knowledge of the situation of the entire industrial process that he/she is managing; Therefore, there are teams that are hidden or small teams, which although they are critical are not shown with sufficient definition. Finally, a visualization of real images of the

industrial process prevents the creation of summary screens, containing the main data of the process.

Currently, virtual reality systems are being used for the training of operators. These simulators are already used in the training of pilots, soldiers, etc..

Virtual reality transports the user to a world of illusions that, in some cases, can correspond to an existing reality, which may be relatively close or far from its physical location. This sensory illusion can be complemented with information about the virtual scene being shown. This will generate virtual scenes that are a hybrid between virtual reality and augmented reality.

The use of virtual reality in industrial environments is being postponed because of the need to use haptics and glasses. In addition, it is not very appropriate to be immersed in a world of virtual illusions, while being near of innumerable risks existing in industrial plants. This demonstrates the need to use virtual reality equipment in closed premises, which is isolated from any risk near its location. Even this closed places must be completely safe, since any incident in its vicinity can happen, that compromises the security of that place. In this case, the virtual user would not be aware of the immense danger that exists outside the place where he/she is, because he/she is inside a world of illusion that prevents him/her from knowing the surrounding reality.

DCS OPERATION SCREEN IN 3D

The usual operating screens of large industrial automation systems have a 2D flow chart format, Figure 15. However, this format has very restricted the amount of information it may contain. This information must be, also very well structured to facilitate the operator can understand it intuitively and with a single glance. This implied that new 2.5D and 3D operation screens have been developed to contain more information and make it more understandable to the operator (Cota, 2013). This application can display 3D operation screens; but you can also display 2.5D displays on computers that do not have the necessary peripherals to view 3D images. Each of these new 2.5D and 3D operation screens may contain information that was previously displayed on various operation screens.

For example, this operation screen, Figure 16 manages to replace a set of 10 old 2D-format DCS screens. A set of 10 screens groups the old steam distribution screen, Figure 15 and the 9 old screens of each of the nine digester lines. The old screen corresponding to digester number 8 is shown in Figure 3. Each digestion line, Figure 17, is composed of a digester, an exchanger, a condensate tank, a recirculation

Figure 15. 2D image of a DCS Screen. Steam Circuit

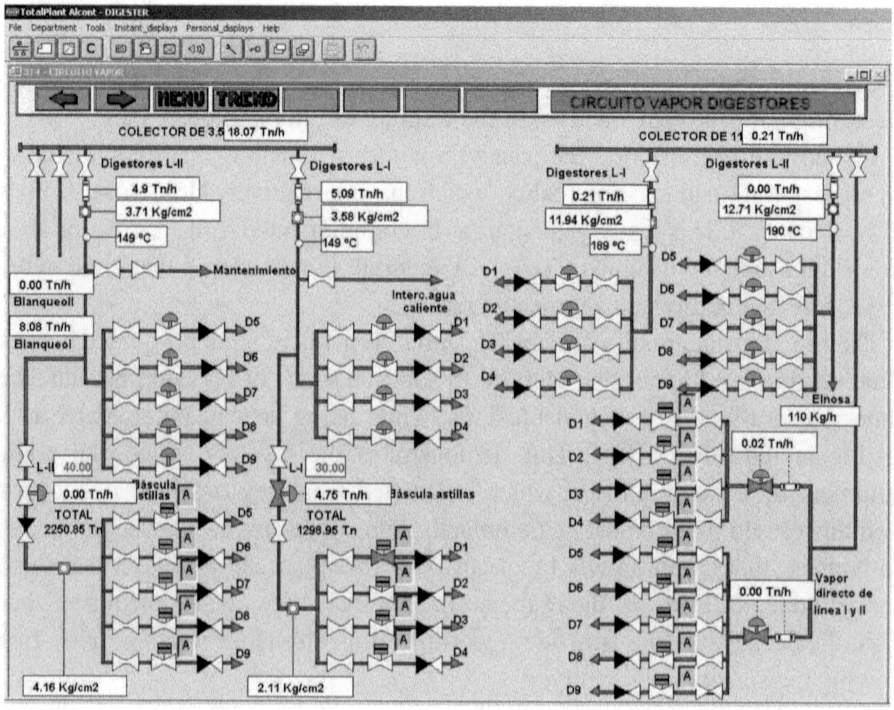

Figure 16. Oblique view of the Industrial Process 2.5D

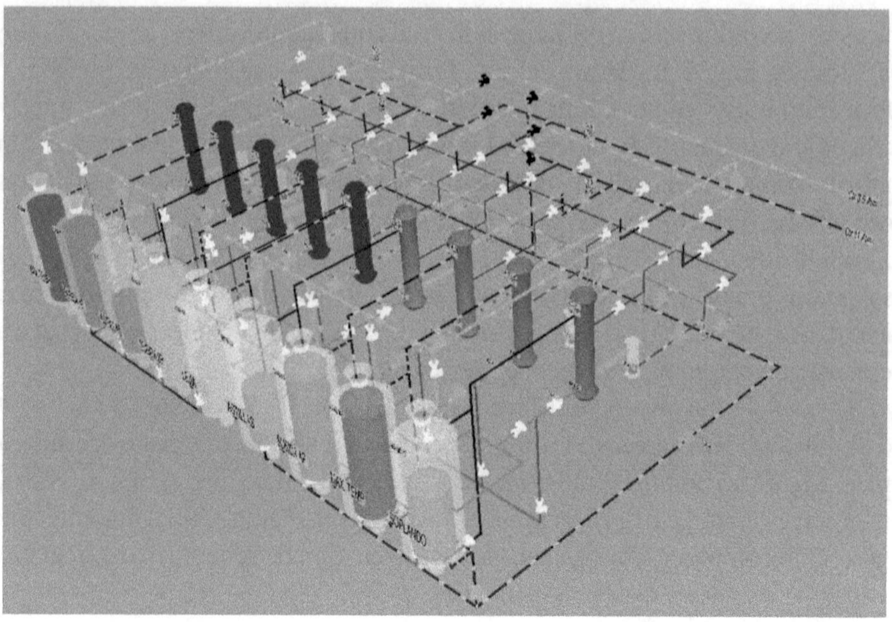

pump, steam valves, liquor valves and all associated pipes. The steam distribution screen shows a set of common facilities for all these lines.

The navigation along the graphic scene is carried out by means of a Joystick, while the selection of a graphic element is done with the mouse and/or Joystick. Likewise, these peripherals facilitate the tasks of rotation, displacement and zoom of the graphic of the industrial process to achieve to visualize the scene from infinite points of view (frontal, lateral, rear, near, far...).

This operating environment also reports the occurrence of an alarm or warning by sending a voice message with emotion. The emission of the vocal messages with emotion facilitates the immediate compression by the operator, of the incidences that are happening; because the emotional intensity indicates the criticality of the alarm and the message indicates exactly which is the component that has generated it. The graphical scene also shows, in textual format, all the physical magnitudes of the process, as well as the state of all industrial apparatuses and equipment (valves, motors, switches, etc.).

The application includes a 2D window of information and command on the components of the process, that have been selected by means of the mouse or the joystick-3D. This window shows in text format the status of the selected component and allows its operation (change of state), by pressing buttons.

The background colour of the graphic scene is decided to be the grey colour, as it is the colour recommended by ASM for the operation screens. The grey colour intensifies the difference between the graphic objects and the vacuum and also allows the use of the operation screen in operating rooms with different luminous intensities.

The graphics components must have a geometric format in 3-dimensions to be inserted in a graphic scene in 3-dimensions. However, all standard symbols to identify a component were designed for use in 2D representations (ISO, 2017). This requires the creation of new designs of 3D graphic symbols, to be assigned to the components of the process, so that they can be used in a graphic scene that represents an actual industrial process. It has been decided that these new 3D graphic symbols must be generated by the axial round evolution of the graphic representation of the 2D component symbol; since this allows them to be recognized or identified in a very simple way, from any spatial position in which the operator is located. Similarly, the creation of these new symbols from an axial evolution of the 2D symbols enables the projection on a 2D plane to exactly reproduce the original 2D symbol. Occasionally, the axial rotation of the representation of a 2D symbol does not generate a 3D geometric figure, which resembles the symbol in 2D. This requires the creation of a new 3D symbol, based on some kind of geometric transformation of the 2D symbol or a new reference model for that component.

The red colour is used only to signal an alarm status; the yellow colour is used to display a warning state and the violet colour is identified with an undefined state

Figure 17. View of one of the industrial process lines

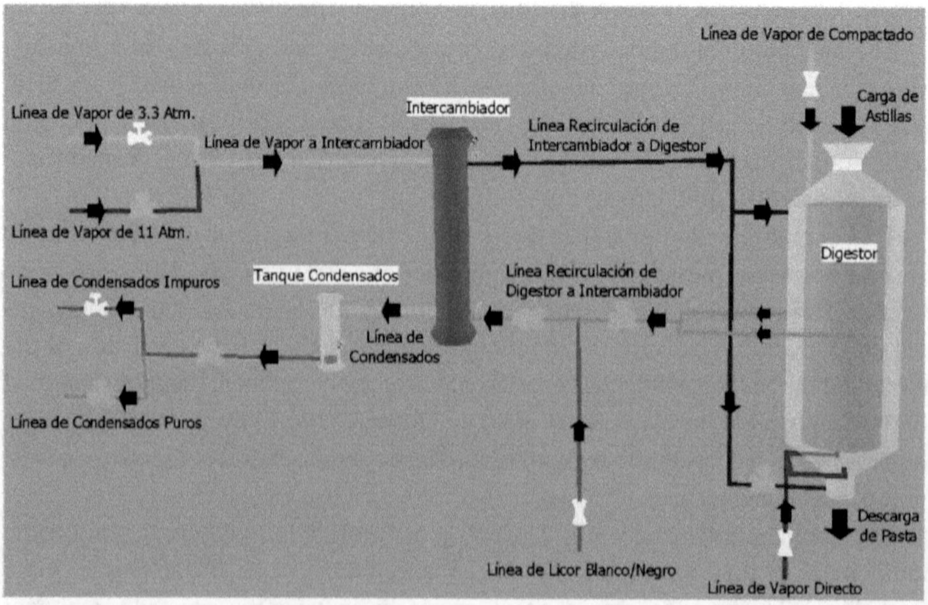

of the component. The green and white colours are used to indicate the different states of operation in which there is a physical component of the industrial process. Green indicates that a pump is running/active or that a valve is open. The white colour warns that a pump is halted/stopped or that a valve is closed.

The pipes have several colours depending on the fluid they carry inside, while a change in a physical characteristic of that fluid is noticed with a variation in its colour shade. The graphic representation of the pipe has an animation to symbolize the flow rate of the liquid it transports.

The graphic scene is contained in a window, which has several menus or tabs, which are used to select different options for modification of the graphic scene. The application allows the individual or grouped display and/or hiding of the digester lines or the common line to all the digesters, Figure 18; as this allows the operator to focus exclusively on a limited group of lines. The pipeline animation is activated/deactivated in a menu option; since its activation is very advisable in tasks of simulation or learning process, as it shows the flow of the different matters involved in the industrial process.

Some components or sections of the circuit must display numeric data or messages to the operator, since a colour code only provides a very limited amount of information. This requires the display of information with information about the

Figure 18. Partial view of the industrial process

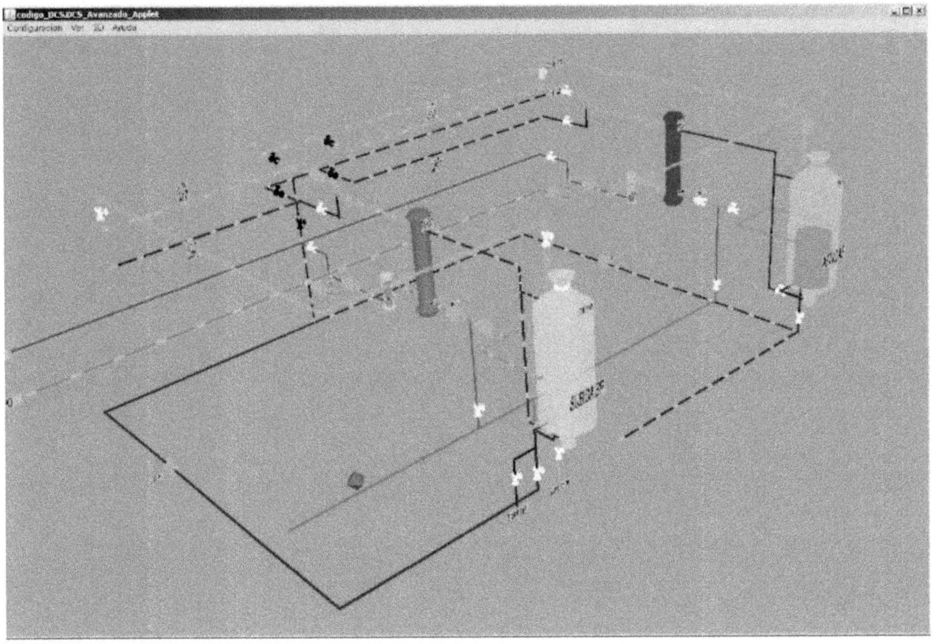

process Figure 19, which informs the state of the digester or the different physical quantities used to keep the process within limits.

The moment in which an alarm or warning of a component arises, the operator may not be concentrated on the display or the colour change of that component; so a voice message is send to tell the operator that there is a circumstance that requires his/her attention. Therefore, whenever a component enters an alarm or warning state, a voice message is send, which contains the unambiguous name of the component and the critical condition (alarm or warning) in which it is present. The menu also has a tab for the operator to activate or deactivate these alarm or warning messages.

The graphic scene, which shows the industrial process, has several options that facilitate its visualization from other points of view. This implies that the graphic scene can be moved to any position, rotated on any axis or modified in size (zoom). These options allow the operator to navigate the inside of the process, to concentrate on specific areas of the process. This facilitates the visualization of the process from other positions and ensures that no part of the process remains hidden or disfigured by another element in front of it. Consequently, the scene can be seen from the lower, posterior, oblique, Figure 16, enlarged, etc. The operator performs these operations using a mouse or a 3D joystick. The latter peripheral is the only device that can be used to interact with scenes shown in 3D, since the graphics card prevents the use

Figure 19. Frontal view of the industrial process, with the command window

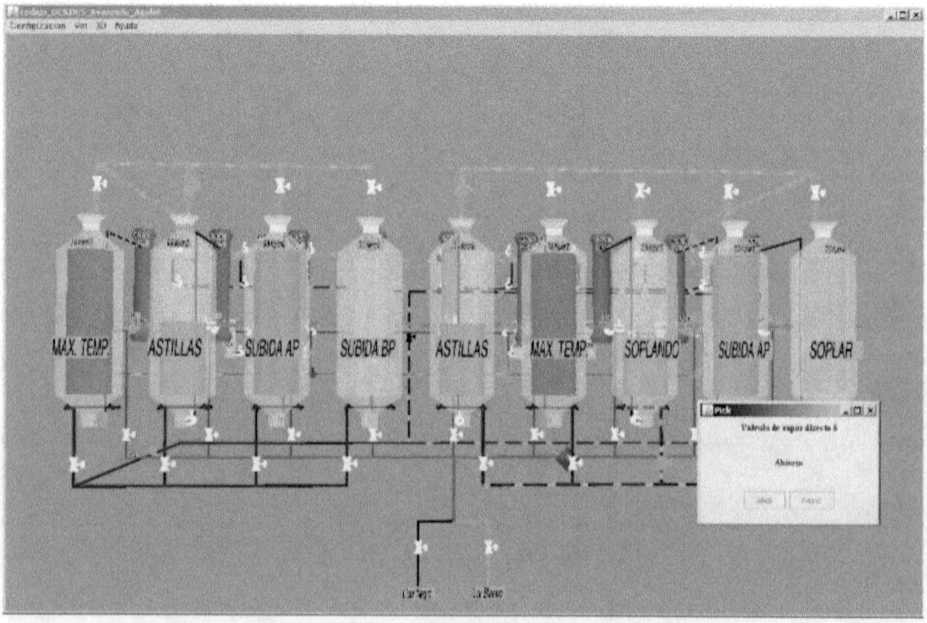

of the mouse. Likewise, a menu option or a Joystick button allows you to place the graphic scene in its initial position and thus, make this task easier for the operator.

The components (digesters, valves and pumps) of the industrial process can be selected so that their information is displayed in a small command window, Figure 19. This window provides a more detailed information about the component, including its full name and operating state. Also, this window can also be used to modify the operating state of the component, as this option was excluded in the requirements of the application. The selection of the component is done with the mouse pointer or by means of an advanced pointer. The advanced pointer is represented on the screen with the geometric octahedron figure and its movement is controlled through the keyboard or the 3D Joystick. This advanced pointer is the only one available in 3D scene visualization.

3D Visualization

Stereoscopic-3D visualization implies that the operator uses his two eyes to quasi-simultaneously perceive a 3D scene. Since, the eyes are separated by a few centimetres between them, causes each eye to perceive the scene from a different angle. The result is that viewing a real scene with both eyes implies a greater perception of the visual information of this scene than if it were perceived exclusively by one eye.

This causes that the information that an operator perceives of a 3D screen is greater than if it were contemplating the same information in 2.5D.

If a valve or pump is hidden behind a bulky display object (digester, tank), it could be partially visible by performing a small rotation of the graphic scene. This small rotation would be the equivalent of perceiving the scene from the viewing angle provided by the operator's other eye. This determines that the visualization of graphical scenes in 3D increases the amount of information that the operator perceives, as to whether this maximum scene is shown in 2.5D.

Visualizing 3D scenes forces the use of 3D devices in the panel operator positions. These 3D devices can be 3D glasses or auto-stereoscopic monitors. The 3D glasses should be of the active type, since the operator must perceive the colours and details of the graphic scene in extraordinary detail. The self-stereoscopic monitors force the user to be positioned exactly in the centre of the screen. However, this is not always possible, as the operator often changes his position during his shift.

EXPERIENCES OF OPERATORS WITHIN 3D ENVIRONMENTS

The application was tested by the DCS display operators of the Digesters Department of the company "Grupo Empresarial ENCE" in Pontevedra (Spain), as well as by technicians from the Engineering Department of this company. This company has installed a Honeywell DCS Alcont that has 2D screens, where each operator is responsible for several operation monitors, in which various operating screens are shown.

It is observed that the application shows an exceptional quantity and quality of information to the visual range of the operators, because in a single screen the same information is presented as in 10 of the old 2D screens of DCS. This prevents the operator from having to navigate between all the screens and ignores what happens on one screen, by watching another different screen. The process chart has a visual representation, which is more natural and intuitive for the user; as it has a great similarity with the actual process and allows it to resemble the augmented reality.

The symbols and colours used in the 3D graphic scene are immediately recognized by the DCS operators; since the symbols used to represent 3D components are an evolution of 2D designs, proposed by international standards. This graphic scene transforms hundreds of status signals from physical devices (valves, pumps, etc.) into visual colour-based information. Formerly, this information is shown in numerical and textual format.

It is observed that the operator requires less mental effort to understand the complete state of the industrial process. This allows us to assert that the operation screen complies with the key concepts of usability; as it is very "easy to use" and very "easy to learn". This is reflected in the fact of "how" the operator visualizes all the components of the graphic scene.

Also, the use of different colours in the representation of figures 2.5D or 3D, which are visualized in the graphic scene, should not be considered strictly incompatible with the application of the principle of usability in computer systems. This is because the "risk assessment" of the workplace of a screen operator indicates that such a position can not be performed by people with colour blindness or other visual or physical impairments. This assessment would also apply to electricians, since an electrician with colour blindness would not be able to perform his job correctly, as he would not differentiate all coloured cables from a cable hose.

It is appreciated that operators and users need a period of adaptation to the new 3D environment, as they are initially surprised by the original presentation format of the process. Also, some people over 55 years or with vision problems are unable to visualize 3D images and indicate that they continue to visualize 2D images; However, some young people are extremely receptive to such 3D images. The position of the user, the distance to the monitor and the angle of distance of the images of each eye decisively influence the perception of the 3D image by the operator; since the presentation has been designed so that it is centred in front of the screen and at a distance of 60 cm.

It is verified that it is dangerous to have the animation of the pipes activated during the process control tasks; since it saturates the operator with an immense amount of visual information, which causes a decrease of its concentration. Likewise, it is detected the convenience of deactivating the sending of the voice warning messages (no alarms) during periods of crisis (for example a start (boot strapping) of the process), so as not to stun the operator.

CONCLUSION

The new advanced visualization systems will drive a great transformation in the way of performing the current maintenance, operation and design tasks in the industrial world. Thus, industrial operators will have at their disposal a universe of information, which will allow them to optimize the work they are doing. Even the operator can retransmit the task that he is executing, to receive help from a group of specialists, who are observing and analysing it from a very distant place.

This group of display devices showed that they should not be used interchangeably for any job; since each of them is more adapted to a specific set of tasks. In addition, it was found that some of these display equipment should not be used inside a factory; because in some situations they increase the occupational risks of the operator who carries them. Likewise, the compatibility of carrying these devices together with personal protective equipment or full protective clothing.

The ARM-G are devices, which are more adapted to tasks where the operator requires information, which does not overlap over their entire field of vision. Likewise, ARB-G are convenient to display information that can be superimposed easily, on the actual scene that the operator is perceiving. However, virtual reality equipment is appropriate for training, teaching and design tasks. In addition, the operator must be located in a very safe place, since he is in a virtual world that distances him/her from the real world that surrounds him/her.

The DCS operation screens are designed to drastically increase the amount and quality of process information that the operator has at his/her disposal. This new operating environment brings together in a single 2.5D or 3D screen the equivalent of 10 of the old 2D screens of DCS. Also, the use of 3D peripherals allows the rotation or displacement of the process on the screen, facilitating their analysis from different angles and positions (front, back, side, oblique, interior, etc.). Likewise, it is verified that there are some functionalities of operation, that are hardly translatable to environments 3D. Finally, it is observed that some methods of design of 2D screens are unassuming in 3D environments, so they have to be adapted to the new environment, but trying to preserve its essence.

REFERENCES

ABB. (2017, March). *System 800xA Extended Automation*. Retrieved from http://new.abb.com/control-systems/system-800xa/800xa-dcs

ASM. (2017, March). Retrieved from http://www.asmconsortium.net

Breibvold, H. P., & Olausson, M. (2010, October). El Operario Eficaz. *Revista ABB, 4*(10), 6–11.

Cámara de Ópticos. (2013, March). *Salud y tendencias visuales de los españoles*. Retrieved from http://camaraopticos.com/salud-visual-y-tendencias-de-los-espanoles/

Cota, M. P., & Castro, M. R. G. (2013). *DCS 3D Operators in Industrial Environments: New HCI Paradigm for the Industry. In Virtual, augmented and mixed reality. Systems and applications* (pp. 271–280). Heidelberg, Germany: Springer.

Cota, M. P., & Castro, M. R. G. (2013). *Usability in a new DCS interface, in universal access. In Human computer interaction. Design methods, tools, and interaction techniques for einclusion* (pp. 87–96). Heidelberg, Germany: Springer.

Daqri. (2017, March). *Smart Helmet*. Retrieved from https://daqri.com/products/smart-helmet/

Dickey, M. R. (2015, March). *How Google Glass Will Revolutionize 9 Industries*. Retrieved from http://www.businessinsider.com/google-glass-will-totally-disrupt-these-tktk-industries-2013-3?op=1

Emerson. (2017, March). *Delta V*. Retrieved from http:// http://www.emerson.com/en-us/automation/deltav

Epson. (2017, March). *Epson Moverio BT-300*. Retrieved from https://epson.com/moverio-augmented-reality-smart-glasses?pg=3#sn

Errington, J. (2005). *Establishing Human Performance Improvements an Economic Benefit for a Human-Centered Operator Interface*. Human Factors and Ergonomic Society.

Google. (2017, March). *Google Glass*. Retrieved from https://developers.google.com/glass/

Honeywell. (2006, October). *TotalPlant Alcont and Printa. Configuration Manual & Application planning guide*. Author.

ISO. (2017, March). Retrieved from http://www.iso.org

Malý, I. (2016, July). Augmented reality experiments with industrial robot in industry 4.0 environment. *IEEE 14th International Conference on Industrial Informatics (INDIN)*, 19-21.

McMahon. (2015, March). *Three decades of DCS technology*. Retrieved from http://www.controlglobal.com/articles/2005/227.html

Metavision. (2017, March). *Meta 2*. Retrieved from https://www.metavision.com

Microsoft. (2017, March). *Hololens*. Retrieved from https://www.microsoft.com/microsoft-hololens/en-us

Olausson, M., Larsson, M., & Alfredsson, F. (2012). Colaborando en un nueva dimensión. *Revista ABB, 2/12*, 6–11.

Omerth. (2017, March). *C-Thru*. Retrieved from http://www.omerh.com/c-thru#0

Pérez Cota M., González Castro M.R. (2011, June). Interfaz Avanzada de Oprador de DCS. *6ª CISTI*, 37-41.

Reising, D. V., Laberge, J., & Bullemer, P. (2010). *Supporting Operator Sitation Awareness With Overview Displays: A Series of Studies on Information vs. Vitualization Requeriments*. ICOCO.

Samsung. (2017, March). *Gear VR*. Retrieved from http://www.samsung.com/global/galaxy/gear-vr/

Siemens. (2017a, March). *Siemens Comos-Walkinside*. Retrieved from http://www.siemens.com/comos

Siemens. (2017b, March). *Simatic PCS7*. Retrieved from http://w3.siemens.com/mcms/process-control-systems/en/distributed-control-system-simatic-pcs-7/Pages/distributed-control-system-simatic-pcs-7.aspx

Silva, M., & Freitas, D. (2014). Glassist: Using Augmented Reality on Google Glass as an Aid to Classroom Management. *XVI Symposium on Virtual and Augmented Reality (SVR)*, 37 – 44. doi:10.1109/SVR.2014.41

Teixeira, J. M., & Ferreira, R. (2014). Teleoperation Using Google Glass and AR, Drone for Structural Inspection. *XVI Symposium on Virtual and Augmented Reality (SVR)*, 28 – 36. doi:10.1109/SVR.2014.42

Vuzix. (2017, March). *Smart Glasses*. Retrieved from https://www.vuzix.com/Products/Series-3000-Smart-Glasses

KEY TERMS AND DEFINITIONS

2.5D: Techniques that are used to represent things in two dimensions, but with an appearance of seeing a 3D representation.

3D: Three-dimensional representation.

Augmented Reality: Computer technology to "augment" the real environment using different technologies in a display that show people the real world with the combination of this technology to give more information or different services about the context.

Computerized Helmet: Helmet with computer abilities to help people in different situations.

Display Device: Output device to present information that can be visual or tactile.

Distributed Control System (DCS): Computerized control system for a process with a large number of control loops and autonomous controllers distributed throughout the system.

Human-Computer Interaction (HCI): Field that is focused on the interfaces that are needed to communicate people with computers.

Virtual Reality: Computer technology that uses headsets or multi-projected environments to generate realistic environments to immerse people in them.

Chapter 2
Developing a Cyber-Physical System for Hybrid Manufacturing in an Internet-of-Things Context

Paul Grefen
Eindhoven University of Technology, The Netherlands

Irene Vanderfeesten
Eindhoven University of Technology, The Netherlands

Georgios Boultadakis
European Dynamics SA, Greece

ABSTRACT

This chapter describes design and development of the HORSE system for process-oriented hybrid manufacturing that seamlessly integrates human and robotics actors in vertical manufacturing cells that are horizontally coupled in end-to-end manufacturing processes. The HORSE system supports advanced dynamic actor allocation to work cells, direct robot control and human actor instruction, closed-loop local event processing, and near-real-time global event processing. The system handles abstract process definitions and status information on the one hand and directly interfaces to industrial sensors and actuators on the other hand, making it a system with a strong cyber-physical character. The physical side of the system is deployed in an internet-of-things context, where the things are the industrial robots controlled by the HORSE system, the sensors feeding data to the system, and the products being manufactured in the industrial process managed by the system. The system will be deployed in real-world, industrial pilot scenarios in a European Horizon 2020 project.

DOI: 10.4018/978-1-5225-3805-9.ch002

INTRODUCTION

The use of advanced robots in manufacturing is becoming more and more commonplace in industry. This is for instance very evident in the German Industrie 4.0 initiave towards smart manufacturing (Germany Trade & Invest, 2014). Where robots used to be applied mainly in large, high-tech manufacturing plants, their application becomes increasingly accessible for a diverse range of manufacturing companies, even if they are small or medium enterprises (SME organizations) or not in a high-tech environment. Robots are used for highly repetitive tasks (such as making large numbers of spot welds), tasks that require strong force (such as lifting of heavy objects) and tasks that are unhealthy or dangerous to human workers (such as working in hazardous atmospheric conditions).

The use of robots in manufacturing is, however, not always very flexible and efficient. Firstly, this is caused by the safety requirements: if robots are not equipped with the right technological context, their use may present a safety hazard for human workers in the same physical space. Consequently, spaces where robots work and spaces where humans work are often physically separated, possibly leading to inflexibility and inefficiency. Secondly, the inflexibility is also caused by the work allocation specification: robots have their specific tasks and human workers too - it is not easy to transfer tasks from one class to the other. In other words: dynamic actor allocation in manufacturing cannot easily cross the human/robot boundary. This may lead to inefficiency where it comes to optimal resource usage. Thirdly, robot control processes are often poorly integrated in overall, end-to-end manufacturing processes. Robot control processes often follow a vertical orientation, focused on the operation within individual manufacturing work cells. End-to-end processes follow a horizontal orientation, focused on the operation across work cells and in the context of enterprise information processing.

The HORSE project is set up to address the three issues identified above. HORSE is a European Research and Innovation Project in the European Union (EU) Horizon 2020 Framework. HORSE runs from 2015 to 2020 and brings together 15 organizations, among which research institutes, technology providers, and manufacturing organizations (see http://www.horse-project.eu/ for more details). HORSE aims at designing, developing and testing an integrated software environment that explicitly supports (1) safe collaboration of human and robotic workers in the same physical environment, (2) flexible, dynamic allocation of manufacturing tasks to robotic workers, human workers, and hybrid teams of both, and (3) integration of vertical, within-cell manufacturing processes with horizontal, across-cell processes and linkage of these to enterprise-wide business processes.

In addressing the three issues above, HORSE integrates the 'cyber' aspect of business information processing with the 'physical' aspect of robotics, arriving at an advanced cyber-physical system for manufacturing. To integrate these two aspects, the digital world has to be connected to the physical world in a bi-directional fashion: the digital world has to be fed with information from the physical world and the physical world has to be fed with commands from the digital world. This is where the HORSE approach meets the world of the Internet of Things (McEwen & Cassimally, 2013).

In this article, we first outline the design of the HORSE system, showing how we have addressed the issues discussed above. In Section 2, we discuss the system design approach used in HORSE, which leads to the distinction between logical and physical architectures. In Section 3, we discuss the high-level design of the HORSE logical system architecture at three levels of aggregation: a context level and two internal levels. In Section 4, we show how the logical HORSE data architecture is used to further refine the logical system architecture. For reasons of brevity, we focus here on one of the four main HORSE subsystems - we choose the one that is most related to the cyber-physical nature of the system. After the discussion of the HORSE logical architecture, we move to the HORSE physical system architecture in Section 5, showing how HORSE relates to the Internet of Things. We end this article with an outlook onto possible future developments and conclusions in Section 6.

SYSTEM DESIGN APPROACH

The HORSE system covers a broad range of advanced functionality that needs to be deployed in an integrated way. This leads to a system structure with considerable complexity. To deal with this complexity in the system design process, we have put a strong emphasis on architecture (Hilliard, 2007). The architecting process is based on two frameworks:

- To deal with the various views of stakeholders and their sequencing in time, we use the well-known software engineering 4+1 framework of (Kruchten, 1995).
- To deal with the set of enterprise information aspects, we use a 5-aspect framework for the design of business information systems (Grefen, 2016), which is based on a framework from practice (Truijens, Oosterhaven, Maes, Jägers, & Iersel, 1990).

In the subsections below, we discuss these two frameworks and show how they have been used in the HORSE system design and how they are reflected in the structure of this article.

Apart from the software engineering point of view, we foster conceptual integration with the manufacturing domain by using the manufacturing control standard of the International Electrotechnical Commission (IEC) (IEC, 2013) in the design of the HORSE architecture.

The Kruchten 4+1 Framework

Kruchten has defined an architecture framework (Kruchten, 1995) that is one of the most important standards in thinking about structuring software architectures (see Figure 1). The framework is based on a separation of concerns with respect to phases of the architecture specification and software realization process. It organizes the description of an architecture around four main views with their respective main stakeholders:

1. The logical view specifies the object/module models of the design, i.e., the structure of the application logic in abstract terms. This view mainly specifies the functionality of a system under design, so what the system should do. The main stakeholders are the end users of the system.
2. The development view specifies the organization of the software in a development environment, i.e., the way the software development is supported to arrive at good software management. This view is concerned with how the system should be realized. The main stakeholders are the software engineers.

Figure 1. Kruchten 4+1 framework (from (Kruchten, 1995))

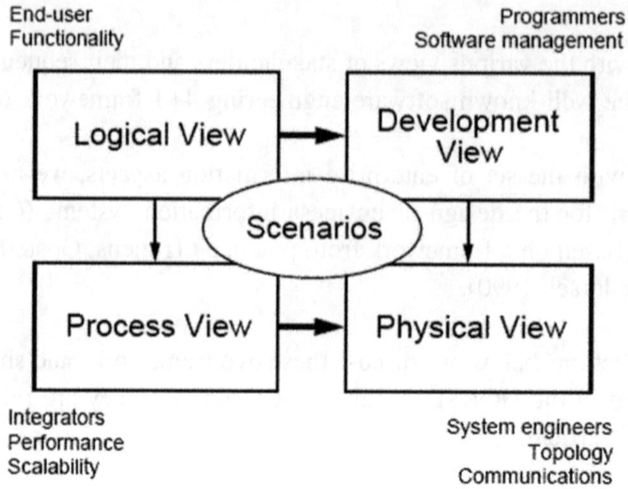

3. The process view specifies the concurrency and synchronization aspects of the software design, i.e., the way objects or modules in the logical view dynamically collaborate in parallel. This view mainly specifies the dynamic mechanisms and performance/scalability of a system under design. The main stakeholders are the integrators of the system.
4. The physical view describes the mapping(s) of software onto hardware, thereby reflecting the distribution aspect. This view mainly specifies the operational deployment of a system. The main stakeholders are the system engineers that are responsible for installing and maintaining the system.

Each of the four views has its prime stakeholders and its major concerns related to these stakeholders. This is a basis for a separation of concerns to reduce complexity in design, but may lead to a content-wise divergence of ideas. To avoid this divergence, the four basic views are illustrated by a fifth element:

5. The scenarios describe a few selected use cases that illustrate the four basic views. The scenarios make things concrete and provide a clear and practical basis for discussions between the various groups of stakeholders in the architecture design or analysis. As such, the scenarios are the 'content glue' that provides convergence of ideas.

The Updated Truijens Framework

The Kruchten 4+1 framework provides a separation of concerns in terms of software development phases, but does not separate various aspects of the description of a complex software system or information system. For this purpose, we adopt an updated version of the 5 aspect framework of Truijens. This framework was originally developed for information system development in the '90s (Truijens et al., 1990) and thereafter updated for information system developed in a modern, networked context (Grefen, 2016). The Updated Truijens Framework is illustrated in Figure 2. It consists of five interconnected aspects, which we describe below.

We distinguish between five interrelated architecture aspects in the design of the HORSE system:

- **Software:** The software aspect describes the structure of the HORSE software under development; it is described for instance in Unified Modeling Language (UML) component diagrams.
- **Process:** The process aspect describes the structure of business/manufacturing processes that the HORSE system supports; it is described for instance in

Figure 2. updated Truijens aspect framework (from (Grefen, 2016))

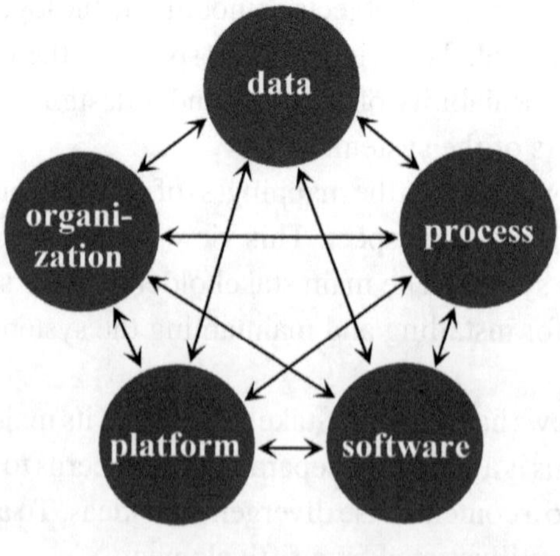

BPMN (Business Process Model and Notation) diagrams or UML activity diagrams.

- **Data:** The data aspect describes the structure of data manipulated by the HORSE system, as well as the structure of the concepts that underlie data definitions (concept model); it is described for instance in UML class diagrams.
- **Organization:** The organization aspect describes the structure of stakeholders in the HORSE context, such as operators of the HORSE system and designers of applications supported by the HORSE system; it is described by organigrams and/or actor models.
- **Platform:** The platform aspect describes the structure of the existing technology that is required to run the HORSE system under design in its operating context; this includes both hardware (such as computer systems and robots) and software (such as existing enterprise information systems, middleware and hardware control software).

The five aspects provide a separation of concerns, but are interrelated as shown by the arrows in Figure 2. For example: if a data structure is changed (in the data aspect), it may be that the software that manipulates this data (in the software aspect) needs to be changed too.

Applying the Frameworks to HORSE

In HORSE, we use the Kruchten 4+1 framework as the leading tool in sequencing the system design steps and involving the stakeholders in these steps. In doing so, we use the sequence of views indicated in Figure 1 and three industrial pilot cases as the basis for the scenarios.

The system design starts with designing the logical architecture. The logical architecture specifies the functional structure of the system under design, without reference to specific implementation techniques, technologies or deployment. The main stakeholders are the users of the system. Consequently, the input for the design is a requirements specification produced with users in pilot cases. Given the complexity of the system, we use a logical architecture design with five system aggregation levels plus one context level (HORSE Architecture Team, 2016). We discuss four of these six levels in Sections 3 and 4 of this chapter. To get to the lowest of these four levels, we need to address the HORSE data architecture as identified in the Updated Truijens Framework, as this defines which concepts need to be managed by the system at this level. We discuss this as well in Section 4.

The operational design and implementation of the HORSE system are covered by the development view and the process view of the architecture. The elaboration of these two views leads to a software system that can be deployed. As software engineering is not the focus of this article, we skip these two views in the discussion below.

In HORSE, software deployment takes place in the physical view of the architecture. Here it is determined what kinds of software and hardware will actually run in concrete scenarios, given the system design in the other three architecture views. We discuss the physical architecture of the HORSE system in Section 5. For reasons of brevity, we limit this discussion to that part of the HORSE architecture that is most connected to its cyber-physical character and therefore best illustrates the Internet-of-Things context.

HIGH-LEVEL LOGICAL SYSTEM ARCHITECTURE

In the HORSE logical system architecture, we have a hierarchical, multi-level design of the functionality of the HORSE system (Grefen, Vanderfeesten, & Boultadakis, 2016a; HORSE Architecture Team, 2016). The complete design comprises six levels. In this section, we discuss three of these six levels, omitting one intermediate level and the two most detailed levels. We label these three levels as follows:

- **Context Architecture:** Describes the HORSE system in its context of other information systems related to manufacturing.
- **Level 1 Architecture:** Describes the HORSE system in terms of its four main functional subsystems.

- **Level 2 Architecture:** Describes the main internal modules of the four subsystems at Level 1.

We discuss the Context Architecture in Section 3.1 and the Level 1 Architecture in Section 3.2. As the Level 2 architecture is complex, we split its discussion into the *design time* half in Section 3.3 and the *execution time* half in Section 3.4. This split is also instrumental to the discussion of the physical architecture in Section 5.

HORSE Context Architecture

HORSE focuses on support for hybrid manufacturing processes, i.e., processes in which human and robotic actors work together tightly and flexibly. For example, in the project we have three industrial pilot cases in the domains of manufacturing car parts, metal casts, and high-end furniture mechanics. In a modern enterprise, these manufacturing processes are embedded in enterprise processes that accept customer orders, create manufacturing planning, handle inbound and outbound logistics, and perform after-sales services (for instance using the value chain model of (Porter, 1985)).

Consequently, the HORSE system needs to be embedded in an enterprise information system landscape supporting these business functions. This is illustrated in Figure 3, where we see the HORSE system in the context of an enterprise business process management system (BPMS), an enterprise resource planning system (ERP), a manufacturing execution system (MES) and a product lifecycle management system (PLMS) (HORSE Architecture Team, 2016). The BPMS controls the end-to-end business processes (i.e., enterprise processes from customer order to delivery or after-sales) across the other systems. We call this architecture the HORSE context architecture (which is in a practical situation typically much more complex than shown in Figure 3).

Figure 3. HORSE simplified context architecture

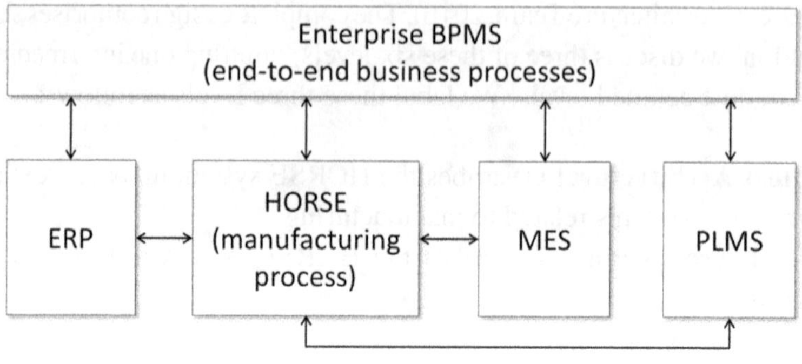

HORSE Architecture Level 1

When we design the HORSE system architecture, we zoom in to the HORSE box of Figure 3 and refine its contents. For this refinement, we make two top-level design decisions.

In the first place, it is important to distinguish between design time and execution time when dealing with hybrid manufacturing activities. These activities are complex in nature, as they can involve many human and robotics actors which need to work highly synchronized. Consequently, support is needed for the well-structured design of these activities. Likewise, the execution of the activities is complex, which requires adequate support. This consideration leads to a design time aspect and an execution time aspect of the system.

In the second place, it is important to distinguish between functionality that is aimed at the support of activities within a single manufacturing work cell and functionality that is aimed at synchronizing activities across multiple work cells. Support within a work cell is closely coupled to the operation of human and robotics workers, geared towards the manufacturing steps they have to perform. The support across cells supports synchronization at the level of manufacturing lines or even manufacturing plants. This distinction is supported by the IEC manufacturing standard (IEC, 2013) that we have mentioned before. This consideration leads to a global level and a local level in the system, i.e., we design a layered architecture (Grefen, 2016). The global level interfaces to the BPMS shown in Figure 3, the local level interfaces to the manufacturing technology such as robots (this is where the cyber-physical nature of the system is most prominent).

When we combine the design time and execution time aspects on the one hand and the global and local levels on the other hand, we arrive at a top-level HORSE architecture with four sub-systems, as shown in Figure 4 (Grefen et al., 2016a; HORSE Architecture Team, 2016). This is a columned architecture embedded into a layered architecture (Grefen, 2016). The two aspects are connected via databases that contain specifications of manufacturing activities and resources, as are the two levels in the design time aspect. In the execution time aspect, the two levels are directly coupled to pass execution command messages from global to local level and status messages from local to global level. Note that we label the local design time support as configuration, as this is a more natural label in the cyber-physical manufacturing domain.

In the two subsections below, we further refine the two aspects of the architecture of Figure 4, first the design time aspect and then the execution time aspect.

Figure 4. HORSE architecture, aggregation level 1

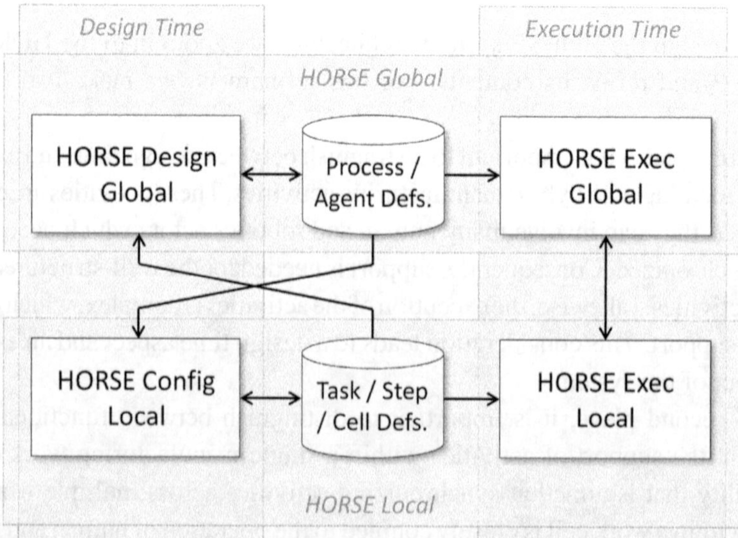

HORSE Design Time Architecture Level 2

We show the elaboration of the design time aspect of the HORSE system in Figure 5, in which the global and local levels are also clearly shown.

The functionality in the global design subsystem focuses on the support of designing manufacturing processes that involve multiple work cells and possibly many agents of various types. As such, the functionality is strongly connected to that of design modules of existing business process management systems, but extended with functionality that can deal with the differences between human and robotic agents and the physical nature of manufacturing processes - as opposed to administrative environments in which business process management systems are traditionally applied (Vanderfeesten & Grefen, 2015). The subsystem contains modules for designing the flow of processes and for designing the characteristics of agents (where agents are any entities that can perform manufacturing activities).

The functionality in the local configuration subsystem is aimed at designing the operation within a work cell, which can involve multiple agents in complex manufacturing activities. This functionality is closely tied to the physical nature of manufacturing. The module for task design supports the specification of synchronization of multiple agents within a cell, like the interplay between a human worker and a robot (possibly even integrated into a so-called cobot). The work cell simulator module is used to evaluate a designed interplay before putting it in actual physical use. There are two modules for the design of manufacturing steps. The

Figure 5. HORSE architecture, design time aspect, aggregation level 2

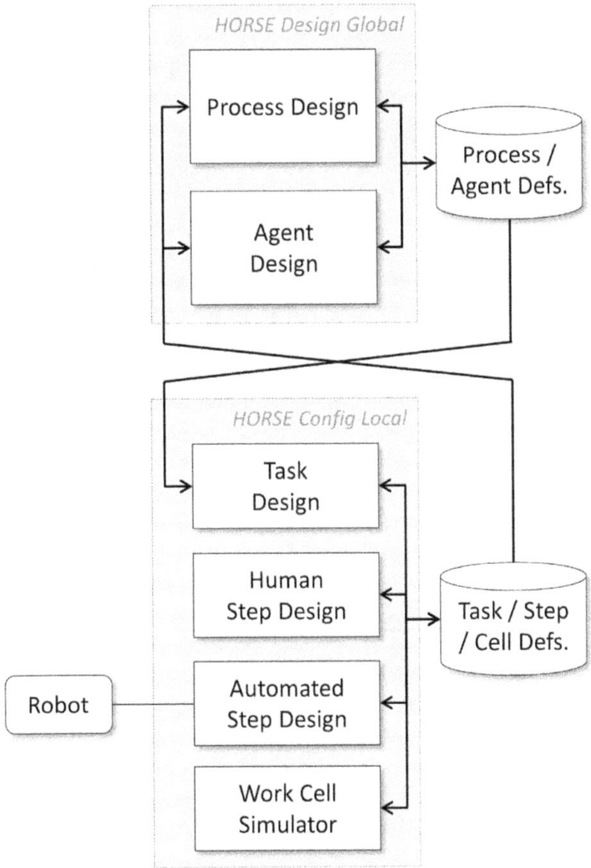

module for the design of human steps creates work instructions for human workers, using advanced technology like augmented reality. The module for the design of automated steps creates execution scripts for robots. This module supports textual scripting, graphical scripting, and scripting by physical manipulation (physically showing the robot what to do, also called programming by demonstration (Dillmann & Friedrich, 2005)). The latter requires a direct connection to the involved robot, as shown in the figure.

HORSE Execution Time Architecture Level 2

The elaboration of the execution time aspect of the HORSE architecture is shown in Figure 6, with the global and local levels clearly distinguished. Both levels contain an execution module and an awareness module. The levels are connected to each

Figure 6. HORSE architecture, execution time aspect, aggregation level 2

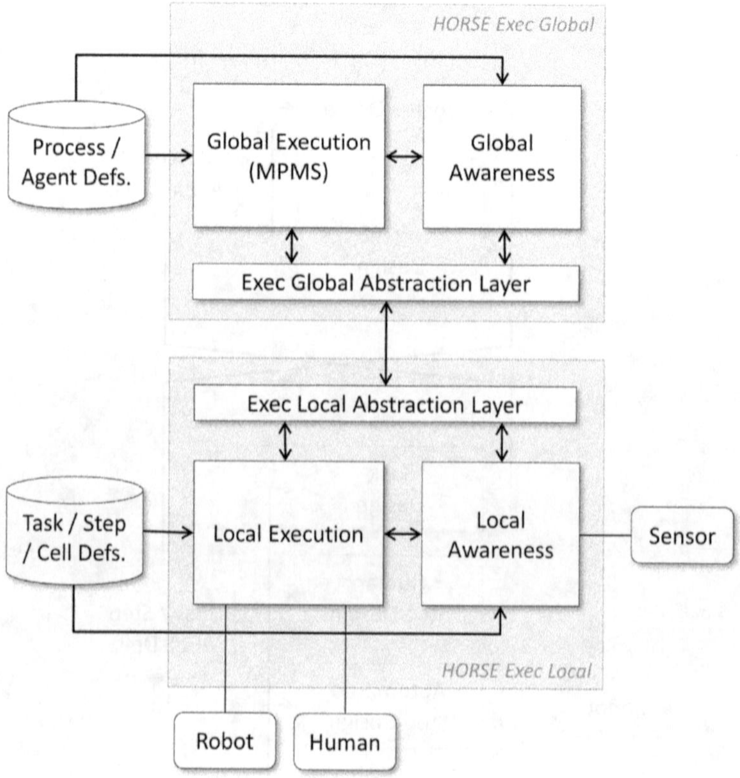

other via abstraction layers to allow easy portability across various technology platforms from either side.

The global execution module is responsible for the execution of the overall manufacturing processes across work cells. Analogous to the global design subsystem, this module is based on extensions to existing BPMS mechanisms, taking the specifics of robotic manufacturing environments into account (Vanderfeesten & Grefen, 2015). The local execution module directly interacts with the agents in a manufacturing environment (as shown in the figure). The interaction with human agents differs greatly from the interaction with robotic agents. Human agents typically receive high-level work instructions that may be complemented with augmented reality support. They execute these instructions using their interpretation. Robots receive detailed step scripts that describe the desired activities in low-level, physical parameters.

Both awareness modules support context awareness in the manufacturing environment. Awareness is used for both regular activity monitoring and for exception detection. The latter is an important element in providing safety in the cyber-physical environment, for example to avoid collisions between robots and human workers. Local awareness provides context awareness within a manufacturing cell, providing a direct control loop between sensor readings and execution control. It can escalate exceptions that it cannot handle to global awareness. Global awareness provides context awareness at the manufacturing process or manufacturing plant level, either on the basis of global observations or escalated local observations.

DETAILED LOGICAL EXECUTION ARCHITECTURE

In this section, we further refine part of the logical system architecture as discussed in the previous section to the Level 3 Architecture. For reasons of brevity, we limit our discussion of the Level 3 Architecture to one of the four main functional subsystems (as identified in the Level 1 Architecture): the subsystem that directly controls local manufacturing functionality in the cyber-physical context. This partial Level 3 Architecture is discussed in Section 4.2. It is the basis for the discussion of the physical architecture in Section 5.

Before we can discuss this refinement of the logical system architecture, we need to discuss the HORSE data architecture. This data architecture defines the concepts to be handled by the system architecture and hence the detailed structure of this system architecture. We discuss the HORSE data architecture in Section 4.1.

HORSE Logical Data Architecture

The high-level HORSE logical data architecture consists of three concept models:

- An *agent concept model*, which specifies the concepts and relations between concepts that describe actors in a manufacturing context, i.e., entities that can perform manufacturing activities;
- An *activity concept model*, which specifies the concepts and relations between concepts that describe the activities to be performed in a manufacturing context by agents;
- An *event concept model*, which specifies the concepts and relations between concepts that describe events that require reactions in a manufacturing context; this concept model is included because monitoring and safety are important aspects in HORSE.

The high-level logical data architecture is shown in Figure 7. Here we see the three concept models and the way they are linked.

Figure 7. HORSE overall logical data architecture

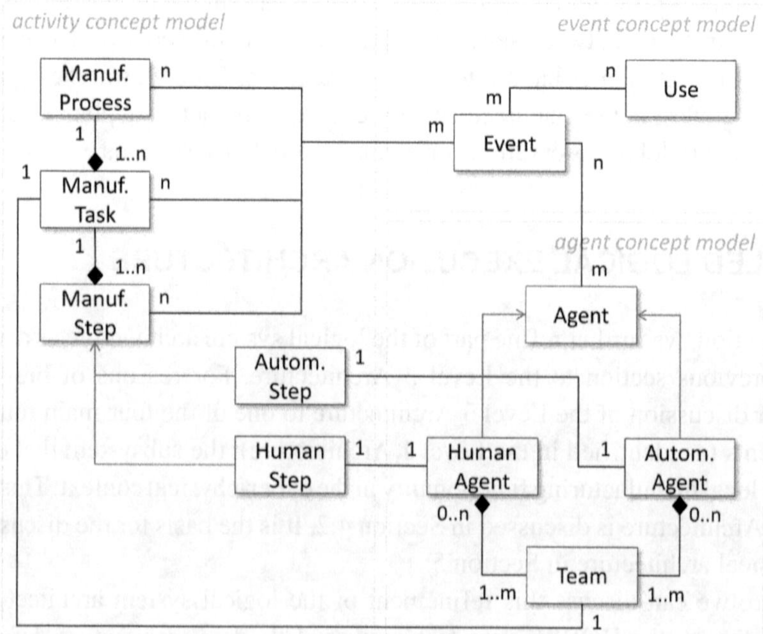

In the activity concept model, we see that manufacturing processes consist of manufacturing tasks. A process is executed across manufacturing work cells, a task within a single work cell. Manufacturing tasks consist of manufacturing steps. In the agent concept model, we see that manufacturing teams consist of manufacturing agents, which can be human or automated in nature. The coupling between these two concept models determines how the HORSE system manages manufacturing in detail:

- Manufacturing tasks are linked to manufacturing teams consisting of one or more agents.
- Manufacturing steps (as parts of tasks) are linked to manufacturing agents (as parts of teams).

This implies that manufacturing in work cells is primarily controlled at the team level and within that at the agent level. At the latter level, the distinction is made between human agents and automated agents. In the next subsection, we will see how this is directly reflected in the structure of the Level 3 Logical System Architecture.

When we refine the agent concept model of Figure 7, we see the different kinds of agents in the HORSE cyber-physical context - and thus the kind of 'active things' that are present in the HORSE Internet of Things context. This is shown in Figure 8. Here we see that we distinguish between configurable automated agents (intelligent robots) and non-configurable automated agents ('dumb' devices like industrial conveyors and turntables). Robots can be static (fixed to a location) or mobile (able to move around a factory). Both can take the form of a so-called *cobot*: a robot that is closely coupled to a human (for example a wearable exo-skeleton for lifting heavy loads). Mobile robots can be automated guided vehicles (AGVs).

HORSE Local Execution Time Architecture Level 3

The HORSE execution time aspect logical architecture at aggregation level 2 is shown in Figure 6. In this section, we further elaborate the local part of this architecture (indicated as *HORSE Exec Local* in the figure). This part of the overall architecture most explicitly shows the cyber-physical aspect of the HORSE system. The refinement of this architecture is shown in Figure 9.

Within the box *HORSE Exec Local* in Figure 9, we see the software modules that directly manage the cyber-physical manufacturing environment. The modules are divided into a *Local Execution* subsystem and a *Local Awareness* subsystem, which are both connected to the global execution level through an abstraction layer. The modules obtain their information from the definitions database (the same database as

Figure 8. HORSE detailed agent logical data architecture

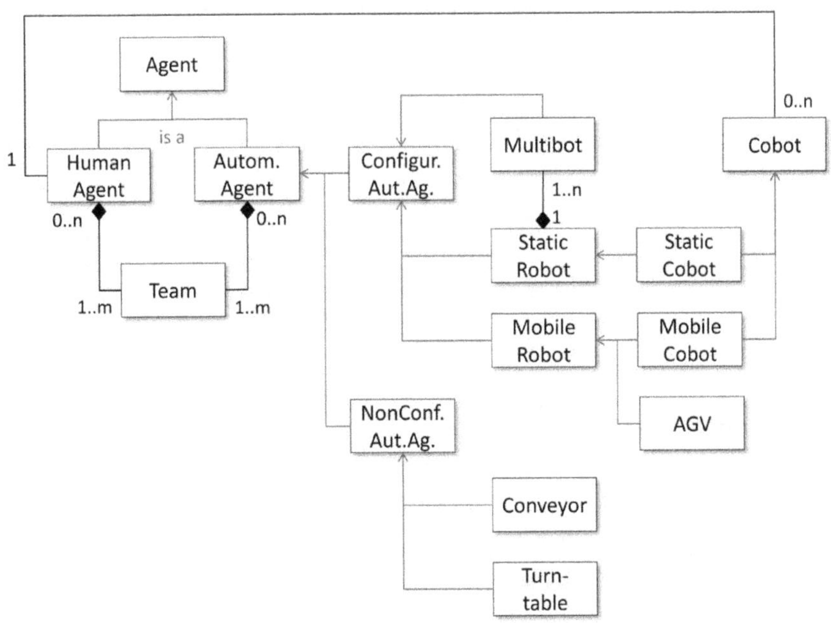

Figure 9. HORSE architecture, local execution time aspect, aggregation level 3

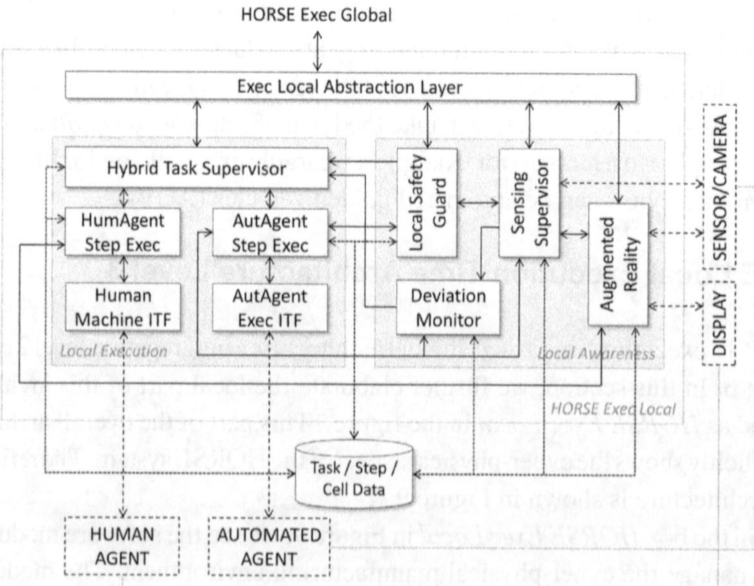

shown at the local level in Figure 4) and communicate through direct interfaces. As can be seen easily, this is a fairly complex architecture. For easier understanding, we show a simplified architecture in Figure 10, in which we have omitted the connection to the global level and the definitions database with its connections.

Figure 10. Simplified version of Figure 9

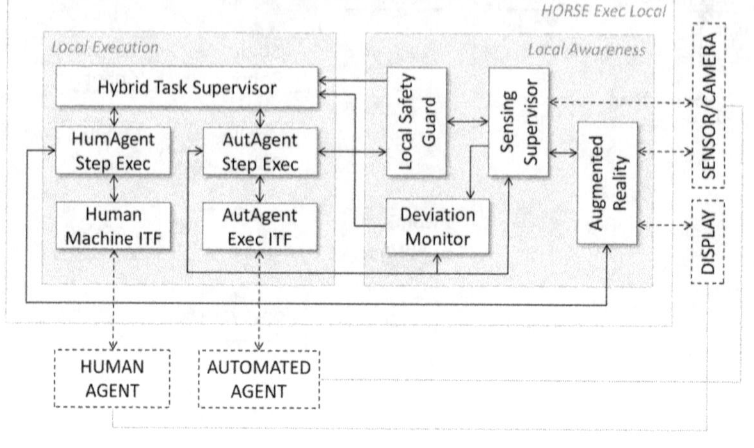

In Figure 10, we see the physical context of the HORSE software system (indicated by the dashed boxes). It consists of human agents (factory workers), automated agents (intelligent industrial robots and 'dumb' automated devices like conveyor belts), sensors and cameras that observe the state in a manufacturing cell, and displays that instruct human agents. The dashed interfaces between software modules and physical elements 'define' the cyber-physical nature of the system. Note that physical elements are also connected to each other in the physical world (indicated by the thin gray lines): sensors and cameras may be attached to automated agents, displays may belong to human agents (such as tablet computers) or may even be attached to these (such as head-mounted displays or smartwatches), and even human agents and automated agents may be physically connected (in the form of so-called *cobots*, i.e., combinations of humans and robots like wearable robots).

The *Local Execution* subsystem consists of three types of modules. The *Hybrid Task Supervisor* controls the interplay of multiple agents executing a task within a manufacturing work cell. The two *Step Execution* modules control the execution of individual manufacturing steps by a single agent. The relation between the Hybrid Task Supervisor and the Step Execution modules is directly dictated by the HORSE logical data architecture, as we have seen in the previous subsection. The two *Execution Interface* modules contain the logic to actually drive the various types of agents (via detailed task lists for human agents and control scripts for automated agents).

The *Local Awareness* subsystem consists of a *Local Safety Guard* that monitors whether all activities in a work cell remain within safe boundaries, a *Sensing Supervisor* that interprets all signals from sensors and cameras, a *Deviation Monitor* that compares sensor and camera readings with permitted values, and an *Augmented Reality* module that provides augmented reality awareness to human agents via displays connected to these agents.

After having discussed the logical architecture of the HORSE system in this section, we move our attention to the physical architecture in the next section.

PHYSICAL SYSTEM ARCHITECTURE

In Section 3, we have outlined the logical architecture of the HORSE system, coinciding with the logical view of the Kruchten 4+1 framework introduced in Section 2. In this section, we continue with the physical view of this framework, i.e., we discuss how the logical architecture can be physically deployed in an execution environment to obtain a running system in a specific manufacturing context.

In this section, we focus on the cyber-physical aspect of the HORSE system. As discussed before, we limit ourselves in this section to that part of the HORSE system that is closest related to this cyber-physical character of the system (and of manufacturing in general): the Local Execution subsystem of which the logical architecture is discussed in Section 4.1.

Below, we first discuss several categories of non-functional requirements to the HORSE system that must be reflected in its physical system architecture. Next, we show how this leads to the HORSE technology stack.

Response Time Requirements to the HORSE System

The HORSE system is developed to support hybrid manufacturing processes in which humans and robots collaborate in close physical proximity. Mostly, this has the form of multi-agent manufacturing cells, where one or more agents are human and one or more agents are robotic. But this can also have the form of mobile robots operating in a work space where humans do their work.

This hybrid manufacturing approach offers many advantages compared to a manufacturing context where human agents and robotic agents are physically separated (by fences or even walls). It does, however, also pose safety risks – primarily for the human agents. For this purpose, the HORSE system is functionally equipped with global and local awareness modules (see Figure 6). To make meaningful use of these modules, nonfunctional requirements have to be taken into account, in this case predominantly requirements with respect to response times to effectively deal with critical real-time events, such as safety breaches.

This is most important for the local awareness module that controls safety aspects within a work cell, for instance by making sure robots do not collide with humans. To do so, the local awareness module observes physical movements in a work cell, analyzes them in real-time and instructs the involved actors to take immediate action (such as halting the robot) in case of an imminent collision through the local execution module. Execution of the entire procedure must take place within a small fraction of a second. Consequently, this needs to be executed very efficiently in a communication path as illustrated in Figure 11 with real-time interconnection between the various modules and sufficient computation power.

Interoperability Requirements to the HORSE System

From a cyber-physical and Internet of Things point of view (McEwen & Cassimally, 2013), there are complex interoperability requirements to the HORSE system. This is partly attributable to the fact that the HORSE context includes robotic manufacturing agents, as we have seen in the previous subsection. But this is also attributable to the fact that the HORSE approach includes advanced support for human actors. The latter is most clearly visible in the support for augmented reality (AR).

Figure 11. Local communication path in case of an observed safety breach

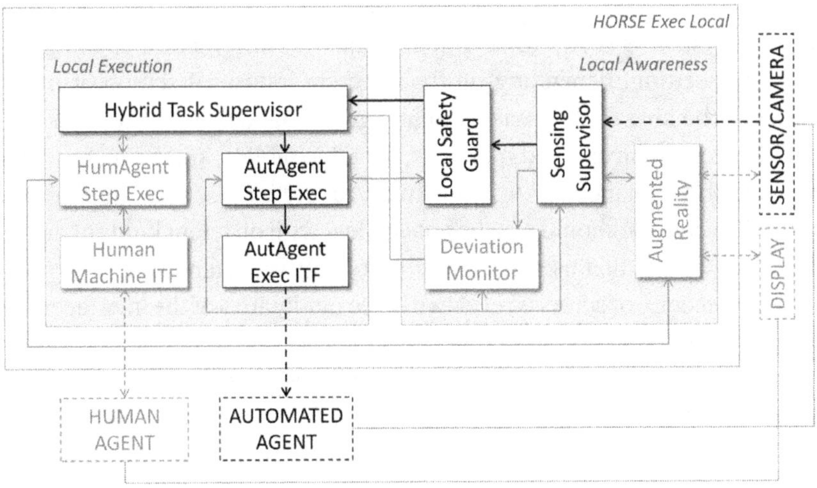

Using AR functionality, human workers receive real-time, graphical step execution instructions that are projected onto real-world observations (through wearable displays). This means that the HORSE system must be able to communicate with cameras to record the real-world observations (and possibly with other sensors for aspects like detailed geo-location) and displays to provide the task-dependent, real-time instructions, controlled by the HORSE step execution engine. This is illustrated in Figure 12. This has consequences for the physical architecture technology stack that we discuss later in this section.

Figure 12. Local communication path for execution of an AR supported step

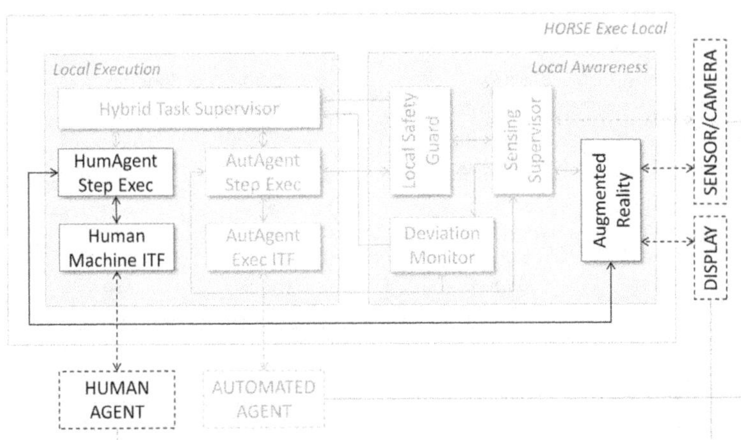

Portability Requirements to the HORSE System

The HORSE system is set up to be able to deal with different kinds of agents in a manufacturing setting, depending on the concrete industrial setting at hand. The system should be able to deal with human agents that are instructed via different physical channels, such as fixed monitors, portable tablets, smartwatches, or smart glasses - possibly enhanced with augmented reality as discussed in the previous subsection. The system should also be able to deal with different kinds of automated agents, such as robots that use different control software standards.

This heterogeneity of actors is reflected in the modularity of the interfaces towards these actors in the logical architecture. This means that for physical architectures, these interfaces modules can be chosen depending on the exact agent configuration in a specific manufacturing setting. This is illustrated in Figure 13, in which we show to alternative setups for the local execution subsystem (the left-hand side of Figure 10).

Technology Stack for the HORSE System

Given the complexity of the HORSE system, a middleware approach is required to implement the interfaces between the modules. The HORSE design approach uses, amongst other interfaces, the OSGi (Open Services Gateway initiative) specification for general module interconnection. OSGi (Hall, Pauls, McCulloch, & Savage, 2011) is a modular system architecture and a service platform for the Java programming language that implements a complete and dynamic component model. It also provides a universal publish-subscribe messaging bus for system modules to communicate.

Figure 13. Alternative agent interface modules

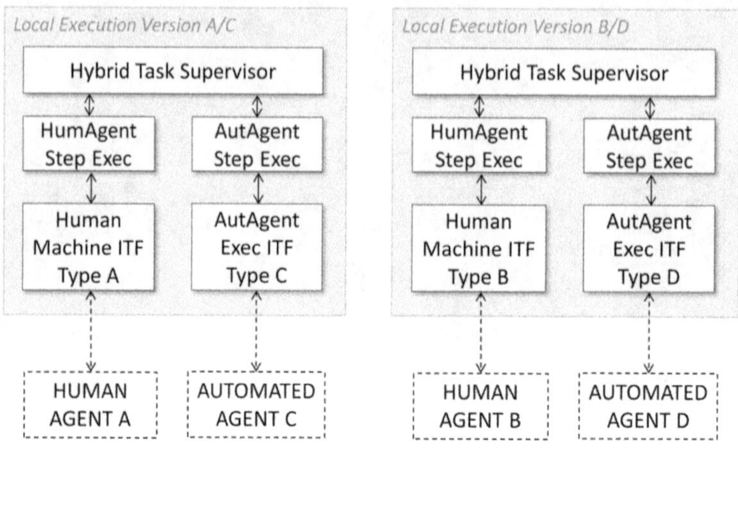

Therefore, OSGi is the basis for an interconnect that satisfies the high response time requirements that we have discussed in Section 5.1.

To develop modules to communicate with automated agents, several software frameworks are used.

The KUKA Sunrise software platform provides all functions to operate lightweight KUKA robots. These functions cover, for instance, graphical programming, force and torque monitoring, safe collision detection, and velocity monitoring.

The tailor made HORSE OSGi Apps are software packages that offer powerful and sophisticated component management and interoperability, as well as context-aware assistance of agents (workers, robots) on the production floor in the execution of their tasks. Some of the key HORSE components (like messaging infrastructure, device management and others) are provided as OSGi products or modules.

The Robot Operating System (ROS) (O'Kane, 2013) is an open-source, meta-operating system for robots and provides functionality such as hardware abstraction, low-level device control, implementation of commonly used functionality, message-passing between processes, and package management (Open Source Robotics Foundation, 2017b). Within the ROS environment, several applications are used: an extended version of ROS FlexBE (Open Source Robotics Foundation, 2017a), which is a graphical language for design and execution of complex automated agents behavior; ROS MoveIt! (Chitta, 2016) for force feedback control to enable more precise handling (gripping, placing, etc.) of objects; ROS Kinetic for simple operating system functionality and the interfacing between the above mentioned ROS applications and the robot.

Another software package used for advanced robot motion planning is GPU Voxels (Hermann et al., 2014). To provide the processing power required by GPU Voxels, nVidia CUDA (Storti & Yurtoglu, 2015) is used. CUDA is a parallel computing platform and application programming interface model, allowing software developers to use a CUDA-enabled graphics processing unit for general-purpose, high-performance processing. Using this kind of parallel computing is required to deliver the computation power required to do real-time 3D projections as mentioned in Section 5.1.

On the robotic hardware level, HORSE supports various options: the CEA Sybot and various Kuka offerings. To work with Kuka robots, the Kuka Sunrise robot software platform includes a specific Kuka robot interface. Next to that, OPC UA (Rinaldi, 2016) is used as the interface to advertise and invoke robotic services, both on Kuka and Sybot robots. And the ROS kinetic operating system includes an interface to the Sybot.

To support augmented reality, the use of Light Guide Systems (LGS) is considered in the HORSE physical architecture.

All the technology choices above determine the HORSE local execution technology stack, which is shown in Figure 14. Note that the overall HORSE technology stack (including the other three main subsystems of Figure 4) is considerable more complex.

OUTLOOK AND CONCLUSION

In this section, we first provide an outlook for further extension and embedding of the technology described in this chapter. Then, the chapter is concluded with a short conclusion.

Outlook: Manufacturing Networks

The HORSE framework as discussed in this article has in principle an intra-organizational scope, i.e., it covers the automation of a single manufacturing organization at a single location. Modern manufacturing, however, typically takes place in manufacturing chains or even manufacturing networks (IDC, 2014). These chains and networks consist of several (and possibly many) autonomous manufacturing organizations that collaboratively manufacture a complex product.

This principle of cross-organizational manufacturing has for example been developed in the CrossWork project (Grefen, Eshuis, Mehandjiev, Kouvas, & Weichhart, 2009; Grefen, Mehandjiev, Kouvas, Weichhart, & Eshuis, 2009), be

Figure 14. HORSE local execution technology stack

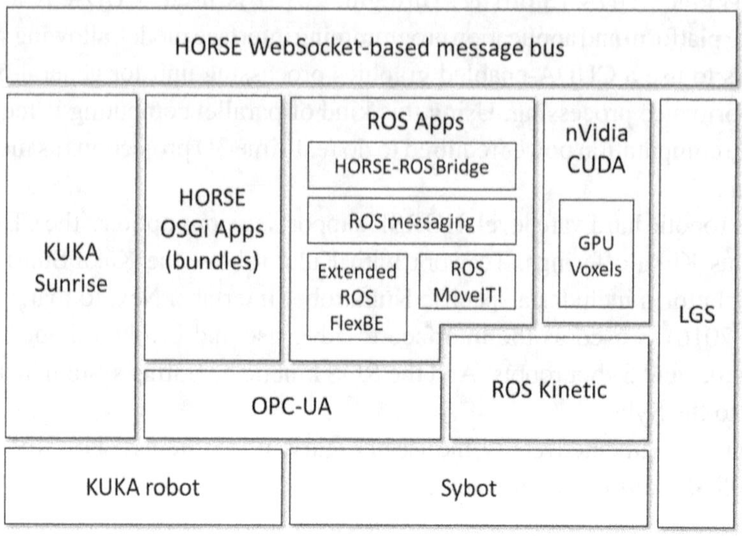

it without the coupling to the local level as in the HORSE project. In CrossWork, networks of manufacturing organizations connect their local manufacturing processes into a global process that is synchronized by process management technology. This leads to the creation of so-called instant virtual enterprises, temporary collaborations for the production of series of products, which use networked business process management (Grefen, 2013). The CrossWork approach has been prototyped in the automotive industry (which provides a similarity with one of the pilot cases of the HORSE project). CrossWork relies on a centralized process management engine that executes a shared global business process, which controls local processes in the collaborating organizations. This is illustrated in Figure 15, which shows one global process that connects the local processes of four manufacturing organizations in a specific market (Grefen, Eshuis, et al., 2009). The local processes are abstractions of HORSE manufacturing processes.

Adding this inter-organizational level to manufacturing even widens the cyber-physical scope of the resulting approach, covering the spectrum from internet-based, global electronic business to local industrial robot control. This can lead to full automation support for concepts like virtual manufacturing enterprises (Hans, Abels, Zöller, Miede, & Steinmetz, 2013; Schulte et al., 2014) and plug-and-play virtual factories (Steinmetz, Schuller, Schulte, & Abels, 2012).

Outlook: Cloud Computing

One of the points of departure of the HORSE project is that its results should be also applicable in an SME context. This SME context often implies limited on-site

Figure 15. Inter-organizational manufacturing business process (Grefen, Eshuis, et al., 2009)

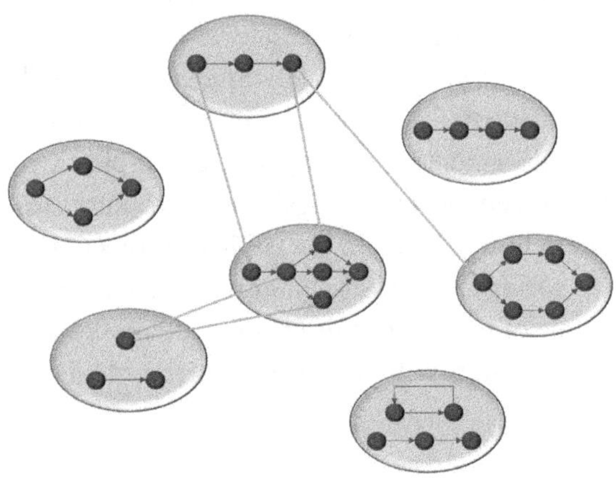

availability of a full-blown enterprise information system context, limited availability of high-level manufacturing control systems, and limited availability of high-end computing resources for advanced robot usage and control (think for example of simulation environments for robot programming or the use of augmented reality for instruction of human workers in robotic environments). Therefore, the use of cloud services can be an important enabling factor in the application of HORSE concepts and technology in SME environments. This implies the coupling of manufacturing control technology as discussed in this article with cloud computing technology (Shawish & Salama, 2013). The use of cloud computing can also further enable inter-organizational manufacturing as discussed above (Hans et al., 2013; Schulte et al., 2014).

Note however that not all manufacturing control can always be brought to the cloud because of performance and timing constraints. The latter we have discussed in Section 5 of this article. This implies that different cloud computing paradigms, such as Software-as-a-Service (SaaS) and Platform-as-a-Service (PaaS), can apply to different parts of the HORSE architecture (Grefen, Vanderfeesten, & Boultadakis, 2016b). Where timing constraints do not allow the direct application of cloud computing (most specifically in the local execution subsystem), it may be combined with a local infrastructure for fog computing (Bonomi, Milito, Zhu, & Addepalli, 2012).

A high-level overview of the possible application of cloud computing and fog computing paradigms in the HORSE system is given in Figure 16 (as an overlay of Figure 4).

CONCLUSION

In this article, we have outlined the architecture design of the HORSE system. We have shown how a structured, hierarchical system design leads to a modular architecture with clear subsystems and interfaces at several levels of aggregation (with additional levels covered in (Grefen et al., 2016a; HORSE Architecture Team, 2016)). The HORSE system integrates aspects of typical enterprise information systems (such as explicit process management) and of typical cyber-physical systems (such as real-time interaction with connected 'things' such as robots, sensors and cameras).

The HORSE system is developed in the HORSE project, which is scheduled to run from fall 2015 to spring 2020. Consequently, the HORSE system is still under development at the time of writing of this chapter and complete application results are not yet available. The system will be first tested in three real-world manufacturing pilot cases:

Figure 16. HORSE architecture and possible cloud computing paradigms

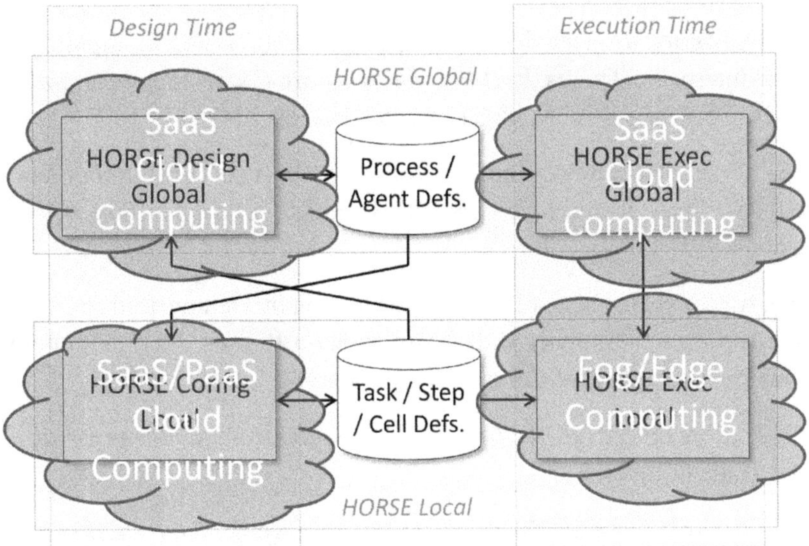

- A pilot case in manufacturing large series of car parts (wind screen wiper systems).
- A pilot case in manufacturing medium series of high-end telescopic sliders.
- A pilot case in manufacturing small series of metal castings.

These pilot cases define the details of the scenarios in the Kruchten framework as discussed in Section 2 (see Figure 1). After collecting feedback from these first tests, an updated version of the HORSE system will be used in an open call phase, where it will be used in ten more industrial cases.

ACKNOWLEDGMENT

The HORSE project has received funding from the European Union's Horizon 2020 Research and Innovation Programme under Grant Agreement No. 680734. All members of the HORSE project team are acknowledged for their contribution to the system development process. Jonnro Erasmus, Kostas Traganos and Venelin Arnaudov are thanked for their help with lining up the technical details for this chapter.

REFERENCES

Bonomi, F., Milito, R., Zhu, J., & Addepalli, S. (2012). Fog Computing and its Role in the Internet of Things. In *Proceedings 1st MCC workshop on Mobile Cloud Computing* (pp. 13–16). ACM. doi:10.1145/2342509.2342513

Chitta, S. (2016). MoveIt! An Introduction. In A. Koubaa (Ed.), *Robot Operating System (ROS): The Complete Reference* (Vol. 1, pp. 3–27). Springer. doi:10.1007/978-3-319-26054-9_1

Dillmann, R., & Friedrich, H. (2005). Programming by Demonstration: A Machine Learning Approach to Support Skill Acquisition for Robots. Artificial Intelligence and Symbolic Mathematical Computation, 87–108.

Germany Trade & Invest. (2014). *Industrie 4.0: Smart Manufacturing for the Future*. Germany Trade & Invest.

Grefen, P. (2013). Networked Business Process Management. *International Journal of IT/Business Alignment and Governance*, *4*(2), 54–82.

Grefen, P. (2016, Fall). *Business information system architecture*. Eindhoven University of Technology.

Grefen, P., Eshuis, R., Mehandjiev, N., Kouvas, G., & Weichhart, G. (2009). Internet-Based Support for Process-Oriented Instant Virtual Enterprises. *IEEE Internet Computing*, *13*(6), 65–73. doi:10.1109/MIC.2009.96

Grefen, P., Eshuis, R., Mehandjiev, N., Kouvas, G., & Weichhart, G. (2016). *Business Information System Architecture, Fall 2016 Edition*. Eindhoven University of Technology.

Grefen, P., Mehandjiev, N., Kouvas, G., Weichhart, G., & Eshuis, R. (2009). Dynamic Business Network Process Management in Instant Virtual Enterprises. *Computers in Industry*, *60*(2), 86–103. doi:10.1016/j.compind.2008.06.006

Grefen, P., Vanderfeesten, I., & Boultadakis, G. (2016a). *Architecture Design of the HORSE Hybrid Manufacturing Process Control System* (Beta Working Paper Series No. 518). Eindhoven University of Technology.

Grefen, P., Vanderfeesten, I., & Boultadakis, G. (2016b). Supporting Hybrid Manufacturing: Bringing Process and Human/Robot Control to the Cloud. In *Proceedings 5th IEEE International Conference on Cloud Networking* (pp. 200–203). IEEE. doi:10.1109/CloudNet.2016.39

Hall, R., Pauls, K., McCulloch, S., & Savage, D. (2011). *OSGi in Action: Creating Modular Applications in Java*. Manning Publications.

Hans, R., Abels, S., Zöller, S., Miede, A., & Steinmetz, R. (2013). Enabling collaboration in virtual manufacturing enterprises with cloud computing. *Proceedings 19th Americas Conference on Information Systems, AMCIS 2013 - Hyperconnected World: Anything, Anywhere, Anytime*, 2, 1341–1350.

Hermann, A., Drews, F., Bauer, J., Klemm, S., Roennau, A., & Dillmann, R. (2014). Unified GPU voxel collision detection for mobile manipulation planning. *IEEE International Conference on Intelligent Robots and Systems*, 4154-4160. doi:10.1109/IROS.2014.6943148

Hilliard, R. (2007). *All About IEEE Std 1471*. Retrieved from http://www.iso-architecture.org/ieee-1471/docs/all-about-ieee-1471.pdf

HORSE Architecture Team. (2016). *Complete System Design; HORSE Deliverable D2.2 (complete version, confidential)*. Author.

IDC. (2014). *IDC Reveals Worldwide Manufacturing Predictions for 2015, IDC Manufacturing Press Release*. IDC.

IEC. (2013). Enterprise-Control System Integration - Part 1: Models and Terminology (2nd ed.). Geneva, Switzerland: IEC.

Kruchten, P. (1995). Architectural Blueprints—The "4+1" View Model of Software Architecture. *IEEE Software, 12*(6), 42–50. doi:10.1109/52.469759

McEwen, A., & Cassimally, H. (2013). *Designing the Internet of Things*. Wiley.

O'Kane, J. (2013). *A Gentle Introduction to ROS*. CreateSpace Independent Publishing Platform.

Open Source Robotics Foundation. (2017a). *ROS FlexBE*. Retrieved April 27, 2017, from http://wiki.ros.org/flexbe

Open Source Robotics Foundation. (2017b). *ROS Introduction*. Retrieved April 27, 2017, from http://wiki.ros.org/ROS/Introduction

Porter, M. (1985). *Competitive Advantage: Creating and Sustaining Superior Performance*. Free Press.

Rinaldi, J. (2016). *OPC UA - Unified Architecture: The Everyman's Guide to the Most Important Information Technology in Industrial Automation*. CreateSpace Independent Publishing Platform.

Schulte, S., Hoenisch, P., Hochreiner, C., Dustdar, S., Klusch, M., & Schuller, D. (2014). Towards Process Support for Cloud Manufacturing. *Proceedings IEEE 18th international Enterprise Distributed object computing conference*, 142–149.

Shawish, A., & Salama, M. (2014). Cloud Computing: Paradigms and Technologies. *Inter-Cooperative Collective Intelligence: Techniques and Applications*, 39–67.

Steinmetz, R., Schuller, D., Schulte, S., & Abels, S. (2012). Plug and play virtual factories. *IEEE Internet Computing*, *16*(5), 78–82. doi:10.1109/MIC.2012.114

Storti, D., & Yurtoglu, M. (2015). *CUDA for Engineers: An Introduction to High-Performance Parallel Computing*. Addison-Wesley Professional.

Truijens, J., Oosterhaven, A., Maes, R., Jägers, H., & van Iersel, F. (1990). *Informatie-Infrastructuur: een Instrument voor het Management*. Kluwer Bedrijfswetenschappen. (in Dutch)

Vanderfeesten, I., & Grefen, P. (2015). *Business Process Management Technology for Discrete Manufacturing* (Beta Working Papers No. 486). Eindhoven University of Technology.

KEY TERMS AND DEFINITIONS

Business Process: An ordered set of business activities to achieve a specific business goal; the order is specified as the control flow (i.e., the required precedence relation between the activities).

Cyber-Physical System: An automated system that is part of both the digital world (as it processes digital information) and the physical world (as it observes and/or manipulates physical objects).

Logical Data Architecture: The specification of the structure of the data elements used in an automated system in a form that is independent of specific data management technology.

Logical System Architecture: The specification of the structure of the functionality of an automated system in terms of abstract functional components and the connections between these components without any reference to specific technologies for the realization of these components.

Manufacturing Process: A business process in a manufacturing context geared towards the production of specific products, including tasks that perform physical manufacturing activities.

Manufacturing Work Cell: A part of a manufacturing plant dedicated to the execution of one specific manufacturing step; a work cell typically is related to a specific task in a manufacturing process.

Physical System Architecture: The specification of the structure of the functionality of an automated system in terms of concrete functional components and the connections between these components with references to specific technologies for the realization of these components.

Technology Stack: A hierarchy of specific technologies that are used in the implementation and deployment of a system following a physical system architecture.

Chapter 3
Low Power Communication Protocols for IoT–Enabled Applications

Manoj Devare
Amity University – Mumbai, India

ABSTRACT

The industrial IoT marching towards the digital twin and the broad spectrum of applications need the specialized low power protocols for communication and data transfer. This chapter provides a comprehensive discussion on the challenges, opportunities, use cases, platforms, and protocols for the deployment of low power protocols in the context of IoT applications. Moreover, discussion extends to the various custom techniques for energy saving in the communication of sensors to hardware, hardware to Cloud, and deferred data pushing in edge computing. The traditional wireless data transfer and communication protocols are suitable in case of the hardware platforms connected with seamless power supply. However, there is need of low power protocols 6LoWPAN, LoRaWAN, Sub 1, ZigBee, BLE, NFC, and other telecommunication protocols across several IoT applications. The SBCs and micro-controllers are not always equipped with these protocol-enabled hardware. This chapter addresses the suitable hardware and combination with low energy options as per the budget, range, and specifications.

DOI: 10.4018/978-1-5225-3805-9.ch003

INTRODUCTION

The emergence of the Internet of Things (IoT) has brought forth new opportunities by seamlessly integrating the physical world using computing, sensing, and wireless networks, transforming it into a Cyber-Physical System (CPS). An essential building block enabling the IoT is a sensing system. The industrial automation, Machine to Machine (M2M) communication are always there for making the life of the industrial workers more better. However, the use of the energy-saving products in the IoT is an important aspect of the Smart City, Smart Factory, and Digital Twin (DT) creation.

The Cloud Computing enabled by virtualization, Edge Computing and Fog Computing are also energy-saving technologies. Although these technologies are not directly related to the energy harvesting concepts, unlike the generation of the energy for the device to device communication through the motion, pressure, or temperature differences. But indirectly the public Cloud infrastructure solves the energy utilization problem as shared by many users, and reduces the cooling cost. Hence it highly contributes to the energy saving. In case of the edge computing, where the computations are happening near to the data sources like in Micro-controller units or other Single Board Computers. In case of Fog Computing the network devices like routers and gateways having the capability to store some data on the interval basis.

(Tata, Jain, Ludwig, & Gopisetty, 2017) Discusses on the availability of low-cost, low-power SBCs, it is possible to perform certain business logic at the edge of the network utilizing such computers. This way the IoT application is distributed across many devices, some running at or near the edge of the network, at different locations and some running in the public or private Cloud.

The energy consumption rate of one joule per second is called as One watt. One watt is also defined as the current flow of one ampere with a voltage of one volt. (IEA, 2016) Discusses the IoT devices used in the various applications consume the power ranging from the 0.4 to 8.0 watt. The low energy technologies are available for interfacing with the low-cost open source or commercial SBC, micro-controllers. There is need to find the industrial buses interfacing with the different resource constrained situation, and lacking in the main platform facilities. The transfer range may start from the Personal Area Network (PAN) having a smaller range of data communication like creating Piconet or Scatternet, like in Bluetooth or BLE. The communication may range up to the range of the home indoor or outdoor like up to the backyard and garden premises of the home. The normal Wi-Fi is suitable to use in the large range up to few meters, but not specially designed for the low energy needs.

There are wireless technologies related to the concept of ambient intelligence where the home automation is done for the comfort of the human beings. The M2M,

CPS, and the IoT are closely related to each other. Most of the wireless low power communication protocols work on IEEE 802.15.4 protocol. Other protocols are used for the communication in various parts of the IoT communication. Few protocols are used in the industrial automation. Like Infrastructure protocols 6LowPAN, IPv4/IPv6, and RPL. The identification protocols like EPC, uCode, IPv6, and URIs, the communication and transport protocols like Wi-Fi, Bluetooth Low Energy (BLE), and LPWAN. The discovery protocols like Physical web, Mdns, and DNS-SD. The data protocols like MQTT, CoAP, AMQP, and WebSocket. The device management protocols like Technical Report (TR-069), and Open Mobile Alliance Device Management (OMA-DM). Other than this there are some other protocols like Neul, Z-Wave, Sub-1, Zigbee, LORA, LoRAWAN, LORAPAN, RFID & NFC. There are Open Source protocols like WirelessHART, Dash7, and some Proprietary protocols like MiWi, DigiMesh, EnOcean, and ANT & ANT+.

The Digital Twin (DT) IoT is a real-time visualization of the product like formula one car, a spacecraft, a turbine, and digital visualization of heart and much more. The DT IoT needs the 3D design of the physical asset, system or process for forecasting the planning. The DT IoT is highly dependent on the rich computational infrastructure to represent the real-time, visualized model of the physical asset. However, collecting the data from the battery supplied or a batteryless sensor needs a systematic choice of the low power communication protocols. The model needs the sensor readings and collecting data, analyze it, and find optimal solution strategies. In this process the assets connected to the sensors that need to send the data to the nearest gateway or data collection point. The assets perhaps located in deep inside the jungle, farthest distance away from the city, or in the deep basements. In any case, the data transmission using the short range, or long range affordable, low power, wired or wireless communication technologies play an extremely important role.

In the IoT based projects, the choice of the connectivity can be either customer supplied options like Wi-Fi and Bluetooth. But these options having the provisioning and security concerns. Another option is vendor managed LPWAN, i.e., LoRAWAN or Symphony Link. The connectivity perhaps networks operator LPWAN, i.e., LTE-M, NB-IoT, Sigfox or Ingenu. The cost of either of the connectivity technology includes the module, connectivity and infrastructure cost. Table 1 shows the various low-power wireless technologies and their important features.

(IEA, 2016) Discussed that the technologies with low standby power are already established or emerging for the prioritized IoT applications. The comparatively high standby power found in some products is the result of either a poor implementation of the technology or use of an inappropriate technology. Further, the low efficiency of AC or DC power supplies at low loads may contribute to unnecessary high standby power in mains-connected devices. Figure 1 shows the summary of the low power wireless protocols with their range and power consumption characteristics.

Figure 1. Range of the Low Power Protocols and their power consuming characteristics

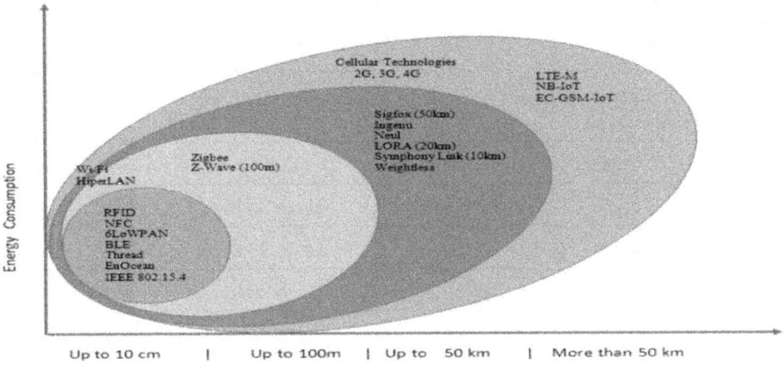

Although the range of each protocol is mentioned in Figure 1 and Table 1, the last device in the topology may further extend the range by connecting further, due to support to act in mesh topology by most of the protocols discussed here. The power consumption also varies on the use in different context.

The remaining chapter covers various low-power energy concepts. The discussion covers battery and energy-related concepts, energy harvesting concept, short-range wireless protocols, medium range protocols, i.e., Low Power Wide Area technologies. The next section covers long-range cellular protocols especially designed for the IoT devices. There is few platform-independent low power consuming techniques and protocols, and automation related the IoT friendly protocols also discussed in next sections. Few protocols are royalty-free, and few are proprietary. The selection of the protocols for the IoT applications highly influences the decisions and affects the budget of the product and services of the IoT.

BATTERY AND ENERGY CONCEPTS

The energy stored in a battery called the battery capacity is measured in either Watt-hours (Wh), kiloWatt-hours (kWh), Ampere-hours (Ahr), or milli-Ampere-hours (mAh). The most common measure of battery capacity is Ah, defined as the number of hours for which a battery can provide a current equal to the discharge rate at the nominal voltage of the battery. There are different batteries like AAAA, AAA, AA, C, D, L, S, P, or W. The most popular batteries are AAA, AA and coin cells.

For low power, wirelessf communication entities, mostly AAA cell is used. These batteries are a low drain, portable, and dry. AAA is smaller in size and contains a few electrochemical materials, whereas AA is large and contains a larger amount of electrochemical material. AA batteries cannot fit in AAA slot. The AAA can fit in

Table 1. Wireless technologies characteristics for the IoT applications

Low Power Protocols	Power Source / Life	Range	Throughput	Communication/ Topology
RFID	No Battery for Passive Type	100 m	--	Point-to-point
NFC	Not Required	20 cm	424 kbps	Point-to-point
ZigBee	No Battery	100 m	Up to 20 kbps	Mesh, Star
6LowPAN	No Battery	116 m	Up to 20 kbps	Mesh, Star
BLE	Coin Cell	50 m	Up to 20 kbps	Peer-to-Peer, Star
Classic Bluetooth	AAA	10-50 m	2.1 MBps	Peer-to-Peer, Star
Wi-Fi	AA	100 m	20 MBps	Peer-to-Peer, Star
SigFox	10 Years	30 km to 50 km	100 - 600 bps	Star
Sub-1 GHz	Coin Cell	10 km	Up to 20 kbps	Mesh, Star, Peer-to-Peer
EnOcean	No Battery	30 meter in Buildings & 300 meter Outdoor	125 kbps	Bi-directional, Range extension with Repeater.
Thread	AA	Up to one home	250 kbps in the 2.4 GHz band	Mesh
LTE-M	10 Years	10 km	--	Cellular
NB-IoT	15+ Years	30-50 km	--	Cellular
EC-GSM	10 Years	50 km	--	Cellular
LORA	10 Years	15 to 20 km	--	LPWA
Neul	10 Years	20 km	--	LPWA
Ingenu	20 + Years	482 km	--	LPWA

AA slot through suitable adapters. AAA is a single cell, 12 gm in weight, 44 mm in length, provides 540-1250 mAh, and used in TV remotes. The chemical composition of the batteries consists of Alkaline, Zinc-Carbon, Silver cell, Mercury, Zinc-air batteries, Lithium, Nickel Oxyhydroxide type of materials.

The coin cell or button cell batteries are from 5 to 25 mm in diameter, with anode material as Zinc or Lithium and Cathode with Manganese Dioxide, Silver oxide, Cupric Oxide or Oxygen. It is used in portable electronic devices such as wrist watch, cardiac pacemakers, and hearing aids. If there is a requirement of performance in case of the IoT devices, then it consumes the power. The systems are either always ON, battery powered, or battery-backed. Each type of the IoT devices and applications are having the different needs, such as the light metering and camera require the stable voltage. The M2M communication devices need the more sleeping time, as no frequent data transfer happens.

The battery life cycle is expressed regarding the hours or number of months. This can be expressed regarding the equation, formed with several parameters. The electrical load is one such a parameter which is having two parts as circuit load and an active load. The circuit load is one, i.e., power draw when the product is not being used. The active load is one, i.e. when drawing while in use. Active load is subdivided if the product has multiple settings for elements like brightness or duration, in case of screens. The designer considers how long the product is in activation and how many times the product is activated per day.

The M2M communication is different from the normal voice-data type of communication. The voice-data type of communication needs the video, streaming with high throughput, with low latency requirement. The humans need the data frequently whereas, the machine needs not. The message frequency, packet size, and data transmission protocols have an impact on device battery life. The longer a device is ON and sending a signal, the more the power it consumes. The power needed to send a signal is called Active Transmit Power. The time of transmitting a signal should be minimum to save the battery charge. A radio module can have the greatest physical (PHY), or hardware. The firmware, or Media Access Control (MAC) layer, coordinates the activities of the physical layer.

This communication should be simple, organized and intelligent. The intelligent handling of the acknowledgments for the received message is also a key point to save battery. The typical sensor produces the data of about 10-200 bytes, and the HTTP TCP session adds the approximately 900 Bytes to it. Hence it is necessary to reduce the extra overhead and bring it to the actual payload. The data transmission succinctly, i.e., in short, reduced messages like in the zipped and compressed formats not transmitting frequently can help in energy saving. If data is not required frequently, then sending it after specific interval can save the data pack, in case of cellular data transmission. Whenever a radio module is not transmitting, then it is either sleeping or listening. More a device sleeps, and the deeper that sleeps, the better it is for battery life. The sleep mode is dependent on the chip technology. The sleeping a long time requires good innovation on the MAC. The device not only sends the signal but also collects the information about the other devices. If the chip design is correct, but the application is incorrect, then it consumes lots of energy. The battery selection can give better relief dependent on the form feed and device size (Ingenu, 2017).

BATTERYLESS ENERGY HARVESTING CONCEPT

(EnOcearn, 2015) Discusses that every sensor or device needs energy which can be either consumed from the direct supply of the power through the electrical grid or battery. However, there are some techniques to save the energy, by the intelligent mechanism of communication such as avoiding frequent read-write operations on the disk on communication media. Very few sensor manufacturers' work on the battery less concept where the sensors generated the energy and generated from their surrounding like kinetic motion, light, pressure, and differences in temperature. For example pushing button also generates electro-mechanical energy. The light energy even at the low level of 200 Lux or less. The temperature difference of 2 °C delivers enough energy for electronic devices. The kinetic motion generates electro-dynamic energy with 1,000,000 switching cycles at 25 °C.

EnOcean is energy harvesting wireless standard and patented technology ISO/IEC 14543-3-1X. EnOcean based on the ambient energy, and self-powered wireless sensor solutions and the IoT marketed under the brands Dolphin and Easyfit. The sensors capture measured values, the energy state constantly changes. The different operations such as when a switch is pressed, the temperature alters, or the luminance level varies, it generates enough energy to transmit wireless signals. The Energy harvesting wireless sensors harvest and manage the smallest amount of energy from their environment. Energy management and highly efficient energy storage are keys to wireless technology for ultra-low power consumption and battery-less wireless sensor solutions. EnOcean is used for Buildings, Smart Homes, Industrial Automation, wireless LED control, M2M communication, and the IoT applications.

(Heller, 2015) Explains EnOcean has the battery-less wireless sensor which is having optimization algorithm, control software, energy converter, energy management, microcontroller, sensor, and RF Transceiver. The heat dissipation is used as energy source, with a standard Peltier element in combination with EnOcean ultra-low power DC to DC converter, which uses the minimum temperature difference.

(Hall, 2016) Explains the steps to connect the EnOcean development kit with the Raspberry Pi and FHEM server for the home automation. The EnOcean is used for the switching lamps, scene illumination, or adjusting blinds; it can measure and visualize power consumption, temperature, and humidity. The battery-less vision makes the components maintenance free.

Short Range Wireless Protocols

This section discusses the short-range wireless energy saving protocols. Like RFID, and its recent advancements in NFC, Bluetooth Low Energy (BLE), ZigBee, 6LowPAN, Z-Wave, LWM2M, Symphony link, and Thread protocols. Few of these protocols are proprietary, and few are open standards.

Radio Frequency Identification (RFID) and Near Field Communication (NFC)

The RFID is wireless protocol is the IoT protocol where electromagnetic fields help to identify objects. Reading tags known as Active Reader Passive Tag (ARPT) system that can store information are installed within the device, so it does not require any power to operate. This is also one of the reasons why RFID has become a widely used technology. The technology finds application in road tolls, building access, factory data collection and animal identification.

The use of NFC (Kerem, Vedat, Mehmet, & Aydin, 2010) & (Want, 2011) has gained attention in recent years, as it enables low-power short-range sensing and wireless transfer of low content information. NFC is a short-range wireless communication technology which is evolved from RFID. It enables communication between two NFC enabled devices within few centimeters. There are certain application areas where NFC is used like such as payment, ticketing, supply chain management systems, smart posters, and automated check-in system for hotels. NFC-enabled mobile devices can act as contactless smart cards and are also capable of reading and writing data from and to those cards. The NFC chip operates one part of the wireless link, and once its one part is activated by another chip. It works in 4 cm to 8 cm in range. There are three different operating modes reader-write mode, Card Emulation mode, and Peer-to-Peer mode. The peer to peer mode is easy data exchange and device pairing mode. It is useful for the secure exchange of critical data. The card emulation mode is applicable for the applications such as id-cards, passports, figure-prints, and driver license.

In an NFC model, two devices are involved in the communication, which is called initiator and target. The initiator is an active NFC device which is responsible for starting the communication. Also, it has an embedded energy component whereas target can be either a tag, RFID card or an NFC device which responses the initiator's requests. The devices in the communication share a single RF band in which the communication is half-duplex. When one device is transmitting, the other one has to listen first and should start to transmit after the first one finishes.

The RFID allows compatible hardware to both supply power and communicate with other unpowered and passive electronic tags using radio waves. The device allows data communication between 2 units nearby. Nowadays, the mobile phone also implementing the NFC, such as Android phones are not consisting of Beam function. Android V4.3 has native support for NFC.

(Payam, 2016). The NFC, however, is inapplicable in scenarios where the real-time high-resolution image or video of the object(s) needs to be sensed. The penetration of THz waves through many materials, which are impervious to visible light makes

THz imaging akin to X-Rays, except that THz radiation is non-ionizing and therefore not harmful to the object being imaged, especially living tissues. It addresses the overview of recent advances in the development of silicon-based mm-wave/THz imaging sensors for near-field IoT applications. (Antonio, Miguel & Antonio, 2010) Discusses that, there are some challenges in RFID and NFC were not designed to carry out secure communications, therefore, when its use is extended beyond what is prescribed arises security problems.

(Pascal, 2015) & (Pascal & Xavier, 2016) discussed an innovative and open concept for secure mobile payments, based on payment applications hosted in the Cloud. It details an experimental Android platform, and NFC payment performed with this platform. All the platform components rely on open technologies, i.e., available in commercial devices or specified by IETF drafts. On the mobile side, security is enforced by a dedicated protocol, i.e., based on TLS, running in a secure element. This protocol manages the access to remote payment applications, running in secure elements, hosted on dedicated servers. This approach creates a new entity that collects meaningful and relevant data, dealing with user's purchases. It also increases the level of trust both for consumers and banks.

Electronic Product Code (EPC)

EPC is a standard that seeks to provide unique identification for RFID tags. It was created by MIT's Auto-ID Center and is currently directed by EPCglobal, an organization dedicated to the global standardization of EPC. The EPCglobal stack is the de-facto standard for retail and consumer goods industries. It is designed to be stored on an RFID tag; the EPC is a unique number that identifies a specific item in the supply chain. The EPC can be associated with dynamic data such as the origination point of an item or the date of its production. It is similar to a Global Trade Item Number (GTIN) or Vehicle Identification Number (VIN).

(Hada & Mitsungi, 2011) & (Hisakazu, & Jin, 2011) discusses the use of EPC based the IoT prototype for the energy-saving application in case of collecting the information in the domain of home appliance. It focuses on a ZigBee network and collects the latest information about "Things." The EPC Network provides static information about "Things." To support end-to-end communication between sensor nodes and applications, they used CoAP instead of Hypertext Transfer Protocol (HTTP). A gateway on a LAN converts HTTP and CoAP. A Pseudo-Universal Plug and Play (UPnP) protocol supports join and leaves the management of sensor nodes. This developed prototype provides energy-saving application using home appliances information collected through the system.

Bluetooth Low Energy (BLE)

In classic Bluetooth originally designed for continuous, streaming data applications, i.e., for the exchange of a lot of data at close range. The BLE which was originally invented by Nokia with the name as Wibree, which has the intention to forms the wireless personal area network (PAN). BLE is having various applications including healthcare, fitness, beacons, security, and home entertainment industries by achieving the same range, i.e., 100 m (330 ft) as that of the classic Bluetooth. BLE operates with the same frequency of 24 GHz ISM Band, and compatible with the classic Bluetooth. Data is split into packets and exchanged through one of 79 designated Bluetooth channels. Normally, the Bluetooth having devices like Wireless headsets, File transfers between devices, Wireless keyboards, printers, and Wireless speakers.

The Zigbee, 6LoWPAN, and BLE are always compared. All Bluetooth Smart devices use the Generic Attribute Profile (GATT) based on the client and server is used. BLE 4 is an “always off” technology. It transmits short packages of data and is not able to support audio streaming. It is perfect for devices like a heart rate belt, mouse or keypad.

The Apple’s ibeacons products based on BLE calculating micro-location, region monitoring, co-location, and ranging using data employing little 2.4Mhz transmitters at key locations around a building, or museum. The smartphone or another device automatically picks up the signal from these iBeacons and can calculate the relative position or contextual trigger actions. The signal strength detects the range of the person. The beacon can be anything like third-party BLE emitters, or iOS devices. The advantage of using beacon is its accuracy and range awareness, and one beacon ID can cover multiple locations. The beacon around regions so apps can be alerted when users enter them. The hardware beacons are small wireless sensors placed inside any physical space that transmits data to iPhone using BLE. The technology carries signal strength information, allowing distances to be estimated and triangulation to be used to determine location, assuming that is having enough beacons located throughout the building. The app works in the background it performs the Region Monitoring when it comes to the foreground it applies the ranging. To map the location relative, it has immediate (10 cm), near (2 to 3m away), and far (5m to 70m away).

(Anilkumar, Bhagyalakshmi, Lavanya, & Gowranga, 2016) Developed a fault-tolerant smart system which can render, track and monitor the process of attendance of the students. A smart attendance system is refined in where the students enter the lecture hall with an Android device which possesses a beacon compatible mobile app. The main purpose of this system is to minimize the power consumption using BLE technology, which prevents fraud and favors in an attendance system by using a smart beacon.

Radius Networks offers a wide range of hardware, software and proximity services designed to enable hyper-proximity, micro-location engagement capabilities and analytics. RadBeacon Dot is in the lightweight plastic enclosure, based on coin-cell battery, a fully standalone Bluetooth Smart proximity beacon using iBeacon, AltBeacon and Eddyston technology, implemented in a lightweight package that is powered by a battery. It is the perfect beacon for conferences, trade shows, exhibits and other events where power perhaps not readily available and ultimate flexibility in placement is most important. The configuration of beacon for is possible in two modes, i.e., Nearby or Physical Web.

The Wireless Body Area Network (WBAN) is emerging area to monitor the health (Kenji, Nizar, Fred, & Chakrabartty, 2016) of the patients with monitoring the temperature of the body, heart rate, blood pressure, and emotional status of the person such as Electrocardiograph, electromyography, and electrothermal activity. There are other application areas such as military applications, sports, event management where the wireless low-power protocols such as BLE, and Zigbee. In some cases, the BAN is used implant nodes inside the body or under the skin, and some sensors as the external node.

ZigBee

Zigbee is IEEE 802.15.4 standard based, secure, open, interoperable, global standard, having a lower cost. It is physical and MAC layer specification, and uses AES-128 encryption and built on unlicensed 2.4 GHz. It is useful for suitable operations in harsh radio environments and in isolated locations. ZigBee covers up to 70 to 100 meters range. The Zigbee alliance also developed the Home Area Network (HAN), Neighborhood Area Network (NAN) to extend the Zigbee usage. ZigBee is a networking layer built on top of IEEE standard 802.15.4 MAC. It was designed to provide a standards-based protocol for interoperability of sensor networks. Zigbee connects the widest range of devices and performs the device-to-device communication. The Zigbee uses the mesh networking to eliminate the single points of failure and expand the reach of networks. The mesh networking increases the devices in a home, a network becomes more reliable. The low power door and window sensors useful for the battery-operated devices able to operate up to seven years. It covers few hundreds of yards point to point range coverage. Zigbee is also having green power feature, where no battery is used at all. Some of the electrical switches harvest the energy from the button push. ZigBee defines the communication between 802.15.4 nodes (layer2 in the IP world) and then defines new upper layers all the way to the application. This means ZigBee devices can interoperate with other ZigBee devices, assuming they utilize the same profile. Bridging between ZigBee and non-ZigBee networks requires a more complex application layer gateway.

There are several areas of applications for Zigbee like the smart home applications, the set-top box, satellite transceiver, gateway, light control, HVAC Control, remote control, window control, door control, motion sensor, environmental monitoring, Zigbee retail services, security, and alarm. The Zigbee wireless radio is used in LED lighting and thermostat. The Cloud-based facility can control and monitor the home. The Zigbee often remotely controls the set-top-box. The TV screen is also used to connect the other equipment in the smart home. Zigbee does not need the line of sight; hence the remote controls can be used as per the flexibility. The remote controls are designed with innovation such as motion sensors to browse on-screen content, change channels and volume. One can just wave the remote control. The carbon monoxide leakage, smart lightening control is used for the light intensity changing for watching a movie in the home. There is connected lightening alliance to use the Zigbee for energy management and healthcare management. Philips has designed light dimming kit called HUE personal wireless lighting. Zigbee smart energy products developed the smart meters for saving the energy.

The Zigbee applications are also available in the retail service industry. It improves the business efficiency. The companies like Kroger, Wincor Nixdorf in association with einfochips, developed the useful service industry.

6LoWPAN

6LoWPAN combines the latest version of the Internet Protocol (IPv6) and Low-power Wireless Personal Area Networks (LoWPAN). 6LoWPAN, therefore, allows for the smallest devices with limited processing ability to transmit information wirelessly using an internet protocol. It has 6LoWPAN range is 116 meters. It is a competitor to ZigBee. It is used in the Smart Meters and Smart Home like Lighting, and Thermostats. 6LoWPAN it can run on other PHYs, and it allows for seamless integration with other IP-based systems. It takes the benefits of 128 bit AES encryption.

Interoperability is one of the leading factors when choosing a wireless protocol. Interoperability means that the applications do not need to know the constraints of the physical links that carry their packets. 6LoWPAN offers interoperability with other wireless 802.15.4 devices as well as with devices on any other IP network link such as Ethernet or Wi-Fi, with a simple bridge device. This cuts down on packet overhead and allows more room for the payload data. Also, the typical code size for a full-featured stack is 90KB for ZigBee and only 30KB for 6LoWPAN. ZigBee-IP is also introduced to take advantage of the Internet Protocol, which combines the advantages of the 6LoWPAN.

The semiconductor industry players Texas Instruments, Freescale and Atmel, promote and supply 802.15.4 chips which can be used for either ZigBee or 6LoWPAN.

These same companies even offer free ZigBee stacks. There is one open source stack available, and companies such as Archrock and Sensinode license their 6LoWPAN stacks.

(Jara, 2010) Point out the challenge associated with LoWPAN networks were not designed to handle the IP stack. Therefore, a set of security and mobility problems arises with 6LoWPAN. (Jara, 2010) Designed the system based on the IoT for medical environments to achieve a global connectivity with the patient, sensors and everything around it. The use of 6LoWPAN and RFID and NFC is done. The mobility and security factors have been applied through the use of cryptographic SIM card, the encryption and sign communication is used in the medical devices.

Thread

The thread is open, device to device (D2D), IPV6 based, robust, mesh network, battery friendly, power efficient, designed to connect and control products in the home automation. The devices use 6LoWPAN protocol. However, there are several applications and use-cases like appliances, climate control, security, and healthcare. With the Thread protocol stack devices do not join the Thread Network unless authorized and all communications are encrypted and secure. It operates on AA batteries. A Border Router is a specific type of Router that provides connectivity from the 802.15.4 network to adjacent networks on other physical layers, for example, Wi-Fi and Ethernet. The thread is reliable due to the mechanism where sleepy Child requires a Parent for communications, so this Parent represents a single point of failure for its communications. However, the sleepy device can and will select another Parent if its Parent is unavailable so this transition should not be visible to the user. There are various phases a joining device has to go through before it can participate in a Thread Network like discovery, commissioning and attaching. (Thread, 2015)

Z -Wave

Z-Wave is the leading wireless home control mesh network technology that not interferes with Wi-Fi signal and operates on low power. Z-Wave operates on a different wireless frequency than Wi-Fi. Z-Wave is the smart home technology found in many products such as locks, lights, smart Garage door opener. The Z-Wave enabled products in smart home save energy and provides security with AES128 encryption. It gives alerts like a water leak, fire alarm, and potential break-in. Without any obstacles such as walls and furniture, the range of two Z-Wave products is about 100 meters or 328 feet. When obstacles in the home reduce that range, Z-Wave's mesh networking allows a Z-Wave signal to "hop" through other Z-Wave products to reach the destination device to be controlled. Z-Wave devices work on battery power alone, often for a year or more before needing new batteries The Z-Wave based products are smart locks, smart lighting, smart thermostat, smart plugs and outlets, and smart hubs.

Symphony Link

(Linklabs, 2017) Whenever the BLE, Wi-Fi, Zigbee are not enough due to the range, and cost issue of the cellular network then LPWAN are required for the IoT applications. LPWAN technologies use a star topology network. LPWAN technology is perfectly suited for connecting devices that need to send small amounts of data over a long range while maintaining long battery life. Some IoT applications only need to transmit tiny amounts of information like a parking garage sensor, which only transmits when a spot is open or when it is taken. The low power consumption of such a device allows that task to be carried out with minimal cost.

The end-nodes can be up to 10 kilometers from the gateway, depending on the technology deployed. Less than 5000 bits per second or often only 20-256 bytes per message are sent several times a day. This makes very long battery life, often between five to ten years. The Zigbee cannot solve the problem with mesh topology. They struggled with mesh network solutions because the link budgets for these connections are very limited due to high data rates and low receiver sensitivities. Some ZigBee connections have trouble sending data more than 20-30 meters away because the power coming from the transmitter is lost too quickly. Additionally, others have been surprised by the amount of mesh infrastructure required actually to build a reliable network. Similar to WiFi, the endpoints of star networks are connected directly to the access point. The repeater can be used to fill in gaps in coverage, which, for most applications, is a good middle ground regarding latency, reliability, and coverage.

The Symphony Link is a wireless system developed by Link-Labs which is used by industrial and enterprise customers who need high reliability and advanced features in their LPWA system. It is built on the LORA Chirped Spread Spectrum (CSS) physical layer technology. It is an alternative specification to LORAWAN which is the public network protocol developed by LORA Alliance for carrier networks. Symphony Link overcomes the limitations of the LORAWAN.

(Linklabs, 2017) LORAWAN and Symphony Link both are based on the LORA. Symphony Link provides the range of LORA but needs a level of performance that is not available with LORAWAN. Symphony Link is having the four times the capacity of LORAWAN. Symphony link Use cases in lock control, industrial control System, lighting control, alarm systems, physical security.

Symphony Link, with its Fixed MTU of 256 bytes, is deemed to be a revolutionary wireless system suitable for wide-area IoT networks. Hence, it is ideally used for enterprise and industrial customers who need a highly secure connection to the Cloud. The advantage Symphony Link has over ZigBee and WiFi is that it is much more expensive and reliable. The Nwave, Ingenu, Link-Labs, Sigfox are top technologies in LORAWAN.

Low Power Wide Area iot Protocols

The Low-Power Wide-Area LPWA is the term coined in 2013, for M2M and the IoT communications. The LPWA is different from non-LPWA cellular, Wi-Fi, and mesh where it focuses on low-power and wide coverage and works without line of sight. The Ingenu, Sigfox, and Neul professional players made this technology more popular. (LPWA, 2017) & (Linklabs, 2016) Machine Network is a term declared by Ingenu for a wireless network dedicated exclusively to machines. The cellular industry validated LPWA as the wireless solution for the IoT by announcing a series of its own LPWA candidate standards including EC-GSM, LTE-M (now LTE-M1), and Narrow Band (NB) IoT (then NB-IoT, now LTE-M2). Not every LPWA technology has equally wide or deep coverage, but as a class, LPWA provides a much wider area of coverage. 3G cellular being around 130 ms and LTE around 80 ms, in the US, depending on the carrier. LPWA technologies, by contrast, have latencies from seconds to tens of seconds depending on the technology and conditions. The cost of LPWA dependent on the infrastructure, module (small electronic device) and spectrum. The infrastructure set-up is also low than cellular. The LPWA do not add the cost of the intellectual property ownership as in case of the cellular network. As LPWA uses the non-licensed spectrum, it adds no cost.

Sigfox

The Sigfox is having a very important feature of coverage range of 30 km to 50 km. The Sigfox is Ultra Narrow Band modulation and operates in the 200 kHz of the publicly available band to exchange radio messages over the air. Each message is 100 Hz wide and transferred at the data rate of 100 or 600 bps depending on the region. Hence, long distances can be achieved while being very robust against the noise. SigFox is also a lightweight protocol to handle small messages. As fewer data to send means less energy consumption, hence longer battery life. A device is not attached to a specific base station, unlike cellular protocols. The broadcasted message is received by any base station in the range. LORA and Sigfox are noncellular technologies came from France. Sigfox has extremely low throughputs. LORA is quite good deployments in Europe.

As shown in Table 2, the low power wide-area network technologies are compared on their various characteristics. The LPWA technologies are power efficient that, no need to change the batteries over 5 to 7 years.

Lora

LoRa is a Long Range Wireless Protocol for wireless battery operated the IoT and M2M devices on a regional, national and global network. It has range up to 15 to 20 km, and battery life more than ten years. It is having 868 MHz frequency band in Europe, 915 MHz for North America, and 433 MHz bands for Asia. The LORA gateway received the communication from the LORA endpoints and then transfers them to the backhaul system. The nodes can be established within the building or outside. Cycleo originally developed it, and Semtech acquired it in 2012. It can be optimized for low power consumption, but it can also handle smart city and industrial applications by connecting millions of devices. The data rates can range from 0.3kbps to 50 kbps. The signals can penetrate obstacles and travel long distances, therefore an ideal choice for the IoT connected device. This is made possible through LoRa chips and a spread-spectrum strategy that can transmit through various frequencies and data rates.

(Yan, Xiaoqiang, & Wu, 2017) Discusses the LORA is used for the IoT water meter and remote meter reading to find low power consumption as a part of energy measurement. It uses a multilevel relay and the concentrator based on LoRa communication. It has downlink protocol and a uplink protocol between the concentrator and the data center. The remote data transmission is carried out by the concentrator through GPRS channel. By testing, the system's meter reading distance, the quantity of the meter accessed and the reliability of data communication can meet the application requirements.

Table 2. Low-Power Wide-Area Network Technologies

Technology	Low Power	Bandwidth	Supplier Breadth	Security	Deployments	Technology
LTE-M	Moderate	Yes	Yes	Good	Waiting	Moderate
NB-IoT	Yes	Yes	Yes	Moderate	Moderate	Open LTE
EC-GSM	Yes	Yes	Very Less	Moderate	Less	Moderate
LORA	Moderate	Yes	Moderate	Moderate	Yes	Proprietary
Sigfox	Yes	Moderate	Yes	Limited	Yes	Proprietary
Neul	Yes	Yes	Moderate	Good	Yes	Proprietary
Ingenu	Yes	Yes	Moderate	Good	Yes	Proprietary

Neul

Neul has been a major contributor to the new air-interface, Weightless, designed specifically for the IoT and M2M market, and the open-standard. Neul is the similar word for Cloud is a simple way to "economically connect everything." The concept of Neul is similar to that of Sigfox and operates in the sub-1GHz band. Neul makes use of very small slices of the TV White Space spectrum to deliver highly scalable, wider coverage networks. The Neul is first single-chip baseband, RF implementation of the Weightless standard and Iceni. The Sub-GHz, frequency agile RF transceiver is capable of supporting the advanced modulation schemes and spreading modes employed by the Weightless standard to deliver ubiquitous coverage and sufficient cell capacity.

This is capable of leveraging very small slices of spectrum to deliver high scalability, high coverage, low-power and low-cost wireless networks for the IoT. Low spectral leaking and good adjacent channel blocking performance are mandated, meaning that a Weightless system can be a good neighbor to other spectrum technology incumbents.

Its promoter members including Neul, ARM, and Cambridge Silicon Radio (CSR). Weightless employs a modern set of wireless air interface technologies spanning the PHY and MAC layers, through security, authentication and up through to the application and subscription management layers. At all stages, the air interface has been designed to support path losses much greater than any cellular standard, to provide powerful good in-building penetration together with very long lifetimes from low-cost batteries and ultra-low-cost endpoint modules, to allow the mobile industry to service the full spectrum of the IoT opportunity.

Weightless

Weightless is an open standard protocol operate in sub-1 GHz unlicensed spectrum. Weightless is a wide-area wireless networking technology designed specifically for the IoT, achieving coverage, battery life, module cost and efficiency goals that far out-reach today's GPRS, 3G, Code Division Multiple Access (CDMA) and LTE WAN solutions. It can communicate data in the range from few bits per second to 100 kbps using the same link with very less power consumption. It runs the Weightless Special Interests Group (SIG), a nonprofit organization formed to develop its open standards, and test upcoming technologies.

Weightless-N offers a simple one-way directional standard with a very long (10-year) battery life and a low overall cost. Weightless offers two-way communication, but it has a shorter battery life and higher network cost. Weightless-W is the most extensive option, and it runs off of unused TV spectrum but has some drawbacks. Its most extensive open standard, Weightless-W, has a shorter battery life (three-five years) and a higher cost for both the terminal and the network.

Ingenu

Ingenu supported the M2M communication long-range, two-way, reliable connectivity and based on Random Phase Multiple Access (RPMA) technology (RPMA, 2017). It covers more than 300 square miles per access point. Transmission gains can come from augmenting power to a transmitting antenna or increasing receiver sensitivity and antenna gain. Transmission losses are incurred through obstructions, such as topography and human-made objects; cable loss, and other deleterious elements. RPMA gains its largest chunk of coverage from receiver sensitivity. RPMA's smart modules use transmits power control so that as more access points and endpoints are added, they can adjust accordingly.

The Ingenu worked with General Electric to solve the problem in association with Consorcio Energético Punta Cana Macao (CEPM) of providing the real-time monitoring problem with a network that enables over 24,000 smart meters to speed power restoration and increase the reliability of services to customers in the Dominican Republic as island country. The solutions are providing accurate reporting and monitoring of energy operation and consumption using RPMA access points, which served as the communication device between the meters and head-end system, were installed in strategic locations to obtain ideal RF performance, allowing a single RPMA access point to serve as many 20,000 GE smart meters. (CEPM, 2017)

Use of Cellular Technologies for IoT

The IoT devices that need to communicate over long distances can use Global System for Mobile (GSM), 3G, or 4G cellular communications. With 4G, it is possible to send high quantities of data but it is expensive, and the devices might consume too much power. To avoid such a situation, it would be better to use cellular applications for sensor-based, low-bandwidth-data requirements. After the emergence of LPWA technologies, the mobile cellular providers have announced the NB-IoT, LTE-M, EC-GSM, and eMTC (enhanced Machine-Type Communication). This section discusses these cellular technologies specially designed for the IoT and M2M communication. It is interesting to see the sun rising of these technologies, despite the sunset predictions by Machina Research for the 1G, 2G and 3G in developed countries shortly.

LTE-M

The Long-Term Evolution (LTE) is a complex system capable of carrying high data rates. LTE cellular system is well placed to carry a lot of the traffic for the M2M communications. LTE-M (also referred to as LTE Cat-M1) is a Low-Power Wide-Area (LPWA) technology deployed by AT&T to support today's IoT devices, even in the most challenging environments. It is highly secure, has features that can lower power consumption to extend battery life, enhances coverage to connect hard-to-reach devices, and comes at a lower cost than standard LTE. LTE-M can be installed in underground and deep inside buildings to enhance the coverage area. It is the first network on a dedicated spectrum that is optimized for the IoT. LTE-M offers coverage enhancement to penetrate better walls and underground, plus power-saving features that extend battery life to last up to ten years. These are a few ways how LTE-M offers positive changes in utilities monitoring and services.

LTE-M allow for tower handoff, giving it the same strong mobility characteristics found in the traditional cellular network. It is helpful to track movement over local or wide areas, tracking and asset monitoring from shipping containers to fleet vehicles, and even in locating valuable assets, children, or pets.

There are some challenges with the LTE-M such as it should support to the wide spectrum of devices. Another challenge is M2M devices need to be small and fit into equipment that is very cost sensitive. With many low-cost M2M systems already available. LTE-M should provide the benefits of a cellular system, but at low cost. Many LTE-M needs to understand the problem of M2M devices where the battery needs to work up to many years.

Narrow-Bandwidth IoT (NB-IoT)

NB-IoT & LTE-M are low bandwidth cellular protocols. There are few deployments found using NB- IoT in the Europe. The LTE-M deployments found in the North America used for voice data transfer also. NB-IoT is cellular 3GPP. Vodaphone deployments of NB-IoT has shown footprints.

The are several examples of case studies where the NB-IoT is used for various purposes. Like making Las Vegas a smart City, smart metering and tracking in Brazil and Connected sheep in Norway. In China, ZTE, and three carriers, China Mobile, China Unicom and China Telecom used the NB-IoT Successfully.

(Mads, Istvan, Preben, Mads & Steffen, 2016) Analyze the coverage probability, the number of supported devices, and the device battery life in networks equipped with either of the newly standardized technologies, i.e., LTE-M and NB-IoT. The study is made for a site-specific network deployment of a Danish operator, and the simulation is calibrated using drive test measurements. The results show that

LTE-M can provide coverage for 99.9% of outdoor and indoor devices if the latter is experiencing 10 dB additional loss. However, for deep indoor users, NB-IoT is required and provides coverage for about 95% of the users. The cost is support for more than ten times fewer devices and 2-6 times higher device power consumption. Thus both LTE-M and NB-IoT provide extended support for the cellular Internet of Things, but with different trade-offs.

Extended Coverage Global System for Mobile IoT (EC-GSM-IOT)

EC-GSM is standard for IoT communication based on eGPRS, and LPWA technology. It is high capacity, long range, low complexity for the cellular system in IoT communications. It has battery life up to 10 years. Supported by all major mobile equipment, chipset, and module manufacturers. Its networks will co-exist with 2G, 3G, and 4G mobile networks. The Ericsson and Orange made few trials for the use of EC-GSM-IoT.

(Saahithyan, Samir & Debabrata, 2016) Shows the results that, using the stealing bits as Paging Indicator in a GSM system can predominantly reduce the power consumption. An IoT device which functions using GSM/GPRS/EGPRS system can achieve a better battery life by mitigating the stealing bits in a

Normal Burst of a paging channel. EC-GSM with its potential for Extended Coverage in building basements can use this effectively to increase the battery life of the IoT devices.

INDUSTRIAL AUTOMATION PROTOCOLS

There are several useful automation friendly protocols mature and widely used in the IoT applications. This section discusses the Domotics supporting X10 protocol, BACnet as building automation protocol, and Modbus as a serial communication protocol for the electronics devices.

X10

The name of the protocol comes into existence after the series of the project taken by Pico Electronics. It is communication protocol for Power Line Control (PLC) for signaling and control for home automation called as Domotics. It is used for the remote control of home devices and appliances, in 1975 by Pico Electronics Company. X10 enables the electronics devices to communicate over the 120V existing housing wiring (EnOcean, 2016) & (Technica,2005).

In case of X10 for wireless, the wireless transceiver (TM751) receives wireless RF signals from wireless remotes, then sends that signal to homes existing power lines then trigger modules that are attached to lamps and appliances. The signal then turns them off, on or dims them to a level of choice. For Wired operations, with a kit like the Mini Timer starter kit directly sends a signal through the existing power line which triggers modules that are attached to appliances.

(Sean, David, & Prashant, 2016) Discussed that many existing IoT-enabled devices operate through low-cost, convenient power line networks, using protocols such as X10 and Insteon for communication. These technologies have targeted low bandwidth device control; they are often not readily suited to higher bandwidth uses such as continuous energy monitoring. They are leveraging existing low bandwidth PLC networks for energy monitoring, and present several techniques that enable reliable, high-resolution monitoring in such networks. The Insteon protocol is observed, and results show that intelligent polling and event detection methods can reduce the bandwidth requirements and undetected power events in a real-world Insteon network by 50% or more versus naive methods.

Building Automation and Control Networks (BACnet)

It is open source data communication protocol stack for embedded systems, Windows, Linux, or another operating system. It is a standard way to send and receive messages on the wire containing data that is understood by other BACnet compliant devices. It works as a backbone for carrying building automation information, wired BACnet bus systems have become a norm. It defines a way to communicate over some wires, known as Data Link and Physical Layers: Ethernet, EIA-485, EIA-232, ARCNET, and LonTalk. The BACnet standard also defines a standard way to communicate using UDP, IP, and HTTP (Web Services).

The BACnet and EnOcean enable Energy Efficient Buildings Integration of batteryless wireless sensors offers amazingly new opportunities for BACnet building automation. When the wired and wireless scenarios are compared, then wired provides greater range, and better data volumes, better reliability, moderate cost benefits. Whereas, the wireless provides advantages in installation efforts and flexibility, moderate reliability, and with better cost. Combining these two features is an idea to combine use BACnet and EnOcean technology. (EnOcean, 2016)

Modbus

It is an open protocol and hence freely available to the manufacturers to build into their equipment, without paying royalties, developed by Modicon Systems. It is useful for connecting industrial electronic devices, transmit signals from instrumentation and control devices. It is a method used for transmitting information over serial lines between electronic devices. The device requesting the information is called the Modbus Master, and the devices supplying information are Modbus Slaves. In a standard Modbus network, there is one Master and up to 247 Slaves, each with a unique Slave Address from 1 to 247. The Master can also write information to the Slaves. Modbus is often used to connect a supervisory computer with a Remote Terminal Unit (RTU) in Supervisory Control and Data Acquisition (SCADA) systems. Versions of the Modbus protocol exist for serial lines (Modbus RTU and Modbus ASCII) and Ethernet (Modbus TCP).

(Kuo, Chin & Yun, 2015) The automation application is generally having UI system for, observing or monitoring existing systems. Due to low functional requirements provided in the system, the operational staff cannot manage the system very well. It requires a lot of funding and time to rebuild a new system, and replacing is also difficult. The supporting system can be useful in this case like with enhanced additional functionalities like data storage, analysis, or even achieve the purpose of control; the system optimization can be realized. The intervention of a Modbus protocol arbitration device can effectively solve the problem by building a new monitoring system in parallel to the existing system, which allows more than two hosts to operate in the same automation system.

APPLICATION LAYER DATA TRANSFER TECHNIQUES

In general, the IoT protocols having real-time communication ability problems. There are three real-time communication protocols namely MQTT, XMPP, and CoAP. XMPP is based on TCP and XML. The other useful low energy consuming protocols are AMQP, RPL and LWM2M are also discussed in this section. Table 3 shows the comparison of the application layer protocols.

Table 3. Comparison of Application Layer IoT Protocols.

Application Protocol	RESTful	Transport	Publish-Subscribe	Request Response	Security	QoS	Header Size (Bytes)
COAP	Yes	UDP	Yes	Yes	DTLS	Yes	4
MQTT	No	TCP	Yes	No	SSL	Yes	2
XMPP	No	TCP	Yes	Yes	SSL	NO	-
AMQP	No	TCP	Yes	No	SSL	Yes	8
DDS	No	UDP	Yes	No	DTLS	Yes	-

Constrained Application Protocol (CoAP)

The CoAP is internet application protocol for constrained devices intended for use in resource-constrained internet devices, such as wireless sensor nodes. It is useful in case of the low power lossy networks where less memory and power is available. It is most suitable for the IoT and M2M devices. CoAP is similar to HTTP, where it can be integrated with XML, JSON, CBOR or other data format of choice. CoAP works with the microcontrollers with less memory even with 10KiB. CoAP suitably runs on in request and response fashion. For programming purpose C, Java and Python are suitable as API libraries are available in these languages. CoAP provides the good security using DTLS parameters equivalent to RSA keys. CoAP works on UDP rather than TCP and uses the Datagram Transport Layer Security (DTLS) for encryption. But, the CoAP is one-to-one protocol, so the broadcasting feature is not available.

(Khattak, Ruta & Eugenio, 2014) Discussed the CoAP is Supporting resource constrained devices and easy integration with the existing TCP/IP standards. They have solved the problem of healthcare domain where creating healthcare WSNs utilizing IPv6 and CoAP for real-time monitoring purpose.

(Iulia, Razvan, Laura, & Dan, 2017) Discusses the various low-power IoT protocols from application layer like CoAP, and MQTT. The service discovery protocols mDNS, DNS-SD, uBonjour. The infrastructure protocols are IEEE 802.15.4, 6LoWPAN, LoRaWAN.

Multi-Queue Telemetry Transport (MQTT)

The MQTT is application layer protocol based on the publishing and subscribes mechanism. It is built on top of the TCP layer, and it is suitable for low resource devices. It consists of three elements, subscriber, publisher, and broker. The publisher is the one that sends data, and it forwards through the Broker and to subscribers. When a device or service publishes data to a topic, all of the devices subscribed will automatically get the updated information.

The MQTT uses TCP connections to an MQTT broker. The connection is always on which puts constraints on some device connections. The MQTT-S is another protocol which works with UDP. The MQTT also lacks encryption since the protocol was intended to be lightweight and encryption would add significant overhead. Choosing the right real-time protocol like XMPP, CoAP and MQTT depend largely on the needs of a given developer and the IoT devices.

(Priyanka &Yoohwan, 2016) Express through the experiment that MQTT is more suitable for the IoT messaging and nodes with no power constraints would prefer MQTT. MQTT and CoAP are having tree architectures and lightweight M2M protocols. Depending on the hardware of the IoT node and data requirements either MQTT or CoAP can be used. When data flows in from one client to multiple nodes, MQTT is much suited for such environments. The CoAP is found more reliable due to the re-transmission process and less packet loss while delay stays high. CoAP has efficient power management and is more applicable in utility field area networks.

The AWS IoT uses the MQTT to push the messages on the Cloud system. One can connect the Raspberry Pi SBC to the AWS Cloud, and easily the JSON format messages can be stored on the DynamoDB database.

Extensible Messaging and Presence Protocol (Xmpp)

XMPP is a streaming XML protocol, open, secure, standards-based, freely-available technology for real-time communication. The chat network which powers a wide range of applications including instant messaging, presence, collaboration, voice & video calling, IoT, military messaging, and mobile Cloud push. There are successful implementation use case applications like Google Cloud Messaging, Facebook Chat integration, NATO tactical chat, and IETF use it in their meetings.

It is considered as one of the Alternatives to the Skype, WhatsApp, Google Hangouts, and Jabbar. Someone can choose the XMPP because of better security with own server and share the data with the colleagues, without knowing communication data to the single company. XMPP has been deployed to thousands of websites and has had pure Java-Script libraries. XMPP typically uses reliable stream transports. The use of XML makes XMPP slower than, as compared to it would be with JSON.

XMPP supports different communication patterns like Request-Response, Asynchronous Messaging, Publish-Subscribe, Event Subscription (Observe) and Delayed delivery. XMPP also has support for different Quality of Service levels for messaging.

Advanced Message Queuing Protocol (AMQP)

It is open, interoperable, reliable, standardized, and safe. AMQP is message-oriented, application layer, transport protocol like TCP for exchange messages. It supports reliable communication via message delivery including at-most-once, at-least-once and exactly once delivery (Ala, Mohsen, Mehdi, Mohammed, & Moussa, 2015). The latest version provides the efficient wire protocol, supports multiple brokers, message security, global addressing, and extensible addressing. AMQP defines two types of messages, i.e., bare massages that are supplied by the sender and annotated messages that are seen by the receiver. (Ala, Abdallah, Mohsen, Ammar, & Mehdi, 2015) & (Muneer, Mohammed, & Dua, 2016). discusses the several application layer protocols including REST, Data Distribution Service (DDS), and gateway interfaces.

AMQP allows messages to pass between applications, especially designed by the financial companies like JPMorgan and Berkley. Using AMQP, these type of applications exchange messages between new and legacy applications. It works as the messaging middleware to exchange messages. The companies like CISCO, Microsoft, Redhat are also involved in the development of AMQP for the Cloud-based message exchange.

(Zoran, Jelica, & Veljko, 2016) Few IoT applications need the real-time sensor data and rich interfaces. The strong graphics need the browser plug-ins such as Adobe Flash and Microsoft Silverlight. The IoT Web application performance is measured latencies induced by different communication protocols and message encodings, as well as graphics rendering performance. The comparison is also performed with the IoT messaging protocols such as MQTT, AMQP, XMPP, and DDS by measuring the latency of sensor data message delivery and the message throughput rate. The Adobe Flash has the best performance at the moment, the HTML5 platform is also very capable of running real-time IoT Web applications, whereas Microsoft Silverlight is noticeably behind both platforms. MQTT is the most appropriate messaging protocol for a wide set of the IoT Web applications. The IoT application developers should be aware of certain MQTT message broker implementation shortcomings.

Routing Over Low Power and Lossy Networks (RPL)

There are some constrained nodes having power, memory, and processing resources limitations lead to hard upper bounds on state, code space, and processing cycles, making optimization of energy and network bandwidth usage a dominating consideration in all design requirements. RPL works on the intra-domain distance vector routing protocol. This protocol frequently informs to the neighbored about the changing topology.

Light Weight Machine to Machine (LWM2M) Protocol

The Open Mobile Alliance developed the Light Weight M2M remotely managing the IoT and M2M embedded devices and application management. It works in client-server fashion. Fixed network broadband routers and smartphones are not suitable for limited bandwidth, memory, and energy. It works on the wireless connection. It is designed to provide device management functionality over the sensor or cellular networks, transfer service data from the network to devices.

The LWM2M protocol based on REST, to be used for remote management of M2M devices and related service enablement. It defines a resource and data model that is extensible, modern architectural design, better performance and the constraints of M2M devices in mind, builds on an efficient, secure data transfer. It has benefits like to reduce the degree of fragmentation in the area of remote management for M2M. It provides the plug-and-play functionality. Open interfaces between the M2M device/client side and the M2M service platform side have benefits for many parties in the value chain. It avoids repetitive implementation of bespoke, vendor-proprietary or customized protocol endpoints on their systems. M2M application and equipment developers will embrace an open off-the-shelf standard that enables them to get their products remotely managed and connected to any M2M management platform that implements that open interface. The LWM2M client can communicate with the LWM2M server either using 6LoWPAN, Wi-Fi, Cellular mechanism. The server is having the responsibility of discovery, security, and communication. The server mechanism may reside on public or private Cloud. (Guenter, Friedhelm, Zach, Sandeep, & Jan 2014) & (Chang & Lin, 2016).

(Rao, Chendanda, Deshpande, & Lakkundi, 2015) Developed the client side mechanism using LWM2M as an emerging standard that defines a fast deployable client-server specification to provide various M2M services. It provides both efficient device management as well as security workflow for the IoT applications, making it especially suitable for use in constrained networks. However, most of the work focuses on the server domain of LWM2M. Enabling relevant LWM2M functionalities on the client side is not only critical and important but challenging as well since these end-nodes are invariably resource constrained. Its implementation framework carried out over Contiki-based the IoT nodes.

(Chang & Lin, 2016) Discussed that the device management protocols OMA LWM2M has been adopted by the global M2M standards. However, OMA LWM2M supported devices are still not widely available because the standard is relatively recently published. On the other hand, there are millions of legacy devices and sensors that do not support the OMA LWM2M protocol. Consequently, how to integrate non-OMA LWM2M devices so that OMA LWM2M Server can manage them. Moreover, how to exercise OMA LWM2M device management from the M2M standards is also not well addressed by the standard. The designing of an OMA LWM2M gateway between OMA LWM2M server and legacy non-OMA LWM2M devices.

SUMMARY

The wireless sensor network is connecting the different devices in the mesh topology up to quite larger scale. The data transfer is possible due to hopping process of the involved devices. Hence the hassle-free wireless techniques and protocols are always a choice of the system implementers for the IoT. However, it brings new challenges along with the facilities.

There are several wireless low-energy technologies developed either in open or commercial basis. The interoperability and interfacing of the data communication and transfer units are always a topic of research for next at least one decade. Finding the compatibility of the low energy wireless data transfer technologies using industrial buses is a challenge in the field. Always finding the storage unit of energy, i.e., battery for the devices is not the only solution. However, the battery-less devices generating the energy for the communication from the environment itself like EnOcean is one of the key technology. Generating the energy from the motion, temperature level, pressure, light source, solar energy are another source of energy for the sensors and the edge devices.

Interfacing of the units of data transfer from the available for very few centimeters up like RFID and NFC to few kilometers range using the infrastructure establishment protocols like LORAWAN and Sigfox. It has the necessity to find the suitable options of the communication. Finding the feasibility of the interfacing of the standard protocols and wireless technologies with the popular and well-tested hardware units like Raspberry Pi or Arduino need to be tested. The interoperability of the protocols will be the subject of research and investigation for next decade.

REFERENCES

Ala, A. F., Abdallah, K., Mohsen, G., Ammar, R., & Mehdi, M. (2015). Toward Better Horizontal Integration Among IoT Services. *IEEE Communications Magazine Communications Standards*, (Supplement), 72–79.

Ala, A. F., Mohsen, G., Mehdi, M., Mohammed, A., & Moussa, A. (2015). Internet of Things: A Survey on Enabling Technologies, Protocols, and Applications. *IEEE Communications Surveys and Tutorials*, *17*(4), 2347–2376. doi:10.1109/COMST.2015.2444095

Anilkumar, B. G., Bhagyalakshmi, K. C., Lavanya, K., & Gowranga, K. H. (2016). A Bluetooth Low Energy Based Beacon System for Smart Short Range Surveillance. *IEEE International Conference on Recent Trends in Electronics Information Communication Technology*, 1181-1184.

Antonio, J. J., Miguel, A. Z., & Antonio, F. G. S. (2010). An Architecture Based on Internet of Things to Support Mobility and Security in Medical Environments. *IEEE CCNC Proceedings*, 1-5.

CEPM. (2017). *Case Study – CEPM*. White Paper by Ingenu,1-2.

Chang, W. G., & Lin, F. J. (2016). Challenges of Incorporating OMA LWM2M Gateway in M2M Standard Architecture. *IEEE Conference on Standards for Communications and Networking (CSCN),* 1-6.

EnOcean. (2015). *The True Cost of Batteries, Why Energy Harvesting Is The Best Power Solution For Wireless Sensors*. White Paper, EnOcean, 1-6.

EnOcean. (2016). *BACnet and EnOcean enable Energy Efficient Buildings*. White Paper of EnOcean Alliance, 1-16.

Guenter, K., Friedhelm, R., Zach, S., Sandeep, A., & Jan, H. (2014). *Lightweight M2M: Enabling Device Management and Applications for the Internet of Things*. White Paper, Open Mobile Alliance.

Hall, R. (2016). *Raspberry Pi Talks EnOcean-How to combine your Raspberry Pi board with the EnOcean Developer Kit*. Dolphin White Paper.

Heller, W. (2015). *Daylight Harvesting based on EnOcean Finished Products*. White Paper, 1-3.

Hisakazu, H., & Jin, M. (2011). EPC based Internet of Things Architecture. *IEEE International Conference on RFID-Technologies and Applications*, 527-532.

IEA. (2016). *Energy Efficiency of the Internet of Things*. Technology and Energy Assessment Report, IEA 4E EDNA.

Ingenu. (2017). *The Six Secrets of Extremely Long Battery Life*. A White Paper By Ingénue, 1-3.

Iulia, F., Razvan, R., Laura, R., & Dan, D. (2017). Survey of Standardized Protocols for the Internet of Things. *21st International Conference on Control Systems and Computer Science*, 190-197.

Kenji, A., Nizar, L., Fred, F., & Chakrabartty, S. (2016). Infrastructural Health Monitoring Using Self-powered Internet-of-Things. IEEE.

Kerem, O., Vedat, C., Mehmet, N., & Aydin, B. O. (2010). Current Benefits and Future Directions of NFC Services. *International Conference on Education and Management Technology*.

Khattak, H. A., Ruta, M., & Eugenio, D. S. (2014). CoAP-based Healthcare Sensor Networks: a survey. *IEEE Proceedings of 11th International Bhurban Conference on Applied Sciences & Technology (IBCAST)*, 499-503. doi:10.1109/IBCAST.2014.6778196

Kuo, H. T., Chin, L. H., & Yun, F. L. (2015). A solution of a Newly Built Monitoring Automation System In Parallel to the Original Automation Management System. IEEE.

Linklabs. (2016). *A Comprehensive Look at Low Power, Wide Area Networks, For 'Internet of Things' Engineers and Decision Makers*. LinkLabs.

Linklabs. (2017). *LoW Power wide area network technology, Symphony Link Vs. LoRaWAN, A Guide for Engineers and Decision Makers*. Linklabs.

LPWA. (2017). *What Is LPWA? An IoT Connectivity Guide*. A White Paper By Ingenu, 1-3.

Mads, L., Istvan, Z. K., Preben, M., Mads, S., & Steffen, H. (2016). Coverage and Capacity Analysis of LTE-M and NB-IoT in a Rural Area. IEEE.

Muneer, B. Y., Mohammed, Q. S., & Dua, A. Z. (2016). Application Layer Protocols for the Internet of Things: A survey. IEEE.

Pascal, U. (2015). RACS: Remote APDU Call Secure Creating Trust for the Internet. IEEE.

Pascal, U., & Xavier, A. (2016). Secure Mobile Payments Based on Cloud Services Concepts And Experiments. *IEEE 2nd International Conference on Big Data Security on Cloud, IEEE International Conference on High Performance and Smart Computing*, 333-338.

Payam, H. (2016). Integrated Millimeter-Wave/Terahertz Sensor Systems for Near-Field IoT. ACM.

Priyanka, T., & Yoohwan, K. (2016). Implementation and Comparison of M2M Protocols for Internet of Things. *Proceedings of 4th International Conference on Applied Computing and Information Technology*, 43-48.

Rao, S., Chendanda, D., Deshpande, C., & Lakkundi, V. (2015). Implementing LWM2M in Constrained IoT Devices. *IEEE Conference on Wireless Sensors*, 52-56.

RPMA. (2017). *An Educational Guide How RPMA Works*. A White Paper By Ingenu, 1-4.

Saahithyan, R., Samir, K. M., & Debabrata, D. (2016). Efficient Algorithm for Less Power Consumption in Extended-Coverage-GSM for Low Data-Rate IoT Devices. IEEE.

Sean, B., David, I., & Prashant, S. (2016). Pervasive Energy Monitoring and Control through Low-Bandwidth Power Line Communication. *IEEE Internet of Things Journal*, 1-10.

Tata, S., Jain, R., Ludwig, H., & Gopisetty, S. (2017). Living in the Cloud or on the Edge: Opportunities and Challenges of IoT Application Architecture. *IEEE 14th International Conference on Services Computing*, 221-225.

Technica, P. (2005). *Easy X10 Projects for Creating a Smart Home*. Indy-Tech Publishing.

Thread, G. (2015). *Thread Stack Fundamentals*. Thread Group.

Want, R. (2011, July). Near Field Communication Smartphones. *Pervasive Computing*, 1-4.

Yan, Y. L., Xiaoqiang, L. Z., & Wu, H. (2017). Research on Water Meter Reading System Based on LoRa Communication. *IEEE International Conference on Smart Grid and Smart Cities*, 248-251.

Younghwan, C., Yunchul, C., Dongmyoung, K., & Jungsoo, P. (2017). Scheme to Guarantee IP Continuity for NFC-based IoT Networking. *ICACT2017*, 695-698.

Zoran, B. B., Jelica, P., & Veljko, M. (2016). Web Performance Evaluation for Internet of Things Applications. *IEEE Translations and Content Mining*, *4*, 6974–6992.

KEY TERMS AND DEFINITIONS

6LoWPAN: It is the combination of best features of internet protocol (IPv6) and low-power wireless personal area networks that allows limited processing smallest devices to transmit information wirelessly using an internet.

BLE: Low energy version of Bluetooth necessarily made for the IoT applications.

CoAP: Constrained application protocol especially designed for IoT web-enabled applications where the nodes and networks are constrained due to low energy, bandwidth, and memory.

Digital Twin IoT: A digital twin IoT is a dynamic digital representation of an industrial asset, processes, and systems that enable companies to better understand and predict the performance of their machines and find new revenue streams, and change the way their business operates.

LoRaWAN: Is a low power wide area network (LPWAN) that provides the internet of things such as secure bi-directional communication, mobility, and localization services.

LTE-M: Long-term evolution technology for the IoT devices to connect directly to a 4G network without a gateway and on batteries with less service cost.

LWM2M: Lightweight M2M is a protocol for M2M and the IoT device management functionality over the sensor or cellular networks.

MQTT: Publish-subscribe basis, JSON-enabled, energy-efficient multi-queue telemetry transport protocol for sending the message from the IoT devices and Cloud infrastructure.

SIGFOX: It is proprietary wireless technology which connects low-energy objects such as electricity meters, smart watches, and washing machines, which need to be continuously on and emitting small amounts of data.

Zigbee: It is IEEE 802.15.4 protocol to create wireless PAN with low power, low data rate with 10–100 meters line-of-sight range.

Chapter 4
Bluetooth Low-Energy-Based Applications:
The State of Art

Smita Sanjay Ambarkar
Lokmanya Tilak College of Engineering, India

Rakhi Dattatraya Akhare
Lokmanya Tilak College of Engineering, India

ABSTRACT

This chapter focuses on the comprehensive contents of various applications and principles related to Bluetooth low energy (BLE). The internet of things (IoT) applications like indoor localization, proximity detection problem by using Bluetooth low energy, and enhancing the sales in the commercial market by using BLE have the same database requirement and common implementation idea. The real-world applications are complex and require intensive computation. These computations should take less time, cost, and battery power. The chapter mainly focuses on the usage of BLE beacons for indoor localization. The motive behind the study of BLE devices is that it is supported by mobile smart devices that augment its application exponentially.

INTRODUCTION

Localization is locating any object or person in a space which may be open (outdoor) or limited (indoor/closed). Localization has become an intense research area for the past decade because of its real life application in various domains. During this

DOI: 10.4018/978-1-5225-3805-9.ch004

tenure of intensive research in the area of localization, earlier the focus was limited to outdoor localization but during the past few years. Recently indoor localization has also acquired focus of many researchers from industry and academia and thus intensifying research in the area of indoor localization (Liu, Darabi, Banerjee, and Liu, 2007).

There exist various technologies that have been used for outdoor localization. Global Positioning System (GPS) has been recognized to be the most efficient technology for outdoor localization, but it has some drawbacks that limit its application impossible for indoor localization and proximity detection. The major limitations of GPS are required of specialized hardware and demand for line-of-sight between sender and receiver. An additional limitation of GPS is that the accuracy of the result is also affected by the interference and noise in the environment (*Zahid F., Rosdiadee N., & Mahamod I,2013*).

The proximity detection and location detection is furthermore tedious with the existing satellite system when object or person moves into the closed loop architecture like inside the building or in the area where the line of sight is not available. The situation is also complicated in high-density urban areas with rare line-of-sight to the satellites. The solution to the above problem, which can solve the indoor localization and proximity detection, is the use of radio network like Wi-Fi, IEEE 802.11 etc. But during the literature survey, it is learned that few technologies were developed in order to be used for indoor localization. However, these technologies are not in usage due to cost and performance. Thus, it concurs that wireless systems can be implemented for indoor localization considering that many buildings have existing WLAN infrastructure. This wireless system for indoor localization can be coalesced with GPS to escalate and broaden its application. As already stated, despite rigorous research in indoor positioning, it is deprived of its extensive application. The major reasons that deject its widespread application are expensive, cost, excess battery power consumption and inadequate accuracy.

Research must thank the IoT(*García, Espada, Valdez, García-Díaz, Midgar,2014)* which comes up with the advanced technology like Bluetooth Low Energy (BLE) which can be used effectively for solving the above problem. Bluetooth Low Energy (BLE) technology is a very good alternative for indoor location detection, which augments Wi-Fi access points for indoor localization. Bluetooth low energy is a promising technology developed by SIG group the leverage of BLE is through its properties which dominate the existing Wi-Fi techniques, i.e. low power consumption, small size, connectivity to mobile phones, low cost, robust, efficient, multi-vendor interoperability, global availability, license free. One of the leading advantages of BLE it is cost effective and it consumes very less power as compared to Wi-Fi. One of the prominent motives behind the beacon popularity is, it is possible to place the beacons in the spots where Wi-Fi access points would be difficult to power. As the implementation cost is very low, it can be effectively used for many applications like asset tracking, hospitals, object detection, etc. It can also be used for facilitating the business or improving the sales.

The success of any methodology is measured in terms of various performance metrics. Few performance metrics that have been identified in the literature are accuracy, cost, precision, complexity, robustness, scalability etc. These performance metrics can be used to perform the comparative analysis of any two techniques. The rest of the chapter broadly discusses the following points, the Literature survey, the procedures used by BLE for Indoor Localization section, proximity detection and the various challenges involved in sales enhancement using BLE schemes. Comparisons between various indoor localization techniques like Wi-Fi, BLE &.at last the conclusion.

BACKGROUND

During the recent past, Bluetooth Low Energy (BLE) has emerged as an effective means for indoor localization. As the name itself implies, BLE is low energy, low cost and flexible technology for indoor localization. BLE uses Received Signal Strength Indicator (RSSI) to estimate the location of missing person or object in the indoor space. The major limitation of RSSI is that the accuracy of the result is easily affected by the various environmental factors and thus may produce incorrect results sometimes (*Yeob Kim, Hyung Kim, Choi & Jin, 2015*). It affects the widespread application of BLE for indoor localization.

According to the literature that authors have surveyed, existing approach sets up the threshold range for RSSI to evaluate if every single RSSI value measured lies within the specified range at a time (Aislelabs, 2015)(Bluetooth SIG. Bluetooth Technology Basics, 2015)(Peng and Sichitiu, September 2006). The authors in (Bluetooth SIG. Bluetooth Technology Basics, 2015) strongly recommend the usage of BLE technology for indoor localization as it is supported by the mobile devices like smart phones and tablets. During usage of BLE technology, a fingerprint database is created which is used during a later phase to locate the object.

BLE devices are used along with Wi-Fi access points. As these devices consume less energy, it can be placed in the spots where Wi-Fi points are difficult to power. Here BLE beacons can be used to transmit the radio signals which can be received by the mobile device. The signal strength is directly proportional to the distance of a beacon to the mobile device while transmission time is inversely proportional to the distance of beacon and mobile device. As the distance between the mobile device and transmitter increases, the signal strength weakens and transmission time increases.

In order to effectively employ the beacons for indoor localization, beacons need to be installed in the building so that no region of the building remains out of the range of a beacon. Let us consider a beacon to be installed at some point P in the building, its visibility range will be a circular disk of radius α' centered at P where α is the threshold value of the distance within which the beacon may receive a signal of strength not less than Δ. The same can be illustrated in Figure 1 shown. As observed in Figure 1, four beacons have been installed in the rectangular area. BLE beacons are devices made by estimate, Kontakt, Gimbal, and other manufacturers (*Zhao K., Li B., Andrew D. & Chen, 2013*). A beacon consists of a Bluetooth chipset (including its firmware), a battery providing power supply, and an antenna. Texas Instruments, Nordic Semiconductor, Bluegiga, and Qualcomm are the main current producers of the BLE chips. The visible area of a beacon is represented by a circular disk of radius α. Here α represents the range beyond which BLE is unable to receive a signal. The portion of the rectangular region that is outside any circle (shown by white area) represents the region that will not be localized as it remains outside the range of any beacon. Therefore, placement of beacons is also an important issue that needs to be focused upon in order to completely cover the building with any of the circle and thus effectively and efficiently perform localization.

The two most commonly used techniques for indoor localization and proximity detection are triangulation and fingerprinting. In triangulation method (19), the information from multiple transmitters is used to estimate the location of an object or

Figure 1. Illustration of Beacons and its range

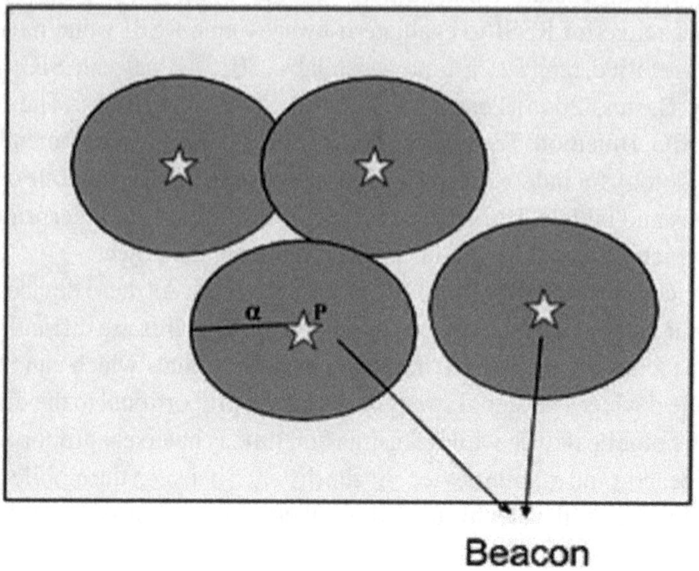

person. Few used techniques are Time of Arrival, Time Difference of Arrival, Angle of Arrival etc. as mentioned earlier. It has various limitations. The first limitation is that all the devices should be perfectly synchronized else may derive incorrect results. Another limitation of using a time to travel is that it may not give a correct estimation as these are affected by various environmental factors in the building like walls, other obstacles etc. and thus making distance estimation bit intricate.

Another popular approach for indoor localization using beacons is by creating a fingerprint database. This approach works in two phases. During first phase also known as training phase, vectors for location and RSSI are collected. This collected vector (specific to the building) is later used to estimate the location of mission object or person in the building during the second phase of the approach. The commonly used comparison algorithms for localization are the k-nearest neighbor algorithm, neural networks, probabilistic method, SVM, M vertex polygon etc.

In compliance with research in the field of Wi-Fi technology proximity detection which includes measuring the strongest signal strength from the Wi-Fi access point to detect the proximity can be achieved, but the cost of high implementation aids so there is need to implement the proximity detection at the low cost which can be possible by the use of the BLE.

Bluetooth-based indoor localization is an innovative approach. According to research specified in (*Bruno & Delmastro, 2003*) (*Muñoz-Organero, Muñoz-Merino & Kloos,2012*), Bluetooth can be used for indoor localization and proximity detection techniques but its performance is not satisfactory as it follows the long process of discovery and consumes the battery life quickly hence the total cost of implementation is high as compared to the BLE.

BLE TECHNOLOGY

Bluetooth Low Energy also called as Bluetooth Smart, is a wireless technology, uses low power or energy, low cost, long battery life, and ease of deployment. It can be connected with any product like a Smartphone or tablet easily used in widespread applications from personal networks for industrial or The IoT networks, Bluetooth low energy wireless ICs and certified modules can also be worked in long life battery-powered or in battery-less systems. BLE is an efficient technology for infrequent short-range wireless data communication at very low cost (*Venkatesh,n.d.*).

The BLE was started by Nokia, which was called as "Wibree" in 2006. In 2010, the Bluetooth Special Interest Group combined Wibree with the Bluetooth standard as a part of the 4.0 core specification. BLE is not treated as same protocol as Bluetooth even both are part of Wireless Personal Area Network (WPAN) standards. Bluetooth

Low Energy is designed for sending small chunks of data to run the IoT devices using coin cells(*Ji, Anwen,2010).*

Bluetooth is used for network requiring data exchange as well as wireless headset and other consumer devices where as BLE is used for applications such as mobile payment, healthcare, ticketing or access controls. Bluetooth and BLE networks involve master and slave devices.

Bluetooth and Bluetooth Low Energy are used for very different purposes. Bluetooth can manage a lot of data but consumes more battery life quickly at high costs. BLE is used for applications where a large amount of data transfer is not required and can, therefore, run on battery power for years at a cheaper cost. Bluetooth is not suitable for all kinds of wireless communication, whereas BLE can be integrated into any type of projects easily. BLE is designed in such a way that anyone who needs to send some data, it can be sent in any way they want. So it became most popular radio communication module which is low cost and energy efficient. BLE commonly used in mobile phones which run Android, OS X, Windows Phone, iOS and BlackBerry, as well as Linux, and Windows 8.

Bluetooth Low Energy (BLE), sometimes referred to as "Bluetooth Smart", is a lightweight subset of classic Bluetooth and was introduced as part of the Bluetooth 4.0 core specification. While there is some overlap with deciding Bluetooth, the basic idea applications and advantages of BLE are almost completely different from traditional Bluetooth. BLE communication is better understood by considering two types of devices central and peripheral (like master and slave) central mode where the device is in scanning mode and peripheral is in advertising mode. Peripheral broadcast the advertisement after every 20 ms to 10 ms intervals. The battery consumption depends upon the rate of transfer of the advertisement packet if the interval is short then battery life is also short, but the device is discovered faster. The BLE devices (Peripheral and central) are operated in GAP role and GATT profile. The GAP is a generic access profile and GATT is a generic attribute, the details of the protocol stack, GAP & GATT layers are included in the chapter. The GAP layer is responsible for communication establishment and maintaining it. When a central device captures the advertisement packet and asks for scanning response the peripheral has to send the scan response packet and hence the connection is established. It is then possible to read the services that the BLE device offers, and for each service there are characteristics. Each characteristic provides some value, which can be either read, written, or both read/written (*Nathan J. Muller,September 8, 2000*).

As shown in Figure 2 BLE consists of three main layers: Application, Host, and Controller. Application layer works as an interface between the user application and BLE protocol stack. Host Layer which is the upper layer consists of Generic Access Profile (GAP), Generic Attribute Profile (GATT), Security Manager Protocol (SMP),

Figure 2. Basic Overview of BLE Protocol Stack

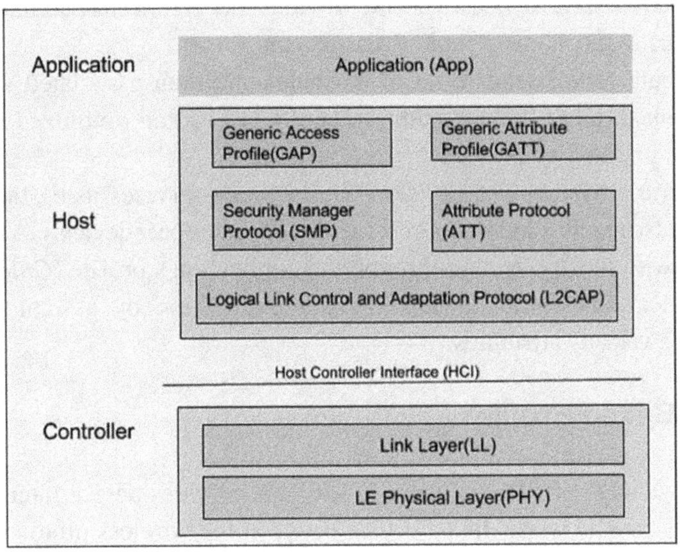

Attribute Protocol (ATT) and Logical Link Control and Adaptation Protocol (L2CAP). Host layer can communicate with the BLE module through the Host Controller Interface (HCI). HCI allows interfacing wide range of Hosts with the controller. The controller is the lowest layer of the stack, which consists of Link Layer (LL) and LE Physical layer (PHY). The controller is responsible handling physical layer packet transmission within time and it is implemented in integrated Bluetooth radio as a small source (*Townsend, Cufi, Akiba & Davidson,2014*). The host is nothing but hardware part runs on the application processor along with the user's application. Time restriction is much lesser than the controller. Host Controller Interface (HCI) matches different combinations of host and controller implementations. Sometimes HCI is not required, instead of it, complete Bluetooth SoC runs user applications and chip provides needed peripherals.

The Link Layer (LL) manages communication over a Physical Layer (PHY) interface. It handles sequence and timing of transmitted and received frames in advertising or scanner modes using link layer protocol to control data flow. The LL also works as gateways to limit data exchange with other devices and to protect data. The LL plays a major role in security and less power consumption.

The logical link control and adaptation layer protocol (L2CAP) layer manages services like security manager protocol and attribute protocol of upper layer protocols. L2CAP works LL controller. It performs data segmentation into smaller packets and protocol multiplexing and on the other side reassembly operation and de-multiplexing.

The SM architecture increases resource utilization by assigning more tasks to master device than slave devices. The SM provides encryption and data authentication using the pairing mechanism for key distribution.

The attribute server sends a set of attributes and their associated values in an attribute client through the attribute protocol (ATT) in an optimized way. These attributes are updated by peer devices.

The generic attributes profile (GATT) discovery services using the attributes protocol and also reading and writing characteristics of the peer device. GATT provides an interface with the application through the application's profile (*Galeev, n.d.*).

The application profile handles the communication by assigning different permission to various attributes.

Attribute-Based Profiles

The main advantage of BLE technology is that it provides device interoperability. The Attribute profile works like a bridge between the wireless protocol stack and the application devices. It provides a common format for data representation. So that different types of devices which want to share their data with each other can communicate using attribute profile in BLE.GATT -based profiles give the efficient data exchange among devices using low power. Also, Implementation of GATT is easy and it saves energy. Many GATT-based profiles will be available during upcoming years for BLE applications like proximity profiles, indoor localization etc (5).

APPLICATION IMPLEMENTATION CHALLENGES IN BLE

In this section, let us discuss the existing problems and challenges encountered in indoor positioning systems and corresponding algorithms (*Kul a,Ozyer, ba, Cankaya,Ankara,S ̈og ̈ut ̈oz ̈u & Ankara, 2014*).

The *Accuracy* of a positioning system is challenging and the required parameter as the result of the exact location of indoor objects depends upon accurate measuring of the received signal strength. The *Range* of existing system depends on received signal strength. The *Complexity* of a positioning system can be attributed to involved hardware, software, and operation factor. Various indoor localization systems can vary in the levels of complexity of the system. A positioning technique with high *Robustness* could function normally even if some signals are missing, or when some of the RSS value or angle character is never seen before. The positioning system must be *Scalable* in terms of size, geographic area, and administration. Size means a number of objects need to localize in the area. The geographic means scope may be increased geographically by implementing more beacons. Administration means even though the signals will interfere with the accuracy of detection of the object must need to be same. The **Cost** of a positioning system involves various factors like money, time, space, weight, and energy. The time factor is related to installation and maintenance. Mobile units may have limited space and weight constraints. Measuring unit density is considered to be a space cost. Sometimes, it necessitates considering some sunk costs, e.g. a position positioning system layered over a wireless network may be considered to have no hardware cost if all the necessary units of that network have already been purchased for other purposes. Energy is an important cost factor of a system. Some mobile units (e.g., Electronic Article Surveillance (EAS) tags and passive RFID tags (which are addressed later) are completely energy passive. These units only respond to external fields and, thus, could have an unlimited lifetime. Other mobile units (e.g., devices with rechargeable battery) have a lifetime of several hours without recharging. The time required for localization of wireless based indoor localization varies for the different methods. For methods that support localization for an immobile object, the **Localization time** can be very small in comparison to the localization of highly mobile objects.

APPLICATIONS

Implementation of Indoor Localization Using BLE

Localizing the thing or object inside the closed loop architecture (like inside the building/campus/room/mall, etc.) where the line of sight is very poor is termed as Indoor Localization. Implementing the indoor localization is a tedious and complicated application. This chapter focuses on the implementation details of indoor localization with the use of new Bluetooth Low Energy technology. As this technology brace contemporary mobile devices, especially by Smart phones and tablets.

Setup

The Setup of this application required to install the Bluetooth Low Energy transmitter at the every strategic point on the floor. All the Wi-Fi access points are might be considered as the strategic points for implementing the BLE transmitter or “Art Gallery Theorem” (*Hopcroft, Plotkin,Scott & Vuillemin,n.d.*) can be used as a novel approach to deciding the points for transmitter placement of a beacon transmitter. The setup also required the digitized map of the building previously installed in the mobile operating system.

Connection Establishment Using BLE

BLE Beacons are operated in two different modes advertising mode and scanning mode. In advertizing mode, a beacon advertises the Bluetooth packets with identification data called as advertisements, at regular intervals. Advertising is the only way of communication with surrounding the device. Advertisements contain the following data:

1. MAC address.
2. A UUID that identifies the beacon.
3. A Major number -identifying a subset of beacons within a large group.
4. A Minor number -identifying a specific beacon.

During BLE advertisement, at a physical layer, BLE transmits in the 2.4 GHz ISM band with 40 channels Each 2.0 MHz wide. The BLE Peripheral device transmits packets on the 3 advertising channels one after the other. A Central device (BLE enabled Smartphone) which is in the scanning mode scans for devices or beacons will listen to those channels for the advertising packets, and without forming connections it can ask for the scan response packet from peripheral. The scan Response packet contains the same information as the advertisement which helps to discover the peripherals name or other services which are not mentioned in the advertisement packet such as TX power or advertisement interval.

When a connection is established, the central device supplies the peripheral device with a set of critical data defining the channel and timing of the central -peripheral data exchange. These data state two important parameters: connection interval and slave latency. The central device decides the how frequently to synchronize with the peripherals which are called as connection interval. Latency, on the other hand, is a number of communication interfaces that a slave may ignore without losing the connection. It gives the slave an option of skipping a number of connected events. This gives the peripheral device some flexibility, in that if it does not have any data to send, it can choose to skip connection events and stay asleep, thus providing some power savings. The decision is up to the peripheral device.

Localization Methods

Localization involves exact positioning of the object for this purpose there is a need to map signal strength into the distance measurement, Trilateration method.

Trilateration

Trilateration method shown in figure 3 calculates the distance between the receiver's device and Wi-Fi access point. Trilateration method requires 3 such measurements. The circle is drawn by considering the Wi-Fi access point at the center and the distance measured above as the radius of the circle (T1, T2, T3) from all three decided access point. The position is discovered if the receiver's device lies in the area of intersection of all the three circles otherwise another access point should be considered in the calculations. The circles drawn are nothing but the range of wireless access point. As the direct line of sight is not possible in indoor localization and the signal propagation is affected by interference, hence there is inaccuracy in measuring the signal strength which gives incorrectness in the calculation of the radius for trilateration method; therefore, this method is not appropriate for indoor positioning applications.

In addition to this other method which is specified like AOA, TOA, TDOA [9] used in Wi-Fi require the direct line of sight and the accuracy in measurement, which is difficult to achieve in indoor localization. Thus, there is need to specify some other techniques. Fingerprinting is the technique which gives the more accuracy for implementing indoor applications

Fingerprinting

Fingerprinting techniques are the more suitable method where the line of sight propagation is poor. This method operates in two phases 1) offline database collection phase2) online positioning, discovery phase.

Figure 3. Trilateration method

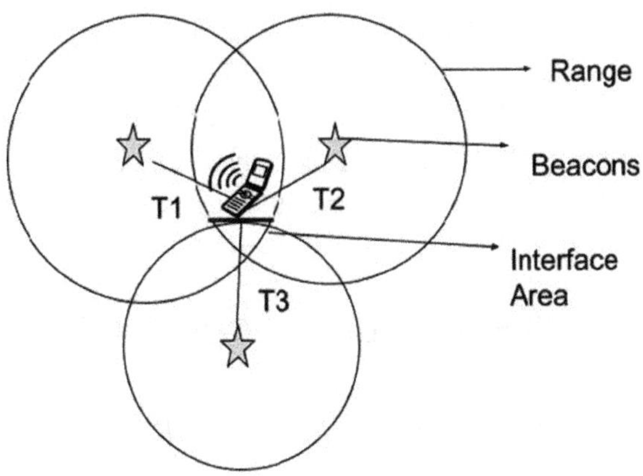

Database Collection Phase

The database collection phase is also called as training it involves selecting the reference beacons and locating receiver at one location, the signal strength from all the reference beacons is measured which is nothing but the digital map of the localization area (i.e. Digital map of the building/room/campus etc.).This measurement reveals the characteristic features of the beacons, which is then recorded in the database. This process is repeated at another reference beacon, and so on until all reference beacons are visited. For further reference of the collection of fingerprint database reader can refer approaches suggested by Bahl and Padmanabhan (*Bahl & Padmanabhan 2000*) or Azizyan et al. (*Azizyan, Constandache, & Choudhury, 2009*).

Positioning Phase

Locating the exact position of an object is called positioning. For finding the positions of an object its fingerprint measurement needs to be taken by the Smartphone consider, this measurement as the reference fingerprint. This reference fingerprint is then matched with the database and one or more fingerprints with the highest similarity are searched. As the digital map is previously stored the fingerprint value can be mapped to the position. The accuracy of position estimation depends upon the algorithm used for searching and the quality of the collection of fingerprint values in the database. There are probabilistic ways and deterministic way to for searching in the database. The deterministic method includes NN (Nearest Neighbor), KNN, WKNN (Weighted KNN), and probabilistic methods include the Bayesian probabilistic algorithm. The most commonly used distance metric is the Euclidian distance.

The Euclidean distance of the measured vector of the fingerprint $m = (m_1, m_2, \ldots, m_n)$ from the ith fingerprint $S_i = (s_i 1, s_i 2, \ldots, s_{in})$ in the database can be expressed by the following formula:

$$\text{Distance } (D_i) = | \sum^{n}_{i=1} (m_i - s_{ij})^q |^{1/q}$$

The q value determines the type of the distance: Manhattan Distance for q=1and Euclidean distance for q=2 (*Ault A., Zhong X. & Coyle E. J., 2005*).

Figure 4 shows the positioning method by using KNN

EVALUATION OF Wi-Fi AND BLE TECHNOLOGY

Evaluation of Wi-Fi and BLE technology can be done by considering the following parameters.

Figure 4. Positioning Method

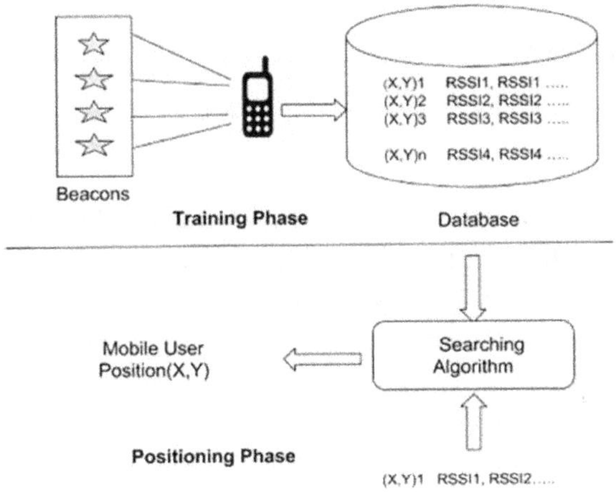

Signal Strength

The signal strength is an important parameter while preparing the collection database. The database will be accurate only if the signal strength received (i.e. RSS value) from the access point or beacon is proper. It is observed from the experimental result (*Kriz, Maly & Kozel,2016*) that Wi-Fi and BLE both are having equal signal strength. But the battery consumption and the cost of Wi-Fi is high as compared to beacon hence BLE implementation is preferred.

Scanning Interval

Scanning includes two factors recording of signals from the transmitters into the database and searching the database and according to the experimental setups BLE are faster in locating devices than Wi-Fi.

Beacon/Access point Density

The beacon /access point density highly affects the accuracy and performance of the system. As the number of beacons/access points is placed, more accuracy will be achieved. But if the localization is performed by using Wi-Fi and the density of access point increases the cost will also gradually increased. This is not the case with beacon density, the increase of beacon density will increase the performance but not the cost hence beacons will be preferred over Wi-Fi.

OTHER BLE APPLICATIONS

Proximity Detection Using BLE

Introduction

Proximity detection is an important issue which leads to the development of many real time applications like finding the missing person, localization of object, context-aware service, hands-free system, assistance to blind persons and so on. BLE is an effective and more flexible technology for implementing above mentioned applications in a low cost and low energy. The literature survey reveals that the most of the work in this domain is restricted to RSSI values (Received signal strength indicator) but the problem with this approach is RSSI may return inaccurate values because of interference in the surrounding and increase the error rate in proximity detection. Hence BLE detection is more promising over the existing technology (*Dae Kim, Soo Kim, Choi & Jin, 2015*).

As discussed in section (BLE Technology), BLE is operated in four mode master, slave, advertising, and scanning, the beacon is acting in advertising mode and smart phone is in scanning mode. The beacon will continuously advertise the signal which will be detected by scanning devices. These values will be continuously increasing as scanning device approaches near to the advertizing device and it is calculated approximately by using radio propagation model.

$$P_r(d) = \frac{P_t G_t G_r \lambda^2}{(4\pi)^2 d^2 L}$$

where, Pt is the transmitted signal power. G_t and G_r are the antenna gains of the transmitter and the receiver respectively. L ($L \geq 1$)is the system loss, and λ is the wavelength(2.4GHz). It is common to select $G_t = G_r = 1$ and L=1.

Enhancing Sales Using BLE

iBeacon, working in conjunction with Bluetooth Low Energy (BLE), can integrate the physical and mobile channels, enabling a bank's mobile app to deliver highly tailored digital promotions, coupons or offers directly to the consumer's Smartphone when the customer is in the general vicinity of an office, at any specific location within an office or at an ATM.

iBeacon technology is designed to deliver continuous content based on the precise location of a customer within a branch, allowing for highly relevant messaging or special offers on products to be sent to Smartphone users at the exact time and place they are most useful. This immediacy is a big advantage over other technology like NFC or QR codes that are either less accurate or require additional steps by the customer.

In order for iBeacon to work in banking, customers must first install the mobile app of the bank, they are visiting and opt-in for personalized promotional alerts. By providing the bank access, the bank could track activities performed both online and in the branch in the past to customize both mobile and in-person communication the moment they step inside the branch (Chen, Zhu, Jiang, and Soh, June 2015).

DISCUSSIONS AND FUTURE WORK

BLE is a powerful technology and can be used for a widespread application. The limitations of above technology are very high scanning rate, which ultimately increases the battery consumption, the power consumption and lowers the throughput of the system. Hence, in future, there is need to develop the techniques which start scanning only when the object is in the proximity. Another limitation is that the location of Smartphone is not considered. For instance, users can carry their device in pocket, bags and so on. In future, the BLE can also be combined with sensors to increase the usability of the technology. However, it additionally utilized sensor values and the main technique was the same with the existing techniques. Our goal was to improve the above-discussed applications.

CONCLUSION

The chapter Bluetooth Low Energy based applications-The state of art discussed an improved way to use the indoor localization, proximity detection application which was initially based on Wi-Fi. Chapter elaborated the BLE technology in detail along with its protocol stack and considerable deliberation of BLE and Wi-Fi. BLE beacons are placed in the same positions as Wi-Fi and it is observed that BLE gives more accurate results. BLE uses Fingerprinting database, as discussed above gives precise results as compared to Wi-Fi as there is less variance in signal strength. The BLE has many interesting and advantageous characteristics like higher scan rates, lower power and ability to be deployed unobtrusively on key objects and locations. For deployment of beacons various positioning method is also elaborated. The cost of BLE transmitter and receiver is very less; hence dense beacon placement is possible for more accuracy. As BLE uses simple star topology and silicon footprints, it reduces the implementation complexity as well as cost too.

It provides high security by using 128 bit AES encryption method. As compared to other wireless technologies, BLE is very robust through frequency hopping and popular for low power consumption. So this chapter helps to conclude that BLE is more approachable and dominant technology for indoor localization and proximity detection applications.

REFERENCES

Aislelabs. (2015). *The Hitchhikers Guide to iBeacon Hardware: A Comprehensive Report*. Retrieved from www.aislelabs.com/ reports/beacon-guide

Ault, A., Zhong, X., & Coyle, E. J. (2005). K-nearest-neighbor analysis of received signal strength distance estimation across environments. *Proceedings of the First Workshop on Wireless Network Measurements*.

Azizyan, M., Constandache, I., & Choudhury, R. R. (2009). Surround-sense: mobile phone localization via ambiance fingerprinting. *Proceedings of the 15th Annual International Conference on Mobile Computing and Networking, MOBICOM 2009*.

Bahl, P., & Padmanabhan, V. N. (2000). RADAR: an in-building rf-based user location and tracking system. *Proceedings of the INFOCOM*, 775–784. doi:10.1109/INFCOM.2000.832252

Bluetooth SIG. (2015). *Bluetooth Technology Basics*. Retrieved from www. bluetooth.com/what-is-bluetooth-technology/bluetooth-technology-basics/low-energy

Bruno & Delmastro. (2003). Design and analysis of a Bluetooth-based indoor localization system. In *Lecture Notes in Computer Science: Vol. 2775. Personal Wireless Communications* (pp. 711–725). Springer.

Chen, Z., Zhu, Q., Jiang, H., & Soh, Y. C. (2015). Indoor localization using smartphone sensors and ibeacons. *Proceedings of the IEEE 10th Conference on Industrial Electronics and Applications (ICIEA '15)*, 1723–1728. doi:10.1109/ICIEA.2015.7334389

Galeev. (n.d.). *Bluetooth 4.0: An Introduction to Bluetooth Low Energy-part II*. Z-Focus Consulting.

González García, C., Espada, J. P., Valdez, E. R. N., & García-Díaz, V. (2014). Midgar: Domain-Specific Language to Generate Smart Objects for an Internet of Things Platform. *2014 Eighth Int. Conf. Innov. Mob. Internet Serv. Ubiquitous Comput.*, 352–357. doi:10.1109/IMIS.2014.48

Hopcroft, Plotkin, Schwartz, Scott, & Vuillemin. (n.d.). *Art Gallery Theorems and Algorithms*. The International Series of Monographs on Computer Science Editor.

Ji, Z., & Qi, A. (2010). The application of internet of things(IOT) in emergency management system in China. *2010 IEEE Int. Conf. Technol. Homel. Secur.*, 139–142. doi:10.1109/THS.2010.5655073

Kim, Kim, Choi, & Jin. (2015). Accurate Indoor Proximity Zone Detection Based on Time Window and Frequency with Bluetooth Low Energy. *The 12th International Conference on Mobile Systems and Pervasive Computing (MobiSPC).*

Kim, D.-Y., Kim, S.-H., Choi, D., & Jin, S.-H. (2015). Accurate Indoor Proximity Zone Detection Based on Time Window and Frequency with Bluetooth Low Energy. *Procedia Computer Science*, *56*, 88–95. doi:10.1016/j.procs.2015.07.199

Kriz, Maly, & Kozel. (2016). *Research Article Improving Indoor Localization Using Bluetooth Low Energy Beacons*. Hindawi Publishing Corporation. doi:10.1155/2016/2083094

Kula, Ozyer, Tavliba, Cankaya, & S˙og˘ut˙oz˙u. (2014). IEEE 802.11 WLAN Based Real Time Indoor Positioning: Literature Survey and Experimental Investigations. *9th International Conference on Future Networks and Communications.*

Liu, H., Darabi, H., Banerjee, P., & Liu, J. (2007). Survey of wireless indoor positioning techniques and systems. *IEEE Transactions on Systems, Man and Cybernetics Part C*, *37*(6), 1067–1080. doi:10.1109/TSMCC.2007.905750

Muller. (2000). *Bluetooth Demystified*. McGraw-Hill Professional Publishing.

Muñoz-Organero, M., Muñoz-Merino, P. J., & Delgado Kloos, C. (2012). Using Bluetooth to implement a pervasive indoor positioning system with minimal requirements at the application level. *Mobile Information Systems*, *8*(1), 73–82. doi:10.1155/2012/386161

Peng, R., & Sichitiu, M. L. (2006). Angle of arrival localization for wireless sensor networks. *Proceedings of the 3rd Annual IEEE Communications Society on Sensor and Ad Hoc Communications and Networks (Secon '06)*, 1, 374–382.

Townsend, Cufi, Akiba, & Davidson. (2014). *Getting Started with Bluetooth Low Energy*. O'Reilly.

Venkatesh. (n.d.). *Ultra Low Power 802.11n Wi-Fi – Wireless Connectivity for The Internet of Things*. Academic Press.

Zahid, F., Rosdiadee, N., & Mahamod, I. (2013). Recent advances in wireless indoor localization techniques and system. *J. Comput. Netw. Commun., 2013*. doi:10.1155/2013/185138

Zhao, K., Li, B., Andrew, D., & Chen, L. (2013). A Comparison of algorithms adopted in fingerprinting indoor positioning systems. *Proceedings of the International Global Navigation SatelliteSystems Society IGNSS Symposium*.

KEY TERMS AND DEFINITIONS

Beacon: A beacon is a small Bluetooth radio transmitter that can send radio frequency signals and notify nearby Bluetooth devices of their presence.

BLE: Bluetooth low energy (BLE) is a wireless technology standard for personal area networks. BLE is targeted for very low power devices, devices that can run on batteries.

Fingerprint Database: It is a database used in indoor positioning. Updated fingerprints of interested locations are kept in fingerprint database.

iBeacon: iBeacon is a communication protocol developed by Apple on top of Bluetooth smart technology.

Indoor Localization: Indoor localization refers to tracking objects in an indoor environment.

IoT: The vast network of devices connected to the internet, including smart phones and tablets and almost anything with a sensor.

Proximity: Proximity sensor, a sensor able to detect the presence of nearby objects without any physical contact.

Signal Strength: Signal strength refers to the transmitter power output as received by a reference antenna at a distance from the transmitting antenna. It is radio frequency.

Wi-Fi: Wi-Fi is the name of a popular wireless networking technology that uses radio waves to provide wireless high-speed internet and network connections.

Chapter 5
An Introduction to IWoT:
How the Web of Things Helps Solve Industry 4.0 Challenges

Ángel Retamar
CTIC Technology Centre, Spain

Daniel Ibaseta
CTIC Technology Centre, Spain

Andrés G. Mangas
CTIC Technology Centre, Spain

Iván Gallego
CTIC Technology Centre, Spain

Irene Alonso Canella
CTIC Technology Centre, Spain

Lucía Fernández
CTIC Technology Centre, Spain

ABSTRACT

The major drawback of the industrial internet of things is the lack of interoperability across the plethora of IoT platforms. Cross-platform services often require the development of complex software components for protocol translation, device discovery, and thing lifecycle management. As a result, these systems are too expensive and hard to develop. The W3C Consortium launched the Web of Things Working Group to develop the standards for open interoperability in the internet of things. This chapter presents the web of things specifications for systems architecture and communication protocols and how they can be applied in industrial domains, building the industrial web of things. Finally, this chapter shows that this industrial web of things is built upon a network of systems and devices linked with universal open standards such as enterprise systems, which are nowadays communicated through the conventional "web of pages," as a key player in the Industry 4.0 revolution.

DOI: 10.4018/978-1-5225-3805-9.ch005

INTRODUCTION

The Internet of Things (The IoT in its acronym) integrates a series of techniques and technologies that allow common objects and any kind of device to gather data from the environment, store and expose it. A Thing can be defined as any physical object or entity with a unique identifier, an embedded system and able to communicate with other things in its surroundings. Common daily use objects like fridges, TVs and phones have become Things, integrated into an intelligent environment and connected to the internet.

This also applies to the industry, where all kind of machinery is, or will be, able to send and capture data about its functioning and the environment or expose a way to control it through the internet. Industrial systems are a composite of different apparatuses, each one of them has its own way of communication, functioning and capabilities. This turns rapidly into a messy pile of devices, nearly impossible to maintain. Furthermore, each equipment has its own application, program or even another device to show its data. At the end, everything is so fragmented that human intervention is often the only way to achieve interoperability between industrial systems. The hyper-fragmentation in The Internet of Things ecosystem is defined by (Chen & Helal, 2008) as "a Sensor Jungle".

This chapter intends to introduce the reader to the World Wide Web's (W3C) Web of Things (WoT) standard to shed some light on its objectives, the problems it addresses, its current status and how it fits simultaneously within the current The Internet of Things (The IoT) and Industrial Systems landscapes.

Along with this chapter, the WoT standards for systems architecture, communication protocols and definition formats for achieving semantic interoperability between Things will be exposed and how they are applied in real industrial use cases.

BACKGROUND

There are some key challenges that The Internet of Things has to face to be adopted by industry: a) aggressive environments, b) real time, c) trust, d) silos and e) lack of standards. Each one of these challenges establishes restrictions and needs in the devices themselves, the companies and the people.

Aggressive Environments

Industrial platforms for data gathering, for example, a production chain, are designed to resist the aggressive industrial environment where it might be exposed to high temperatures, electrical noise, electromagnetic fields, dust and many other threats.

However, the integration of The IoT in the industry requires, in many cases, the integration of microprocessors very sensitive to temperature, electrostatic and/or hits. These apparatuses might be suitable for an office environment, but they are not really appropriate for a hazardous environment. Device protection, as hardening or waterproofing, is essential in an industrial environment.

This all concerns physical requirements, but there are some other problems to take into account in an industrial environment, like connectivity. One of the key factors of The IoT is, obviously, the internet connection: no device is an The IoT Thing until it is connected. However, a public regulation, such as ATEX normative for hazardous and potentially explosive environments, usually restricts wirelessly connectivity. It might not be an internet access point (Ethernet cable) or a wireless connection (Wi-Fi) in key areas of a given industrial facility; it might even not be possible to deploy one. Because of this lack of conventional connectivity, devices must rely on other ways of communication, stronger, wider and shielded from the environment.

Real Time

In terms of industry, The IoT has strict requirements such as bandwidth, latency, and determinism. Industrial machines often need a millisecond precision for decision-making, so the thing that monitors it must react, at least, with that precision. It also has to be scalable and adaptive, for example, a bakery industry that needs a lot of sensors to measure ovens temperatures and control them, so that each oven must be accessible and respond to temperature updates quickly. Also if a new oven was added it should not affect the rest of them or the whole system.

Trust

The IoT opens industrial machinery, usually designed to be used manually or from a local panel, to be worldwide accessible via the internet, with the risks this entails. They are classified in the following areas: Privacy, Security, and Safety.

As any device that has internet connectivity, a Thing is vulnerable to external attacks and is hardly capable to be protected by itself due to its lack of computing capacity. In many cases, poor capabilities are the main threat to security because, in a majority of devices, they are absolutely impossible to be even implemented. An attacker could enter into one device and control other systems connected to it, read the collected data, remove or replace it or simply turn the machine off. The number of poorly secured devices connected to the internet is growing daily and they represent a vast field of attack for hackers.

Security involving The IoT, and particularly in an industrial deployment, have to cover the following areas to maximize security:

- **Switching On:** A device must be able to check if the software that is going to execute is the one it was meant to execute and abort its execution if it is not.
- **Access:** Each application running in the machine must be credential locked, so that each one of them has access only to a certain functionality of the device, limiting attack area even if the credentials are obtained.
- **Connection:** Each connection with a network must be credential-locked in a machine-to-machine way so that no human intervention is required.
- **Actualization:** Any device must be able to get updates and assure that they are legitimate. It must also not stop giving service while updating if it is a critical mechanism.

The IoT is designed to affect all kind of scenarios, for example, a car that has integrated sensors and actuators and is controlled via internet. If this car was hacked, the attacker might be able to shut down the car or disable the breaks.

But not everything is that dangerous: workers safety can be improved by The IoT applied to the industry. For example, an The IoT network that monitors vitals from the workers, hazardous gasses, movements, etc. Combining this with data coming from the machinery and other ambient sensors it would be easy to detect if the worker is going to a dangerous place, suffered a fainting or is in the path of a machine. This data can be accessible not only by a supervisor but to every worker, to know for themselves the threats that can be present.

Silos

The IoT generally suffers from fragmentation and isolation, named by Ensor P. (1988) as "Information Silos". An information silo is a "conjunct of data under the control of a person or organization, where it stays hidden and/or inaccessible". Applied to The IoT, a silo is a set of devices which information is not accessible from other devices. Silos are a bigger problem when they are inside a company because this is not only a technical problem to communicate devices, but also a barrier between people. The majority of The IoT platforms focus on capturing its own data and does not contemplate sharing it, and this lack of information sharing creates inefficiencies and diminishes data usefulness.

Silos are also caused by the vast amount of The IoT solutions, platforms and different standards that are out in the field. To fully obtain the total value of The IoT it is needed to be able to access, process and correlate all the data gathered, and then, the principal obstacles are the technical barriers between departments, systems and people.

Lack of Standards

The IoT ecosystem is absolutely fragmented, no solution has become dominant yet and every company implements different The IoT products, most of them incompatible. A lack of some dominant solutions leads to a lack of reliable standards, as it can be seen in mobile technologies or internet protocols where a technology has overcome all the others. This lack of standards slows down the estimated growth of The IoT and contributes to create silos and make product development harder.

The IoT communication protocols are a representative example of incompatibility, where Bluetooth, ZigBee or LTE are common communication solutions that cannot be able to interact with each other. Which one of them must a device designer pick up in order to make the invention as much compatible as possible in the future? None? All of them? Maybe a new one? Nobody knows. And it is not only a matter of compatibility but also a matter of the particular use case. For example, Bluetooth is designed to connect with half a dozen or less nearby devices, but ZigBee is able to manage for more devices, and LTE can access to Things located farther away from the Hub.

There may also be use cases where all of them would be needed. A standard must cover all these cases, and this is hard to overcome and standardize. Standardization must also cover the gathered data, how it is collected and stored so that access to data is predictable due to a standardized format. This also enables device-to-device communication, because every device knows how the data is represented and can use it without translations.

No manufacturer alone is going to be able to solve the standardization problem and to create a viable standard. The solution is a coordinated joint effort to come together to a solution that can be widely accepted.

OPEN STANDARDS FOR SEMANTIC INTEROPERABILITY: THE WEB OF THINGS

As described in a previous section, the cost of integrating The IoT devices from multiple vendors using a huge set of protocols and technologies grows in an impractical and unacceptable manner. The W3C WoT standards aim to solve this problem using the Web, these Web technologies serve as the foundation of the Internet, and as such are well-known, widely supported and established. The main objective is to define the set of entities that may appear in a WoT environment standardizing the interactions between them and focusing on using the protocols present in the Web stack, mainly HTTP.

One of the most prominent arguments commonly used against this approach is the fact that many The IoT devices are constrained by their computational power and Web protocols (mainly HTTP) are too heavy to properly run on that hardware. This is addressed by focusing on protocols such as CoAP which are explicitly designed to solve this issue. Devices that are completely blocked from using any Web protocol, even CoAP, could use an intermediate bridge to integrate them in the WoT environment. Advances in hardware, battery efficiency and the upcoming HTTP/2 protocol should also be of help. It seems reasonable to think that this will be a lesser concern as time passes.

The standard aims to fulfill three basic requirements:

- It must be flexible to represent and expose the multitude of possible physical devices.
- It must be compatible with all currently existing legacy The IoT solutions and architectures (the standard would be bound to fail otherwise due a number of resources that have already been invested in these solutions).
- It must provide room to implement the appropriate security mechanisms to address all security concerns that stem from The IoT applications.

Thing Description

Each of the devices in a WoT network has an associated Thing Description (TD): a document that defines all the device properties and interactions in a standardized format. In order to interact with a Web of Things device, an external client or device should obtain its Thing Description to understand the semantics associated with the device.

The Thing Description can be stored in the device itself or hosted by an external system, which would allow extending legacy devices with Web of Things functionality. All the Thing Descriptions in a system could be registered in a centralized repository (Thing Repository), which would enable the process of discovering new devices, in addition, to providing search methods on the registered devices.

Each WoT device should implement a web interface that allows access to its Thing Description. This interface, known as the WoT interface, would allow the devices to consume and provide information to other devices or clients that follow the WoT standard. The WoT interface must expose at least one endpoint for each of the interactions defined in its Thing Description. Additionally, the WoT interface must adhere to the communication and security protocols established in the Thing Description.

The Thing Description of a device is represented as a JSON document enhanced with a semantic context that uniquely identifies all the fields in the Thing Description. To this end, the Thing Description is defined as a JSON-LD (Lanthaler & Gütl, 2012), a serialization format based on the JSON specification that adds a semantic context to a JSON document, associating each of the fields present in the JSON document to a unique URI present in a shared vocabulary.

Thing Metadata

The top level of the Thing description contains generic metadata fields related to the device, such as the device name, accepted communication protocols or security concerns. It also defines the semantic context of the document, which univocally defines each of the JSON fields present in the Thing Description.

Additional fields related to the device can be defined at this level, if they are present in the semantic context of the Thing, as explained in the next chapter.

The context of a Thing Description is represented by a set of associations between the fields present in the Thing Description document and their concept URI's, as defined in a shared vocabulary.

These associations are specified with the key @context, which must be present at the top level of the Thing Description. The value of @context can be defined as a JSON object in which the keys are fields in the document and the values its context URI's. Additionally, its value could be a string with the URI of a publicly exposed context defined previously. In case that a device involves several contexts, the @context field can be defined as an array of URI's. This format also allows extending predefined contexts with additional concepts. Once defined with the @ context keyword, all the fields can be referenced in the Thing Description document.

Table 1. Thing metadata

Field	Optional	Description
name	No	Name of the Thing
@context	No	Semantic context of the Thing
base	Yes	Base URI valid for all the Thing defined interactions.
security	Yes	Security related information to interact with the Thing

The following Thing Description contexts show the accepted @context formats:

```
        {
"@context": {
"name": "http://schema.org/familyName",
"address": "http://schema.org/address"
}
        }

        {
"@context": "http://w3c.github.io/wot/w3c-wot-td-context.
jsonld"
        }
        {
"@context": [
"http://w3c.github.io/wot/w3c-wot-td-context.jsonld",
{"address": "http://schema.org/address"}
        ]
        }
```

Thing Interactions

The resources exposed in the Thing Description to interact with the device are not limited to endpoints provided by the device itself. If necessary, all interactions could refer to resources exposed by external devices or servers, which would enable the following scenarios:

- Provide an external WoT interface to legacy devices that do not provide WoT capabilities by themselves.
- Enhance device data with additional information that cannot be hosted on the device itself.
- Build a meta-thing that combines all the interactions of different devices on the same interface.

There are three main interaction patterns: Property, Action and Event. According to their type, the interactions could result in either some action performed on the device or some information returned from the device. The interaction types expect or produce different value types on invocation, which are defined as a valid JSON Schema.

Table 2. Thing Property definition parameters

Field	Optional	Description
@type	No	Interaction type, which defines its semantic fields. Defaults to "Property"
name	No	Name of the property
outputData	No	Data type of the property
writable	No	Whether the property can be modified (true/false)
links	No	Links to access the property through different protocols
stability	Yes	Milliseconds in which the property is expected to change its value (-1 for static properties, 0 for an irregular stability)
security	Yes	Specific security restrictions for the property, in addition to the measures to be applied to the device itself

Properties

Properties allow direct access to device information that could be static or dynamic in nature. If allowed by the device, static properties could be overwritten by the client. Each property must define the format of its output data as a valid JSON schema to allow clients to interpret their response.

Additionally, properties can define security policies that could be applied at the interaction level, or set its stability to communicate the client the frequency of the property changes. This could be used for polling routines to avoid overloading the device with requests if the property is not expected to change. The stability could also be included in the cache control headers of the HTTP protocol.

Following code shows an excerpt from the Thing Definition for a WoT-enabled Weather Station device:

```
{
  "@context": "http://w3c.github.io/wot/w3c-wot-td-context.
jsonld",
  "name": "weather-station",
  "interactions": [
    {
      "@type": ["Property"],
      "name": "device-model",
      "outputData": {"valueType": { "type": "string" }},
      "writable": false,
      "links": [{
        "href": "http://example.com:80/device-model",
```

```
        "mediaType": "application/json"
        }],
      "stability": -1
    },
    {
      "@type": ["Property"],
      "name": "wind-speed",
      "outputData": {"valueType": { "type": "number" }},
      "writable": false,
      "links": [{
        "href": "http://example.com:80/wind-speed",
        "mediaType": "application/json"
        }],
      "stability": 60000
    }
  ]
}
```

Two properties are defined: "device-model" and "wind-speed". Both can be accessed through HTTP protocol at their respective endpoints and return a JSON document. "device-model" is defined as a non-writable static string property, as defined by the -1 stability. "wind-speed" is defined as a non-writable numeric property expected to change each 60 seconds.

Actions

Actions result in device processes or changes that are not expected to complete instantly like Property changes do. The state of this long-running processes could be monitored through a sub-resource created on action received, and may generate some output or receive input information.

The sub-resource generated could provide methods to modify or cancel the action process if the device allows stopping queued processes. Once the process finishes, the sub-resource is removed and could be stored for traceability reasons.

Following code shows the Thing Description for a car barrier device with two actions to raise or lower the barrier. Both actions return a string with an endpoint sub-resource to monitor the state of the task.

```
{
  "@context": "http://w3c.github.io/wot/w3c-wot-td-context.
jsonld",
```

Table 3. Thing Action definition parameters

Field	Optional	Description
@type	No	Interaction type, which defines its semantic fields. "Action" by default.
name	No	Name of the Action
links	No	Array of links to access the action through different protocols
inputData	Yes	Input data related to the action
outputData	Yes	Data type returned by the action
security	Yes	Specific security restrictions for the action

```
  "name": "car-barrier",
  "interactions": [
    {
      "@type": ["Action"],
      "name": "raise",
      "outputData": {"valueType": { "type": "string" }},
      "links": [{
        "href": "http://example.com:80/barrier/raise",
        "mediaType": "application/json"
        }]
    },
    {
      "@type": ["Action"],
      "name": "lower",
      "outputData": {"valueType": { "type": "string" }},
      "links": [{
        "href": "http://example.com:80/barrier/lower",
        "mediaType": "application/json"
        }]
    }
    ]
}
```

Events

Events provide a method for a client to be notified by the device on a specific condition (e.g. alarm). Some protocols provide this natively, such as WebSockets or CoAP, and others could be adapted to offer it.

This following code describes a temperature alarm event for a Weather Station Thing. The alarm should be notified to each client subscribed to the event through the CoAP protocol. The value return could be a string with the encoded alarm payload.

```
{
  "@context": "http://w3c.github.io/wot/w3c-wot-td-context.
jsonld",
  "name": "weather-station",
  "interactions": [
    {
      "@type": ["Event"],
      "name": "temperature-alarm",
      "outputData": {"valueType": { "type": "string" }},
      "links": [{
        "href": "coap://example.com:80/alarms/temp",
        "mediaType": "application/json"
        }]
    }
    ]
}
```

THE WEB OF THINGS ARCHITECTURE

WoT Architecture: The WoT Servient

The WoT Servients are the building blocks for the Web of Things (as Web Servers are the main building blocks for conventional World Wide Web). WoT Servients have the responsibilities of provide open access to physical things, define their semantics

Table 4. Thing Event definition parameters

Field	Optional	Description
@type	No	Interaction type, which defines its semantic fields. "Event" by default
name	No	Name of the event
links	No	Array of links to access the event through different protocols
outputData	Yes	Data associated to the event
security	Yes	Specific security restrictions for the event

and ensure non-functional requirements such as privacy, security, performance, etc. (Guinard et al. 2011).

At the date of writing of this chapter (April 2017), the W3C is actively working to generate a recommendation with the goal of standardizing the internal architecture and building blocks of WoT servients.

The WoT servients are the main actors in a WoT environment, and represents a virtual entity that is both a WoT client and a WoT server at the same time.

- WoT servers are Web servers that possess capabilities to access underlying The IoT devices and expose a public interface, named the WoT Interface, that may be used by other clients.
- WoT clients are entities that are able to understand the WoT Interface to send requests and interact with The IoT devices exposed by other WoT servients or servers using the capabilities of a Web client such as Web browser.

It is important to note that WoT servients represent a powerful abstraction tool that may be used to encapsulate and expose an The IoT device using multiple different views, i.e. a WoT Servient may interact with The IoT devices through other WoT servients without the need to access physical devices. A WoT environment may consist of multiple interrelated WoT servients with multiple layers of functionality that provide a way to grow in a scalable and horizontal manner.

- **Resource Model:** Thing interactions are defined as resources. These resources are represented by conventional web URIs (Unified Resource Identifier) and serve as a suitable abstraction that is contained in the Resource Model block. URIs composition for each kind of thing interaction (thing properties, actions or events), are defined using the design principles behind REST (Representational State Transfer) protocol (Feng, Shen & Fan, 2009).
- **Protocol Binding:** A resource is just a logical, high level, representation and has to be mapped to the actual protocols used in the lower layers of the stack. Any given resource may have different representations depending on the protocol. The WoT Servient's Protocol Binding layer has the responsibility of interpreting communications and applying the required transformations to get from interactions based on any of the supported protocols. For example, subscribing to an event in HTTP could be defined as an initial POST request followed by a series of GET polling requests, the same interaction when using the WebSockets protocol would require sending a message from client to server to initiate the subscription and waiting for event messages originated from the server.

Figure 1. Overview of the inner composition of a WoT Servient

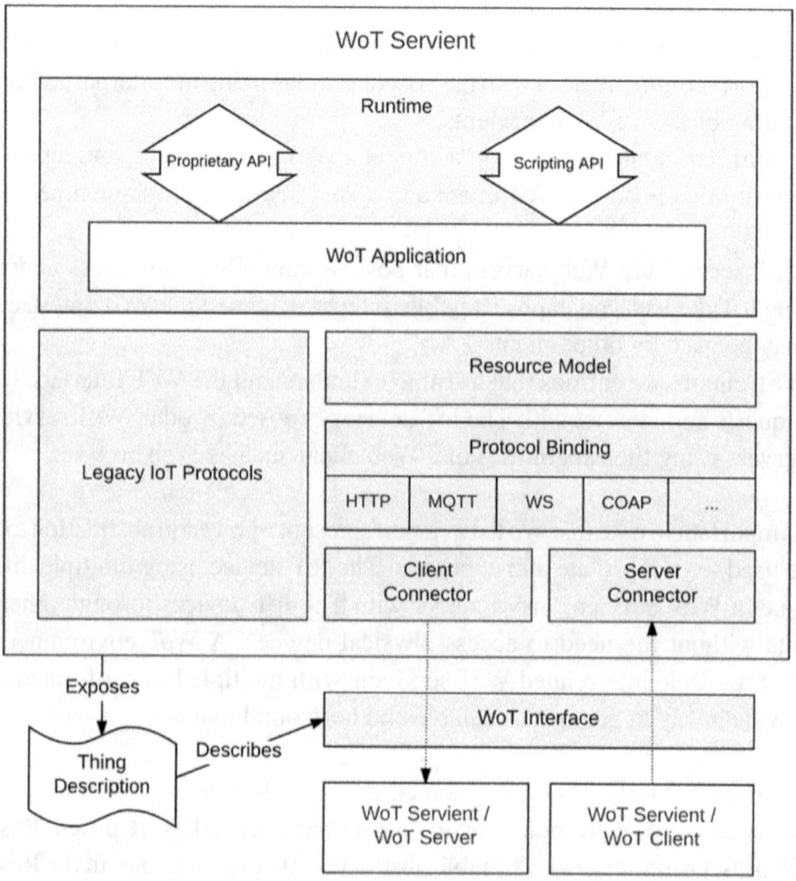

- **Client & Server Connectors:** WoT servients contain both a Client Connector and a Server Connector that are able to handle communications in each of the protocols defined in the Protocol Binding layer (this is the case on servients, WoT clients or servers would only define client or server connectors respectively). Client Connectors initiate connections to other servients or servers while Server Connectors accept requests from servients or clients.
- **WoT Interface:** Interactions between WoT entities handled by Client or Server Connectors follow the rules established by the WoT Interface. The WoT Interface is a standardized Web API that defines how to interact with the properties, events and actions of a Thing and stems from the Thing Description documents intrinsically linked to every WoT servient or server. These documents contain information about the URIs, along with supported protocols, parameters and other metadata for each resource.

WoT Applications

WoT applications sit at the top of the pyramid and contain the servient logic. These are the software components in charge of communicating with underlying sensors, actuators or The IoT devices in general to expose their capabilities. They may also serve as proxies to other Things (WoT servients or servers) by adapting or aggregating the WoT Interfaces of said Things.

WoT applications rely on two kind of APIs: the standard Scripting API and proprietary APIs. Proprietary APIs represent all APIs provided by private The IoT equipment vendors or other third parties that fall outside of the scope described by the WoT standard, e.g. an API to manage a ZigBee-based wireless temperature sensor. These two types are not exclusive; in fact, many servients would probably make use of both: proprietary APIs would handle the details of communicating with each The IoT device while the Scripting API would wrap and expose that functionality in a manner that is understandable by the rest of the WoT network. This would lead in turn to a higher degree of encapsulation, restricting the knowledge about the protocols and the finer details of the inner workings of each Thing to its own servient.

The Scripting is at the foundations of the future WoT applications ecosystem.

The API intends to be language-agnostic and defines a global object that is the single entry point to a group of factories whose objective is to expose and consume Things. Clients may consume Things by discovering previously unknown devices that match a set of filters or by using the Thing Descriptions of said Things in

Figure 2. Overview of the Scripting API design

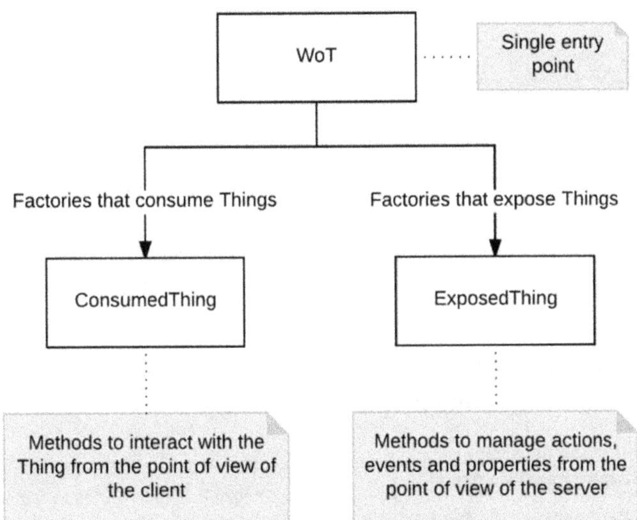

case the application knows of its existence in advance. It is interesting to note that discovery mechanisms are up in the air and much work still needs to be done, although the current consensus is tending towards a central Things repository exposing a REST interface. Servers may expose Things from Thing Description documents or by initializing empty objects and programmatically adding interactions, events and properties. All these methods focus heavily on the Promise pattern that is commonplace in the Javascript ecosystem.

Following code shows the Scripting API entry point WebIDL definition; as was published by WoT Scripting Task Force on May 2017 (WoT Scripting, 2017):

```
interface WoT {
 Observable<ConsumedThing> discover(optional ThingFilter
filter);
 Promise<ConsumedThing> retrieve(USVString url);
 Promise<ExposedThing> createLocalThing(ThingInit init);
};

dictionary ThingInit {
 DOMString name;
 USVString url;
 Dictionary description;
};

enum DiscoveryType {
 "any",
 "local",
 "nearby",
 "directory",
 "broadcast",
 "other"
};
dictionary ThingFilter: ThingInit {
 (DiscoveryType or DOMString) type = "any";
};
```

Consumed Things provide methods that may be used by clients to interact with the Thing, i.e. getting or setting properties, listening to events or invoking actions.

```
interface ConsumedThing {
 readonly attribute DOMString name;
```

```
 readonly attribute USVString url;
 readonly attribute Dictionary description;
 Promise<any> invokeAction(DOMString name, sequence<any>
parameters);
 Promise<void> setProperty(DOMString name, any value);
 Promise<any> getProperty(DOMString name);
 ConsumedThing addListener(DOMString eventName,
ThingEventListener listener);
 ConsumedThing removeListener(DOMString eventName,
ThingEventListener listener);
 ConsumedThing removeAllListeners(DOMString eventName);
};

callback ThingEventListener = void (Event event);

[Constructor(PropertyChangeEventInit init)]
interface PropertyChangeEvent: Event {
 readonly attribute PropertyChangeEventInit data;
};

[Constructor(ActionInvocationEventInit init)]
interface ActionInvocationEvent: Event {
 readonly attribute ActionInvocationEventInit data;
};

[Constructor(ThingDescriptionChangeEventInit init)]
interface ThingDescriptionChangeEvent: Event {
 readonly attribute ThingDescriptionChangeEventInit data;
};

dictionary PropertyChangeEventInit {
 DOMString name;
 any value;
 any oldValue;
};

dictionary ActionInvocationEventInit {
 DOMString actionName;
 any returnValue;
};
```

```
dictionary ThingDescriptionChangeEventInit {
 TDChangeType type;
 TDChangeMethod method;
 DOMString name;
 TDChangeData data;
};

enum TDChangeMethod {
 "add",
 "remove",
 "change"
};

enum TDChangeType {
 "property",
 "action",
 "event"
};

typedef (ThingPropertyInit or ThingActionInit or
ThingEventInit) TDChangeData;
```

Exposed Things live on the server and contain a superset of the Consumed Thing method set. Additional actions available in the server include emitting events, creating or removing actions, events or properties and defining the callbacks that must be called on action invocation or property update.

```
interface ExposedThing {

ExposedThing addProperty(ThingPropertyInit property);
 ExposedThing removeProperty(DOMString name);
 ExposedThing addAction(ThingActionInit action);
 ExposedThing removeAction(DOMString name);
 ExposedThing addEvent(ThingEventInit event);
 ExposedThing removeEvent(DOMString name);
 Promise<void> register(optional USVString directory);
 Promise<void> unregister();
 Promise<void> start();
 Promise<void> stop();
```

```
 Promise<void> emitEvent(DOMString eventName, any payload);
 ExposedThing onRetrieveProperty(PropertyRequestHandler
handler);
 ExposedThing onUpdateProperty(PropertyRequestHandler handler);
 ExposedThing onInvokeAction(ActionRequestHandler handler);
 ExposedThing onObserve(ObserveRequestHandler handler);
 };

 ExposedThing implements ConsumedThing;

 callback PropertyRequestHandler = any (PropertyRequest
request);
 callback ActionRequestHandler = any (ActionRequest request);
 callback ObserveRequestHandler = any (ObserveRequest request);

 dictionary PropertyRequest {
 USVString from;
 ThingPropertyInit property;
 Dictionary options;
 };

 dictionary ActionRequest {
 USVString from;
 ThingActionInit action;
 any inputData;
 };

 dictionary ObserveRequest {
 USVString from;
 ObserveType type;
 boolean subscribe;
 DOMString name;
 };

 enum ObserveType { "property", "action", "event", "td" };

 dictionary SemanticType {
 DOMString name;
 DOMString context;
 };
```

```
dictionary ThingPropertyInit {
DOMString name;
boolean configurable = true;
boolean enumerable = true;
boolean writable = true;
SemanticType[] semanticTypes;
Dictionary dataDescription;
any value;
};

dictionary ThingEventInit {
DOMString name;
SemanticType[] semanticTypes;
Dictionary outputDataDescription;
};

dictionary ThingActionInit {
DOMString name;
Dictionary inputDataDescription;
Dictionary outputDataDescription;
SemanticType[] semanticTypes;
Function action;
};
```

There are experimental implementations currently available for Java and Node on the W3C Exploratory WoT Implementations GitHub page (https://github.com/w3c/wot). It seems probable that in the near future Web browsers could implement this API to enable them as application hubs and control centers of WoT deployments.

This API should facilitate the creation of a rich ecosystem where developers would be able to build applications that interact with the WoT environment in a flexible manner, with minimal configuration and without the need of dealing with multiple protocols or having previous knowledge of the types of devices that are present. Third party vendors would also be able to launch interoperable products that would, in turn, allow end users to mix and match pieces from multiple providers without being restricted to a specific brand, as is normally the case nowadays.

WoT Servients for Industrial Applications: PLC/OPC WoT Servient

OPC is a set of standards for data interchange on industrial environments that is comprised of a series of specifications grouped into two families:

- OPC Classic was the first to appear and its components are based on Microsoft COM/DCOM technologies, this generates some problems related to the impediments for integrating with non-Windows systems and the inherent difficulties of properly configuring communication between hosts using COM/DCOM.
- OPC Unified Architecture (UA) is more recent and attempts to address these issues by moving to a future-proof service-oriented architecture based on open-source well-known protocols and serialization formats, one of the most noticeable downsides to OPC UA is the fact that its adoption rate is somewhat slow in the industry.

OPC is commonly used as a means of exposing and interacting with data captured from industrial processes and stored in industrial PLCs. An approach based on Web of Things could remove the majority of barriers and challenges related to data access, facilitate the operation and extraction of value, and lay the foundation for innovative applications further down the line.

Figure 3 provides a diagram that identifies the actors and interactions involved in this theoretical WoT + OPC infrastructure.

The OPC WoT Servient is the cornerstone of an OPC WoT deployment and contains the logic to interact with the OPC server. It exposes all OPC variables as properties, which may be retrieved or updated depending on their writable status, i.e. there is a property resource for each variable stored in the OPC server. It also provides a set of events that emit notifications each time an OPC variable change.

The main building blocks for an OPC WoT Servient are;

- **The Protocol Binding Layer:** Contains definitions for both the HTTP and WebSockets protocols. This way, clients may choose between the familiar and widely supported HTTP or the real-time capabilities and performance of WebSockets. This component could run in an independent host connected to the same LAN as the PLC or even in the machine that contains the OPC server if the appropriate resources can be spared.
- **The Historical WoT Servient Component:** Has the responsibility of subscribing to the events provided by the OPC WoT Servient to store the historical evolution of the OPC variables. To that end, it uses the WebSockets

Figure 3. OPC WoT Servient

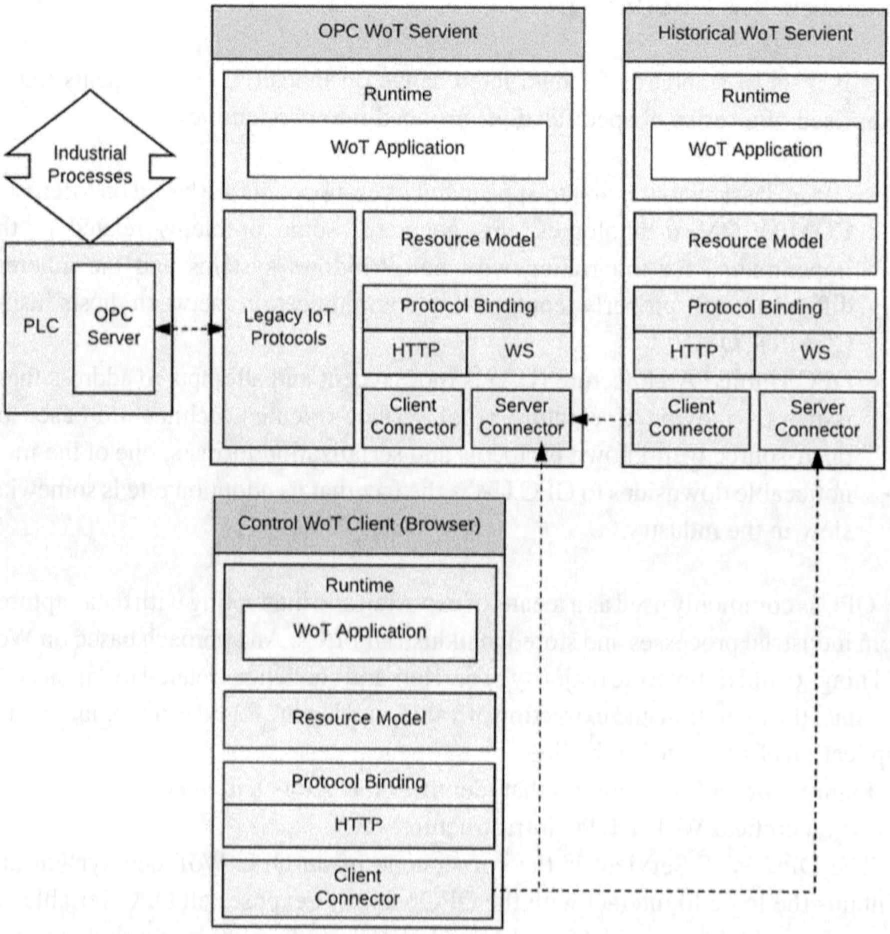

protocol binding, which is better suited for the continuous streaming of notifications initiated from the server-side. It should be noted that this component does not have any knowledge about the OPC protocol; all interactions adjust to the guidelines defined by the WoT Interface.

- **The Control WoT Client Component:** Functions as the interface between the end-user and the data exposed by the other servients. It would send requests to the OPC WoT Servient to check or update the current values of the OPC variables and to the Historical WoT Servient to review their trends and evolution. This component could take one of two forms: A standard WoT client with an application developed on top of the Scripting API running in a browser that provides such implementation. The second option would be a regular Web application with the capability of directly accessing the WoT Interface of the other servients over HTTP.

USE CASE: SMART GRIDS AND RENEWABLE ENERGY SOURCES

Introduction

(EISA, 2007) introduces the concept of "Smart Grids" which are defined as intelligent power networks supported by digital technologies, real-time communications and data analytics in order to optimize the relation between energy generators and consumers. A major difference between conventional and smart grids lays in the flexibility in the network topology. Smart grids are able to handle bidirectional energy flows, allowing consumers to act as nodes in a distributed generation network using renewable energy generators such as photovoltaic panels, biomass generators, wind turbines, etc. In two-way flows of electricity, the excess of energy production from any local sub-network can be reverted to the main grid, raising safety and reliability.

Each node in sub-networks for energy co-generation is designated as a DER (Distributed Energy Resource). DER systems are typically power generators using renewable energy sources but also can be classified as a DER system any grid-connected device for energy storage. DER systems have reduced generation capacities (up to 10 MW or less).

In a sunny location (i.e. in Southern Europe), a photovoltaic based DER system have to deploy more than 50.000 solar panels to reach a 10 MW generation capacity (Magtel, 2017). By using the eolic power source, around 9 wind turbines are needed to generate the same 10MW (Menz & Vachon, 2006).

Renewable energy sources, such as PhotoVoltaic (PV) and eolic, due to its dependency on weather conditions, show very high variability rates in output power generation (i.e. the fluctuations in PV generators because of the shading effects caused by moving clouds).

To maintain necessary power quality and reliability in the network, several national-wide grid operators are imposing regulations limiting the variability of generated output power by DER systems (Marcos et al, 2014). I.e. the (Gevorgian & Booth, 2013) imposed a 10% per minute rate of charge of output power and, in Germany (Franz & Barth, 2013), a PV system can only inject power up to 70% of its rated capacity to the grid.

The diagram in Figure 4 shows the usual process for renewable energy based power generation (at least, for weather dependent energy sources such as photovoltaic, thermal solar, eolic or hydroelectric).

1. Based on weather forecasting, plant assets are properly configured to optimize energy generation or even, to protect them if weather conditions are potentially dangerous. i.e. solar panels have to be abated if the wind is too high or dam floodgates have to be opened when rain rates are too high.
2. The energy generated by natural processes (kinetic, thermal, etc.) is transformed into electrical power by converter devices.
3. If a converter device produces direct current (DC) electricity, it is usually converted to alternating current (AC) using inverters.
4. To smooth fluctuations in power generation, it can be stored prior to being injected to the main grid.
5. Energy is distributed to regional-wide grids though provided access points by grid operators.

Technological Challenges

Renewable energy DER nodes, in a region-wide smart grid, are usually framed by the following issues:

Figure 4. Renewable energy power generation

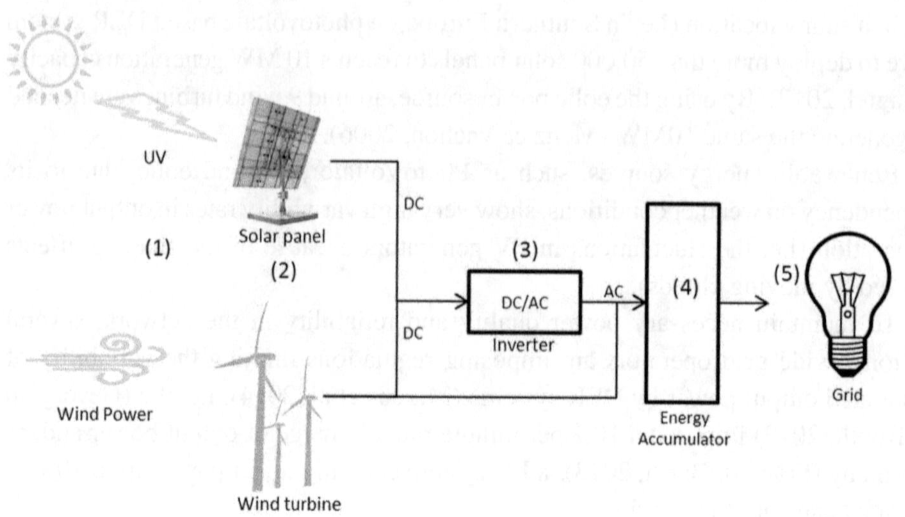

- As they have a strong dependency on weather, they have to perform real time monitoring of weather forecasting to prevent adverse conditions, failures and/ or damages in plant assets.
- Negotiations/collaborations with grid operator are common issues to DER managers.
- They have to perform real time controls on fluctuations in power generation to fit into the regulations imposed by grid operators.

As a result in (WoT Use Cases, 2017), the following technological challenges for energy generation scenarios were identified:

1. **Multi-Stakeholder Operation:** The business case for power generation and distribution involve several systems provided by different actors. DERs, grid operators, device vendors and IT service influence, or are influenced, by the whole system.
2. **Device Lifecycle Management:** Device networks inside DER facilities cannot be broken when one of them is suddenly switched-off. The sensor network has to be able to manage a dynamic ensemble of heterogeneous devices that can dynamically appear or disappear.
3. **Embedded Runtime:** Due to restrictions in connectivity, it couldn't be possible to maintain a close couple control loop over systems and devices. To overcome this scenario, a sandboxed runtime with a standardized API1 should be provided to offload the control logic to the device itself.
4. **Ensemble Discovery:** To be able to dynamically manage the lifecycle of sensors and devices, the ability to discover single components at runtime is crucial. New sensors and devices, from any vendor, should be detected and gathered into the network at runtime.
5. **Content-Negotiation:** As power generation involve multi-stakeholder operations, it is necessary to agree on a common data exchange format.
6. **Resource Description:** Sensors and devices have to be described or being described by themselves so their provided services can be understood by other systems with no (or little) engineering effort.
7. **Push Services:** Real time monitoring systems usually follow the publisher/ subscriber pattern (Bender, 2007). Many sensors can fan-out data to a single central unit even under limited connectivity conditions.
8. **Object Memory:** As sensors can be replaced, exchanged or updated, it is beneficial to track a history of changes of each one.
9. **Privacy:** Fine grained metering data provide sensitive information about energy generation and consumption. A high degree of privacy should be granted.

10. **Trust:** Since data exchanged leads to physical actions that involve currents and monetary flows, the integrity of data is crucial.
11. **Layered L7 Communication:** Due to the high variety of sensors, devices and vendors, using different The IoT protocols for data exchange, a clear and consistent separation of information from the used serialization and application protocols is required.

The IoT at Work: Devices and Sensors

The wide variety of sensors deployed in DER facilities for real time data gathering can usually be classified as a) industrial control systems or b) The IoT devices.

- **Industrial Control Systems:** Electrical industries typically use industrial control systems, and its associated instrumentation, for automatic control and data acquisition. SCADA systems, distributed control systems (DCS) and programmable logic controllers (PLC) are often installed for local operations and environment controlling, monitoring and data collecting from sensor systems.

Wind turbines, solar trackers and power inverters are usually controlled and monitored by PLCs.

- **Conventional the IoT Devices**: The IoT devices are any non-standard device that has the ability to record and transmit data through a WSN (Wireless Sensor Network), using any kind of open or proprietary M2M (Machine – to Machine) protocol, such as MQTT protocol for telemetry transport.

Examples of The IoT-enabled sensors commonly used in renewable energy power generation industries are (ambient or contact) thermometers, pyranometers, anemometers and weather stations.

WoT Based Architecture

The WoT based architecture for monitoring industrial facilities will lay (in a near future, once the W3C recommendations are published) on a network of WoT-enabled sensors and platforms.

WoT-enabled devices are expected to reach the market following W3C's WoT standards. They will host their own embedded runtime for describing by themselves, providing the Thing Description document specifying the semantic information needed for access to thing's services, protocol negotiation and security requirements.

Table 5. Examples of the most usual devices and variables registered by PLC devices.

Device	Measures
Inverter	• Input Voltage • Input Current • Output frequency • Output Voltage in Phase A, B or C • AC Active / Reactive / Apparent Power in each Phase • 1st Harmonic in each Phase • Cos(φ)in each Phase
Solar Tracker	• Heading Angle (Azimuth) • Roll Angle • Elevation Angle • Accumulated tracker movement • Engine temperature • Accumulated tracking time
Wind Turbine	• Wind speed • Survival wind speed • Angle of attack for each blade • Accumulated yaw rotation • Temperature in gear box • Temperature in brake disks • Drag value in each blade • Engine speed • Tip speed ratio • Electromagnetic torque

Table 6. Examples of the most usual variables registered by conventional The IoT devices.

Device	Measures
Weather Station	• Wind speed • Wind direction • Pressure • Temperature • Humidity
Thermometer installed on solar panels	• Ambient temperature • Contact temperature
Pyranometer	• Irradiance

Legacy The IoT devices (not compliant with the WoT recommendations), are managed by proxy WoT Servients, hosted by regular computers, which can be deployed in the same plant.

Proxy servients can be configured with libraries for each legacy-protocol mapping. I.e:

- A PLC device can be accessed using the OPC legacy-protocol binding API.
- A conventional The IoT device can be accessed using the MQTT legacy-protocol binding API.
- Any The IoT device or service can be accessed using a REST API over HTTP protocol.

Third party developers can also implement legacy communication libraries for The IoT or Industrial (de-facto) standard protocols or even for any other privative communication protocols and systems.

As Things, under the Web of Things paradigm, are only logical abstractions, other entities apart from real-world devices, such as databases, data analytics services or business entities can be deployed in any WoT-enabled industrial network. So, WoT-enabled control and monitoring systems are ensembles of heterogeneous components like sensors, devices, industrial systems, actuators, data analytics, presentation services, applications and enterprise systems.

Figure 5. Web of Things solution for photovoltaic plant monitoring

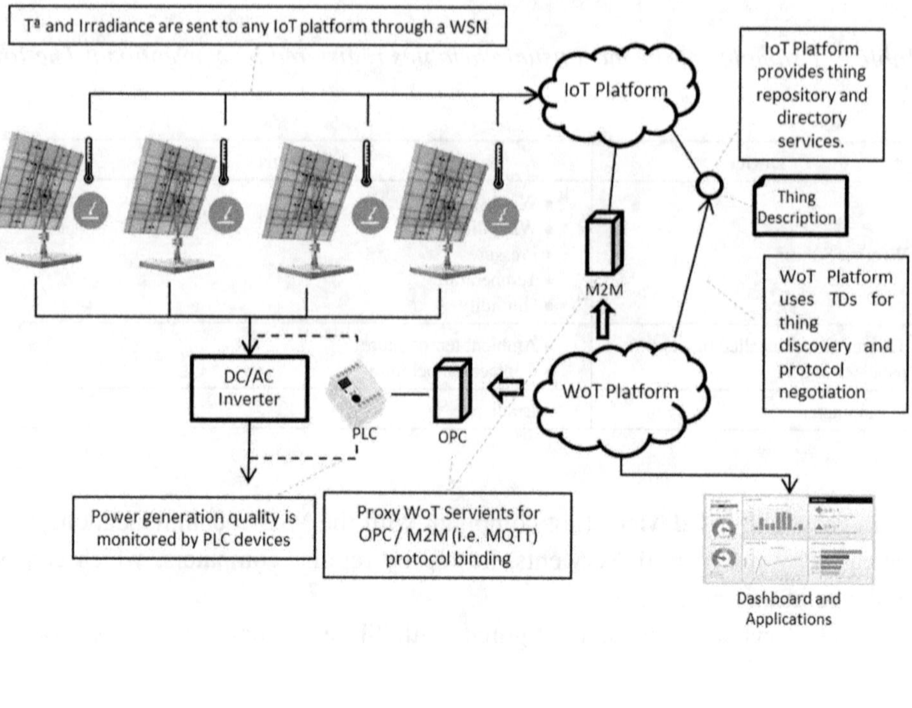

FUTURE RESEARCH DIRECTIONS

The information technologies, the telecommunications and the manufacture are facing in such a way that the production is becoming increasingly autonomous. Nevertheless, it is impossible to predict exactly how they will be the intelligent plants in the future. A possible approach: the machines are organized in an autonomous way and they communicate between them, while the orders are applied directly. At the foundations of this new model for smartly connected industries, is a stack of open standards for interoperability between enterprise and industrial systems and a wide range of sensors, devices and actuators. The W3C's Web of Things initiative, aims at going further the "web of pages" model, by designing a new framework for interoperability in The Internet of Things; and unifying both two models: the World Wide Web and The Internet of Things.

Already, the virtual production of products, the impression in 3D of tools or using interconnected robots makes the industry 4.0 a reality. Research areas for Web of Things applied to industrial scenarios are:

- **Autonomous Machine 2 Machine Communication, Coordination and Orchestration:** Machines can search and discover other machines or devices in the same local area network, access the exposed API by each other, and automatically create smart service aggregations and mashups (Guinard & Trifa, 2009), (Stribu, 2008), (Patel et al., 2016) providing value added for industrial processes.
- **The Semantic Web of Things:** To allow Things (being things systems, devices, sensors or even abstract entities) to be fully interoperable, semantic descriptors for its exposed services and APIs are needed. New rich methods for semantic denotation which allow machines to perform discovery and reasoning are being researched (Pfisterer et al. 2011).
- **Mixing Real and Virtual Worlds:** As Things, under the Web of Things paradigm, can be anything described by a Thing Descriptor, abstract entities such as social network groups or profiles can be also considered as "things". Research actions in mixing social networks (or VR worlds) with real-world sensors and devices are being carried on (Guinard & Trifa, 2010), (Gyrard et al., 2016). The Wisdom Web of Things (W2T) is the term for define

The organic amalgamation and harmonious symbiosis among humans, computers and things in the hyper world, which consists of the social world, the physical world and the information world. (Zhong et al., 2016)

- **Dynamic Software Updates:** Applications in The Internet of Things have strict requirements in processing time, availability and security; but they usually rely on software which has to be maintained and updated on a regular basis. Research on dynamic (an even smart) software updates are being done in order to allow devices to automatically update their firmware without human intervention (Neuman al., 2016), (Mukhopadhyay et al., 2017).

CONCLUSION

The industrial IT sector is playing a role increasingly important worldwide. It is considered to be an engine of the innovation, growth and social stability. Nevertheless, the competition is increasingly intense. The clients demand high quality and personalized products, with a time of minor production.

Only those that manage to obtain products customized and that reduces the time of production, with the maximum efficiency in his plants, will be capable of being competitive. The solution is in the union of the real and virtual world: the industry 4.0. The Web of Things initiative, fostered by W3C Consortium, are aimed at defining the new standards for interoperability between devices and systems of any kind, mixing virtual and real-world entities, in a unique World Wide Web.

The main Industry 4.0 characteristics that can be supported by the Web of Things standards are the following ones:

1. Adaptable products, by allowing processes and plant configurations to be easily adaptable to include personalized features in products.
2. Process digitalization, connecting and integrating the different phases and actors of the productive process.
3. Smart processes and big data analytics, allowing Artificial Intelligence Systems to be integrated into industrial systems, accessing devices and sensors and performing real time reasoning over gathered data.
4. Cyber-physical systems are all the devices that have capacities of computation, storage and communication, monitoring and control of objects in the physical world.
5. Collaborative robotics, which allows a simple, flexible way and without safety complications to easy work humans with robots.
6. Augmented reality. Across a WoT enabled device, it will be possible to see the physical real world. It means, the real world is combined with the virtual one creating an augmented real time reality

7. Artificial vision. WoT enabled devices can be able to capture, process and analyze the images of the real world and translate them into a numerical or symbolic information to be sent over a WoT network.

In summary, most of the Industry 4.0 practices are demanding a common infrastructure for data sharing between control systems, sensors and devices, but also involving other high level systems such as MES (Manufacturing Execution System), ERP (Enterprise Resource Planner), CRM (Customer Relationship Manager), even the enterprise web portal or event social networks.

The W3C's Web of Things work group is defining this common framework for interoperability of "everything", which is based on a stack of well-known open standards: the World Wide Web protocols and documents.

REFERENCES

Atzori, L., Iera, A., & Morabito, G. (2010). The Internet of Things: A survey. *Computer Networks*, *54*(15), 2787–2805. doi:10.1016/j.comnet.2010.05.010

Bender, M., Michel, S., Parkitny, S., & Weikum, G. (2007). A Comparative Study of Pub/Sub Methods in Structured P2P Networks. *Lecture Notes in Computer Science*, *4125*, 385–396. doi:10.1007/978-3-540-71661-7_37

Castellani, A. P., Bui, N., Casari, P., Rossi, M., Shelby, Z., & Zorzi, M. (2010). Architecture and protocols for the Internet of Things: A case study. In *2010 8th IEEE Int. Conf. Pervasive Comput. Commun. Work*. IEEE. doi:10.1109/PERCOMW.2010.5470520

Chen, Ch., & Helal, S. (2008, October-December). Sifting Through the Jungle of Sensor Standards. *IEEE Pervasive Computing*, *7*(4), 84–88. doi:10.1109/MPRV.2008.81

EISA. (2007). *Energy Independence and Security Act of 2007 (H.R. 6)*. EISA.

Ensor, P. (1988). The Functional Silo Syndrome. *Association for Manufacturer Excellence (AME) Target*, *16*, 1988.

Feng, X., Shen, J., & Fan, Y. (2009). REST: An alternative to RPC for Web services architecture. *2009 First International Conference on Future Information Networks*, 7-10. doi:10.1109/ICFIN.2009.5339611

Franz, O., & Barth, B. (2013). Results from PV GRID Research for Germany. *PV GRID EU Project Deliverables*. Available: http://www.pvgrid.eu/fileadmin/6.Germany_131022_PVGRID_RWE_BSW.pdf

Gevorgian, V., & Booth, S. (2013). Review of PREPA Technical Requirements for Interconnecting Wind and Solar Generation. National Renewable Energy Laboratory Technical Reports. NREL/TP-5D00-57089, pp. 12-13 (Nov 2013).

González García, C., Meana-Llorián, D., Pelayo G-Bustelo, C., & Cueva-Lovelle, J. M. (2017). A review about Smart Objects, Sensors, and Actuators. *Int. J. Interact. Multimed. Artif. Intell.*, *4*(3), 7–10. doi:10.9781/ijimai.2017.431

Granjal, J., Monteiro, E., & Silva, J. S. (2015). Security for the Internet of Things: A Survey of Existing Protocols and Open Research issues. *IEEE Commun. Surv. Tutorials. PP*, *25*. doi:10.1109/COMST.2015.2388550

Guinard, D., Fischer, M., & Trifa, V. (2010). Sharing using social networks in a composable Web of Things. *2010 8th IEEE International Conference on Pervasive Computing and Communications Workshops (PERCOM Workshops)*, 702-707. doi:10.1109/PERCOMW.2010.5470524

Guinard, D., & Trifa, V. (2009). Towards the Web of Things: Web Mashups for Embedded Devices. Workshop on Mashups, Enterprise Mashups and Lightweight Composition on the Web (MEM 2009). *Proceedings of WWW (International World Wide Web Conferences)*.

Guinard, D., Trifa, V., Mattern, F., & Wilde, E. (2011). From The Internet of Things to the Web of Things: Resource Oriented Architecture and Best Practices. In D. Uckelmann, M. Harrison, & F. Michahelles (Eds.), *Architecting The Internet of Things* (pp. 97–129). Berlin, Germany: Springer. doi:10.1007/978-3-642-19157-2_5

Gyrard, A., Patel, P., Datta, S., & Ali, M. (2016, October). Semantic web meets internet of things (The IoT) and web of things (wot). *The 15th International Conference on Semantic Web (ISWC)*.

H, Z., A, H., & M, M. (2015). Internet of Things (IoT): Definitions, Challenges and Recent Research Directions. *International Journal of Computers and Applications*, *128*(1), 37–47. doi:10.5120/ijca2015906430

Lanthaler, M., & Gütl, Ch. (2012). On Using JSON-LD to Create Evolvable RESTful Services. *Proceedings of the 3th International Workshop on RESTful Design (WS-REST) at the of the 21st International World Wide Web Conference (2012)*, 25-32. doi:10.1145/2307819.2307827

Magtel, S. A. (2017). *Photovoltaic Solar with Tracker*. Retrieved from http://www.magtel.es/en/projects/photovoltaic-solar-with-tracker/

Marcos, J., Storkël, O., Marroyo, L., García, M., & Lorenzo, R. (2014). Storage requirements for PV power ramp-rate control. *Solar Energy*, *99*, 28–35. doi:10.1016/j.solener.2013.10.037

Menz, F., & Vachon, S. (2006, September). The Effectiveness of Different Policy Regimes for Promoting Wind Power: Experiences from the States. *Energy Policy*, *34*(14), 1786–1796. doi:10.1016/j.enpol.2004.12.018

Mukhopadhyay, D., Saha, S., Rao, R., & Paranjpe, A. (2017). A Web-of-Things-Based System to Remotely Configure Automated Systems Using a Conditional Programming Approach. In *Proceedings of the 5th International Conference on Frontiers in Intelligent Computing: Theory and Applications* (pp. 303-311). Springer. doi:10.1007/978-981-10-3153-3_30

Neumann, M., Bach, Ch., Miclaus, A., Riedel, T., & Beigl, M. (2016). Always-On Web of Things Infrastructure using Dynamic Software Updating. In *Proceedings of the Seventh International Workshop on the Web of Things*. ACM. doi:10.1145/3017995.3017997

Nguyen, K. T., Laurent, M., & Oualha, N. (2015). Survey on secure communication protocols for the Internet of Things. *Ad Hoc Networks*, *32*, 17–31. doi:10.1016/j.adhoc.2015.01.006

Patel, P., Gyrard, A., Thakker, D., Sheth, A., & Serrano, M. (2016). SWoTSuite: A Toolkit for Prototyping Cross-domain Semantic Web of Things Applications. *Proceedings of the 15th International Semantic Web Conference (ISWC).*

Pfisterer, D., Romer, K., Bimschas, D., Kleine, O., Mietz, R., Truong, C., ... Richardson, R. (2011, November). SPITFIRE: Toward a semantic web of things. *IEEE Communications Magazine*, *49*(11), 40–48. doi:10.1109/MCOM.2011.6069708

Sánchez-Arias, G., González García, C., & Pelayo G-Bustelo, B. C. (2017). B.C. Pelayo G-Bustelo, Midgar: Study of communications security among Smart Objects using a platform of heterogeneous devices for the Internet of Things. *Future Generation Computer Systems*, *74*, 444–466. doi:10.1016/j.future.2017.01.033

Stirbu, V. (2008). Towards a RESTful Plug and Play Experience in the Web of Things. *2008 IEEE International Conference on Semantic Computing*, 512-517. doi:10.1109/ICSC.2008.51

Web of Things (WoT). (2017). *Use Cases and Requirements for the Web of Things.* W3C Editor's Draft May 2017. Retrieved from https://w3c.github.io/wot/wot-ucr.html

Web of Things (WoT) Scripting API. (2017). W3C Editor's Draft 16 May 2017. Retrieved from https://w3c.github.io/wot-scripting-api

Zhong, N., Ma, J., Huang, R., Lui, J., Yao, Y., Zhang, Y., & Chen, J. (2016). *Research Challenges and Perspectives on Wisdom Web of Things (W2T). In Web Information Systems Engineering and Internet Technologies Book Series* (pp. 3–26). Springer.

Zhong, N., Yau, S. S., Ma, J., Shimojo, S., Just, M., Hu, B., & Anzai, Y. (2016). Brain Big Data in Wisdom Web of Things. In *Wisdom Web of Things* (pp. 339–349). Springer International Publishing. doi:10.1007/978-3-319-44198-6_15

KEY TERMS AND DEFINITIONS

Industry 4.0: Industry 4.0, also known as "the 4th industrial revolution," is a paradigm shift in industrial organization and management to a new model based on smart connected systems, additive manufacturing, and real-time analytics of large data volumes.

Internet of Things: The internet of things (The IoT) is the global network of physical objects that contain embedded technology to communicate and sense or interact with their internal states using internet protocols.

MQTT: Message queue telemetry protocol is an ISO standard (ISO/IEC PRF 20922) for lightweight publisher/subscriber communications on top of TCP/IP protocol stack. MQTT is currently one of the de-facto standards in the internet of things.

OPC: Open platform communications is a series of standards and specifications for industrial telecommunications. OPC specifies the communication of real-time data between control devices and between them and the control data panels (SCADA).

PLC: A programmable logic controller is a digital computer adapted for high reliability and real-time control of industrial processes.

REST: Representational state transfer is a simple stateless architecture and a protocol set for web services.

Semantic Interoperability: Is the ability of computer systems to exchange information (data and control) with unambiguous shared meaning.

W3C: World Wide Web Consortium is the organization where member organizations, full-time staff, and public sector work together to develop the internet standards.

Web of Things: The web of things is the upcoming set of W3C's recommendations for interoperability in the field of the internet of things.

Web Servient: A web servient is a soft-defined virtualization middleware for physical (or abstract) things. Web servients are the main building blocks in the web of things and they can act simultaneously as a data server and consumer.

ENDNOTE

1 Application Programming Interface

APPENDIX

Complete Thing Description for a connected Weather Station device.


```
{
"name": "Weather Station 3",
-
"interactions": [
-
{
"name": "cell-temperature-with-wind-correction",
-
"links": [
-
{
"href": "/properties/weather-station_3/cell-temperature-with-
wind-correction",
"mediaType": "application/json"
},
-
{
"href": "tcp://wot-cluster-10:1883/weather-station_3/cell-
temperature-with-wind-correction",
"mediaType": "application/json"
}
],
"@type": "Property",
"unit": "qudt:DegreeCentigrade",
"@id": "59c1d0c1-ea2a-329b-aad9-4805679c8e43",
"uuid": "59c1d0c1-ea2a-329b-aad9-4805679c8e43",
"stability": "25000"
},
-
{
"name": "module-temperature",
-
"links": [
-
{
"href": "/properties/weather-station_3/module-temperature",
```

```
"mediaType": "application/json"
},
-
{
"href": "tcp://wot-cluster-10:1883/weather-station_3/module-
temperature",
"mediaType": "application/json"
}
],
"@type": "Property",
"unit": "qudt:DegreeCentigrade",
"@id": "55ff3622-31d9-36f8-a0e4-8d71f076ba85",
"uuid": "55ff3622-31d9-36f8-a0e4-8d71f076ba85",
"stability": "25000"
},
-
{
"name": "model",
-
"links": [
-
{
"href": "/properties/weather-station_3/model",
"mediaType": "application/json"
},
-
{
"href": "tcp://wot-cluster-10:1883/weather-station_3/model",
"mediaType": "application/json"
}
],
"@type": "Property",
"@id": "e0f1eeab-010d-3e44-8500-dcc6ac1d2978",
"uuid": "e0f1eeab-010d-3e44-8500-dcc6ac1d2978"
},
-
{
"name": "rain-rate",
-
"links": [
```

```
-
{
"href": "/properties/weather-station_3/rain-rate",
"mediaType": "application/json"
},
-
{
"href": "tcp://wot-cluster-10:1883/weather-station_3/rain-
rate",
"mediaType": "application/json"
}
],
"@type": "Property",
"unit": "om:litrePerHour",
"@id": "ba2c35d1-2fe2-35fd-8ca3-44e1d4bb8b6b",
"uuid": "ba2c35d1-2fe2-35fd-8ca3-44e1d4bb8b6b",
"stability": "25000"
},
-
{
"name": "irradiance-sensor-1",
-
"links": [
-
{
"href": "/properties/weather-station_3/irradiance-sensor-1",
"mediaType": "application/json"
},
-
{
"href": "tcp://wot-cluster-10:1883/weather-station_3/
irradiance-sensor-1",
"mediaType": "application/json"
}
],
"@type": "Property",
"unit": "qudt:WattPerSquareMeter",
"@id": "6d9997a8-f61a-349e-9653-288b549b613f",
"uuid": "6d9997a8-f61a-349e-9653-288b549b613f",
"stability": "25000"
```

```
},
-
{
"name": "relative-humidity",
-
"links": [
-
{
"href": "/properties/weather-station_3/relative-humidity",
"mediaType": "application/json"
},
-
{
"href": "tcp://wot-cluster-10:1883/weather-station_3/relative-
humidity",
"mediaType": "application/json"
}
],
"@type": "Property",
"unit": "qudt:Percent",
"@id": "7e191b57-1cce-3b1d-893b-6d3a73b38cb1",
"uuid": "7e191b57-1cce-3b1d-893b-6d3a73b38cb1",
"stability": "25000"
},
-
{
"name": "description",
-
"links": [
-
{
"href": "/properties/weather-station_3/description",
"mediaType": "application/json"
},
-
{
"href": "tcp://wot-cluster-10:1883/weather-station_3/
description",
"mediaType": "application/json"
}
```

```
],
"@type": "Property",
"@id": "eabb9cb3-8d2b-3ef6-8b8d-fa98307a5761",
"uuid": "eabb9cb3-8d2b-3ef6-8b8d-fa98307a5761",
"stability": "-1"
},
-
{
"name": "pressure",
-
"links": [
-
{
"href": "/properties/weather-station_3/pressure",
"mediaType": "application/json"
},
-
{
"href": "tcp://wot-cluster-10:1883/weather-station_3/pressure",
"mediaType": "application/json"
}
],
"@type": "Property",
"unit": "qudt:Millibar",
"@id": "60730509-4ee6-3c4a-8258-51dfc9ead49f",
"uuid": "60730509-4ee6-3c4a-8258-51dfc9ead49f",
"stability": "25000"
},
-
{
"name": "devicetype",
-
"links": [
-
{
"href": "/properties/weather-station_3/devicetype",
"mediaType": "application/json"
},
-
{
```

```
"href": "tcp://wot-cluster-10:1883/weather-station_3/
devicetype",
"mediaType": "application/json"
}
],
"@type": "Property",
"@id": "c7a03a50-11a2-3fe5-b889-57601fedf1fb",
"uuid": "c7a03a50-11a2-3fe5-b889-57601fedf1fb",
"stability": "-1"
},
-
{
"name": "manufacturer",
-
"links": [
-
{
"href": "/properties/weather-station_3/manufacturer",
"mediaType": "application/json"
},
-
{
"href": "tcp://wot-cluster-10:1883/weather-station_3/
manufacturer",
"mediaType": "application/json"
}
],
"@type": "Property",
"@id": "dbd370ed-188f-3ee0-b3eb-a100b08bb589",
"uuid": "dbd370ed-188f-3ee0-b3eb-a100b08bb589",
"stability": "-1"
},
-
{
"name": "wind-direction",
-
"links": [
-
{
"href": "/properties/weather-station_3/wind-direction",
```

```
"mediaType": "application/json"
},
-
{
"href": "tcp://wot-cluster-10:1883/weather-station_3/wind-
direction",
"mediaType": "application/json"
}
],
"@type": "Property",
"unit": "qudt:DegreeAngle",
"@id": "09d0aae4-ca87-36ad-b8fb-1dfd94872fa1",
"uuid": "09d0aae4-ca87-36ad-b8fb-1dfd94872fa1",
"stability": "25000"
},
-
{
"name": "cell-temperature",
-
"links": [
-
{
"href": "/properties/weather-station_3/cell-temperature",
"mediaType": "application/json"
},
-
{
"href": "tcp://wot-cluster-10:1883/weather-station_3/cell-
temperature",
"mediaType": "application/json"
}
],
"@type": "Property",
"unit": "qudt:DegreeCentigrade",
"@id": "1c436416-d531-3c54-a2c2-5ad162d4044b",
"uuid": "1c436416-d531-3c54-a2c2-5ad162d4044b",
"stability": "25000"
},
-
{
```

```
"name": "irradiance-sensor-2",
-
"links": [
-
{
"href": "/properties/weather-station_3/irradiance-sensor-2",
"mediaType": "application/json"
},
-
{
"href": "tcp://wot-cluster-10:1883/weather-station_3/
irradiance-sensor-2",
"mediaType": "application/json"
}
],
"@type": "Property",
"unit": "qudt:WattPerSquareMeter",
"@id": "372b56d7-7892-3c02-8985-1870cd0916eb",
"uuid": "372b56d7-7892-3c02-8985-1870cd0916eb",
"stability": "25000"
},
-
{
"name": "temperature",
-
"links": [
-
{
"href": "/properties/weather-station_3/temperature",
"mediaType": "application/json"
},
-
{
"href": "tcp://wot-cluster-10:1883/weather-station_3/
temperature",
"mediaType": "application/json"
}
],
"@type": "Property",
"unit": "qudt:DegreeCentigrade",
```

```
"@id": "1fe2bf09-3037-3304-91ed-1e6d31e36002",
"uuid": "1fe2bf09-3037-3304-91ed-1e6d31e36002",
"stability": "25000"
},
-
{
"name": "wind-speed",
-
"links": [
-
{
"href": "/properties/weather-station_3/wind-speed",
"mediaType": "application/json"
},
-
{
"href": "tcp://wot-cluster-10:1883/weather-station_3/wind-
speed",
"mediaType": "application/json"
}
],
"@type": "Property",
"unit": "qudt:MeterPerSecond",
"@id": "0736067d-ff71-3be9-90cc-ef95f92c2fff",
"uuid": "0736067d-ff71-3be9-90cc-ef95f92c2fff",
"stability": "25000"
},
-
{
"name": "model",
-
"links": [
-
{
"href": "/properties/weather-station_3/model",
"mediaType": "application/json"
},
-
{
"href": "tcp://wot-cluster-10:1883/weather-station_3/model",
```

```
"mediaType": "application/json"
}
],
"@type": "Property",
"@id": "473d5682-dfaa-34e9-94c8-69838a17b77e",
"uuid": "473d5682-dfaa-34e9-94c8-69838a17b77e",
"stability": "-1"
},
-
{
"name": "state",
-
"links": [
-
{
"href": "/properties/weather-station_3/state",
"mediaType": "application/json"
},
-
{
"href": "tcp://wot-cluster-10:1883/weather-station_3/state",
"mediaType": "application/json"
}
],
"@type": "Property",
"@id": "32687c37-13cd-324d-965d-93bf3e8f8c4b",
"uuid": "32687c37-13cd-324d-965d-93bf3e8f8c4b",
"stability": "75000"
},
-
{
"name": "quality-link",
-
"links": [
-
{
"href": "/properties/weather-station_3/quality-link",
"mediaType": "application/json"
},
-
```

```
{
"href": "tcp://wot-cluster-10:1883/weather-station_3/quality-link",
"mediaType": "application/json"
}
],
"@type": "Property",
"@id": "e5bda583-240d-388d-b949-6694ac6c8f0e",
"uuid": "e5bda583-240d-388d-b949-6694ac6c8f0e",
"stability": "75000"
}
],
"base": "http://servient:10050/wot",
"uuid": "f5354c82-597f-3e49-921c-d7f2c77702c8",
-
"@context": [
"http://w3c.github.io/wot/w3c-wot-td-context.jsonld",
"http://w3c.github.io/wot/w3c-wot-common-context.jsonld",
-
{
"qudt": "http://qudt.org/1.1/vocab/unit#",
"om": "http://www.ontology-of-units-of-measure.org/resource/om-2/"
}
],
"@type": "Thing",
"@id": "f5354c82-597f-3e49-921c-d7f2c77702c8"
}
```

Chapter 6
Communication Protocols for the Internet of Things

S. Umamaheswari
Dr. G. R. Damodaran College of Science, India

ABSTRACT

The future internet is expected to be an internet of things (IoT) that makes a huge increase in its capability to collect, investigate, and distribute data that can be turned into information or knowledge. The changeover to IPv6, having a common set of standards and developing energy sources for millions of minute sensors, are the challenges of IoT. The environment can be made smart and self-aware by the direct communication between more and more devices that are part of the IoT. The low power lossy networks (LLNs) that consist of more tiny sensors and low power devices are the elements of the IoT. The TCP/IP reference model is used for the internet connectivity, which is not exactly suited for the network that uses smart objects. There is a need to connect the local network that has the smart objects to the internet. The Internet Engineering Task Force (IETF) has come out with the standardized protocols like 6LoWPAN, RPL, COAP, etc. This chapter provides the various protocols used in the internet of things network with their specifications, benefits, and limitations.

PREFACE

This chapter gives an overview of the Communication Protocols in the Internet Protocol Stack. The devices in the LLNs are resource constrained. The Internet Engineering Task Force designed the protocols like 6LoWPAN, RPL, CoAP, etc. to make the communication more effective. As the devices in the LLNs are small

DOI: 10.4018/978-1-5225-3805-9.ch006

sensor devices and the packets are less in size, the communication is not possible with IPv4. This is overcome by the adaptation layer protocol "6LoWPAN" which communicates through IPv6. Thus, the protocols in the Internet Protocol Stack are not suitable for the LLNs.

This chapter focuses on understanding the architecture and protocol stack of IoT and investigating the behavior of RPL. The performance of RPL is carried out for a Smart Health environment scenario by the simulations done in the Contiki OS Cooja simulator.

OVERVIEW

In this chapter, the IETF RFCs, which are meant for each protocol in the Internet of Things Protocol Stack, is studied. The simulation platform is setup with the Contiki Operating System and the Cooja Simulator.

Contiki is an open source operating system that runs on the tiny low power micro controllers and makes it possible to develop applications that makes efficient use of the hardware while providing standardized low power wireless communication for a range of hardware platform.

Cooja Simulator is a Java-based network simulator specifically designed for Wireless Sensor Networks running on the Contiki Sensor network operating system. The simulator is implemented in Java and the sensor node software can be written in C. Cooja allows the Contiki programs either compiled natively on the host CPU for compiling for any emulator like MSP430.

INTRODUCTION

The computer networks are an interconnection of the computer systems to share the information that has evolved tremendously. The computer networks, which were emerging in the late 1960's, has become the information pool that is available nowadays in the form of Internet from the early 1990s.

The Internet is a network of networks. A software layer, which sits on the top of the operating system, is responsible for implementing the distributed system model. The World Wide Web (WWW) is the distributed system that runs on the top of the internet and offers webpages to the users. The main goal of the network is to share the resources. The resources can be program, physical devices, or data. The communication between the systems on the network can be done by a set of protocols (or rules). Most of the network support layered protocol approach in which each layer provides services to the above layer and protects from the details of the protocols used in the lower layers.

The protocol stacks are based either on the OSI model or the TCP/IP model. Both the models have a set of layers and each layer has its own set of protocols. The Internet Engineering Task Force (IETF) is a standard organization that develops the protocol standards that comprises the Internet Protocol Suite. The IETF is divided into working groups and each work group is meant for a specific application. The Request for Comments (RFCs) are the technical reports that are submitted to the IETF. The RFCs are available online and can be accessed from the websitewww.ietf.org/rfc. The ITU (International Telecommunication Union) is an organization that standardizes the international telecommunications. The communication protocol is very significant irrespective of the physical medium used by the network.

The below sections provide information about the communication protocols used in the Internet of Things network and the protocols at each layer level are discussed.

- Section 1 describes the Internet Protocol Suite and the different layers present in the IoT Protocol Suite.
- Section 2 describes the Physical and Link Layer protocols.
- Section 3 describes the Adaptation Layer and its benefits.
- Section 4 describes the Network layer protocols and its benefits.
- Section 5 briefs the Transport layer.
- Section 6 explains about the Application layer protocols and its simulations.

INTERNET PROTOCOL SUITE (IPS)

The ARPANET was one of the Wide Area Network (WAN) sponsored by the U.S. Department of Defense (DoD) which paves the way to the worldwide internet. It connects hundreds of organizations using leased telephone lines which were then replaced with radio and satellite networks later.

The older protocols had trouble in interconnecting the systems. The IETF has developed two internet protocols, namely, Transmission Control Protocol (TCP) and Internet Protocol (IP) mainly to improve the ability to connect with multiple networks in a seamless way. This model is now popularly known as the TCP/IP Reference Model which is depicted as shown in Table 1.

This model consists of four layers in which the functions of the network communication separate into layers and each layer has their own set of functions. As each layer of the model is arranged on top of each other, this model can also be referred to as Internet Protocol Stack or IPS in short.

Table 1. The TCP/IP Reference Model

Application Layer
Transport Layer
Network Layer
Host to Network Layer

Host to Network Layer

The host-to-network layer is the combination of the Data Link Control and the Physical layers. This layer is responsible for transmitting bits across different kinds of transmission medium as electrical or analog signals and decides how to send finite-length messages between directly connected systems with specified levels of reliability.

Network Layer

The network layer decides the linkage between multiple networks and a network of networks so as to send packets between the remote systems. This layer defines and establishes the internet by describing addressing and routing structures which used in the Internet Protocol Stack. The primary aim of this layer is to transmit datagrams to a next IP router that connects the network closer to the final data destination.

Transport Layer

The Transport Layer forms the network between two network hosts either locally or remotely separated by routers. This layer is responsible for providing a uniform networking interface that hides the underlying connectivity. The protocols of this layer mainly deal with the flow-control and error-correction mechanisms.

Application Layer

The user's application programs such as email and file transfer are available in this layer which is supported by the protocols like SMTP, FTP, SSH, and HTTP.

Limitations of Internet Protocol Stack

1. Even though the TCP/IP model interconnects the networks on the internet with the support of protocols, it has some problems.

2. The services, interfaces, and protocols are not distinguished by this model.
3. The TCP/IP model is not a generic model. For e.g., this model cannot be used in the Bluetooth network.
4. The link layer is not exact layer, but it is just an interface between network and data link layers.
5. There is no differentiation between the Physical and Data link layer.

The Internet of Things (IoT)

The Internet is emerging with a whole lot of smart connected devices today. There is an exponential growth in the number of smart devices connected to the mobile internet. The devices are embedded with high intelligence due to the development of technology. These intelligent (smart) devices are capable of interacting with humans and other smart devices, as well, which led to the development of the "Internet of Things" (IoT). Kevin Ashton has coined the term "Internet of Things" in the context of supply chain management in the year 1999 that describes a technology of the future based on the Internet and involves sharing of information (K. Ashton, 2009).

The IoT can be viewed as a global infrastructure for the information society, enabling advanced services by interconnecting (physical and virtual) things based on existing and evolving interoperable information and communication technologies like ICT and ITU-T 2122. In the year 2050, it is estimated that at least 50 billion smart devices will be connected to the internet. Internet of Things is the Future of the internet and as there are a number of devices connected now, the Internet alone cannot be used for communication.

The IoT enables the communication between various devices. The protocols and standards used in the IoT will be different from the standards used in the present Internet methodology. Low power wireless devices are the main part of the IoT. The IoT protocol stack is different from the TCP/IP stack. The IETF has come out with new protocols for the IoT (Antonio J. et.al. 2013). The end-users of the Internet are the people and the embedded devices.

The People use the internet through the World Wide Web through the interconnected autonomous devices called as the Internet of Things (IoT), which shares the information amongst each other over the Internet. There are no machine equivalent web browsers for these devices and the Development of new tools/services are in progress by the standardization bodies.

Internet of Things Protocol Stack

The Internet of Things (IoT) refers to the interconnection of the IP smart objects, such as sensors and actuators. These devices are used in different fields of the industry, i.e., smart home, smart grid, and in industrial automation to sense the physical parameters like temperature, pressure, and pollution levels. Wireless Sensor Networks (WSN) has become an important block of the IoT. A WSN is also referred as Low power and Lossy Network (LLN).

The LLN nodes are resource constrained in terms of power, memory, and energy. Its main characteristics are,

1. High loss rates.
2. Low data rates.
3. Instability.
4. Consists of up to more than a few thousand nodes.

The IoT deals with a large amount of information, queries, data analysis, and data mining processes with the help of software architectures that maintains the communication standards such as HyperText Transfer Protocol (HTTP) and Internet Protocol (IP). As the IoT objects are battery powered, very low-power consumption is required when they are plugged into the Internet. More energy is wasted by the transmission of unnecessary data and protocol overhead. HTTP and Transmission Control Protocol (TCP) are not suited for very low-power communication due to the high reliability through acknowledgment of packets at higher layers.

The IoT has a wide range of devices such as RFID, Wireless Sensor Networks (WSNs), and has the ability to interconnect objects, things, and machines, etc. The environment can be made smart and self-aware by the direct communication between more devices that are part of the IoT network. The LLNs that consists of tinier sensors and low-power devices are the major elements of the IoT.

The primary requirements related to this ability are listed below:

- **Energy Efficient Protocol Stack:** The devices of the LLN networks are battery powered and are often deployed in the areas where human intervention is not there which makes the frequent battery replacement impossible. So, the protocol stack must utilize low energy.
- **Internet Enabled Protocol Stack:** The machines in the internet network use IP as a universal protocol. Since the LLNs can be connected to the internet to make the IoT a reality, the LLN devices should also have a universal language for their communication.
- **Highly Reliable Protocol Stack:** The LLN networks are lossy in nature in the wireless environments with frequent link failures. The reliability must be guaranteed at different layers of the protocol stack.

Table 2 describes the protocol stack for communications in the LLN network. The bodies like IEEE, IEFT, and W3C are working towards the standardized protocols for the IoT.

PHYSICAL AND LINK LAYER

The most commonly used protocols in the Internet of Things Protocol stack is explained in this section. The protocols for Physical layer and Link (MAC) layer are combined with most of the standards.

Low Power Radio Hardware

The Low-Power Radio Hardware is one of the communication standards for the Physical layer of the Internet of Things (IoT) protocol stack. This hardware translates the digital information into an electromagnetic signal for an effective transmission. The radio uses a modulation scheme for encoding the bytes of data into an analog signal during the transmission. The transmission range of the radios is between -50 dBm and +5 dBm. The transmit current is shown in dBm because 0dBm (i.e., 1 mW) which is the default transmit power for most radios. The Power Amplifier (PA) amplifies this signal before being sent over to the antenna. The energy consumption will not be there when the radio is tipped off. The Radio duty cycle is the time when the radio is on for either transmitting or receiving data. This feature is a good sign of power consumption of the sensor. The communication stack is said to be energy efficient only when the duty cycle is lower than 1%.

Table 2. Internet of Things Protocol Stack

Layer	Protocol
Application Layer	CoAP, MQTT, XMPP, AMQP, REST, Web Sockets
Transport Layer	UDP, DTLS
Network Layer	IPv6/IPv4 Routing, RPL
Adaptation Layer	6LoWPAN
Link Layer	IEEE 802.15.2e Low Power IEEE 802.11
Physical Layer	IEEE 802.15.4 – 2006 (ISM Bands)

IEEE 802.15.4

The underlying Physical Layer and the Media Access Layer (MAC) for the Internet of Things network is the IEEE 802.15.4 standard. The IEEE 802.15.4-2006 standard which has been released after the IEEE 802.15.4-2003 is the physical layer protocol for low-power and low-data rate Low power Lossy Networks (LLNs). The IEEE 802.15.4 concentrates on the transmission of data between the resource constrained devices. The specifications of IEEE 802.15.4 such as low data rate, low cost, and high throughput are suitable for the IoT, machine-to-machine (M2M) and Wireless Sensor Networks (WSNs).

The High levels of security, encryption, and authentication services are the other important features. This is the basis for the ZigBee protocol as both the protocols offer low data rate services on power constrained devices. The IEEE 802.15.4 is providing support for three frequency channel bands and exploits a direct sequence spreadspectrum (DSSS) method.

- **Note:** The data rates of the three frequency channels are 250 KBPS at 2.4 GHz, 40KBPS at 915 MHz and 20 KPBS at 868 MHz.

High-throughput and low latencies are the advantages of higher frequency and wider bands whereas the lower frequencies offer better sensitivity and cover larger distances. The IEEE 802.15.4 utilizes the CSMA/CA protocol to reduce potential collisions (IEEE 802.15.4, 2011).

IEEE 802.15.4e

The IEEE 802.15.4e is an extension of the IEEE 802.15.4 protocol to support low power communication. The main features of this standard are time synchronization and channel hopping to enable high reliability, low-cost, and to meet the IoT communications requirements. The specific MAC features are slot frame structure, scheduling, synchronization, channel hopping, and network formation.

The IEEE 802.15.4e slot frame structure schedules and notifies each node what to do. A node in the network may be either in sleep mode or in send/receive mode. In the sleep mode, the node turns off the radio to save power and stores all information it needs to send during the next transmission. Scheduling handles the mobility scenarios with the help of the manager node by informing the schedule to other nodes to follow. The node's connection with their neighbors and the gateways is maintained well by synchronization. This is done in acknowledgment-based mode and frame-based mode. The IEEE802.15.4e launches channel hopping for time slotted access to the wireless medium. Channel hopping needs changing the frequency channel using a predetermined random sequence. This leads to frequency diversity and reduction of the effect of interference and multi-path fading. The network capacity is added to sixteen channels as two frames and the same link can be transmitted on more than one frequency channel at the same time. The components of the networks are advertised and joined during the network formation process. A new device that needs to join the network will wait for the advertisement command and on receiving the command it can send a join request to the advertising device (M. Park, 2015).

WirelessHART

WirelessHART is a wireless data link protocol based on the Highway Addressable Remote Transducer Protocol (HART) that works on top of the IEEE 802.15.4 PHY and implements Time Division Multiple Access (TDMA) in its MAC. This protocol provides connectivity for a variety of process measurement, asset management, and control applications. As this protocol uses advanced encryption standard to encrypt the messages and calculates the integrity, this is said to be a secure and reliable MAC protocol. This offers end-to-end, peer-to-peer, and per-hop security mechanisms. End-to-end security mechanism implements security of the source devices to destination devices while per-hop mechanism secures only its next hop (A. Kim et al., 2008 and S. Raza, T. Voigt, 2010).

Z-Wave

Z-Wave is a low-power RF communication technology that is mainly designed to create a smart home environment. This protocol is reliable and provides low-latency communication of small data packets up to 100 Kbits/s data rate. As the signal coverage is within 30m, this protocol is very well suited for the small messages in the IoT applications like wearable healthcare, controlling of light, and energy etc. CSMA/CA is used for collision detection and ACK messages are used for reliable transmission. (Z-Wave, 2007).

- **Standard:** Z-Wave Alliance ZAD12837 / ITU-T G.9959
- **Frequency:** 900MHz (ISM)
- **Range:** 30m
- **Data Rates:** 9.6/40/100kbit/s

Bluetooth Low-Energy

Bluetooth Low-Energy (BLE) which is also referred as Bluetooth Smart is a short-range communication protocol, which has become very vital in many consumer products and computing. The signals in BLE can reach ten times less than the classic Bluetooth. The new BLE or Bluetooth Smart is an important protocol for the IoT applications nowadays. The main advantage of Smart/BLE is that the file transfer between personal devices is done with reduced power consumption. Bluetooth Special Interest Group (SIG) predicts that by 2018 more than 90 percent of the Bluetooth-enabled smart phones, including Android, iOS and Window based models are expected to be "Smart Ready". The Bluetooth Version 4.2, the latest version allows Bluetooth Smart sensors to access the Internet through 6LoWPAN connectivity via its Internet Protocol Support profile. This feature enables the use of existing IP infrastructure to handle Bluetooth Smart 'edge' devices (C. Gomez et al., 2012).

- **Standard:** Bluetooth 4.2 core specification
- **Frequency:** 2.4GHz (ISM)
- **Range:** 50-150m (Smart/BLE)
- **Data Rates:** 1Mbps (Smart/BLE)

Zigbee Smart Energy

The Zigbee Smart Energy is devised for a wide range of IoT applications that need relatively uncommon data exchanges at low data-rates over a defined area and within a 100m range such as in a home or building. It supports most of the network topologies like star, peer-to-peer, or cluster-tree. Zigbee PRO and Zigbee Remote Control (RF4CE) are the standards based on the IEEE 802.15.4 protocol. Zigbee/RF4CE is very well suited for complex systems that offer low-power operation, high security and high scalability (ZigBee, 2004).

- **Standard:** ZigBee 3.0 based on IEEE802.15.4
- **Frequency:** 2.4GHz
- **Range:** 10-100m
- **Data Rates:** 250kbps

DASH7

DASH7 is a wireless data transfer protocol devised for active RFID that works in the globally available Industrial Scientific Medical (ISM) band and is suitable for the IoT applications. This protocol works well for scalable, long range and outdoor coverage with high data rate. It is a less-cost solution that supports encryption and IPv6 addressing. The MAC features of DASH7 are filtering, addressing the devices with a unique ID, dynamic network ID, and a well framed Frame format (O. Cetinkaya and O. Akan (2015).

HomePlug

The HomePlug Powerline Alliance has developed a MAC protocol namely HomePlug GreenPHY (HomePlugGP) that is used in home automation applications. This protocol covers both PHY and MAC layers. HomePlug-AV is a basic power line communication protocol. HomePlugGP is devised for the IoT applications, especially for home automation and smart grid applications. It reduces the cost and power consumption (HomePlug Alliance, 2012).

LTE-A

Long-Term Evolution Advanced (LTE-A) is a set of standards devised to fit Machine-to-Machine (M2M) communication and the IoT applications in cellular networks. LTE-A is a lower-cost compared to the cellular protocols. OFDMA (Orthogonal Frequency Division Multiple Access) is used as a MAC layer access technology, which divides the frequency into multiple bands and each one can be used separately. Core Network (CN), Radio Access Network (RAN), and mobile nodes are the components of the LTE-A architecture (M. Hasan, E. Hossain, D. Niyato, 2013).

LoRaWAN

LoRa Alliance, an open-nonprofit association is working on the standardization of LoRa Wide Area Network protocol (LoRaWAN) for Low Power Wide Area Networks. LoRaWAN aims the basic needs of IoT like mobility, localization of services and a secure bidirectional communication. The LoRaWAN network server manages the performance of each end-device individually by means of Adaptive Data Rate (ADR) scheme which increases the battery life of the remote end devices up to 10 years. The overall network capacity is also increased. This protocol supports redundant operation, location free, low-cost, low power, and energy harvesting technologies to support the future needs of IoT while enabling mobility and ease of use features (LoRa Alliance, 2015).

ADAPTATION LAYER

6LoWPAN

The flow of IPv6 packets over 802.15.4 networks that support small packets is taken care by IPv6 over Low Power Wireless Personal Area Networks (6LoWPAN). 6LoWPAN acts as an adaptation layer to transport IPv6 packets over 802.15.4 links. The 6LoWPAN standard is defined by RFC 6282 that bridges the gap between the Internet and Low Power Lossy networks (LLNs) by providing IPv6 networking capabilities through special encapsulation and header compression techniques that allow IPv6 packets to be sent over low-power link layer technologies. IPv6 is the most supported IP in 6LoWPAN because of its large addressing space and the built-in support for network auto configuration. 6LoWPAN networks need a gateway which can be either an Ethernet or Wi-Fi to access the Internet. The nodes of the Internet mostly use IPv4. A 6LoWPAN gateway has an IPv6-to-IPv4 conversion protocol. The 6LoWPAN standard is an adaptation layer between the 802.15.4 link layer and a TCP/IP stack. The main advantages include support to large network size, mesh network topology, reliable communication and less energy consumption. 6LoWPAN is well suited for the applications that have internet-connected sensors, less throughput, and battery-powered. A 6LoWPAN device is capable of communicating with any other IP-based server or device on the Internet, including Wi-Fi and Ethernet devices (Z. Shelby and C. Bormann, 2010).

A single 802.15.4 frame is not capable of holding an IPv6 packet. 6LoWPAN fits an IPv6 packet in 802.15.4 frame by using,

- IPv6 Header Compression
- IPv6 Packet Fragmentation & Reassembly
- IPv6 Packet Encapsulation
- Link layer Packet Forwarding

IPv6 Header of size 40 bytes is compressed into either 2 bytes or 12 bytes or 20 bytes based on the packet transfer scenario. The following table depicts the IPv6 Header and the Compressed Headers for three different packet transfer scenarios.

IPv6 Header

Shown in Table 3.

Table 3.

Ver	Traffic Class	Flow Label	Payload Length	Next Header	Hop Limit	Source address 64-bit prefix, 64 bit HD	Destination address 64-bit prefix, 64 bit HD

Compressed Header 1

Communication between the devices in the same 6LoWPAN network. IPv6 header is compressed to 2 bytes using link-local addresses (Table 4).

Compressed Header 2

Communication outside the 6LoWPAN network. IPv6 header is compressed to 12 bytes if the prefix of the external network is known (Table 5).

Compressed Header 3

Communication outside the 6LoWPAN network. IPv6 header is compressed to 20 bytes if the prefix of the external network is not known (Table 6).

Table 4.

Dispatch	Compressed Header	2 bytes

Table 5.

Dispatch	Compressed Header	CID	Hop Limit	Destination address 64-bit prefix, 64 bit HD	12 bytes

Table 6.

Dispatch	Compressed Header	CID	Hop Limit	Destination address 64-bit prefix, 64 bit HD	Destination address 64-bit prefix, 64 bit HD	20 bytes

In order to facilitate transmission of IPv6 frames over IEEE 802.15.4 links, the IPv6 frames should be divided into a number of smaller segments. Additional data in the headers are produced to reassemble the packets in the proper sequence at the end. The added data is removed when the data packets are reassembled to restore to the initial IPv6 format. The fragment sequence varies depends on the type of routing (P. Thubert, 2011).

NETWORK LAYER

RPL (Routing Protocol for Low Power Lossy Networks)

IETF has come out with a standardized and effective routing protocol known as Routing for Low power and Lossy networks (RPLs), which is capable of quickly building routes, distributing routing knowledge among nodes with little overhead, and adapting topology in an efficient way. RPL is expected to be the standard routing protocol for the majority of the IoT applications including the smart grid. Routing is the primary task of managing the packet forwarding on the efficient route between the sensor nodes. The transceiver part of the nodes which is a short range radio is used to send or receive the packets among the nodes. This radio medium is subject to bit errors and link failures. This makes the LLN nodes difficult in finding the best routes for data delivery. The specific routing requirements of the LLNs have not been satisfied by the existing routing protocols such as OSPF, IS-IS, AODV, and OLSR. The solutions of successful routing should consider the specific application requirements along with the IPv6 behavior and 6LoWPAN mechanisms. The IETF Routing Over Low power and Lossy networks (ROLL) Working Group was formed to design a routing solution for low power and lossy networks (also known as sensor networks). The ROLL working group has proposed the Routing Protocol for Low power and Lossy Networks (RPL), based on a gradient-based approach (T. Winter et al., (2011) and T. Winter, (2012).

The RPL routing protocol is tree-oriented, with RPL topologies generated starting from the Root nodes and organized as directed acyclic graphs. RPL forms non-transitive, nonbroadcast, and multiple access network topologies. RPL offers flexibility in building a topology but is complex as described in detail in the specification of the IETF draft.

The RPL supports three traffic patterns:

- Multipoint-to-point traffic.
- Point-to-multipoint traffic.
- Point-to-point traffic.

For the LLN applications, the dominant traffic is the multipoint-to-point type. Point-to-point traffic is used between the devices within the LLN; the point-to-multipoint pattern is used between a central control point and a set of sensor nodes; the multipoint-to-point pattern is used between a set of sensor nodes and a central control point.

The process of routing optimization and the process of packet routing are isolated. As the verification of the reachability of the router has to be done before using it as a parent, bi-directional links are used by the LLN to run the RPL protocol. There may be a need to connect the 6LoWPAN network to the internet. For this purpose, RPL works out a destination oriented, directed acyclic graph (DODAG) and uses this to route the data traffic. The Trickle algorithm is used by this protocol to exchange the routing information on the DODAG. Objective Functions (OFs) are used to compute the rank value for each node that is a scalar representation of the device location within the DODAG. The nodes determine the parent nodes closer to the graph root by the OFs.

There are three types of RPL messages named DIO (DODAG Information Objects) that contains information about the Rank, the OF and the IDs, DAO (Destination Advertisement Object) messages and DIS (DODAG Information Solicitations) messages. To enable the network formation and the operations of the network, all the nodes execute a set of operations; sending and receiving of DIOs; computation of their own Rank, based on the information included in the received DIOs; joining with a DODAG and selecting a set of parents in that DODAG among all nodes in the neighborhood selection of the preferred parent among the possible nodes. The DAG formed in RPL is split into to one more Destination Oriented DAGs (DODAGs), one DODAG per sink. There are four identifiers to define and maintain the topology and they are RPLInstanceID, DODAGID, DODAGVersionNumber, and Rank.

According to the Objective Functions and the Rank of their neighbors provided in the DIO message, a node can either join a new DODAG or maintain the existing one. RPL uses DAO messages to back-propagate routing information from the child nodes to the parent nodes that are triggered by the reception of DIO message. The RPL control messages are encapsulated into ICMPv6 packets. RPL not only relies on one particular feature of a specific link layer technology, but also to be able to operate over a variety of different link layers, including ones that are constrained, potentially lossy, or typically utilized in conjunction with highly constrained host or router devices, such as but not limited to, low power wireless or PLC (Power Line Communication) technologies.

Implementation of RPL

The RPL protocol implementation is done in the Contiki Operating System. All the protocols in the IoT stack can be simulated with this operating system. As an example, the RPL implementation is done.

Contiki Operating System

Contiki is an open source operating system that runs on the low power micro controllers and makes it possible to develop applications that makes efficient use of the hardware while providing standardized low power wireless communication for a range of hardware platform. It is a wireless sensor network operating system and consists of the kernel, libraries, the program loader, a set of processes.

Contiki is an event-driven system in which processes are implemented as event handlers that run to completion. A Contiki system is the combination of the core and the loaded programs. The core has the Contiki kernel, the program loader, the language run-time, and a communication stack with device drivers for the communication hardware. It is used for networked embedded systems and smart objects (A. Dunkels et al, (2004)).

The Program loader loads the programs into the memory and it can either obtain it from a host using communication stack or can obtain from the attached storage device such as EEPROM. The Contiki operating system provides modules for different tasks (layers). It provides the routing modules in a separate directory "contiki/core/net/rpl" and consists of a number of files. These files are separated logically based on the functionalities they provide for instance rpl-dag.c contains the functionality for Directed Acyclic Graph (DAG) formation, rpl-icmp6.c provides functionality for packaging ICMP messages etc.

Contiki supports a fully standardized IPv6 and IPv4 internet standards. Also supports the recent low power wireless standards 6LoWPN, CoAP, and RPL. Contiki applications are written in C programming language, so it is portable to different architectures like TI MSP430. Since it is an open source operating system, it can be freely used in commercial and non-commercial systems which can run IoT applications. Contiki provides mechanisms for estimating the system power consumption and to understand where the power was spent. The memory allocation module provides memory block allocation and standard C memory application. This implementation is done with the Contiki Operating System Version 2.7.

Cooja Network Simulator

Cooja Simulator is a Java-based network simulator specifically designed for Wireless Sensor Networks running on the Contiki Sensor network operating system. The simulator is implemented in Java and the sensor node software can be written in C.Cooja is a Java-based simulator designed for simulating sensor networks running the Contiki sensor network operating system.

Cooja allows the simultaneous simulations at three different levels:

- Network level.
- Operating System level.
- Machine code instruction level.

Cooja allows the Contiki programs either compile natively on the host CPU or compiles for any emulator like MSP430. The interactions with the simulated nodes in Cooja simulation can be performed via plugins like Simulation Visualizer, Timeline and Radio Logger. The simulation is stored with the extension ".csc" as an XML file. This file has the information about the simulation environment, the nodes and their positions and radio medium, etc. Each platform in Cooja has a separate platform configuration file "platform-conf.h" for each hardware platform which provides the ability to change RPL parameters.

Contiki contains two communication stacks:

- **uIP:** A small RFC-compliant TCP/IP stack that makes it possible for Contiki to communicate over the Internet.
- **Rime:** A lightweight communication stack designed for low-power radios.

Rime provides a wide range of communication primitives, from best-effort local area broadcast to reliable multi-hop bulk data flooding. The radio transceiver must be switched off as much as possible to save energy in the low-power networks. In Contiki, this is achieved by the Radio Duty Cycling (RDC) layer. Contiki provides a set of RDC mechanisms, with various properties. The default mechanism is ContikiMAC(http://www.contiki-os.org/).

Simulation Environment

The main aim of this simulation is to understand the behavior and to evaluate the performance of Routing Protocol for Low Power and Lossy Network (RPL) for the given scenario with respect to different performance metrics such as Packet Delivery Ratio, Signaling Overhead, Power Consumption and Latency. The RPL protocol is evaluated in the Smart Healthcare Environment application. The Smart Healthcare environment includes body sensors attached to the patients, device sensors attached to the devices and sensors attached to the Doctors etc.

Implementing the Smart Healthcare environment needs the integration of collecting the data from various sensors, storing it in the database for monitoring and analyzing the data for making decisions. Also, the emergency care should also be provided. As an initial step, the simulation can be set up to collect the temperature data from the patient. In future, the simulation can be extended for other parameters like a heartbeat, EEG, ECG etc. with appropriate biomedical sensors. A PC based application can also be developed as a front end to monitor and analyze the parameters (S.Umamaheswari and Atul Negi, 2017).

A simulation environment can be set up to read the temperature of the patient from the sensors attached to them and to send it to the server that is connected to the monitors of the Doctors. At the time of sending the data to the server the performance of the network is analyzed. The evaluation of an RPL instance in Cooja simulation has been done. The simulation was carried out for different network sizes such as 10, 20, 30, 40, and 50 RPL nodes with one sink node. The simulation scripts consist of RPL server node and RPL client node programs which are emulated as Tmote sky nodes that are derived from Cooja and uIPv6 module including UDP, ICMPv6, IPv6, SICSLoWPAN and Rime of the Contiki kernel.

The various simulation parameters are set as follows: Objective Function – OF0, RDC Channel Check Rate – 16, TX Range – 50m, Interference Range – 55m and Node Type – Tmote Sky.

The primary function of the RPL protocol is to build the paths between the root node and client nodes either downward or upward. The below figure shows the network topology (1 sink node and 20 client nodes) constructed by the Cooja Simulator. The arrows indicate the direction of packet transmission. As the nodes are mobile, the topology is dynamically changing and the final topology will be different.

At the initial stage when the network is constructed, the control messages transmitted for DODAG construction may flood the network and it will take the time to the construction stage. The analysis of this signaling overhead has been done. The below figure depicts the statistics on control messages and data messages in terms of transmitting network packets sent by WSN nodes .It is observed that the control messages lead most of the construction procedure, whereas UDP and radio data messages are negligible compared to control messages. In the RPL implemented the network, the DODAG root node starts building a network topology by broadcasting RPL control messages to all nodes in its radio range. In turn, the root node receives a large number of messages as a response. But, the UDP messages are sent as a confirmation only after establishing the link path to the DODAG root node.

Figure 1. Network Topology (20 Nodes)

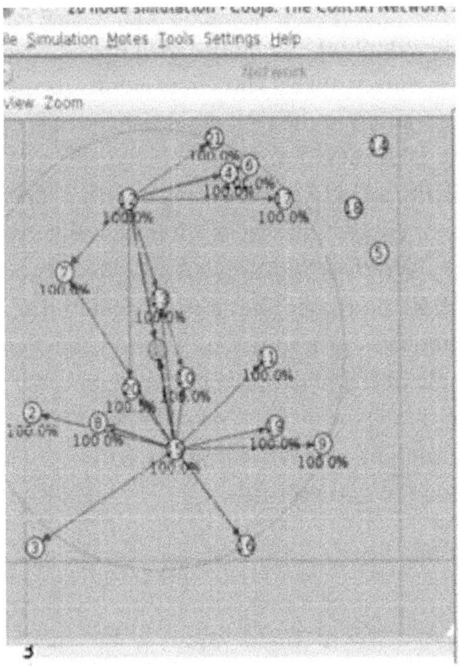

Figure 2. Control and Data Messages

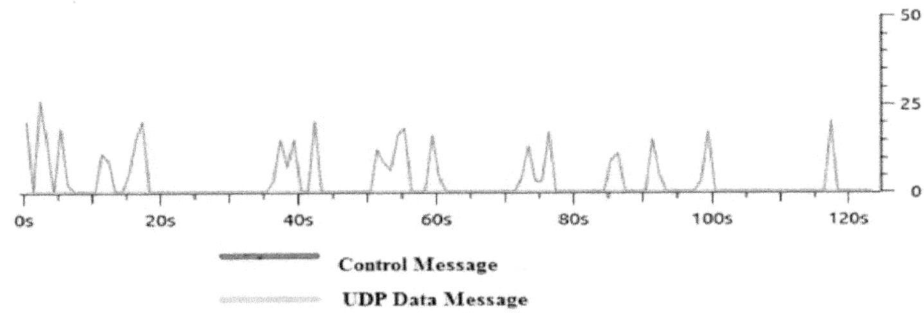

The routing overhead has RPL control messages and data traffic. The RPL signaling is comparatively high if compared to the data traffic. The RPL control messages are divided into three groups, namely the DIO, DAO, and DIS messages.

The breakup of the control messages is presented in the below figure. The DIO messages take the lead, followed by DAO messages and DIS messages. The reason for less number of DIS messages is that only the client nodes beyond the radio range of the root node generate DIS messages requesting for DIO messages from the neighbor nodes. The DAO messages are used to maintain the downward traffic from the root node to the client nodes and the DIO messages are for upward traffic. Our scenario is sending data from all the client nodes to the root node. The DIO messages have to be forwarded to the root node from all the clients that are willing to join or already in the DODAG.

To learn the scalability of RPL with respect to the scale of the network, the increase in the number of control messages (in terms of network packets) with the increase in the number of Wireless Sensor Network (WSN) nodes has been assessed. Figure 3 shows that the RPL protocol has a good scalability, in which the number of control messages increases at a lower speed than the number of WSN nodes, especially when the scale of the network becomes large.

Power consumption is the primary constraint of WSN, and it is necessary to assess the power consumption of a WSN running RPL.

The evaluation is done in two aspects.

Figure 3. Breakup of RPL Control Messages

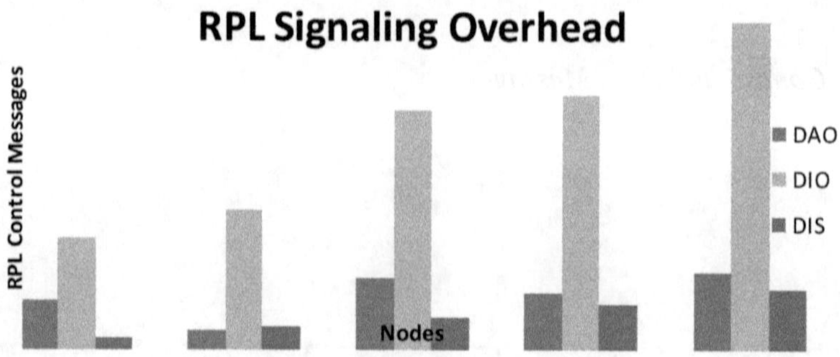

Figure 4. Increase in the number of ICMPv6 Messages

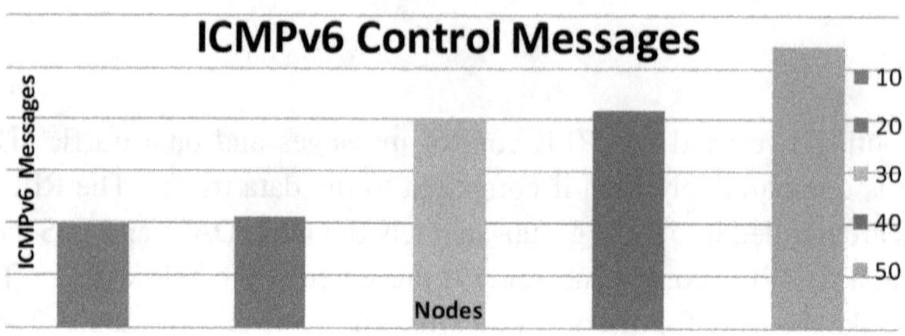

1. Firstly, the power consumption of the whole network is evaluated to get an overall picture of power.
2. Next, the power consumption of individual nodes is studied.

The radio transceiver is the major source of power consumption in a WSN node. For example, the power consumption of the radio is three orders of magnitude larger than that of the CPU for the Tmote Sky platform. So, the focus is set to radio transmission to measure the power consumption. The Contiki operating system has the ContikiMAC as the default duty cycle protocol. As the majority of energy is spent on idle listening, repeated packet sending and receiving, the time of radio on can be used as the metric of power consumption.

The below figure presents the overall usage of radio in the network. It can be observed that the radio keeps off most the time. The power consumption is saved due to the radio duty cycles.

TRANSPORT LAYER

The Transport layer provides end-to-end reliable connectivity over IP based networks. Transmission Control Protocol (TCP) which is the most widely used protocol on internet adopts Automatic Repeat-Request (ARQ) techniques for traffic control and congestion control. The traffic on the internet is maintained and more control overhead is produced for each transmitted packet. The energy consumption is more

Figure 5. The Radio Usage in the Network

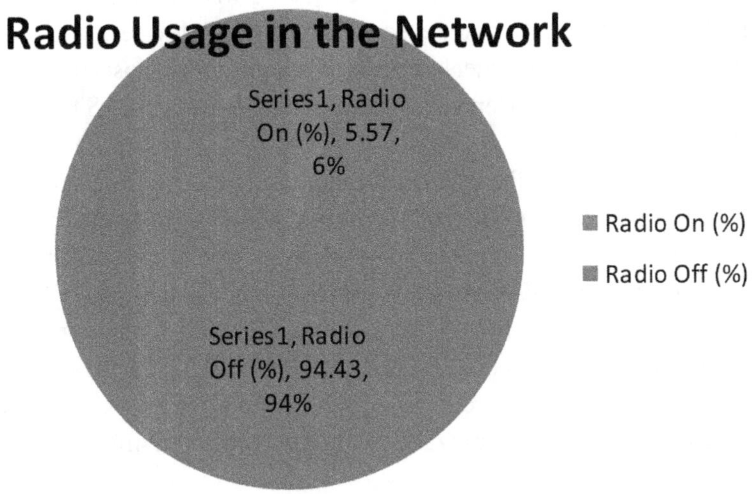

in this protocol and the traffic control and reliability are more expensive in terms of the packet delivery ratio and end-to-end delay. Due to these expensive requirements, the use of User Datagram Protocol (UDP) makes a good changeover between the energy cost and reliability for providing reliable communication in LLNs.

User Datagram Protocol (UDP)

UDP is a datagram-oriented protocol which provides a mechanism for sending messages from one application to other applications with less overhead. This protocol is transaction-oriented and there is no guarantee for the delivery of information and duplicate protection. UDP neither provides a guarantee to its upper layer protocol for information delivery nor maintains a state of sending UDP messages. As in TCP, UDP offers application multiplexing with the port concept. 6LoWPAN eliminates few fields in the IPv6 and UDP headers as they can be assumed from the fields of IEEE 802.15.4 header. UDP is a well-suited protocol for the IoT scenarios. This is a lightweight protocol compared to TCP. Faster transmission rate and smaller header size than TCP make the UDP suitable for constrained environments of devices and sensors. The application layer protocols of the IoT protocol stack like CoAP use UDP than TCP (J. Postel, 1980).

APPLICATION LAYER

CoAP

A Constrained Environment is a workspace with low powered hardware devices, with minimum networking capabilities. The existing web services are extended to the RESTful architecture to provide a service to the IoT devices. The use of web services (web APIs) on the Internet has become ubiquitous in most applications and depends on the fundamental Representational State Transfer [REST] architecture of the Web.

The IoT devices become IP enabled and connected to the Internet and enabled to communicate a language to provide interoperability. Redesigning and optimizations in application protocols are required to implement machine-to-machine (M2M) applications over constrained environments on the IoT. Even though HTTP is widely used with Web Services, it is not the only protocol for M2M communication. The Constrained Application Protocol (CoAP) is designed by IETF Constrained RESTful Environment (Core) working group to provide a lightweight RESTful (HTTP) interface and it incorporates optimizations for constrained environments. REST is the standard interface between HTTP client and servers (Z. Shelby et al. (2014). The below figure depicts the CoAP architecture.

The CoAP is a specialized web transfer protocol for the constrained nodes and constrained networks such as LLNs. The nodes often have 8-bit microcontrollers with small amounts of ROM and RAM, while constrained networks such as IPv6 over Low-Power Wireless Personal Area Networks (6LoWPANs) often have high packet error rates and a typical throughput of 10s of Kbit/s. The protocol is designed for machine-to-machine (M2M) applications such as smart energy and building automation.

The CoAP provides a request/response interaction model between application endpoints, supports the built-in discovery of services and resources, and includes key concepts of the Web such as URIs and Internet media types.

The CoAP comprises of some HTTP functionalities which can be suitable for M2M applications over constrained environments on the IoT, meaning it takes into account the less processing power and energy constraints of small embedded devices, such as sensors. REST results in less overhead and energy consumption of lightweight IoT applications. It makes use of UDP, instead of TCP commonly used in HTTP and has a light mechanism to provide reliability. The CoAP enables low-power sensors to apply RESTful services. Messaging layer and request/response layer are the two layers that are part of the CoAP architecture. It uses the Efficient XML

Figure 6. CoAP Architecture

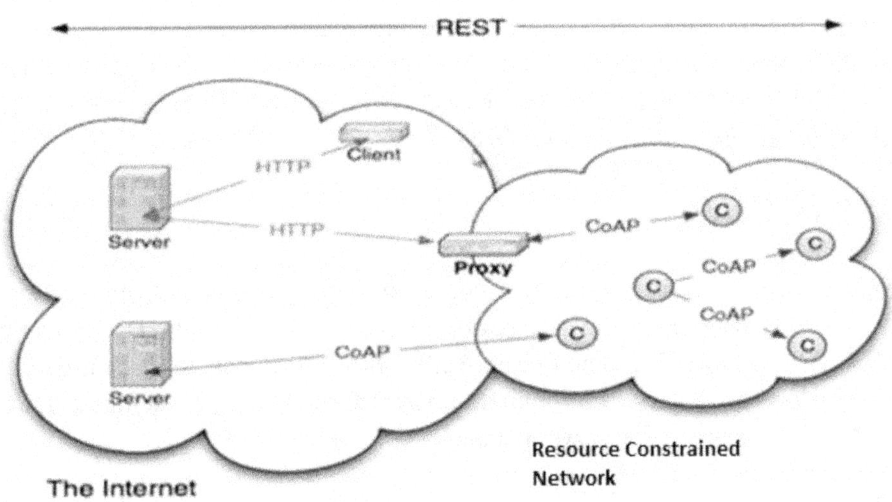

Interchanges (EXI) data format that is far better in terms of space when compared to plain text HTML/XML.

There are four types of messaging modes in CoAP and they are,

- Confirmable
- Non-confirmable
- Separate
- Piggyback.

Reliable and unreliable communication is done in confirmable and non-confirmable modes respectively. Client/Server direct communication is possible in Piggyback mode and the server response is made as a message apart from the acknowledgment in a separate mode. GET, PUT, PUSH, and DELETE are the message requests used in CoAP to retrieve, create, update, and delete, respectively. For reliable transmission over UDP, confirmable messages are used. The response can be piggybacked in the acknowledgment itself (V. Karagiannis and P. Chatzimisios, 2015).

The CoAP is an application layer service discovery protocol for constrained environments. Built-in header compression, congestion control, resource discovery, IP multicast support, native push model, and asynchronous message exchange are other special features of CoAP that are not offered by HTTP.

Service discovery in the constrained environment is an increasingly important issue as we move towards realizing pervasive systems. The user interaction with the service is an important issue once the service is discovered. The service life span is completed only when the communication is proper. A service layer in the form of middleware resolves this issue. CoAP can be used for service discovery in real-time IoT environments. The Integrating Physical world devices in constrained web environments using Constrained Application Protocol (CoAP) together with an end-to-end IP and RESTful Web Services based architecture can be implemented (S.Umamaheswari and K.Vanitha 2016).

HTTP vs. CoAP

As CoAP applies a subset of the HTTP features, there is a direct mapping between HTTP and CoAP. The mapping can be done in either way i.e. CoAP-HTTP mapping or HTTP-CoAP mapping. The former facilitates CoAP clients to make use of the resources on HTTP servers through an intermediate. The latter facilitates HTTP clients to access the CoAP server resources.

Similarities Between HTTP and CoAP

- Request-Response pattern.
- Device addressing with the IP address and Port number.
- Usage of methods like Get, Post, Put and Delete, Status Codes, URLs, and content-type.
- Support for Service/Resource discovery at the IoT network.
- Simple proxy and caching.

Differences Between HTTP and CoAP

CoAP libraries are available for the programming languages like C, Java, C#, Python, Ruby, etc. and the mobile operating systems such as iOS and Android.

MQTT

MQTT (Message Queuing Telemetry Transport) is an open source, lightweight messaging protocol for resource-constrained devices in the LLNs which was created by Dr. Andy Standford-Clark of IBM and Arlen Nipper of Arcom (now Eurotech) in 1999 as a cost-effective and reliable protocol to connect monitoring devices used in the oil and gas industries with remote enterprise servers (http://mqtt.org).

This protocol exploits publish/subscribe messaging pattern which is used for M2M communication and plays a vital role in the IoT. It aids in minimizing the

Table 7.

Feature	CoAP	HTTP
Protocol	Uses UDP. UDP is a lightweight protocol	Uses TCP
Communication	Supports multicast	No multicast support
Network Layer	6LoWPAN layer with IPv6	IP Layer
Server Architecture	Support to both Client/Serverand Publish-Subscribe models	Supports only Client/Server Model
Overhead	Less Overhead	More Overhead because TCP is a connection-oriented protocol.
Device Support	Supports resource constrained networking devices inWSN/IoT/ M2M networks	Supports the internet devices where there is no issue of any resources
Notification	"Observe" functionality to notify the changes in the node parameters	No support of notification

resource requirements of the IoT devices and ensures the reliability and degree of assurance of delivery. The main target of this protocol is the large networks with small IoT devices that require monitoring and control from a backbone server on the internet. This protocol is not meant for device-to-device transfer and multicast transfer. MQTT is very simple and offers fewer control options. The below figure gives the working of MQTT protocol.

An MQTT session operates four stages:

- Connection
- Authentication
- Communication
- Termination

The MQTT is implemented with an MQTT client and MQTT Broker. Any device in the IoT network that has an MQTT library running and connected to an MQTT broker is an MQTT client. The MQTT client can either be a Publisher or a Subscriber. MQTT Publisher allows devices to publish information about a given topic to a server that functions as an MQTT message broker. The broker then forwards the information out to the Subscriber clients that have already subscribed to the client's topic. An MQTT broker receives and filters the messages received from the Publisher clients and send them to all the subscribed clients.

The MQTT protocol can be applied in a variety of applications that use sensors and small devices such as Smart Systems for Home Automation, Agriculture, Health Care etc. The implementation of MQTT is available in Java, C, C++, JavaScript, and Python. The origin of these implementations is the codebase of IBM and Eurotech.

There are many industry initiatives for the integration of MQTT and its applications in IoT and prototyping for real time applications. Industries like IBM, Eclipse, and forums like OASIS are working for the resource development for MQTT. The following are some of Broker or Servers released for MQTT application development.

- PAHO
- MOSQUITTO by Eclipse
- WebSphere MQ - Messaging Middleware

Figure 7. Working of MQTT Protocol

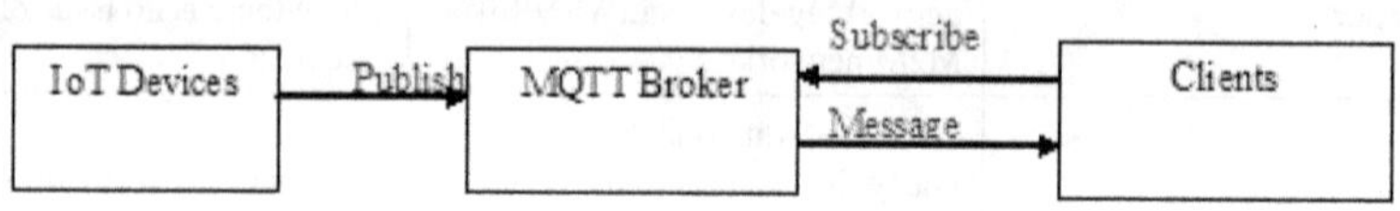

- m2meclipse.org - Server
- Web Sphere Business Integration Message Broker (WBIMB)
- Web Sphere Business Integration Event Broker (WBIEB)
- Web Sphere Connection Server Micro Edition (WCSME)

AMQP

The main objective of the Advanced Message Queuing Protocol (AMQP) was to solve the messaging interoperability problem in the financial industry between the message brokers and heterogeneous platforms which were designed by John O'Hara from JPMorgan. The AMQP specification is an open standard designed by the AMQP working group which includes 20 companies in various segments like financial, technical and network marketing. Similar to MQTT, it runs over TCP and offers a publish/ subscribe architecture.

The main difference between MQTT and AMQP is that the broker component is divided into two segments: Exchange and Queues. The exchange receives publisher messages and distributes them to queues. The queues represent the topics subscribed by the subscribers that get the data which are available in the queue. The below figure depicts the AMQP architecture (OASIS, 2012).

XMPP

Extensible Messaging and Presence Protocol (XMPP) is a messaging protocol that was designed for chatting and message exchange applications. This protocol is used in Software Defined Networks and IoT applications. XMPP supports both the communication models: request/response and publish/subscribe. XMPP is not suitable for M2M communications as there is no support for any quality of service. XMPP messages are in XML format that creates additional overhead and increases the power consumption. So this protocol is not often used in IoT (P. Saint-Andre, 2011).

Figure 8. AMQP Architecture

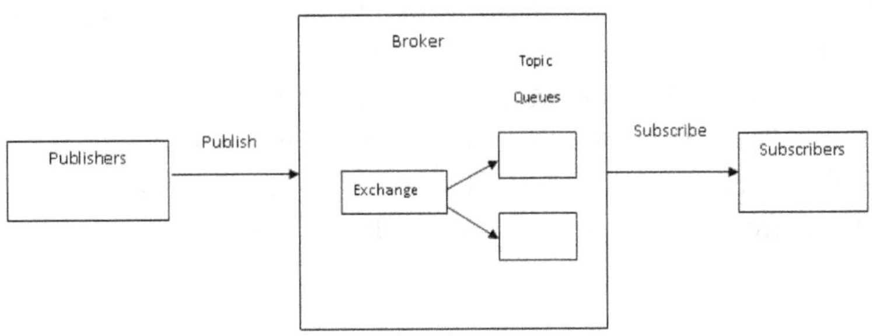

The key XMPP technologies include Core, Jingle, Multi-User Chat, PubSub, and BOSH.

- **Core:** Information about the core XMPP technologies for XML streaming.
- **Jingle:** SIP-compatible multi-media signaling for voice, video, file transfer, and other applications.
- **Multiuser Chat:** Flexible, multi-party communication.
- **PubSub:** Alerts and notifications for data syndication, rich presence, and more.
- **BOSH:** An HTTP binding for XMPP (and other) traffic.

FUTURE DIRECTIONS

The simulation implementation of CoAP and the RPL has been presented in this chapter. The implementation of other protocols can be done with the simulator and in the real time environment by considering various smart environments.

A few authors have come out with some research findings of the challenges and issued faced in the secure communication and security protocols.

- The technologies and communication solutions related to the Internet of Things has been studied and the major issues faced by the research community are addressed by L. Atzori, A. Iera, G. Morabito (2010).
- The Midgar platform evaluates the different traditional security techniques related to cryptography. The evaluation is performed to find the solution for the Internet of Things when there is a usage of insecure protocols. (G. Sánchez-Arias et al. 2017).
- An analysis on the existing security protocols and mechanisms that secure communications in the IoT is carried out. The open challenges in the secure communication are also presented by J. Granjal, E. Monteiro, J.S. Silva (2015).
- The study of existing IP-based Internet Security protocols and other security protocols used in wireless sensor networks checks for the applicability and suitability of these protocols. This study is based on the key distribution mechanism (K.T. Nguyen, M. Laurent, N. Oualha, 2015).
- A practical realization of the IoT architecture is implemented at the University of Padova, Italy. The 6LoWPAN standard is implemented to make nodes reachable from outside networks using IPv6.(A.P.Castellani et.al. 2010)

The issues and challenges faced by these researchers can be considered for the future work.

SUMMARY

This chapter presented the comparison of Internet Protocol Stack and the Internet of Things Protocol Stack. An overview of the Communication Protocols in the Internet Protocol Stack has been presented. The performance of the IETF RPL routing protocol using COOJA simulator under Contiki operating system has been evaluated and analyzed. The performance of network construction process has been analyzed by measuring the metrics like signaling overhead, packet delivery ratio, latency, and energy consumption.

CoAP protocol is suited for a wide range of applications like smart grid, smart buildings, smart lighting system and environmental monitoring. The applications of the MQTT protocol include industrial control systems that access the data from the IoT devices, Smart lighting system, and Facebook Messenger.

The Amazon Internet of Things is based on MQTT. Due to the interoperability feature, the AMQP protocol has been used for complex data processing. The current real time implementations of AMQP include NASA's Nebula Cloud Computing, Google, India's Aadhaar Project and Ocean Observatories Initiative. The instant messaging system is an application of the XMPP protocol. The choice of protocol for the application is purely based on the application. MQTT and CoAP are mostly used as lightweight messaging protocols in the IoT network.

REFERENCES

Ashton. (2009). Internet of Things. *RFiD Journal.*

Atzori, L., Iera, A., & Morabito, G. (2010). The Internet of Things: A survey. *Computer Networks*, *54*(15), 2787–2805. doi:10.1016/j.comnet.2010.05.010

Castellani, A. P., Bui, N., Casari, P., Rossi, M., Shelby, Z., & Zorzi, M. (2010). Architecture and protocols for the Internet of Things: A Case Study. *8th IEEE International Conference on Pervasive Computer Communication*, 678-683. doi:10.1109/PERCOMW.2010.5470520

Cetinkaya, O., & Akan, O. (2015). A dash7-based power metering system. *12th Annual IEEE Consumer Communications and Networking Conference (CCNC)*, 406-411.

Colitti, W., Steenhaut, K., DeCaro, N., & Buta, B., Dobrota, V. (2011). Evaluation of constrained application protocol for wireless sensor networks. In *Proceedings of the 18th IEEE Workshop onLocal and Metropolitan Area Networks (LANMAN '11)* (pp. 1–6) IEEE. doi:10.1109/LANMAN.2011.6076934

Dunkels, Gronvall, & Voigt. (2004). Contiki - A lightweight and flexible operatingsystem for tiny networked sensors. *29th Annual IEEE International Conference on Local Computer Networks*, 455 – 462.

Gomez, J. O., & Paradells, J. (2012). Overview and evaluation of Bluetooth low energy: An emerging low-power wireless technology. *Sensors (Basel)*, *12*(9), 11734–11753. doi:10.3390/s120911734

Granjal, J., Monteiro, E., & Silva, J. S. (2015). *Security for the Internet of Things: A Survey of Existing Protocols and Open Research issues.* IEEE Communication Survey Tutorials.

Hasan, M., Hossain, E., & Niyato, D. (2013). Random access for machine-to-machine communication in LTE-advanced networks: Issues and approaches. IEEE Communications Magazine, 51(6), 86-93.

Hekland, Petersen, & Doyle. (2008). When HART goes wireless: Understanding and implementing the WirelessHART standard. *IEEE International Conference on Emerging Technologies and Factory Automation (ETFA 2008)*, 899-907. doi:10.1109/ETFA.2008.4638503

HomePlug Alliance. (2012). *HomePlug GreenPHY v1.1*. Retrieved from http://www.homeplug.org/tech-resources/resources/ http://www.contiki-os.org/ http://mqtt.org

IEEE 802.15.4. (2011). IEEE Standard for Local and metropolitan area networks--Part 15.4: Low-Rate Wireless Personal Area Networks (LR-WPANs). Retrieved from http://standards.ieee.org/getieee802/download/802.15.4-2011.pdf

ITU-T. (2012). Series Y: Global Information Infrastructure, Internet Protocol Aspects and Next-Generation Networks, Overview of the Internet of things. ITU-T Y.2060.

Jara, A. J., Ladid, L., & Skarmeta, A. (2013). The Internet of Everything through IPv6: An Analysis of Challenges, Solutions, and Opportunities. *Journal of Wireless Mobile Networks, Ubiquitous Computing, and Dependable Applications*, *4*(3), 97–118.

Karagiannis, V., & Chatzimisios, P. (2015). A survey on application layer protocols for the internet of things. *Transaction on IoT and Cloud Computing*, *3*(1), 11–17.

LoRa Alliance. (2015). *LoRaWAN specification.* Retrieved from https://www.lora-alliance.org/portals/0/specs/LoRaWAN%20Specification%201R0.pdf

Nguyen, K. T., Laurent, M., & Oualha, N. (2015). Survey on secure communication protocols for the Internet of Things. *Ad Hoc Networks*, *32*, 17–31. doi:10.1016/j.adhoc.2015.01.006

OASIS. (2012). *OASIS Advanced Message Queuing Protocol (AMQP) Version 1.0.* Retrieved from http://docs.oasis-open.org/amqp/core/v1.0/os/amqp-core-complete-v1.0-os.pdf

Park, M. (2015). IEEE 802.11ah: Sub-1-GHz license-exempt operation for the internet of things. *IEEE Communications Magazine*, *53*(9), 145–151. doi:10.1109/MCOM.2015.7263359

Postel. (1980). *User Datagram Protocol.* Internet Engineering Task Force RFC 768.

Raza, S., & Voigt, T. (2010). Interconnecting Wireless HART and legacy HART networks. *6th IEEE International Conference on Distributed Computing in Sensor Systems Workshops (DCOSSW)*, 1-8. Retrieved from http://ieeexplore.ieee.org/xpl/articleDetails.jsp?arnumber=5593285

Saint-Andre, P. (2011). *Extensible messaging and presence protocol (XMPP): Core.* IETF RFC 6120, 2011. Retrieved from https://tools.ietf.org/html/rfc6120

Sánchez-Arias, G., & González García, C. (2017). Midgar: Study of communications security among Smart Objects using a platform of heterogeneous devices for the Internet of Things. Future Generation Computer Systems, 74, 444–466.

Shelby, Z., & Bormann, C. (2010). *6LoWPAN: The Wireless Embedded Internet.* Wiley.

Shelby, Z., Hartke, K., & Bormann, C. (2014). *The constrained application protocol (CoAP).* Tech. Rep. *IETF RFC*, *7252*, 2014.

Sheng, Z., Yang, S., Yu, Y., Vasilakos, A., Mccann, J., & Leung, K. (2013). A survey on the IETF protocol suite for the internet of things: Standards, challenges, and opportunities. *IEEE Wireless Communications*, *20*(6), 91–98. doi:10.1109/MWC.2013.6704479

Thubert. (2011). *Compression Format for IPv6 Datagrams over IEEE 802.15.4-Based Networks.* Internet Engineering Task Force, RFC 6282.

Umamaheswari, S. (2017). Internet of Things and RPL Routing Protocol: A Study And Evaluation. *IEEE International Conference on Computer Communication and Informatics (ICCCI -2017).*

Umamaheswari, S., & Vanitha, K. (2016). *Interaction Model of Service Discovery Using Visa Processing Algorithm and Constrained Application Protocol (CoAP).* Springer.

Winter. (2012). *IPv6 routing protocol for low power and lossy networks*. Internet Engineering Task Force, RFC 6550.

Winter & Thubert. (2011). *RPL, Internet-Draft, RPL: IPv6 Routing Protocol for Low power and Lossy Networks*. draft-ietf-roll-rpl-19.

Z-Wave. (2007). *Z-Wave Protocol Overview, v. 4*. Retrieved from https://wiki.ase.tut.fi/courseWiki/images/9/94/SDS10243_2_Z_Wave_Protocol_Overview.pdf

Zigbee. (2004). *Zigbee Document*. Retrieved from http://www3.nd.edu/~mhaenggi/ee67011/zigbee.pdf

KEY TERMS AND DEFINITIONS

6LoWPAN: IPv6 over low power wireless personal area networks acts as an adaptation layer to transport IPv6 packets over 802.15.4 links.

AMQP: Advanced message queuing protocol is an open standard application layer protocol for asynchronous messaging.

CoAP: Constrained application protocol is a specifically designed application layer protocol for use with constrained devices and constrained networks in the internet of things.

HTTP: Hypertext transfer protocol is the application level protocol used for defining the messages used by the world wide web.

IETF: Internet Engineering Task Force is a large open international community that develops and promotes voluntary internet standards, in particular the standards that comprise the internet protocol suite (TCP/IP).

IoT: Internet of things refers to the interconnection of the IP smart objects, such as sensors and actuators.

IPv4: Internet protocol version 4 is the fourth version of internet protocol that defines IP addresses in 32-bit format.

IPv6: Internet protocol version 6 is a network layer protocol that enables data communications in the network.

MQTT: Message queuing telemetry transport is a publish/subscribe messaging protocol designed for lightweight M2M communications.

RFC: Request for comments is a formal document released by the Internet Engineering Task Force (IETF) as result of committee drafting.

RPL: Routing protocol for low power lossy networks is capable of quickly building routes, distributing routing knowledge among nodes with little overhead, and adapting topology in an efficient way.

TCP: Transmission control protocol is a standard that establishes the network connection and transfers data streams.

UDP: User datagram protocol is a datagram-oriented protocol that provides a mechanism for sending messages from one application to other applications with less overhead.

XMPP: Extensible messaging and presence protocol is a messaging protocol that was designed for chatting and message exchange applications.

Chapter 7
A Framework for Modernizing Non-Mobile Software:
A Model-Driven Engineering Approach

Liliana Favre
National University of Central Buenos Aires, Argentina

ABSTRACT

New paradigms such as pervasive computing, cloud computing, and the internet of things (IoT) are transforming the software industry and the business world. Organizations need to redesign their models and processes to be sustainable. Smartphones are at the core of these paradigms, letting us locate and easily interact with the world around us. Frequently, the development of mobile software requires of the adaption of valuable and tested non-mobile software. Most challenges in this kind of software modernization are related to the diversity of platforms on the smartphones market and to the need of systematic and reusable processes with a high degree of automation that reduce time, cost, and risks. This chapter proposes a modernization framework based on model-driven engineering (MDE). It allows integrating legacy code with the native behaviors of the different mobile platform through cross-platform languages. Realizations of the framework for the migration of C/C++ or Java code to mobile platforms through the Haxe multiplatform language are described.

DOI: 10.4018/978-1-5225-3805-9.ch007

INTRODUCTION

Today, the use of technology is central to the business world. Organizations need to redesign their processes and models so as not to be left out of the market in the near future. The adoption of new digital technologies offers competitive advantage and performs like a market differentiator. In particular, new paradigms such as Pervasive Computing, Cloud Computing and the Internet of Things are impacting business world.

Pervasive Computing, also called Ubiquitous Computing is the idea that almost any device can be embedded with chips to connect the device to a network of other devices. The goal of Pervasive Computing, which combines current network technologies with wireless computing, voice recognition and Internet capability, is to create an environment where the connectivity of devices is unobtrusive and always available. Cloud Computing is an Internet-based computing for enabling ubiquitous, on-demand network access to a shared pool of configurable computing resources (e.g., networks, servers, storage, applications and services) that can be rapidly supplied with minimal management effort. Cloud Computing has long been recognized as a paradigm for Big Data storage and analytics providing computing and data resources in a dynamic and pay-per-use model. Finally, there is no single universal definition for the IoT which could be defined as the interconnection via the Internet of computing devices embedded in everyday objects, enabling them to send and receive data. The IoT is becoming so pervasive and several studies predict that, in 2020, there will be more than 30 billion of IP identifying connected devices and sensors.

Pervasive Computing, Cloud Computing and the IoT face similar problems related to similar use cases, including smart cities, environmental monitoring, agriculture, home automation, and health. These technologies are possible thanks to the advances in mobile computing and electronic miniaturization that allow cutting-edge computing and communication technology to be added into very small objects. On the one hand, Mobile Computing promoted the globalizations of networks (3G, 4G and 5G) facilitating the development of distributed processing to create a network of billions of devices.

Smartphones are being transformed into a service center for different platforms in science, medicine, education, and the media. With the Smartphone through Wi-Fi and the 5G, we will handle all kinds of objects connected to the network. Just as smartphones have already displaced the camera, the GPS, the music player and the wallet, they will be on-ramp for a new IoT revolution. The IoT is arriving at our everyday life. In this scenario, humans and things act synergistically as a whole. Miranda et al. (2015) state that in a more desirable IoT scenario, technology would take the context of the people into account moving from the IoT to the Internet of

People (IoP). In this situation, smartphones will continue to play a crucial role due to they are the main interface connecting people to the Internet.

Frequently, the development of software component and applications aligned to these new paradigms requires adapting existing non-mobile software to mobile platforms. For instance, there exist valuable software components and libraries implemented in C/C++ or Java that need to be adapted for mobile developments. Most challenges in this kind of software migration are related, on the one hand, to the proliferation of mobile platforms that makes mobile development very difficult and expensive and, on the other hand, to the need to define systematic, reusable processes with a high degree of automation that reduce risks, time and costs.

With respect to the first challenge, the ideal situation is to define multiplatform development. New languages are emerging to integrate the native behaviors of the different platforms targeted in development projects. In this direction, the Haxe language is an open-source high-level cross-platform programming language and compiler that can produce applications and source code for many different platforms from a single code base (Haxe, 2017; Dasnois, 2011).

With respect to the systematic modernization process, novel technical frameworks for information integration, tool interoperability and reuse have emerged. Specifically, Model- Driven Engineering (MDE) is a software engineering discipline which emphasizes the use of models and model transformations to raise the abstraction level and the degree of automation in software development. Productivity and some aspects of software quality such as maintainability or interoperability are goals of MDE.

In the context of MDE, a particular form of reengineering for the functional and technological evolution of software systems is called Model-Driven Software Modernization (MDSM). In this approach, models representing the legacy software are discovered semi-automatically through a reverse engineering process. Next, they are transformed into models that satisfy the modernization requirements which are the input to forward engineering processes that generated new modernized software.

This chapter describes an MDE-based modernization framework defined in the context of a software modernization project aimed at migrating desktop software to various mobile platforms. Realizations of the framework for the migration of C/C++ or Java code to different mobile platforms through the Haxe language are described. The proposal is being validated in the Eclipse Modeling Framework (EMF) considering that some of its tools and environments are aligned with MDE standards (Steinberg et al., 2009).

The structure of the chapter is as follows. The section "*Background*" provides definitions and discussion emphasizing on MDE and multiplatform development. It also presents some relevant literature review related to our approach. The sections "*A modernization framework*" and "*Analyzing different realizations of the framework*" describe the main focus of the chapter: an MDE-based framework for software modernization and different realizations of the framework for the migration of C/C++ or Java code to applications deployed on different mobile platforms and the reverse engineering of Java Code to UML models. The section "*Discussion*" discusses the approach focusing in its advantages and limitations in relation to ad-hoc software migration. Next, conclusion and future work are included.

BACKGROUND

The adaption of non-mobile software to new technologies can be achieved by combining model-driven engineering and multiplatform developments. This section describes the bases of both approaches. Besides, it includes a summary of related work.

Model Driven Engineering

Model-driven Engineering is a software development methodology that focuses on the use of models and model transformations to raise the level of abstraction and automation in software development, either to generate new software or to modernize legacy software. Different acronyms are associated with model-driven developments: MBE (Model Based Engineering), MDE (Model-driven Engineering), MDD (Model-driven Development) and MDSM (Model-driven Software Modernization). Figure 1 shows the relation between the acronyms linked to model-based or model-driven developments.

MBE is the branch of software engineering in which software models play an important role being the basis of development. However, there is no direct link between the models and the generated software defined precisely through transformations.

MDE can be viewed as a subset of MBE. It is the branch of software engineering in which processes are driven by models, i.e. models are the primary artifacts of different software processes. MDE has emerged as a new software engineering discipline which emphasizes the use of models and model transformations to raise the abstraction level and the degree of automation in software development. Productivity and some aspects of the software quality such as maintainability or interoperability are goals of MDE.

Model-driven principles can be summarizes as follows: all artifacts involved in a MDE process can be viewed as models that conform to a particular metamodel, the process itself can be viewed as a sequence of model transformations and, all extracted information is represented in an standard way through metamodels. Then, model, metamodel and transformations are crucial in MDE.

Figure 1. Model-driven acronyms

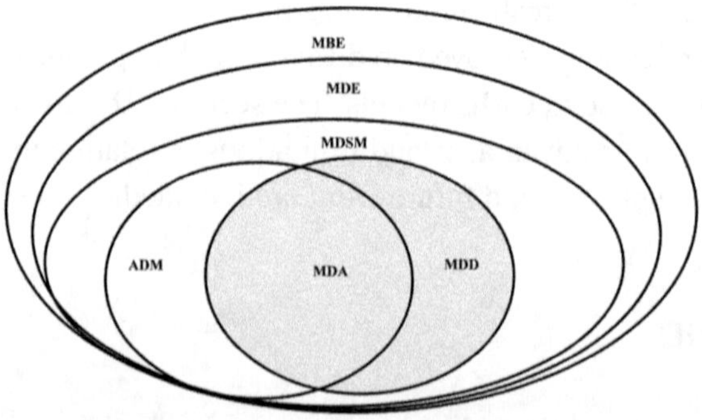

Model-driven Developments (MDD) refer to forward engineering processes that use models as primary development artifacts. A specific realization of MDD is the Model-Driven Architecture (MDA) proposed by the Object Management Group (OMG) (MDA, 2017). The outstanding ideas behind MDA are separating the specification of the system functionality from its implementation on specific platforms, managing the software evolution from abstract models to implementations. Models play a major role in MDA, which distinguishes at least Platform Independent Model (PIM) and Platform Specific Model (PSM). An MDA process focuses on the automatic transformation of different models that conform to MOF (Meta Object Facility) metamodel, the standard for defining metamodels in the context of MDA. It provides the ability to design and integrate semantically different languages such as general-purpose languages, domain specific languages and modeling languages in a unified way (MOF, 2016). MOF can be considered the essence of MDA allowing different kinds of artifacts from multiple technologies to be used together in an interoperable way. The modeling concepts of MOF are classes, which model MOF meta-objects; associations, which model binary relations between meta-objects; Data Types, which model other data; and Packages, which modularize the models. Consistency rules are attached to metamodel components by using OCL (OCL, 2014). MOF provides two metamodels EMOF (Essential MOF) and CMOF (Complete MOF). EMOF favors simplicity of implementation over expressiveness. CMOF is a metamodel used to specify more sophisticated metamodels. The OMG standard related to model transformation is the MOF 2.0 Query, View, Transformation (QVT) metamodel (QVT, 2012).

A particular form of reengineering for the technological and functional evolution of legacy systems begins to be identified in the early 21st century under the designation of Model-driven Software Modernization (MDSM) (Brambrilla et al., 2012). It is based on model-driven processes of reverse engineering, restructuring and forward engineering. In MDSM, models representing legacy software are discovery semi-automatically through a reverse engineering process and then transformed into models that meet the modernization requirements from which it is possible to forward engineering a new modernized software. The OMG Architecture-Driven Modernization Task Force (ADMTF) is developing a set of specifications and promoting industry consensus on modernization. ADM is defined as

The process of understand and evolve existing software assets for the purpose of software improvement, modifications, interoperability, refactoring, restructuring, reuse, porting, migration, translation, integration, service-oriented architecture deployment. (ADM, 2017).

A set of standards (metamodels) to facilitate interoperability between modernization tools are associated to ADM. KDM (Knowledge Discovery Metamodel) is a central metamodel for knowledge discovery in software that allows representing information related to existing software assets, their associations, and operational environments regardless of the implementation programming language and runtime platform (KDM, 2016).

The success of MDE depend on the existence of tools that make a significant impact on software processes such as reverse engineering, restructuring and forward engineering. The Eclipse Modeling Framework (EMF) was created for facilitating system modeling and the automatic generation of Java code (EMF, 2017). EMF started as an implementation of MOF resulting Ecore, the EMF metamodel comparable to EMOF. EMF has evolved starting from the experience of the Eclipse community to implement a variety of tools and to date is highly related to MDE. In this context, the subproject Model to Model Transformation (MMT), hosts model-to-model transformation languages. Transformations are executed by transformation engines that are plugged into the Eclipse Modeling infrastructure. For instance, Atlas Transformation Language (ATL) is a model transformation language and toolkit that provides ways to produce a set of target models from a set of source models (ATL, 2017). Another subproject is Acceleo, which is an implementation of the Model-to-Text (M2T) transformation standard of the OMG for EMF-based models (Acceleo, 2017). Acceleo is used in forward engineering processes.

Multiplatform Development

Today, one of major challenges for software developers is dealing with the rapid proliferation of mobile platforms that entails the high cost, technical complexity and risk of targeting development to a wide spectrum of platforms. Software applications can take full advantage of platforms only when they are built using native codebase. To address this problem a possible solution is to have different teams of developers who are fluent in specific programming language to port an application to a specific platform. Instead of this traditional approach, organizations can use multiplatform or multi-paradigm cross-compiler based languages. In this context, the term "*multiplatform*" is used to refer source-source compilation, that is to say, the source code of these languages can be compiled into source code of other programming language.

Haxe is a good example of multiplatform languages. It allows using the same code to deploy an application on multiple platforms such as iOS, Android or WindowsPhone. In this direction, the Haxe language emerges as an open-source high-level multiplatform programming language and compiler that can produce applications and source code for many different platforms from a single code-base.

The Haxe principles are summarizes at (Cannase, 2014) as follows: "support mainstream platforms", "write once, reuse everywhere", "always native, no wrapper", "generated but readable" and "trust the developer". The Haxe programming language is a high level programming language that mixes features of object oriented languages and functional ones. It is similar (but not pure) to object-oriented languages. Haxe includes a set of common functions that are supported across all platforms, such as numeric data types, text, arrays, binary and some common file formats.

The compiler supports novel features such as type inference, enforcing strict type safety at compile time. To date, Haxe supports nine target languages which allow for different use-cases: JavaScript, Neko, PHP, Python, C++, ActionScript3, Flash, Java and, C#. It provides support for creating interfaces using popular libraries such as OpenFL, HAXEUI and ScableUI (Haxe, 2017). For instance OpenFL is a framework built on Haxe that provides Flash Api on several mobile platforms, and tooling to help compile and test your app on each platform.

The Haxe language can compile to many different platforms being used in a variety of domains such game development, web development and mobile development. In particular, it facilitates mobile development sharing code between key platforms and accessing native functionality without sacrificing performance. This is achieved through the C++ target that allows developers to target major mobile platforms at native speed.

In summary, the idea behind Haxe is to allow developers choose the best platform for a specific development. To achieve this, it provides a standardized language, a standard library that works the same on all platforms and platform specific libraries that allow us accessing the full API for a given platform from Haxe.

A detailed description of the Haxe language may be found at (Haxe, 2017).

Related Work

Several works highlight research directions and challenges on the IoT. The spectrum of research needed to achieve IoT on a large scale requires research along with many different directions. Stankovic (2015) identifies five prominent research communities that involve the smart vision of the world: IoT, mobile computing, pervasive computing, wireless sensors, networks and cyber-physical systems. A basis for discussing open research problems in the IoT and a vision for how the IoT could change the world in the next years are presented.

Miranda et al. (2015) propose an infrastructure that supports the evolution from the "Internet of Things" to the "Internet of People" (IoP).The IoP is used in the sense of bringing the IoT closer to people, for easily integrate them and exploit its benefits.

Gonzalez Garcia et al. (2015) define a domain-specific language (DSL) that allows specifying the coordination and communication between different types of smart objects. Their approach focuses on the IoT as a paradigm that promotes a smart world in which different smart objects, sensors and in general devices are integrated to perform tasks.

Zanella et al. (2014) present a discussion of the IoT for smart cities. The authors describe a general reference framework for the design of an urban IoT. An implementation of an urban IoT that has been realized in the city of Padova is described. Key research topics are enumerated and research problems within these topics are discussed.

Next, existing approaches for the development of mobile applications related in some way with our approach are described.

Braun and Eckhaus (2008) propose a new software architecture with the objective of providing the same service as mobile Web service as well as mobile application. The authors report on the feasibility study that they conducted in order to evaluate whether to use model-driven software development for developing mobile applications. They argue that the architecture is flexible enough to support mobile Web services and mobile applications at the same time. They have develop a metamodel to describe mobile application and have shown how to generate mobile application from that model.

Various authors describe challenges of mobile software development, for example, Dehlinger and Dixon (2011) highlight creating user interfaces for different kinds of mobile devices, providing reusable applications across multiple mobile platforms, designing context aware applications and handling their complexity and, specifying requirements uncertainty. Issues related to ensuring that the application provides sufficient performance while maximizing battery life are remarked in (Thompson et al., 2014).

A proposal for supporting mobile application development by using models as inputs to an emulator is outlined at (Bowen and Hinze, 2011). The authors describe an MDD-based emulator for using in the design of graphical interfaces and interactions. They propose transform functional behavior and requirement models with design restrictions into emulated applications.

Kramer and Clark (2010) describe a DSL (Domain Specific Language), named MobDSL, to generate applications for multiple mobile platforms. They perform the domain analysis on two cases in the Android and iPhone platforms. This analysis allows inferring the basic requirements of the language defined by MobDSL.

ANDRIU, a reverse engineering tool based on static analysis of source code for transforming user interface tiers from desktop application to Android, is described in (Pérez Castillo et al., 2013). ANDRIU has been developed for migrating traditional systems to Android applications although it was designed to be extended for different migrations to others mobile platforms.

Islam (2014) describes six major trends affecting future smartphone design and use: personal computers, the IoT, multimedia delivery, low power operation, wearable computing and context awareness.

Acerbis et al. (2015) describe a comprehensive tool suite called WebRatio Mobile Platform for model-driven development of mobile applications. It is based on an extended version of OMG standard language called IFML (Interaction Flow Modeling Language) empowered with primitives tailored to mobile systems that enable specification of mobile specific behaviors.

Joshi et al (2015) bring out the findings of the experiments carried out to understand the impact of application characteristics, cloud and architecture and the android emulator used, on application performance when the application is augmented to cloud.

Ejarque, Miccsik and Badia (2015) present a solution for facilitating the migration of applications to the cloud, inferring the most suitable deployment model for the application and automatically deploying it in the available Cloud providers.

Favre (2010) describes a reverse engineering approach that fits with MDD. It explains a framework to integrate different techniques that come from compiler theory, metamodeling and formal specification is presented. It emphasizes the use of static and dynamic analysis for generating MDA models.

A reengineering process that integrates traditional reverse engineering techniques such as static and dynamic analysis with MDA is presented at (Améndola & Favre, 2013). The article describes a case study that shows how to move CRM (Customer Relationship Management) applications from desktop to mobile platforms. The proposal was validated in the open source application platform Eclipse, EMF, EMP, ATL and Android platform. Diaz Bilotto and Favre (2016) describe a migration process from Java to mobile platforms through the multiplatform language Haxe.

A migration process from C++ to mobile platforms based on ADM standards such as GASTM and KDM is described at (Martinez, Pereira, & Favre, 2017).

A MODERNIZATION FRAMEWORK

We propose a framework for the modernization of non-mobile software to new technologies. According to the three crucial concepts of MDE, the framework provides sets of models, metamodels and transformations. Figure 2 depicts the main components of the framework.

Three different types of models are distinguished: Platform Independent models (PIM), Platform Specific Model (PSM) and Implementation Specific Model (ISM). A PIM is a model with a high level of abstraction that is independent of an implementation technology. A PSM is a tailored model to specify a system in terms

Figure 2. Modernization framework

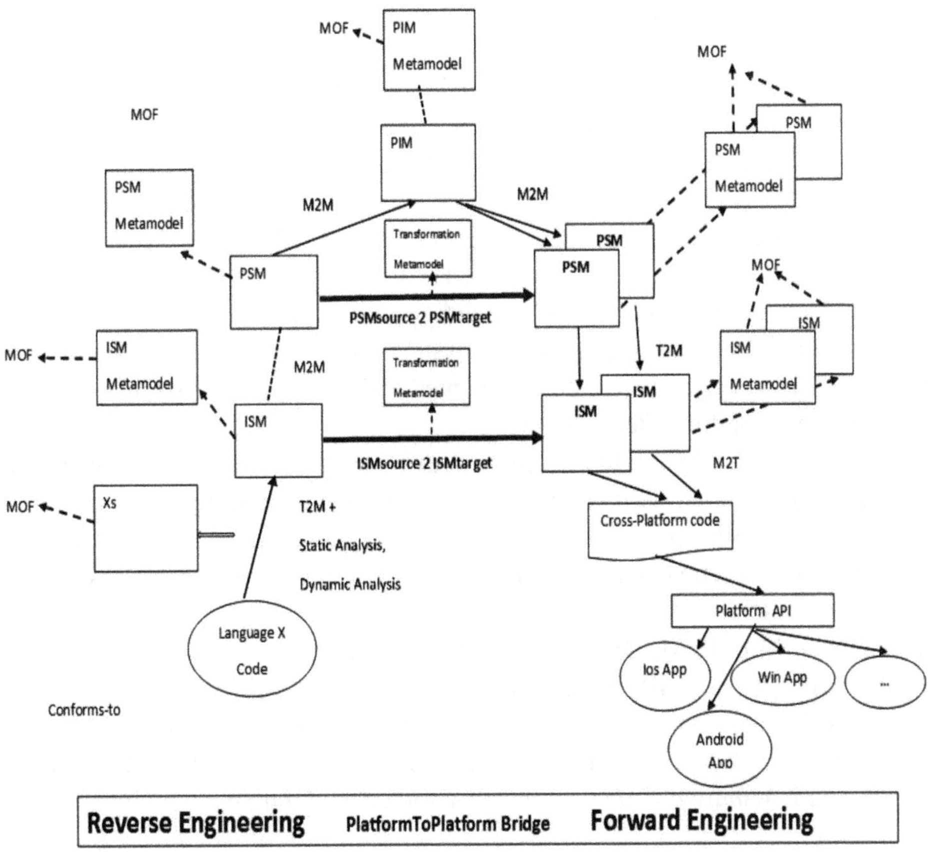

of specific platform. PIM and PSM are expressed in UML and OCL. The subset of UML diagrams that are useful for PSM includes class diagram, object diagram, state diagram, interaction diagram and package diagram. On the other hand, a PIM can be expressed by means of use case diagrams, activity diagrams, interactions diagrams to model system processes and, state diagrams to model lifecycle of the system entities. An ISM is a specification of the implementation (source code) in terms of models.

The framework includes PSMs and ISMs related to the source and target platform. The target PSM and target ISM are related to a cross-platform language that allows writing mobile applications that can be deployed on all major mobile platforms.

Metamodeling is a powerful technique to specify families of models. A metamodel is a model that defines the language for expressing a model, i.e. "a model of models". A metamodel is an explicit model of the constructs and rules needed to build specific models. It is a description of all the concepts that can be used in a model. MOF metamodels use an object modeling framework that is essentially a subset of UML 2.5 core. The modeling concepts are metaobjects, data types which model other data, and packages which modularize the models. At this level MOF metamodels describe families of ISM, PSM and PIM. Every ISM, PSM and PIM conforms to a MOF metamodel.

The framework includes different kinds of transformations: T2M (Text-to-Model), M2M (Model-to-Model) and M2T (Model-to-Text).

T2M transformations allow representing the source code of the program in terms of a model compatible with MOF. They require to have a metamodel that describes the grammar of the source language. First, a representation of the original code in terms of an Abstract Syntax Tree (AST) is built. The next step in the reverse engineering process involves applying traditional techniques for static and dynamic analysis. The basic representation of the static analysis is a direct graph that represents all data flow. Static analysis can be complemented with dynamic analysis that analyses traces of execution for different test cases.

Model-to-model (M2M) transformations provide a mechanism for automatically creating target models based on information contained in existing source models.

The framework distinguishes vertical and horizontal model-to-model transformations. Vertical transformations occur when a source model is transformed into a target model at a different abstraction level. They are useful in reverse engineering processes (ISM-to-PSM, PSM-to-PIM transformations) or forward engineering (PIMtoPSM, PSMtoISM). Horizontal transformations involves transforming a source model into a target model that is at the same abstraction level. They are bridges between different platforms at the same abstraction level (ISM or PSM), for instance *ISMsource2ISMtarget* and *PSMsource2PSMtarget*.

M2T transformations focuses on the generation of textual artifacts from models. In our context, M2T transformations are the processes to extract code from models following the MDE principles.

The framework shows different scenarios of modernization to adapt software to diverse mobile platforms. In the most general form, reverse engineering processes extract PIM models from the code, which are transformed into code through MDD processes for forward engineering. Reverse engineering processes can also recover PSMs that can be restructured at the same level of abstraction through a migration between different platforms. Different realizations of this framework were analyzed. Next we will describe the realizations of the framework for the migration of C / C ++ and Java code to mobile platforms and the reverse engineering of Java code to UML models.

ANALYZING DIFFERENT REALIZATIONS OF THE FRAMEWORK

This section is about customizations of the framework. First, we partially show the metamodels that had to be defined in order to realize the objectives of our project: the C/C++ metamodel and the Haxe metamodel. The section "*From C/C++ to mobile platforms*" describes a realization of the framework for migrating (at ISM level) C/ C++ code to Haxe and the generation of mobile applications that run over different platforms. The section "*From Java to mobile platforms*" describes a realization of the framework for migrating Java to Haxe. Finally, the section "*Reverse engineering Java Code to UML Models*" describes other customization for reverse engineering Java code to PIMs models expressed on UML.

The proposal was validated in the open source application platform Eclipse considering that some of its frameworks and tools are aligned with MDE standards. For example, EMF has evolved starting from the experience of the Eclipse community to implement a variety of tools and to date is highly related to MDE. Ecore is the core metamodel at the heart of EMF that can be considered the official implementation of MOF. The subproject M2M supports model transformations that take one or more models as input to produce one or more models as output. ATL is a model transformation language and a toolkit that provides ways to produce a set of target models from a set of source models develop on top of the Eclipse platform.

The Haxe and C++ metamodels were developed from the grammars of the languages using the Ecore metamodeling graphical language and the OclInEcore textual representation of them that allows us greater readability, modifiability and integration with versioning tools. Other advantage of OclInEcore is allowing to attach OCL expressions in the same file in which the metamodel is written. Ecore metamodels can be integrated with formal specification languages, based on the algebraic formalism. In the context of our research we define the NEREUS language that is a formal notation closed to MOF metamodels that allows meta-designers who must manipulate metamodels to understand their formal specification. The semantic of MOF metamodels (that is specified in OCL) can be enriched and refined by integrating it with NEREUS. This integration facilitates proofs and test of models and model transformations via the formal specification of metamodels (Favre, 2009; Favre and Duarte, 2016).

The C++ Metamodel

The C++ metamodel conforms to ECORE and is partially shown in Figure 3. The root metaclass is *Program* that represents a C++ program, which owns source files, instances of *TranslationUnit*. A translation unit contains declarations such as block declaration, function definitions, template declarations, among others. A *SimpleDeclaration*, instance of *Block-Declaration*, has a *DeclSpecifierSeq* that is a sequence of *DeclSpecifiers* which refers to a declaration specifiers and a type specifier. In addition, a simple declaration has an *InitDeclaratorList* containing a variable declaration list that is a list of specifiers and the name of a variable and its corresponding initialization. A *FunctionDefinition* has a *Declarator* containing the function identifier and the parameter list. *Function* and *CtorOrDestFunction*, instances of *FunctionDefinition*, have a body that contains compound statements such as declarations, iterations, and selections. In addition, a *Function* has a *DeclSpecifierSeq* that is a sequence of *DeclSpecifiers* such as function specifiers and a type specifier. *TypeSpecifier* subclasses are *SimpleTypeSpecifier*, *ClassSpecifier* and *EnumSpecifier* among others. A *ClassSpecifier* has a *ClassHead* containing the class key (class or struct) and a *MemberSpecification* that contains *MemberDeclarations* such as variables, function declarations, function definitions, constructors, destructor and template members. The full C/C++ metamodel may be found at (Duthey and Spina, 2016).

The Haxe Metamodel

The HAXE metamodel conforms to Ecore metamodel. It is partially shown in Figure 4. The main metaclasses of the HAXE metamodel are those that allow specifying an application using HAXE as language.

One of the main metaclasses of the metamodel is *HAXEModel*,that serves as element container used to describe an application and store additional information on it, for example, some options of compilation and different metaclasses for modeling such as modules, classes and packages. *HAXEModel* owns *HAXEModule* and *HAXEPathReferentiable*.

Figure 3. The C/C++ Metamodel

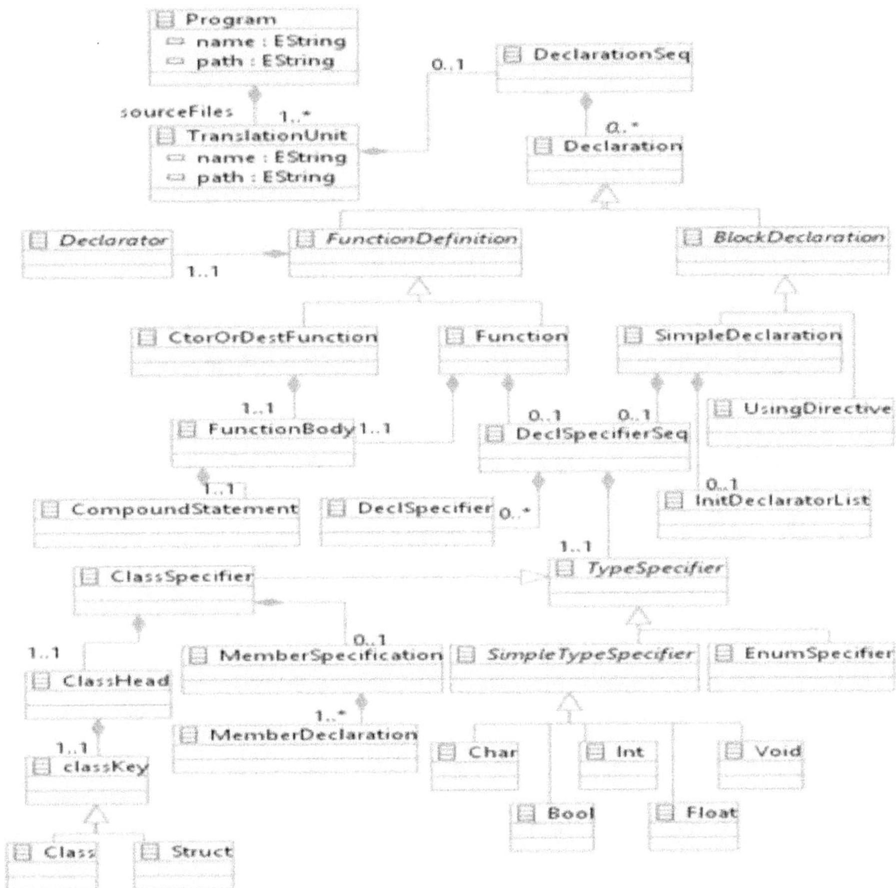

Starting from the relations *HaxeModules*, *referenced* and *elements*, the class *HAXEModel* allows storing different information. Relation *HaxeModules* allows accessing the different

HAXE modules used in the project. Through relation *elements*, it is possible to access the different elements of the package tree. Relation *referenced* provides access to elements, which are referenced in the project but are not defined completely. In the case of relations and referenced elements, the type used is *HAXEPathReferentiable*, which is the parent type of metaclasses such as *HAXEType* and *HAXEPackage*. The HAXE language includes different kind of types such as class (the types class and interface), function, abstract type, enumeration, and anonymous structures. A full description of the Haxe metamodel may be found at (Diaz Bilotto, 2015; Duthey and Spina, 2016).

Figure 4. The Haxe Metamodel

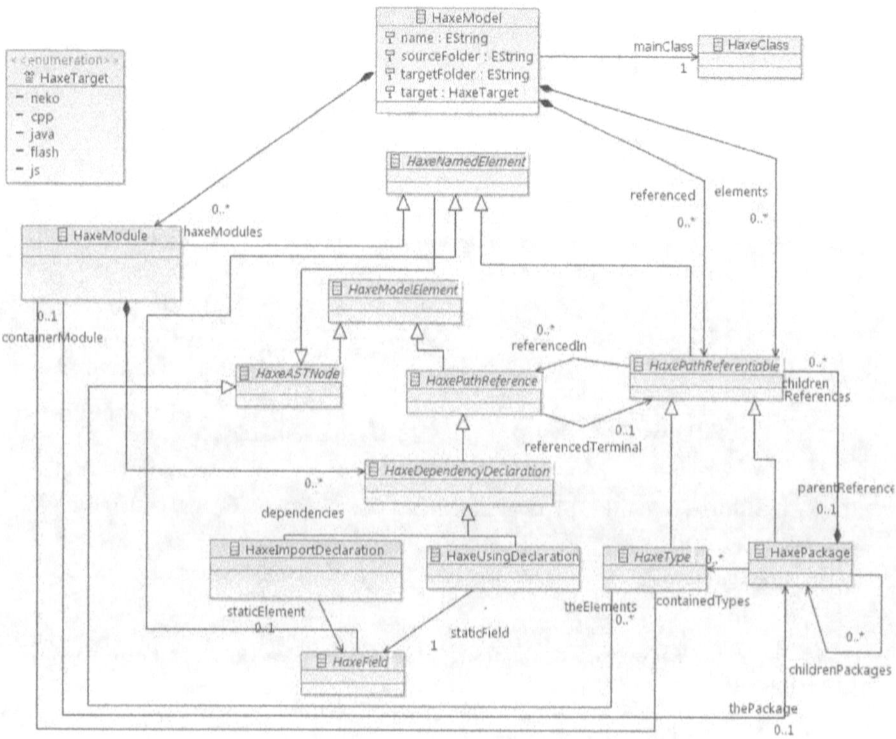

From C/C++ to Mobile Platforms

Figure 5 depicts a framework realization. The initial transformation T2M obtains a code model that conforms to the C/C++ metamodel. This transformation was based on the generation of a parsing tree with the ANTLR tool through the C ++ grammar. Also a discoverer of a C ++ model that conforms to the C ++ metamodel was built. It is a Java program whose input is the syntax tree and its output an ISM, the C++ model of the code.

M2M transformations were defined in ATL, the most mature transformation language in the context of MDE. ATL is a model transformation language and toolkit developed on top of the Eclipse platform. It provides ways to produce a set of target models from a set of source models. The ATL Integrated Development Environment (IDE) provides a number of standard development tools (such as syntax highlighting and debugger) that aims to facilitate the development of ATL transformations. ATL is a hybrid language that provides a mix of declarative and imperative constructs.

A model-to-model transformation from C++ to Haxe, called *C/C++ 2 Haxe*, was defined in ATL. It takes as input the model obtained in the reverse engineering phase

Figure 5. The C/C++ Metamodel

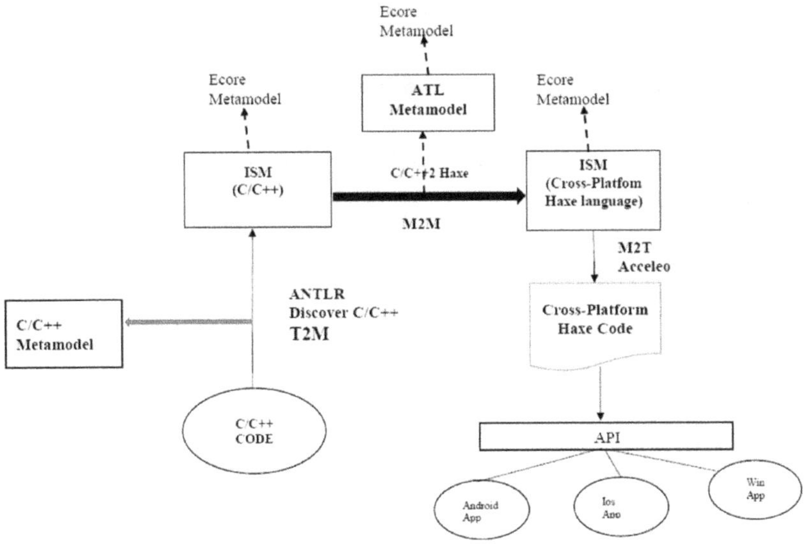

and release a Haxe model. The transformation specifies families of transformations that produce Haxe models (target) from C++ models (source). Both source and target models must conform to the C++ metamodel and Haxe metamodel respectively.

ATL mainly focuses on the model-to-model transformations, which can be specified by means of ATL modules. An ATL module is composed of the following elements:

- A header section that defines the names of the transformation module and the variables of the source and target metamodels.
- An optional import section that enables to import some existing ATL libraries.
- A set of helpers that can be used to define variables and functions.
- A set of rules that defines how source model elements are matched and navigated to create and initialize the elements of the target models.

The *C/C++ 2 Haxe* transformation conforms to the ATL metamodel,that, in the same way conforms to Ecore. Following, we partially show this transformation.

```
module CPP2Haxe ;
c r e a t e OUT: Haxe from IN: cpp;
helper context cpp ! CppPackage def: get_packages () : Sequence
(cpp ! CppPackage) =
self . childrenReferences -> iterate (elem ;acc: Sequence (cpp
```

```
! CppPackage)=
Sequence {} | if(elem. ocl IsTypeOf (cpp ! CppPackage)) then
acc->append (elem)->
union (elem . get_packages ()) else acc->union (Sequence {})
endif) ;
helper context cpp ! CppModel def: get_allpackages (): Sequence
(cpp ! CppPackage) =
self. elements->iterate (elem ; acc: Sequence (cpp !
CppPackage)= Sequence {} |
if (elem.ocl IsTypeOf (cpp! CppPackage)) then acc->append
(elem)->
union (elem. get_packages ()) else acc->union (Sequence {})
endif) ;
helper context cpp ! CppPackage def: get_all classfiles ():
Sequence (cpp ! CppClassFile) =
self.childrenReferences -> iterate (elem; acc: Sequence (cpp !
CppClassFile) = Sequence {} |
if (elem.ocl IsTypeOf (cpp ! CppClassFile))  then acc->append
(elem) else acc->union (Sequence {}) endif) ;
helper context cpp ! CppModel def: get_classfiles(): Sequence
(cpp ! CppClassfile) =
self. get_allpackages () -> collect (package | package . get_
allclassfiles()) ;
helper context cpp ! CppPackage def: get_childrenreferences():
Sequence (cpp ! CppPathReferentiable) =
self.childrenReferences -> iterate (elem ; acc: Sequence (cpp
! CppPathReferentiable) = Sequence {} |if (elem .oclIsTypeOf
(cpp! CppPackage)) then acc->append (elem)
else if (elem. oclIsypeOf (cpp! CppClassFi le)) then acc->union
(elem. elements)
else acc->append (Sequence {}) endif endif) ;
helper context cpp!CppClass def: get_superclass (): Haxe !
HaxeClassifierAccess =
if self . superClass. isEmpty () then OclUndefined
else thisModule.get_generalization (self. superClass ->first
()) endif ;
helper context cpp ! CppClassFile def: get_imports():
Sequence (Haxe! HaxeImportDeclaration)=
if self.imports. isEmpty() then Sequence {} else self.imports
->
```

```
iterate (elem;acc: Sequence (Haxe! HaxeImportDeclaration) =
Sequence {} |
if elem.pathImport.oclIsUndefined () then acc->append (Sequence
{})
else elem.pathImport. elements-> iterate (elem2; acc2: Sequence
(Haxe!HaxeImportDeclaration)=
Sequence {} | if elem2.oclIsTypeOf (cpp!CppClass)
then acc2->append (thisModule.get_classimport(elem2)) else
acc2->append (Sequence {}) endif)
endif) endif ;
helper context cpp!CppForStatement def: get_blockStatements():
Sequence (cpp! CppExpression) =
if self.theBody = OclUndefined then Sequence {} else if self.
theBody. oclIsTypeOf (cpp!CppBlock) then self. theBody. get_
statements () else
if (self.theBody. oclIsTypeOf (cpp ! CppAssignamentStatement)
or self. theBody. oclIsTypeOf(cpp!CppMethodInvocation) or
self. theBody. oclIsTypeOf (cpp!CppPostfixExpression)) then
Sequence { thisModule .statementize (self.theBody)} else
Sequence {self. theBody} endif endif endif ;
…
rule model {
from s: cpp!CppModel
to t: Haxe!HaxeModel (name <- s.name, sourceFolder <- s.
sourceFolder, targetFolder <-
s. targetFolder, referenced <- s. orphanTypes -> select(x |
x.usages InTypeAcces s->
notEmpty () and x.oclIsKindOf (cpp!CppType) and (not x
.oclIsTypeOf (cpp! CppClass))) ->
collect (x | thisModule.Type (x)) ->asSet (), elements <- s .
get_allpackages(),HaxeModules <- s. get_classfiles(), mainClass
<- s. mainClass)}
abstract rule namedElement
{from s: cpp! CppNamedElement
to t: Haxe! HaxeNamedElement (name <- s. name)}
rule packages extends namedElement {
from s: cpp ! CppPackage
to t: Haxe!HaxePackage (parentReference <- s. parentReference,
childrenReferences <- s. get_childrenreferences ())}
rule modules {
```

```
from s: cpp!CppClassFile
to t: Haxe! HaxeModule (name <- s.name,thePackage <-s.
parentReference,
theElement s <- s.elements, dependencies <- s. get_imports ())
}
rule classes extends namedElement {
from s: cpp!CppClass
to t:Haxe! HaxeClass (HaxeFields <- s. cppFields-
>reject (classes |classes. oclIsKindOf (cpp
!CppDestructor)),generalization <- s.get_superclass(),
typeParameters <- s .typeParameters)}
rule typeParameter extends namedElement{
from s: cpp!CppTypeParameter
to t: Haxe ! HaxeTypeParameter (bounds <- s.bounds)}
lazy rule get_generalization {
from s: cpp!CppClass
to t: Haxe ! HaxeClassifierAccess (referencedTerminal <- s) }
lazy rule get_classimport {
from s: cpp ! CppClass
To t: Haxe ! HaxeImportDeclaration (referencedTerminal <- s) }
rule enumTransformation extends namedElement{
from  s: cpp !CppEnum
to t: Haxe !HaxeEnum (HaxeFields <- s.literals)}
```

All models obtained in this chain of transformations are saved in the interchange format XMI, an OMG standard that combines XML, MOF and UML for integrating tools, repositories, and applications in distributed heterogeneous environments (XMI, 2015).

Finally, from a model Haxe, it is possible to generate a source code in Haxe by using an M2T transformation defined in Acceleo which is a code generation system based on MDE standards. More precisely, it is the oficial implementation of MOFM2T, a standard of OMG, for performing model-to-text transformations. Acceleo contains a code generation modules editor with syntax highlighting, completion, real time error detection and incremental code generation. It allows code generation from any kind of metamodel compatible with EMF like UML and Ecore.

Haxe allows writing mobile applications that target all major mobile platforms in a straightforward way. The generated code is syntactically correct, although, it does not compile on other platforms without doing changes due to the code refers to proprietary technologies of C++. To run on mobile environments, these technologies can be replaced with OpenFL and HAXEUI that is an open source, multi-platform application-centric user interface framework designed for HAXE and OpenFL (OpenFl, 2017).

From Java to Mobile Platforms

Figure 6 depicts a framework realization that allows migrating Java to Haxe. It is based on Java and Haxe metamodels and a bridge between them through ATL transformations. The Java metamodel is based on the Eclipse JDT Java model and covers the full abstract syntax ranging from package declarations and classes to method bodies, expressions and statements. A detailed description of the Java metamodel may be found at (Eclipse, 2017).

The initial transformation T2M obtain a code model that conforms to a Java metamodel. Model extraction is performed automatically by the component Java Model Discovery of the Modisco framework (Bruneliere et al, 2014; MoDisco, 2017).

The platform-to-platform bridge is defined as an ATL transformation between the source metamodel Java and the target metamodel Haxe. The main transformations are *java2haxe, javaHaxeRefactoring* and *haxeImports*. The *java2haxe* transformation is central and transforms syntactic elements between the Java metamodel and the Haxe metamodel. The *javaHaxeRefactoring* transformation reorganizes and modifies the syntactic elements in such a way to adapt own behavior of the Java language. The *haxeImports* performs changes in the imports of the own packages of the Java

Figure 6. From Java to mobile platforms

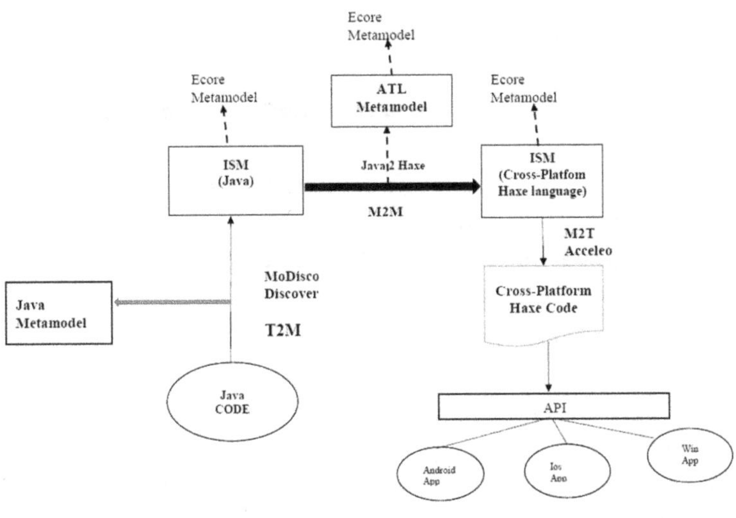

framework, which require a specific treatment. In this transformation, import clauses are added for items belonging to the package *java.lang* which are recognized implicitly by the framework as dependencies in Java but need to be explicit in HaXe classes.

In the following, the *java2haxe* transformation is partially shown. A detail description of the ATL transformations may be found at (Diaz Bilotto, 2015)

```
module java2haxe;
create OUT: haxe from IN: java;
helper context java!BodyDeclaration def: isMainMethod():
Boolean =
if (self.modifier -> oclIsUndefined() or self.name ->
oclIsUndefined())
then  false  else self.name -> matches('main') and self.
modifier.static endif;
helper context java!Model def: hasMainClass(): Boolean =
java!ClassDeclaration.allInstances() -> select(x |
x.isMainClass()) -> isEmpty();
helper context java!Model def: chooseMainClass():
java!ClassDeclaration =
java!ClassDeclaration.allInstances() -> select(x |
x.isMainClass()) -> first();
helper context java!ClassDeclaration def: isMainClass():
Boolean =
self.bodyDeclarations -> exists(x | x.isMainMethod());
helper context java!BodyDeclaration def: isStaticBody():
Boolean =
if (self.modifier.oclIsUndefined()) then false else self.
modifier.static endif;
helper context java!BodyDeclaration def: isAbstract(): Boolean
=
if (self.modifier.oclIsUndefined()) then false else self.
modifier.inheritance = #"abstract" endif;
helper context java!AbstractTypeDeclaration def:
noConstructor(): Boolean =
if (self.bodyDeclarations -> oclIsUndefined())
then true
else if (self.bodyDeclarations -> isEmpty())
        then true
        else self.bodyDeclarations -> select(x | x.oclIsKindOf(
java!ConstructorDeclaration)) -> isEmpty()
```

```
        endif
endif;
helper context java!AbstractTypeDeclaration def:
multipleConstructor(): Boolean =
if (self.noConstructor())
then false
else self.bodyDeclarations -> select(x | x.oclIsTypeOf(java!Con
structorDeclaration))-> size() > 1
endif;
helper context java!AbstractTypeDeclaration def:
isInnerClass(): Boolean =
if (self.abstractTypeDeclaration -> oclIsUndefined()) then
false else true endif;
helper context java!ASTNode def: container():
java!AbstractMethodDeclaration =
if (self.refImmediateComposite()->oclIsKindOf(java!AbstractMeth
odDeclaration))
then self.refImmediateComposite() else self.
refImmediateComposite().container()
endif;
…
rule model {
from javaModel: java!Model
to  haxeModel: haxe!HaxeModel (
name <- javaModel.name,
elements <- javaModel.ownedElements,
referenced <- javaModel.orphanTypes -> select(x |
x.usagesInTypeAccess ->
notEmpty() and x.oclIsKindOf(java!Type) and
(not x.oclIsTypeOf(java!ParameterizedType)) and
(not x.oclIsTypeOf(java!WildCardType))) -> collect(x |
thisModule.Type(x))-> asSet(),
haxeModules <- javaModel.compilationUnits,mainClass <-
javaModel.chooseMainClass())
do {thisModule.targetModel <- haxeModel;}}
abstract rule ASTNode {
from  s: java!ASTNode
to t: haxe!HaxeASTNode (comments <- s.comments)}
abstract rule namedElement extends ASTNode{
from s: java!NamedElement
```

```
to t: haxe!HaxeNamedElement (
name <- s.name)}
rule packages extends namedElement {
from s: java!Package
to t: haxe!HaxePackage (
parentReference <- s.package,
childrenReferences <- s.ownedPackages)}
abstract rule typeDeclaration extends namedElement {
from s: java!AbstractTypeDeclaration
to t: haxe!HaxeType (
commentsAfterDeclaration <- s.commentsAfterBody,
commentsBeforeDeclaration <- s.commentsBeforeBody,
parentReference <- s.package)}
```

The forward engineering from a model Haxe is based on M2T transformations defined in Acceleo in the way described at previous section.

Reverse Engineering Java Code to UML Models

Reverse Engineering is the process of analyzing available software artifacts such as requirements, design, architectures, code or byte code, with the objective of extracting information and providing high-level views on the underlying system (Canfora, Di Penta and Cerulo, 2011) (Favre, 2010).

The reverse engineering process begins with two crucial steps *model discovery* and *static analysis* that provide as a result a refined model (Figure 7). This Java model is the input to the *model transformation* step. Next, we describe them.

Model Discovery

In this step, the source code of the program is represented through a model of the Java language, which is a representation of the input program. This is a very important step, since it allows obtaining the implementation of the program in terms of a model compatible with an Ecore metamodel.

Figure 7. Reverse engineering: From Java to PIM

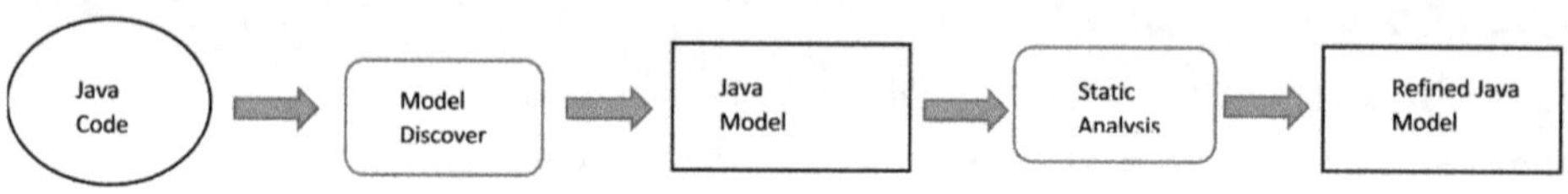

The resulting model is an equivalent representation of the original program by an abstract syntax tree, and therefore, any reverse engineering task to be performed on the system can be performed, with the same result, using this model as a valid input representation (ASTM, 2011).This step requires to have a metamodel that describes the grammar of the source language. In our case the Java metamodel used is provided by the MoDisco tool. This metamodel is based on the Eclipse JDT Java model, and covers the full abstract syntax tree of a Java program, ranging from package declarations and classes to method bodies, expressions and statements.

Model extraction is performed automatically by the component Java Model Discovery of the MoDisco framework. The resulting model is called *initial model* since it has a direct correspondence with the elements of the original system. In the context of MoDisco this phase of the reverse engineering process is called *Model Discovery*. The idea is to represent the original system using a set of models without loss of information.

Static Analysis

The next step in the proposed reverse engineering process involves applying traditional static analysis techniques on the Java model obtained in the previous step.

The concepts and algorithms of data flow analysis described in (Tonella and Potrich, 2005) are adapted for reverse engineering object-oriented code. Data flow analysis infers information about the behavior of a program by only analyzing the text of the source code.

The basic representation of this static analysis is the Object Flow Graph (OFG) that allows tracing information of object interactions from the object creation, through its assignments to variables, attributes or their use in messages (method invocations). OFG is defined as a direct graph that represents all data flows linking objects in a program.

The static analysis is data flow sensitive, but control flow insensitive. This means that programs with different control flows and the same data flows are associated with the same analysis results. The choice of this program representation is motivated by the computational complexity of the involved algorithms. On the one hand, control flow sensitive analysis is computationally intractable and on the other hand, it is aligned to the “nature” of the object-oriented programs whose execution models impose more constraints on the data flows than on the control flows. A consequence of the control flow insensitivity is that the construction of the OFG can be described with reference to a simplified, abstract version of the object-oriented languages in which instructions related to flow control are ignored. On this OFG different types of propagation are performed. They allow obtaining information used to generate the various UML diagrams in the next step. The information resulting from this analysis is stored in the original model, either in the form of modifications to existing elements or as additional elements incorporated into the model.

Model Transformation

The "refined" Java model obtained in the previous step conforms to the input of the third and final step in the process of reverse engineering called *Model Transformation.* They are defined as model-to-model (M2M) transformations and specified in ATL.

We describe, as an example, the extraction of a representation of the interactions that occur among objects in an object-oriented system. Starting from a Java Project a Java code model (an abstract syntax tree that conforms to an Ecore metamodel) is obtained. This step is performed automatically by using the component Java Model Discovery of MoDisco.

The static recovery of the interactions among objects is done, on the one hand, inferring from the code the objects created by the program that are accessible through program variables. On the other hand, each call to a method is solved in terms of the possible source and target objects involved in the message interchange.

This information can be obtained by means of the propagation through the OFG of the objects generated at each point of the program that represents the creation of a new instance. The result of this stage will provide for each node of the OFG the set of objects to which the node can be linked at some point.

Following, we exemplify the ATL transformation called *Java2SequenceDiagram* transformation. It allows recovering a sequence diagram for each selected Java method. Different ATL rules specify the mappings that allow to generate elements of the sequence diagram from the input Java model. As an example we show a rule included in this transformation that express that for each interaction in a Java program represented by *MethodDeclaration*, an Interaction in UML is created.

```
rule javaInputMethodDeclaration2UMLInteraction {
from
javamethod: java!MethodDeclaration (javamethod.proxy = false
and thisModule.isInputMethod(javamethod))
using {
sourceLifeline: UML!Lifeline =
thisModule.getInitialLifeline(javamethod);
callerStack: Sequence(java!AbstractMethodDeclaration) =
Sequence{javamethod};
sourceMethodActivation: UML!ActionExecutionSpecification =
thisModule.createActionExecutionSpecification(sourceLifeline,ja
vamethod.name);
```

```
}
to
umlinteraction: UML!Interaction (name <- javamethod.name)
do {
thisModule.model.packagedElement <- thisModule.model.
packagedElement ->
including(umlinteraction);
thisModule.addExecutionEventToModel(sourceMethodActivation.
start.event);
 thisModule.addExecutionEventToModel(sourceMethodActivation.
finish.event);
umlinteraction.lifeline <- umlinteraction.lifeline
->including(sourceLifeline);
umlinteraction.fragment <- umlinteraction.fragment -> including
(sourceMethodActivation);
umlinteraction.fragment <- umlinteraction.fragment -> including
(sourceMethodActivation.start);
thisModule.translateStatements(umlinteraction,umlinteraction,
sourceLifeline,javamethod.body.statements, callerStack);
umlinteraction.fragment <- umlinteraction.fragment ->
including(sourceMethodActivation.finish);
}
}
```

A plugin tool integrated to Eclipse that provides support for reverse engineering UML diagrams from Java code was developed (class diagram, sequence diagrams and use case diagrams). It was implemented in Java using the infrastructure provided by EMF and PDE (Plug-in Development Environment). Besides, it uses other framework and technologies such as MoDisco and ATL. The full description may be found at (Galitiello and Rolandi, 2015).

DISCUSSION

The validation of the process showed that it is possible to migrate Java or C / C ++ software to mobile platforms semi-automatically. In particular it is possible to migrate the logic of software applications and run them on mobile platforms without having to completely rewrite them. Due the fact that the objective of the migration is not only "compile" an application in a mobile platform but also to create a fully functional version of the application using quality criteria, small adjustments had to be made.

We believe that our approach provides benefits with respect to ad-hoc migration. One of the benefits of applying MDE techniques is to increase productivity in software development due to the automation that is introduced in the generation of artifacts. Besides, to use MDE in migration projects is more cost-effective when the same process must be repeated frequently as the case of migrations to different platforms.

A migration process must be independent of the source and target technologies. In our approach, the intermediate models act as decoupling elements between source and target technologies. The independence is achieved with injectors and, M2M and M2T transformations. Besides, in a transformation sequence, models could be an extension point to incorporate new stages.

The migration process is based on MOF-like metamodeling that is a powerful approach for interoperability. It outperforms XML due to its expressive power and, the existence of powerful model transformation languages to implement the transformations required at the different stages of the migration process. MOF-like metamodeling also includes the possibility to attach OCL restrictions to complete the model specification. In addition, MOF-like metamodels allow a clear separation of abstract and concrete syntax and thus, associate different notations for a model. It is worth mentioning that the generation of models by ATL transformations, aims to generate models "*Correct-by-Construction*" with respect to metamodel specifications.

Our approach involves preliminary activities that require time and cost, for instance the developer need to define metamodels and transformations if they do not exist. It is assumed that using a brute-force redevelopment, developers do not need training to write metamodels and model transformations. However, model transformations allow developers to concentrate on conceptual aspects of the relations between models and then to delegate most of the migration process to the transformation rules, whereas in the brute-force redevelopment, developers need to migrate by hand the legacy systems, making over and over again the same task.

The following limitations our approach were observed. The set of metamodels and discovers that can be used is limited. In our project it was necessary to define metamodels for the C / C ++ and Haxe languages and, a discoverer for C/C ++. In addition, although Eclipse provides its modeling framework, the tools are not yet mature, especially for the transformation phase and forward engineering, limited by scalability problems. Another aspect to consider is that the graphic interfaces of the programs are not migrated if they are linked to specific libraries of languages and their code is not accessible, meaning that it is not possible to perform a fully automatic migration in many cases.

Beyond the previous issues, we consider that mobile application developers need frequently adapt software components and applications developed in languages such as Java or C/C++. Then, model-driven migration processes could be reused and the cost of preliminary activities is recovered.

CONCLUSION AND FUTURE WORK

This chapter describes a modernization framework that allows migrating software to new technologies in which smartphones are its great facilitators such as the IoT. An integration of the MDE principles with the multiplatform language called Haxe is described. Different realizations of the framework for the migration of C/ C++ or Java software to different mobile platforms are presented. Our approach covers a migration method and the presentation of models, metamodels and model transformations that can be reused, modified for evolution purposes or extended for other purposes. The proposal is validated in the open source platform Eclipse, notably the projects built around EMF metamodeling framework.

The main results of the project are mentioned below. Regarding the definition of metamodels, the major contribution had to do with the specification of Ecore metamodels of the C / C++ and Haxe languages. These metamodels allowed that both, C / C ++ and Haxe languages, can be integrated into MDE processes. They are an important contribution to both the Eclipse community and the MDE community since there were no complete metamodels of these languages.

Regarding the implementation of discoverers, a discover C/C++ implementation was implemented. This allows to obtain an ISM model of the C ++ language through the reverse engineering of source code in C / C ++. In addition, reverse engineering processes from object-oriented code to PIM and PSM models expressed in UML models that follow MDE principles were defined.

As regards the definition of transformations, two bridge transformations were defined in ATL: *ISMJava2 Haxe* and *ISMC/C++ 2 Haxe*. They allow integrating the Java and C / C ++ languages with the Haxe language.

It is expected to continue working on the definition of metamodels and transformations. Rather than defining a tool that supports specific technologies, the idea is to define a pool of metamodels and transformations that can be reused in different modernization processes.

Starting from the gained experience in the metamodel definition, we propose to analyze the semiautomatic transformation of language grammars to Ecore metamodels. With regard to reverse engineering, it is proposed to define T2M transformations that integrate static analysis with dynamic one. In addition, an Haxe code generator from UML models is being developed to enrich forward engineering processes.

REFERENCES

Acceleo. (2017). *Obeo. Acceleo Generator*. Retrieved April 25, 2017 from http://www.eclipse.org/Acceleo/

Acerbis, R., Bongio, A., Brambilla, M., & Butti, S. (2015). *Engineering the Web in the Big Data Era*. In Lecture Notes in Computer Science: Vol. 9114. *Model-Driven Development Based on OMG's IFML with WebRatio Web and Mobile Platform* (pp. 605–608). Berlin: Springer-Verlag.

ADM. (2017). *Architecture-driven modernization task force*. Retrieved April 25 from http://www.adm.org

Améndola, F., & Favre, L. (2013). Adapting CRM Systems for Mobile Platforms: An MDA Perspective. *International Journal of Computer & Information Science*, *14*(1), 31–40.

ASTM. (2011). *Abstract Syntax Tree Metamodel, version 1.0, OMG Document Number: formal/2011-01-05*. Retrieved April, 25, 2017 from http://www.omg.org/spec/ASTM

ATL. (2017). *Atlas Transformation Language Documentation*. Retrieved April 25, 2017 from http://www.eclipse.org/atl/documentation/

Bowen, J., & Hinze, A. (2011). Supporting mobile application development with model-driven emulation. *Journal of the ECEASST*, *45*, 1–5.

Brambilla, M., Cabot, J., & Wimmer, M. (2012). *Model-Driven Software Enginneering in Practice, Synthesis Lectures on Software Engineering*. Morgan & Claypool Publishers.

Braun, P., & Eckhaus, R. (2008). Experiences on model-driven software development for mobile applications. In *Proceedings of Engineering of Computer-Based Systems, IEEE International Conference and Workshop on the Engineering of computer Base Systems* (pp. 490-493), Washington, DC: IEEE Computer Society. doi:10.1109/ECBS.2008.50

Bruneliere, N., Cabot, J., Dupé, G., & Madiot, F. (2014). MoDisco: A Model Driven Reverse Engineering Framework. *Information and Software Technology*, *56*(8), 1012–1032. doi:10.1016/j.infsof.2014.04.007

Canfora, G., Dipenta, M., & Ceruelo, L. (2011). Achievements and Challenges in Software Reverse Engineering. *Communications of the ACM*, *54*(4), 142–151. doi:10.1145/1924421.1924451

Cannasse, N. (2014). Haxe. Too good to be True? *GameDuell Tech Talk*. Retrieved April 25, 2017 from http://www.techtalk-berlin.de/news/read/nicolas-cannasse-introducing-Haxe/

Dasnois, B. (2011). *Haxe 2 Beginner's Guide*. Packt Publishing.

Dehlinger, J., & Dixon, J. (2011). Mobile application software engineering: Challenges and research directions. In *Proceedings of the Workshop on Mobile Software Engineering* (pp. 29-32). Berlin: Springer-Verlag.

Diaz Bilotto, P. (2015). *Software development for mobile applications through an integration of MDA and Haxe* (Undergraduate thesis). Computer Science Department, Universidad Nacional del Centro de la Provincia de Buenos Aires, Argentina.

Diaz Bilotto, P., & Favre, L. (2016). Migrating JAVA to Mobile Platforms through HAXE: An MDD Approach. In A. M. Cruz & S. Paiva (Eds.), *Modern Software Engineering Methodologies for Mobile and Cloud Environments* (pp. 240–268). Hershey, PA: IGI Global. doi:10.4018/978-1-4666-9916-8.ch013

Duthey, M., & Spina, C. (2016). *Migrating C/C++ to mobile platforms through MDD* (Undergraduate Thesis). Computer Science Department, Universidad Nacional del Centro de la Provincia de Buenos Aires, Argentina.

Eclipse. (2017). *Eclipse-The Eclipse Foundation open source community*. Retrieved from http://eclipse.org/

Ejarque, J., Micsik, A., & Badia, R. (2015). Towards Automatic Application Migration to Clouds. In *Proceedings IEEE 8th Int. Conf. on Cloud Computing (CLOUD)* (pp. 25-32). New York: IEEE.

EMF. (2017). *Eclipse Modeling Framework (EMF)*. Retrieved April 25, 2017 from http://www.eclipse.org/modeling/emf/

Favre, L. (2009) A Formal Foundation for Metamodeling. In *Proceedings of 14th Ada-Europe International Conference. Lecture Notes in Computer Science* (Vol 5570, pp.177-191). Berlin: Springer-Verlag. doi:10.1007/978-3-642-01924-1_13

Favre, L. (2010). *Model Driven Architecture for Reverse Engineering Technologies: Strategic Directions and System Evolution*. IGI Global. doi:10.4018/978-1-61520-649-0

Favre, L., & Duarte, D. (2016). Formal MOF Metamodeling and Tool Support. In *Proceedings of the 4th International Conference on Model-Driven Engineering and Software Development. MODELSWARD 2016* (pp. 99-110). Roma, Italy: SCITEPRESS (Science and Technology Publications).

Galitiello, E., & Rolandi, B. (2015). *Reverse engineering of Object-Oriented Code* (Thesis). Computer Science Department, Universidad Nacional del Centro de la Provincia de Buenos Aires, Argentina.

González García, C., & Espada, J. (2015). MUSPEL: Generation of Applications to Interconnect Heterogeneous Objects Using Model-Driven Engineering. In V. G. Díaz, J. M. C. Lovelle, & B. C. P. García-Bustelo (Eds.), *Handbook of Research on Innovations in Systems and Software Engineering* (pp. 365–385). Hershey, PA: IGI Global. doi:10.4018/978-1-4666-6359-6.ch015

Haxe. (2017). *The Haxe Language.* Retrieved April 25, 2017 from https://haxe.org/

Islam, N., & Want, R. (2014). Smarthphones: Past, present and future. *Pervasive Computing, 13*(4), 82–92. doi:10.1109/MPRV.2014.74

Joshi, P., Nivangune, A., Kumar, R., Kumar, S., Ramesh, R., Pani, S., & Chesum, A. (2015). Understanding the Challenges in Mobile Computation Offloading to Cloud through Experimentation. In *2nd ACM Int. Conf. on Mobile Software Engineering and Systems* (pp.158-159). Florence, Italy: ACM. doi:10.1109/MobileSoft.2015.43

KDM. (2016). *Knowledge Discovery Meta-Model (KDM), OMG Document Number: formal/2016-09-01*. Retrieved April, 25, 2017 from http://www.omg.org/spec/KDM/1.4

Kim, H. (2008). Frameworks of process improvement for mobile applications. *Engineering Letters, 16*(4), 550-555. Retrieved April 25, 2017 from http://www.engineeringletters.com/issues_v16/issue_4/EL_16_4_13.pdf

Kramer, D., Clark, T., & Oussena, S. (2010). MobDSL: A domain specific language for multiple mobile platform deployment. In *Proceedings of IEEE Int. Conf. on Networked Embedded Systems for Enterprise Applications* (pp. 1-7). Perth, Australia: IEEE. doi:10.1109/NESEA.2010.5678062

Martinez, L., Pereira, C., & Favre, L. (2017). Migrating C/C++ Software to Mobile Platforms in the ADM Context. *International Journal of Interactive Multimedia and Artificial Intelligence, 4*(3), 34–44. doi:10.9781/ijimai.2017.436

MDA. (2017). *The Model-Driven Architecture*. Retrieved April 25, 2017 from www.omg.org/mda/

Miranda, J., Makitalo, N., Garcia-Alonso, J., Berrocal, J., Mikkonen, T., Canal, C., & Murillo, J. (2015). From the Internet of Things to the Internet of People. *IEEE Internet Computing, 19*(2), 40–47. doi:10.1109/MIC.2015.24

MoDisco. (2017). *Model Discovery*. Retrieved April 25, 2017 from https://eclipse.org/MoDisco/

MOF. (2016). *Meta Object Facility (MOF) Core Specification, Version 2.5, OMG Document Number: formal/2016-11-01*. Retrieved April 25, 2017 from http://www.omg.org/spec/MOF/2.5.1/

OCL. (2014). *OMG Object constraint language (OCL), version 2.4. OMG Document Number: formal/2014-02-03*. Retrieved April, 25, 2017 from http://www.omg.org/spec/OCL/2.4

OPEN FL. (2017). *OPEN FL 4.7*. Retrieved April 25, 2017 from http://www.openfl.org/

Pérez Castillo, R., García Rodriguez, I., Gómez Cornejo, R., Fernández Ropero, M., & Piattini, M. (2013). ANDRIU. A Technique for Migrating Graphical User Interfaces to Android. In *Proceedings of The 25th International Conference on Software Engineering and Knowledge Engineering* (pp. 516-519). Academic Press.

QVT. (2012). *QVT: MOF 2.0 query, view, transformation: Version 1.1*. OMG Document Number: formal/2011-01-01. Retrieved from http://www.omg.org/spec/QVT/1.1/SMM

Sánchez Cuadrado, J., Cánovas, J., & García Molina, J. (2014). Applying model driven engineering in small software enterprises. *Science of Computer Programming*, *89*, 176–198. doi:10.1016/j.scico.2013.04.007

Stankovic, J. (2014). Research Directions for the Internet of Things. *IEEE Internet of Things Journal, 1*(1), 3–9.

Steinberg, D., Budinsky, F., Paternostro, M., & Merks, E. (2009). *EMF: Eclipse Modeling Framework* (2nd ed.). Addison-Wesley.

Thompson, C., Schmidt, D., Turner, H., & White, J. (2014). *Analyzing Mobile Application Software Power Consumption via Model-Driven Engineering. In Advances and Applications in Model-Driven Engineering* (pp. 342–366). Hershey, PA: IGI GLOBAL.

Tonella, P., & Potrich, A. (2005). *Reverse engineering of Object-Oriented Code. Monographs in Computer Science*. Springer-Verlag.

XMI. (2015). *XML Metadata Interchange (XMI) Specification*. OMG Document Number: formal/2015-06-07. Retrieved April 25, 2017 from http://www.omg.org/spec/XMI/2.5.1

Zanella, A., Bui, N., Castellani, A., Vangelista, L., & Zorzi, M. (2014). Internet of Things for Smart Cities. *IEEE Internet of Things Journal*, *1*(1), 22–32. doi:10.1109/JIOT.2014.2306328

KEY TERMS AND DEFINITIONS

Atlas Transformation Language (ATL): A model transformation language and toolkit developed on top of the Eclipse platform that provides ways to produce target models from source models.

Ecore Metamodel: The de-facto reference implementation of EMOF (essential meta-object facility), a subset of MOF. It is the core metamodel of EMF.

HaXe: An open source toolkit based on a modern, high level, strictly typed programming language, a cross-compiler, a complete cross-platform standard library and way to access each platform's native capabilities.

Metamodeling: The process of generating a "model of models"; the essence of model-driven development approaches.

Mobile Technology: The technology used for cellular communication.

Model Transformation: A mechanism for automatically creating target models based on information contained in existing source models.

Model-Driven Architecture (MDA): An initiative of the OMG for the development of software systems based on the separation of business and application logic from underlying platform technologies. It is an evolving conceptual architecture to achieve cohesive model-driven technology specifications.

Model-Driven Engineering: Software engineering discipline that emphasizes the use of models and model transformations to raise the abstraction level and the degree of automation in software development.

Model-Driven Software Modernization: A particular form of reengineering for the functional and technological evolution of software systems that follows the MDE principles.

Software Migration: The process of moving from the use of one operating environment to another operating environment that is, in most cases, thought to be a better.

Chapter 8
Big Data and Machine Learning:
A Way to Improve Outcomes in Population Health Management

Fernando Enrique Lopez Martinez
University of Oviedo, Spain

Edward Rolando Núñez-Valdez
University of Oviedo, Spain

ABSTRACT

IoT, big data, and artificial intelligence are currently three of the most relevant and trending pieces for innovation and predictive analysis in healthcare. Many healthcare organizations are already working on developing their own home-centric data collection networks and intelligent big data analytics systems based on machine-learning principles. The benefit of using IoT, big data, and artificial intelligence for community and population health is better health outcomes for the population and communities. The new generation of machine-learning algorithms can use large standardized data sets generated in healthcare to improve the effectiveness of public health interventions. A lot of these data come from sensors, devices, electronic health records (EHR), data generated by public health nurses, mobile data, social media, and the internet. This chapter shows a high-level implementation of a complete solution of IoT, big data, and machine learning implemented in the city of Cartagena, Colombia for hypertensive patients by using an eHealth sensor and Amazon Web Services components.

DOI: 10.4018/978-1-5225-3805-9.ch008

INTRODUCTION

Big Data and artificial intelligence are currently two of the most important and trending pieces for innovation and predictive analysis in health care. For big data, Internet of Things (IoT) is one of the primary sources for data acquisition nowadays in health care, allowing patients with network connectivity to send and receive data in real-time to patient-centric platforms that collect and monitor patient information. The health care industry represents significant opportunities for machine learning (ML), big data and IoT. These paradigms, tools, and techniques are helping providers around the world to produce better outcomes for patients, communities and population health management.

Because many health care organizations are already working on developing their own intelligent big data analytics systems based on machine learning principles, this paper will discuss how these two components are the new pillars of population health management, value-based care and upcoming challenges in health care.

We are experiencing a new era of information in health care, a decade of progress in digitalization of medical records, usage of health wearables and monitoring devices. Electronic pharmaceutical services, insurance claims, conversations about health in social media and years of research of organizations aggregating data in electronic databases has generated according to Harvard business review magazine since 2012, 2.5 quintillion terabytes of data every day. This vast amount of data generated and collected comes in multiple forms making the extraction and integration a real challenge. The actual value of big data and IoT can be captured easily in health care and is very important to review how this data can be usable, searchable and actionable by the health care industry and specifically in the area of population health management. This collection, integration, and treatment of data will require collaboration between the public and private sector to enable the research community to better access, manage, and utilize IoT objects (smart devices, sensors, smart beds, etc.) and big data.

IoT is gaining more attention every day, and the demand for intelligent and connected devices provides a new level of opportunities to collect data at home and improve the interaction with the health care professionals.

On the other hand, generating new knowledge and predictive analysis is where Machine learning takes action in our article. The generation of machine learning (ML) algorithms that can use these immense data sets generated in health care and collected by interconnected devices might improve the quality and efficiency in several health care areas such as readmissions, treatment optimization, and population health management.

This article will show how the primary goal of health care data analytics is the combination of technologies, strategies, and techniques that allow analyzing clinical data from different sources to determine appropriate insights to improve the outcome of health care and to improve population health management. This article also shows how transforming this knowledge into practice is another challenge, this will require a change in current practices and most important practice-changing decisions.

For several years researchers have been working with health care organizations trying to improve the process of data collection, data aggregation, data analysis and decision-making process. A lot of them has succeeded enabling clinicians and health care facilities to generate insights from big data and the use of machine learning algorithms straight to the care of an individual patient or to a group of people by analyzing the data of their treatment, their socio – economic environment and their health habits. The expectation is to show what is out there that works and for whom, the complexities, needs, and challenges.

BACKGROUND

Population health management is the aggregation of patient data across multiple health information technology resources, the analysis of that data and the actions that care providers can use to improve clinical and financial outcomes of a group of individuals (Kindig, 2003). A population health management objective is to give real-time insights to health providers based on clinical, operational and financial data from a population and provides analytics to improve efficiency and patient care.

The first challenge is to aggregate and normalize the enormous amount of data across different EHR platforms and external sources like wearables and sensors. The data in health care is typically so vast and complex that it is hard to manage with traditional data management methods (Priyanka, 2014) and some of this data by its nature needs to be collected and analyzed in real-time. When the data exceeds the traditional capacity of conventional database systems, and it is generated and collected too fast, the concept of big data appears in the scene. Big data is a term that describes large volumes of high velocity, complex and variable data that requires advanced techniques and technologies to enable the capture, storage, distribution, management and analysis of the information (TechAmerica Foundation paper, 2012). Big data in health care is massive amounts of generated genomic, clinical, behavioral, business, and financial data. And, information generated from sensors and wearable's devices. Internet of Things (IoT), is a powerful paradigm that provides to healthcare, tools, and mechanism for data acquisition, data gathering and data transferring (Mustafa Abdullah, 2016). This healthcare monitoring includes body and environmental sensors, communication and networking devices and processing and analyzing nodes.

Population health management usually requires the collection of heterogeneous data from multiple sources plus the application of advanced analytics models to improve clinical operations and public health. These advanced analytics models refer to predictive modeling and transformation of this data into actionable information.

Colombia is creating personalized care programs to reduce healthcare costs to the government, reduce the number of hospitalizations in healthcare facilities and to reduce the number of patients in the emergency rooms. To do what has been mentioned before, the government is providing incentives to use technology for patient monitoring at their homes. Several research groups are creating Wireless Body Area Networks (WBAN) and Wireless Personal Area Networks (WPAN) to track and monitor population health. The data generated in this networks are large in volume, and some of the research groups need assistance and supervision on how to retrieve and analyze patient's information in real time, and how to generate meaningful statistics and visualizations with this data.

Big data analytics has been used in personalized care in different countries (Patidar, 2017) with a huge success with sensors and wireless networks in patient's health monitoring. This information in the form of "big data" is complex to analyze and store and requires specialized frameworks and architectures to be manipulated, treated and obtain insights of it.

IoT IN POPULATION HEALTH

Internet of Things (IoT) has been used in healthcare since the 2000s but just recently is taking the importance it deserves. Health care professionals know the potential and value that comes from patient data about personal health. IoT provides a perfect tool to observing patient behavior thru the use of personal health devices and sensors, allowing healthcare providers to monitor patient's health proactively. Health care is taking advantage of IoT to gather patient's information from various devices and integrate and analyze that information to provide insights and recommendations for healthy behaviors.

The devices used in IoT in health care can be categorized in:

- **Clinical Monitoring:** Are integrated and discrete sensors and signal conditioning technology used for study monitoring at the healthcare facility (Dan S Karbing, 2017). Some samples are Smart beds, Smart pumps, Smart monitors, ECG Patient Monitoring, Pulse transit time capture with many different methodologies such as bio potential and optical sensors, Respiration Measurement.

- **At Home Monitoring:** Are all wearable and sensors that can measure critical physiological indicators such as activity levels, sleep, blood pressure, heart rate, EEG and ECG at the patient's home. Some samples are, glucose monitor, oximetry monitor, weight and blood glucose monitors
- **Personal Health:** All personal devices used to track and monitor personal health. Some samples are, smart watches to monitor resting heart rate (RHR), heart rate (HR), recovery time, V02 max, movement, sleep, wireless-connected scale to measure weight, fat mass, bone mass, muscle mass, water and blood pressure monitors.
- **Ingestible Devices:** these are all kind of ingestible sensors that wirelessly reports body's vital signs (Raed Shubair, 2017). Some samples are, sensors to track what drugs patients have taken, sensors that can measure pH, temperature, and pressure and can transmit those measurements to an external data receiver.

The interest of this chapter is in the suite of wearable and sensors that can be combined and deployed in a nonclinical home (home monitoring) setting used for remote data collection and monitoring.

Hospitals are looking for strategies to minimize costs of the patient care (Itamir de Morais, 2017), and IoT provides a broad range of opportunities to offer patient monitoring at home. Smart home environments can use a network of sensors connected via Zigbee wireless (Ghamari, 2016) to a local hub that connects to the internet to transmit the data collected by the sensors to a cloud-based big data platform that will clean, transform and analyze this data. The previously mentioned network is called Wireless Body Area Network (WBAN) as described in (Bo Yu, 2009). This type of network will facilitate the early detection and prevention of several diseases by a continuous monitoring of health conditions. All the data gathered by this devices and sensors like an electrocardiogram (ECG), electroencephalography (EEG), respiratory rate, body temperature and movement will be collected and communicated to a base station wirelessly to be further analyzed and processed.

APPLICATIONS OF BIG DATA IN POPULATION HEALTH

Population health management is the aggregation of health care data across multiple health information technology systems and the analysis of this data to improve health care outcomes. The use of big data can generate multiple benefits as follows:

1. **Earlier Disease Detection:** Nowadays a lot of sensors are being used to monitor patient health, these sensors produce a vast amount of information

that can be aggregated and analyzed in real-time. This analysis can predict disease outbreaks and detect early development of infections.

2. **Fraud Detection and Prevention:** Big data predictive analytics can be used by health care payers to check the accuracy of claims and payments and to verify compliance with Medical policies (Remus, 2012).
3. **Personalized Patient Care:** Health care is moving from disease-centered model to a patient-centered model (Yang, 2014). Data from medical evidence and electronic medical records (EMR) are needed, and big data will facilitate aggregate and analyze this personalized patient care data to improve clinical outcome.
4. **Genomics Analytics:** A huge number of diseases are genetic in nature, genomic data can provide a better understanding of these diseases and conventional data-driven technologies can't treat this complex type of data.
5. **Clinical Outcomes Analytics:** Collection of data from clinical systems, clinical operations, and financial systems through big data provide improvements in health outcomes (Helm-Murtagh, 2014).
6. **Smart Health and Wellbeing:** With the current sensor technologies the adoption of wearable's devices and smart home environments the amount of data collected from patients and their conditions need big data technologies to turn this massive amount of data in useful information having a profound impact on population health.

Figure 1 shows a conceptual architecture of big data analytics that includes the Hadoop and MapReduce framework capable of storage and analyzes different

Figure 1. An applied conceptual architecture of big data analytics (Raghupathi and Raghupathi, 2014)

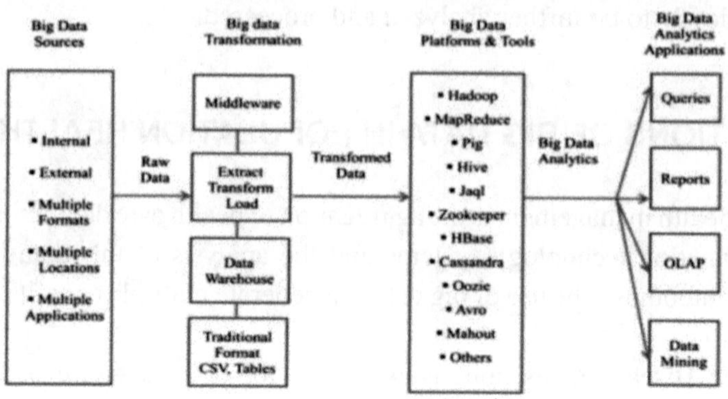

Figure 1. An applied conceptual architecture of Big Data analytics (Raghupathi and Raghupathi, 2014)

types of medical data and intelligent, functional machine learning (ML) modules for diagnosis and analysis (Ngufor & Wojtusiak, 2013).

In this architecture, Hive will support queries in HiveQL which will be compiled into map-reduce jobs that will be executed using Hadoop. Hive will provide the initial data mining, log processing, and document indexing and initial predictive modeling. For data storage will be utilized Hadoop Distributed File System (HDFS).

MACHINE LEARNING AND CLINICAL PREDICTION MODELS

While massive data is becoming very familiar in health care, data mining and machine learning (ML) techniques can be implemented to generate knowledge from this data and machine learning has a significant opportunity to be applied in population health management. However, health care organizations before investing in Machine learning (ML) technologies should have a clear and concrete idea of how they will use it to improve health outcomes and a better population health management.

Based on the formal definition of Machine learning stated by (Mitchell, 1986). "*A computer program is said to learn from experience E with respect to some class of tasks T and performance measure P if its performance at tasks in T, as measured by P, improves with experience E*". is clear that ML refers to a particular type of algorithm that can learn from data in order to create a general model that produce accurate predictions.

Machine learning algorithms were designed and used to analyze medical data sets (Kononenko, 2001). And still today ML provides several tools for intelligent data analysis. There are three types of learning, supervised, unsupervised, and semi-supervised learning. This chapter will focus on the first type. In supervised learning, the data contains the response to be modeled, and the goal is to predict the value of the hidden data. Through the years advance ML methods have been used to analyze clinical data sets, and clinical prediction models are one of the most important branches of health care data analytics, the following is a list of the learning methods that have been used successfully for clinical prediction tasks:

1. **Linear Regression:** Is a supervised regression where the dependent variable or outcome is assumed to be a linear combination of the attributes with corresponding estimated regression parameters as explicated in (Trevor, 2009).
2. **Logistic Regression:** Supervised two class and multi-class classification. This binary classification method assumes that there is a linear relationship between the features and the log-odds of the probabilities as explicated in (Dreiseitl, 2002).

3. **Bayesian Models:** Supervised two class and multiclass classification model. Bayesian model is one of the most important principles in probability and mathematical statistics; it provides a link between the posterior likelihood and the prior probability. Is possible to see the probability changes before and after accounting for a particular random event. This theorem is explained in details in (Kononenko, 2007).
4. **Decision Trees:** Supervised two class and multi-class classification. One of the most widely used clinical prediction model (Aspinall, 1979). The prediction is made by asking a series of questions about a test record and based on the answers; the test record falls into a smaller subgroup where the individuals are similar to each other concerning the predicted outcome as explained in (Long, 1993).
5. **Artificial Neural Networks:** Supervised regression. This method is inspired by biological neural systems. Simple artificial nodes called "neurons" are combined via a weighted connection to form a network that simulates a biological neural network as explained in (Dreiseitl, 2002) and (Rosenblatt, 1958).

There are many other methods and future trends where ML in medical diagnosis could take place. The important part here is that with all the advance in computer technology and devices to collect data researchers have a lot of opportunities to improve health outcomes and the medical diagnosis that will affect population health management positively.

PROJECT IMPLEMENTATION

An initial one home monitoring platform has been implemented in Cartagena, Colombia to track and monitor hypertensive data for one patient and validate the infrastructure. For this research, a total of 150 family's homes were selected, and one hypertensive patient for each home has been chosen for the study to use the sensor shield device. Figure 2 shows the architecture utilized for this project and the following are the specifications of the data and the platforms.

- **Location:** Cartagena, Colombia
- **Universities Contributing:** University of Cartagena (Colombia) and University of Oviedo (Spain).
- **Healthcare Facility Contributing:** Clinic of Caribbean
- **The Object of the Study:** Track and treat Hypertension population in Cartagena Colombia.

- **Initial Features for Study:** Age, Race, Height, Weight, Blood pressure, daily step count, BMI index.
- **IoT Infrastructure:**
  - Arduino Uno R3
  - e-health sensor shield v2.0 (Arduino compatible)
  - Radio signal supported (BT, ZigBee, 4G / 3G / GPRS)
  - Oxygen in the blood (SPO2) sensor
  - Body temperature sensor
  - Sphygmomanometer sensor
  - DHT22 sensor (ambient humidity and temperature)
  - XBee breakout board
  - XBee 2mW Wire Antenna - Series 2
  - Raspberry Pi 2
  - Antenna Wireless Network Dongle
- **Big Data Frameworks:** Hadoop & Spark Amazon EMR
- **Machine Learning:** Amazon Machine Learning Platform.
- **Result:** A Data Analytics visualization tool and a healthcare dashboard will be created that will enable clinicians, and healthcare executives improve their decision support process for a hypertensive population.

The high-level diagram in Figure 2 shows the basic WPBN and the AWS (Amazon Web Services) services that were configured for this project. AWS IoT is a managed cloud platform that allows IoT gateways communicate easily and securely to AWS, and to gather device data based on business rules that should be defined. AWS IoT has been integrated to Amazon S3 (Amazon Simple Storage Service) to store the data from the IoT sensors and devices. Then, an EMR cluster is created to pull the data from S3 and use Hive and Hue to analyze and display the data collected from the devices. Once the data is stored in a Hive table, some transformations are needed it to prepare and clean the data. In the last step, Amazon ML is used to create and train an ML model using Amazon EMR as the data source. The trained ML model will be used to generate predictions for the test data set, and this is output back to another S3 bucket. A web application will be created to create the dashboards based on the generated prediction to support population health management decisions.

RECOMMENDATIONS

The collection and transmission of health care related data in a WBAN network is a challenge, the designers of this type of environments should keep in mind that this information is private and confidential. Encryption technologies must be used in the

Figure 2. IoT, big data and ML infrastructure

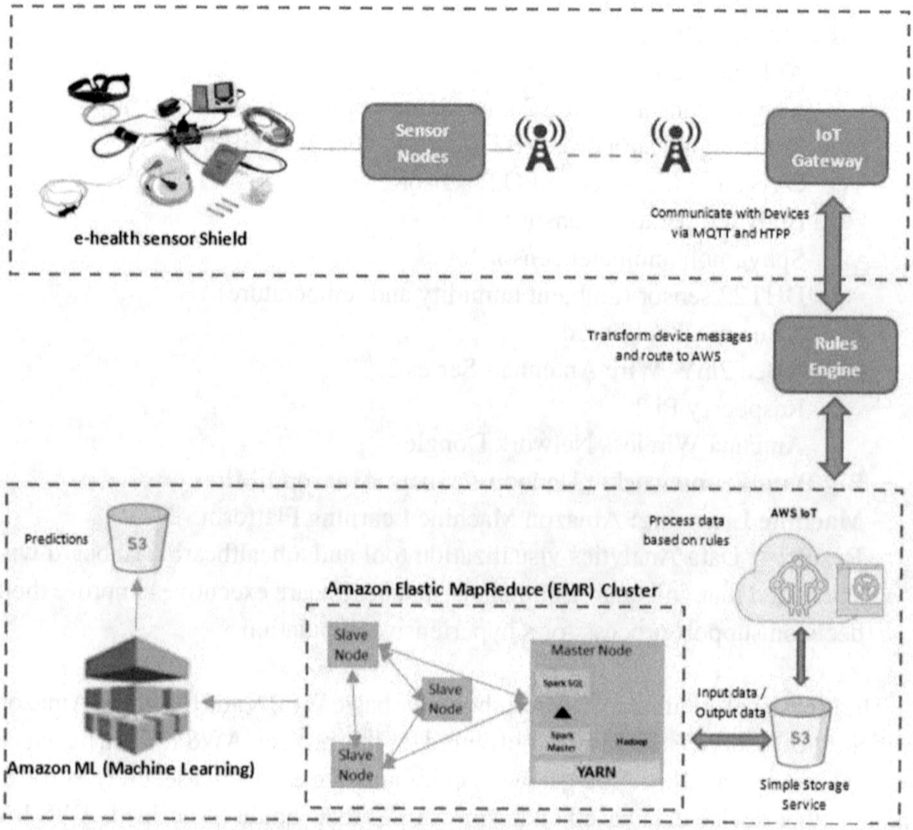

Figure 2. IoT, Big Data and ML Infrastructure

transmission between sensors and monitoring devices, and healthcare professional must be sure this information is protected from not authorized access. In addition, big data and machine learning allow performing sophisticated data analysis in the medical diagnosis and health care outcomes based on the secured collected data. Healthcare institutions should take advantage of all the new technologies and systems that have emerged to help medical providers to find interesting and complex relationships in clinical data to improve population health management. Technological research groups need to create strategic alliances with Clinical research groups to gain clinical knowledge and exploit the technical and practical possibilities of IoT, big data frameworks and machine learning methods applied to the medical field. This type of technology has a measurable impact on population Health allowing health care providers improve health outcomes in their communities.

FUTURE RESEARCH DIRECTIONS

The Colombian government is providing incentives to clinical research groups in Cartagena to explore technological opportunities and learn about different technologies like IEEE 802.15.4, Bluetooth devices, low-power wireless technology, Radio-Frequency Identification (RFID), and ZigBee networks to promote the building and use of WBANs for home-centric patient monitoring. Big data frameworks and machine learning methods should be incorporated in prevention and management of chronic diseases. The researchers will help improve population health management in Colombia using these technologies to aggregate data and provide a comprehensive clinical picture of an individual in a population group in the city of Cartagena, using this data to track and improve health outcomes while trying to lower the costs of health care treatments. The research will provide a general picture of the population health to health care providers and the government to identify care gaps, disease outbreaks and patient treatment deficiencies within the patient population in Cartagena.

The creation of clinical prediction models for health care institutions in Cartagena, Colombia could make a tremendous impact in terms of diagnosis and treatment of diseases. In order to promote this type of research, Cartagena local government is giving incentives to research projects that includes linear regression, logistic regression, Bayesian models and neuronal networks in the solution of clinical health care problems. This incentives also includes any other machine learning model not mentioned in this chapter that can be adapted to the health care domain.

FUTURE WORK

Scientists in Cartagena, Colombia are working with healthcare facilities and local government to implement WBAN networks for patient tracking and monitoring, and the implementation of an artificial intelligence (AI) platform for detection and diagnostic of diseases in the population. The vital objective is to create a technological platform that integrate all electronic medical record (EMR) systems from different healthcare facilities in Cartagena and all the collected patient information thru the WBAN networks. This clinical information will be accessed by authorized users (health physicians) at any time and from anywhere. Population health management in Cartagena will be improved by the analytical tools provided on this platform that will allow healthcare stake holders and physicians to identify value and opportunities to improve healthcare outcomes in the population.

CONCLUSION

Population health management is the collection and aggregation of health care data across multiple health information technology systems and the analysis of this data to improve health care outcomes. In this definition was only include data collection and aggregation but there are other components like patient stratification, care coordination, patient engagement, performance and reporting and administration of the new value-based model.

IoT, data collection, data aggregation, and analytics are at the center of all other components, and these are the pillar because the data drive clinical decisions and strategies to turn information into actionable insights supported by IoT technologies, big data frameworks and machine learning methods. Data analytics has been heavily used in the past few years and are continuing gaining importance and interest at all levels. Some of the interest areas where data analytics is gaining importance are pervasive health, health care fraud detection, pharmaceutical discoveries, computer-aided diagnosis, mobile imaging for biomedical applications and clinical decision support systems (CDSS). Another key component in this field of research is the support of health care institutions. Due to the privacy of the clinical data, this research work in the health care data analytics field should be done with a particular hospital or health care facility. There are a wide variety of public repositories in health care to validate the models, but it is important to validate the models with data collected from the nominated study population. Hardware, software, and communication technologies are no excuses anymore. Nowadays these technologies to collect and analyze health care data have significantly increased, allowing solutions to collect high volumes of data and process them in real-time, producing real-time analysis and insights.

The chapter points to articles that provide more details about IoT technologies and how effectively use Big data and prediction models in Clinical environments to improve health outcomes.

ACKNOWLEDGMENT

This research was supported by the Organization Sysdevelopment LLC. USA; University of Oviedo, Spain.

REFERENCES

Aspinall, M. J. (1979). Use of a decision tree to improve accuracy of diagnosis. *Nurs Res., 28*(3), 182–185. PMID:254902

Dreiseitl, S., & Ohno-Machado, L. (2002). Logistic regression and artificial neural network classification models: A methodology review. *Journal of Biomedical Informatics, 35*(5-6), 352–359. doi:10.1016/S1532-0464(03)00034-0 PMID:12968784

e-Health Sensor Platform V2.0 for Arduino and Raspberry Pi. (n.d.). Retrieved from https://e-class.teilar.gr/modules/document/file.php/CS103/IOT%20-%20 SENSORS%20-%20ACTUATORS/e-Health%20Sensor%20Platform%20V2.pdf

Ghamari, M., Janko, B., Sherratt, R. S., Harwin, W., Piechockic, R., & Soltanpur, C. (2016). A Survey on Wireless Body Area Networks for eHealthcare Systems in Residential Environments. *Sensors (Basel), 16*(6), 831. doi:10.3390/s16060831 PMID:27338377

Hastie, T., Tibshirani, R., & Friedman, J. (2009). *Elements of Statistical Learning: Data Mining, Inference and Prediction* (2nd ed.). New York: Springer-Verlag. doi:10.1007/978-0-387-84858-7

Helm-Murtagh, S. C. (2014). Use of Big Data by Blue Cross and Blue Shield of North Carolina. *NCMJ, 75*, 195–197. PMID:24830494

Itamir de Morais, B. F., & Gibeon, S. A. J. (2017). IoT-Based Healthcare Applications: A Review. Lecture Notes in Computer Science. DOI: doi:10.1007/978-3-319-62407-5_4

Karbing, Rees, & Jaffe. (2017). *Journal of Clinical Monitoring and Computing 2016 end of year summary*. DOI: 10.1007/s10877-017-0008-0

Kindig, D., & Stoddart, G. (2003). *What Is Population Health*. American Journal of Public Health, *93*(3), 380–383.

Kononenko, I. (2001). Machine learning for medical diagnosis: History, state of the art and perspective. *Artif Intell Med., 23*(1), 89-109.

Kononenko, I. (2007). Inductive and Bayesian Learning. In *Medical Diagnosis* (pp. 317–337). Journal Applied Artificial Intelligence.

Long, W. J., Griffith, J. L., Selker, H. P., & D'Agostino, R. B. (1993). A comparison of logistic regression to decision-tree induction in a medical domain. *Computers and Biomedical Research, an International Journal*, *26*(1), 74–97. doi:10.1006/cbmr.1993.1005 PMID:8444029

Mitchell, T. M., Carbonell, J. G., & Michalski, R. S. (1986). *Machine Learning: A Guide to Current Research* (1st ed.). The Springer International Series in Engineering and Computer Science. Original. doi:10.1007/978-1-4613-2279-5

Ngufor, C., & Wojtusiak, J. (2013). *Learning from Large-Scale Distributed Health Data: An Approximate Logistic Regression Approach*. Academic Press.

Patidar, P., Praneeta, S., Kataria, R., & Vidhyasagar, B. S. (2017). Analysis of Multi-Disease & Prediction of Suitable Drug for Healthcare Application using Big data. *International Journal of Research in Applied Science & Engineering Technology, 5*(4).

Priyanka, K., & Kulennavar, N. (2014). A survey on big data analytics in health care. *Int. J. Comput. Sci.Inform. Technologies*, *5*, 5865–5868.

Remus & Kennedy. (2012). Special Focus on Nursing Informatics. *Innovation in Transformative Nursing Leadership: Nursing Informatics Competencies and Roles*, 14-26. doi:10.12927/cjnl.2012.23260

Review on Internet of Things (IoT) in Healthcare. (n.d.). Available from: https://www.researchgate.net/publication/309718253_A_Review_on_Internet_of_Things_IoT_in_Healthcare

Rosenblatt, F. (1958). The Perceptron: A Theory of Statistical Separability in Cognitive Systems (Project Para). Buffalo, NY: Cornell Aeronautical Laboratory.

Shubair & Kiourti. (2017). *In-Body Devices for Wireless Biotelemetry: Implants and ingestibles*. Special Session organized at the 2017 IEEE AP-S Symposium on Antennas and Propagation and USNC-URSI Radio Science Meeting (AP-S/URSI 2017), San Diego, CA.

Tech America Foundation. (2012). *Demystifying Big Data: TechAmerica Foundation paper*. Retrieved from http://www1.unece.org/stat/platform/pages/viewpage.action?pageId=80053387

Yang, S., Njoku, M., & Mackenzie, C. F. (2014). 'Big data' approaches to trauma outcome prediction and autonomous resuscitation. *British Journal of Hospital Medicine*, *75*(11), 637–641. doi:10.12968/hmed.2014.75.11.637 PMID:25383434

Yu, B. (2009). *Wireless Body Area Networks for Healthcare: A Feasibility Study*. Available from: https://www.ieee.org/documents/Yu_Final_Published_Paper_March2009.pdf

KEY TERMS AND DEFINITIONS

Arduino: Is an open source electronic platform to build interactive projects receiving inputs from sensors and controlling actions by using the development environment.

AWS: Is Amazon Web Services, a platform that offers on-demand cloud computing.

Big Data: Extremely large data sets, generated by humans, applications, or machines.

Cloud Computing: Is the practice of using remote servers and services hosted on the internet to store, manage, and process data.

Data Mining: Specific algorithms for extracting patterns from data.

Descriptive Analytics: Technology that focuses less on the precise details of every piece of data, and instead focuses on an overall description.

Disease: Is a disorder of a function in a human or a particular abnormal condition.

Electronic Health Record: An electronic health record contains your health information.

Hadoop: Open-source framework for processing a large volume of data in a clustered environment.

Hypertension: Is an abnormally high blood pressure.

IoT: Internet of things is the interconnection of physical devices that enable these devices to collect and exchange data.

Machine Learning: Computer programs that automatically improve with experience.

Population Health: Population health is defined as the health outcomes of a group of individuals, including the distribution of such outcomes within the group.

Predictive Analytics: Technology that learns from experience to predict the future behavior of individuals in order to drive better decisions.

Prescriptive Analytics: Generally follows prediction, in that actions can be prescribed based on what has been collected from predictive modeling.

Raspberry Pi: Is a small single-board computer.

Sensor: Is a device that detects or measures a physical property.

Chapter 9
Smart City Based on MQTT Using Wireless Sensors

Monika Bharatbhai Patel
Charotar University of Science and Technology, India

Chintan Bhatt
Charotar University of Science and Technology, India

Hamed Vahdat-Nejad
University of Birjand, Iran

Hardik B. Patel
Epsilon Electronics, India

ABSTRACT

The internet of things can involve a huge number of connected devices and sensors for the betterment of our lives and businesses. Sensors are the main part of IoT. The main target of this chapter is to develop an IoT-based information observing system for specific areas like home, cities, industries, hospitals, etc. In this system, the environmental data of different elements, for example, temperature, humidity, pressure, should screen and get a redesign with a particular time interval. The authors use Raspberry Pi 3 and MQTT to observe information over a remote area and get an update with it anyplace in the world. They transmit the environmental data to the cloud server sent by Raspberry Pi 3. There, the authors can monitor data in both modes (online and offline).

DOI: 10.4018/978-1-5225-3805-9.ch009

INTRODUCTION

The Internet of Things (IoT), which is based on Machine to Machine (M2M) communication, can possibly change our life. It is based on client-server architecture as well as publish/subscribe transport protocol. Message Queuing Telemetry Transport (MQTT) is a lightweight open source protocol, which is easily implemented in IoT-based applications. It makes it perfect to use an IoT application, implemented system, and M2M devices (Atzori, lera & Morabito, 2010).

The main parts of IoT are sensors and the MQTT protocol. By various sensors we can easily get environmental data and can process them. Using this data, we can make our life more comfortable.

Right now these elements are encountering particular necessities that identify striking topics, such as business and work, economic, energy and water, open security, environment, healthcare, education and open administrations, all of which are, in some frame or another, progressively encouraged and empowered by ICT. Simultaneously, the most recent turbulent worldwide monetary downturn is progressively setting weight on urban areas to cut spending plans. It brings about malicious impacts not just on the upkeep and update of current ICT framework and offices, but additionally on future advancement policies. Notwithstanding, the idea of a "keen city", additionally known as astute city, data city, advanced city, e-city and virtual city, has been recognized just like a commendable case of a reaction to address the present and future complex difficulties of expanding asset proficiency, lessening emissions, providing sustainable human services administrations for maturing populations, empowering youth and incorporating minorities (Shah & Bhatt, 2014).

Smart sensors are the major aspect of the IoT (Bhayani, Patel & Bhatt, 2016). Once you have real-time data of various environments, then actions can be taken easily into account based on that Wi-Fi based smart connected sensors. With the help of the smart sensors, Wi-Fi module, MQTT protocol and IoT-based various applications, we are making systems that could be used for monitoring sensors data like temperature, humidity, pressures, and altitude of selected areas where the system is placed.

The IoT devices can collaborate with each other without or with human intercession. The IoT involves the things that are implanted in frameworks, and it can possibly change our reality with the assistance of them. The IoT is an assuming part for brilliant urban areas, shrewd frameworks, keen wellbeing checkings, and savvy garments and so on. Each one of these advances of IoT will change the living way of human beings. (Bhatt, Dey & Ashour, 2017)

MQTT

IoT is a keen system, which associates all things to the web with the final goal of trading data with concurred conventions. In this way, anybody can get to anything, whenever and from anyplace. In the IoT system, things or items are remotely associated with shrewd sensors. (Singh, Rajan, Shivraj, & Balamuralidhar, 2015)

MQTT (Message Queue Telemetry Transport) is a lightweight messaging protocol. It is a broker-based publish/subscribe messaging protocol designed to be simple, open and straightforward to implement. In 1999, Dr.Andy Stanford-Clark from IBM and Arlen Nipper from Arcom invented the MQTT protocol. In MQTT protocol the session layer is used for IoT (Garcia, Espada & Midgar, 2014). The IoT devices are inter-connected with each other using the light-weight MQTT communication. The IoT applications typically use C, Python, Java as well as an MQTT scripting language (Andy Banks, 2012).

MQTT Broker controls the distribution of information (Gibbons, 2017). It stores, forwards, filters and prioritizes public requests from the publisher to the subscriber clients. Client switch between publisher and subscriber depends on the desired functionalities. There are many MQTT brokers available and they are different in their features; they can be set as per our requirements. MQTT brokers are Web sphere MQ, MQTT.js, Apache ActiveMQ, IBM Message Sight, Solaee Message Routers, Apache Apollo, Mosquitto, JoramMQ, HiveMQ, mosca, etc. For some of them, we can also implement additional features (Collina, Bartolucci, Vanelli-Coralli, & Corazza, 2014).

MQTT Client and MQTT Broker

MQTT client can act as a publisher and subscriber or sometimes both. MQTT library running on the MQTT client is any micro controller device that could be connected to an MQTT broker over any network. MQTT client libraries are available in a variety of programming languages like C, C++, C#, Android, Arduino, iOS, Go, .NET, JavaScript, Java, and etc. Using MQTT protocol client implementation is straight forward and really reduces to the embodiment. For this purpose, MQTT is suitable for small devices ("Sensor, Types of sensor,").

MQTT broker can handle hundreds of connected MQTT clients, concurrently. The broker is responsible for receiving MQTT client messages, it then filters them and decides who is interested in and forwards them, accordingly. MQTT clients are authenticated and authorized by MQTT broker. The MQTT broker is extensible; it easily incorporates some integration, authorization and authentication in the system backend ("Sensor, Types of sensor,").

Figure 1. MQTT Broker and Client

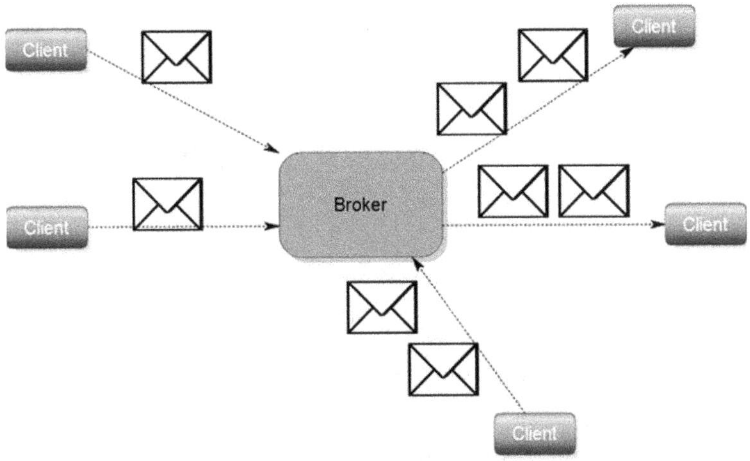

MQTT Connection

MQTT protocol is based on TCP/IP and client-broker scheme. The message is wrapped inside the TCP packet. It uses port number 1883 for MQTT. In MQTT no client can directly connect to another client, but the connection is always between one client and the broker. The MQTT client sends a CONNECT message to the broker for initiating the connection. The MQTT broker sends the CONNACK message as the response and also sends the status code. The broker keeps the connection alive till the client sends disconnect message to broker or the client loses the connection ("Sensor, Types of sensor,").

Each MQTT client has its unique identification number. The broker provides the client with its own unique id "Client ID" and by this id, manages the client connection and exchanges messages. The broker is answerable for managing messages persistence so that it can send them to the clients that were temporarily disconnected; this feature is called "retain message", which is important on unreliable networks with fragile connections.

When a client does not need to send any message or it does not receive messages for a long time, it must periodically send a "keep-alive" message to the broker to keep the connection alive; otherwise the broker terminates the connection after a timeout. The entire architecture is based on TCP/IP, so that each message exchanged between clients is wrapped inside TCP segments.

For connection between client and broker, there is MQTT connection command:

Figure 2. MQTT Broker and Client Connection

Figure 3. MQTT Publisher and Subscriber connection

```
MqttClient client =new MqttClient("tcp:// brokerid:portnum",
MqttClient.generateClientId(),
                new  MemoryPersistence());
client.connect();
client.disconnect();
, where
          brokerid=IP address of broker,
          portnum=Broker port number(default 1883)
```

MQTT Publish/Subscribe Architecture

MQTT is based on “publish/subscribe” and “topic”. A client can act as a publisher, subscriber or both. If it acts as a publisher, it publishes a message on a topic; if it acts as a subscriber, it subscribes to a specific topic. From this specific topic, it can receive the entire messages that are published on the topic (Locke, 2010).

MQTT protocol has a message queue mechanism; and all subscriptions to the topics are managed by the MQTT broker. The broker has to transfer the message from the publishing client to those who are subscribed to the topic. MQTT allows one-to-one and one-to-many dispersion and the subscriber does not need to worry about the subscribers (Locke, 2010).

The following is the MQTT publish command for publishing a message:

```
client.connect();
client.publish(subscribetopic,message);
 where
              subscribetopic= Name of the subscribed topic
```

In the above example, Client A publishes a message on the specific topic “current_temp”, and other clients Client B and Client C who have subscribed on that topic name “current_temp” and through MQTT broker, receive the message.

Figure 4. MQTT Publish architecture

Client B and Client C also publish messages on the same topic, so at this time they become a publisher and client A becomes receiver.

A subscription can be durable or non-durable. In the durable mode, the broker transfers a message to a subscribed client immediately, (if they are connected) or it stores the message till the subscriber connects. In the non-durable mode, if the subscriber is not connected, it loses that message.

The following is the MQTT subscribe command for the subscribe topic:

```
client.connect();
client.subscribe(subscribeTopic,QoS);
client.unsubscribe(subcribeTopic);
, where
          subcribeTopic=Topic name for subscription
          QoS=Quality of service
```

Quality of Services (QoS) of MQTT

QoS is an agreement between the sender and receiver of a message. It gives surety for delivering messages. The quality of services of a publication is an attribute of MqttMessage (Luzuriaga et al., 2015).

There are 3 levels of QoS in MQTT.

1. QoS 0
2. QoS 1
3. OoS 2

Figure 5. MQTT Subscription architecture

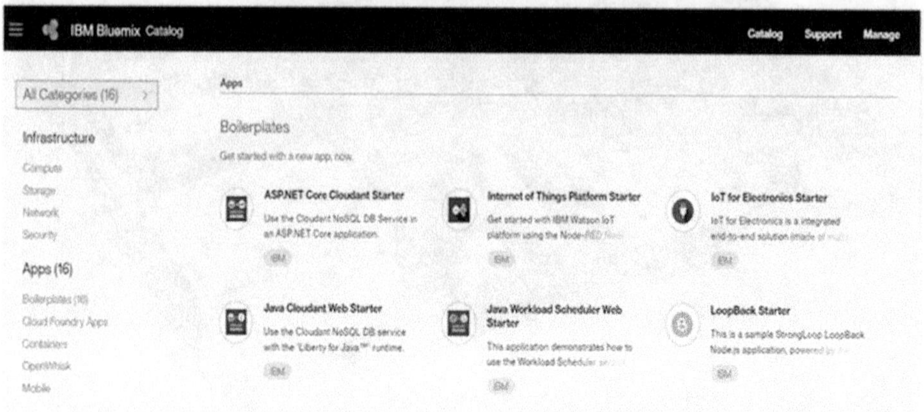

QoS 0: At Most Once

In this level, the message is delivered at most once, so it may not be delivered at all. Its delivery across the network is not acknowledged. At time of disconnection, the message might be lost. if the server fails, it receives the publication but it might be discarded, depending on the server. It is called "fire and forget" ("Sensors: Different Types of Sensors,").

There is the MQTT subscription command qos-0 to connect broker:

```
client.connect();
client.subscribe(subscribeTopic,qos-0);
, where
          subcribeTopic=Topic name for subscribe
          qos-0=Quality of service level
```

Use of QoS 0

- At the time of stable connection between sender and receiver or when there is wired connection between them, one can use this level of QoS.
- When data is not much important, loss of data is not important or message quality is not needed, this QoS level might be used.

QoS 1

It guarantees that the receiver gets messages successfully. In this case, the message can be delivered more than once. Sender stores the message until it gets PUBACK as acknowledgement from the receiver. PUBLISH and PUBACK are adapted by their

Figure 6. MQTT Quality of Service level 0

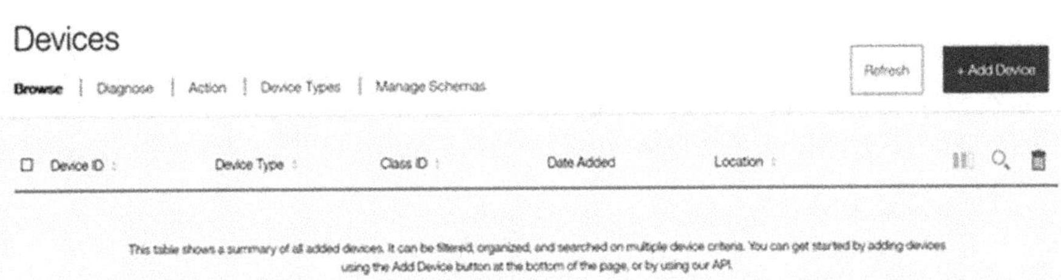

packet identifier that is placed in the packet. If PUBACK is not received in some fix amount of time, the sender resends the PUBLISH message. When receiver receives the PUBLISH message, it immediately replies PUBACK as acknowledgement to the sender.

At the time of redelivering message, the duplicate (DUP) flag is set by broker or client. Receiver sends PUBACK for DUP flag ("Sensors: Different Types of Sensors,").

There is the MQTT subscription command qos-0:

```
client.connect();
client.subscribe(subscribeTopic,qos-1);
, where
            subcribeTopic=Topic name for subscribing
            qos-1=Quality of service
```

Use of QoS 1

- OoS 1 is typically used when you have to get each message and your utilization case can deal with copies. The QoS-1 ensures the message touches base at least once.
- Obviously, the application must endure copies and process them appropriately. QoS 1 is a great deal quick in conveying messages.

QoS 2

It ensures that every message is received just once by the counterpart. It is the most secure and furthermore the slowest QoS level. Between the sender and receiver, it provides two flags.

It replies PUBREL and stores PUBREC. The receiver discards all packets that are stored and replies PUBCOMP when getting PUBREL ("Sensors: Different Types of Sensors,").

Figure 7. MQTT Quality of Service level 1

There is the MQTT subscription command qos:

```
client.connect();
client.subscribe(subscribeTopic,qos-2);
, Where
          subcribeTopic=Topic name for subscribing
          qos-2=Quality of service
```

Use of QoS 2

- When you need every message once use this QoS level, but duplication may harm your application.
- In this QoS level, one must take care of the overhead, because it takes longer to be completed.

Types of MQTT Control Packet

MQTT control Packets are shown in table 1.

MQTT Features

1. TCP/IP port 1883 is used for MQTT.
2. The use of TCP/IP to provide basic network connectivity.

Figure 8. MQTT Quality of Service level 2

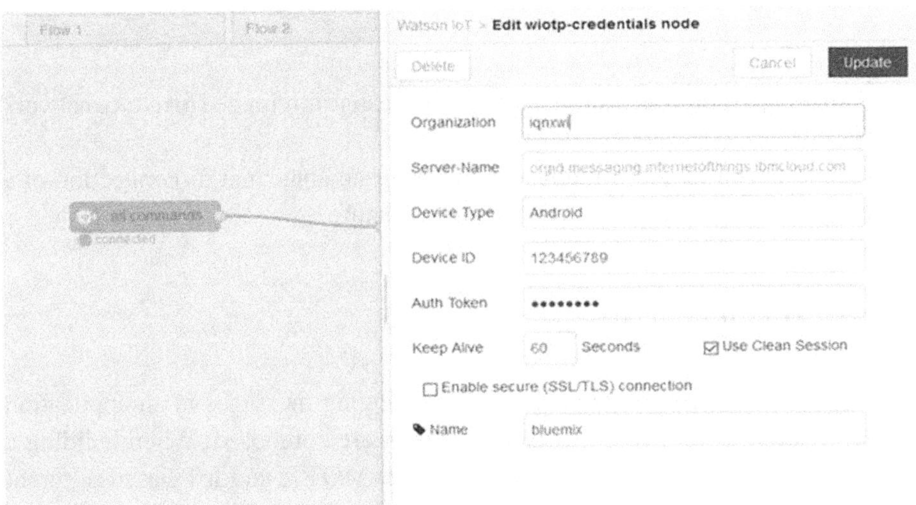

Table 1. MQTT control Packet

Packet Name	Packet Value	Flag Direction	Description
Reserved	0	Forbidden	Reserved
CONNECT	1	Client → Server	Client request to connect to Server
CONNACK	2	Server → Client	Connect acknowledgment
PUBLISH	3	Client → Server Or Server → Client	Publish message
PUBACK	4	Client → Server Or Server → Client	Publish acknowledgment
PUBREC	5	Client → Server Or Server → Client	Publish received
PUBTREL	6	Client → Server Or Server → Client	Publish release
PUBCOMP	7	Client → Server Or Server → Client	Publish complete
SUBSCRIBE	8	Client → Server	Client subscribe request
SUBACK	9	Server → Client	Subscribe acknowledgment
UNSUBSCRIBE	10	Client → Server	Unsubscribe request
UNSUBACK	11	Server → Client	Unsubscribe acknowledgment
PINGREQ	12	Client → Server	PING request
PINRESP	13	Server → Client	PING response
DISCONNECT	14	Client → Server	Client is disconnecting
Reserved	15	Forbidden	Reserved

3. A small transport overhead and protocol exchange minimized to reduce network traffic.
4. A mechanism to notify interested parties of an abnormal disconnection of a client using the Last Will and Testament feature.

PROBLEM SOLUTION

The MQTT is lightweight. The degree of exchanging messages in an application relies upon the way an MQTT broker and client are composed. When building a system with the help of sensors, Raspberry Pi 3, MQTT, and IoT based different applications and executing it, issues happen.

Without MQTT and IoT establishment and connection, it will be difficult to interfacing with client and server as well as machines that are utilized for M2M correspondence. MQTT is particularly used for installed devices as well as M2M and IoT availability protocol.

MOSQUITTO

MQTT is a broker-based public and subscription TCP/IP messaging protocol. It is designed for connections with remote locations, where a small code footprint is required or the network bandwidth is limited. Mosquitto is an open-source message brokering service that uses the MQTT protocol for sending and receiving messages. This broker is based on open source software that implements MQTT v 3.1 and v3.1.1.

Mosquitto Installation

For Broker

- The Raspberry Pi normal "apt-get" archives do not contain the latest version of the Mosquitto software. Do the followings:

Figure 9. Device with MQTT broker

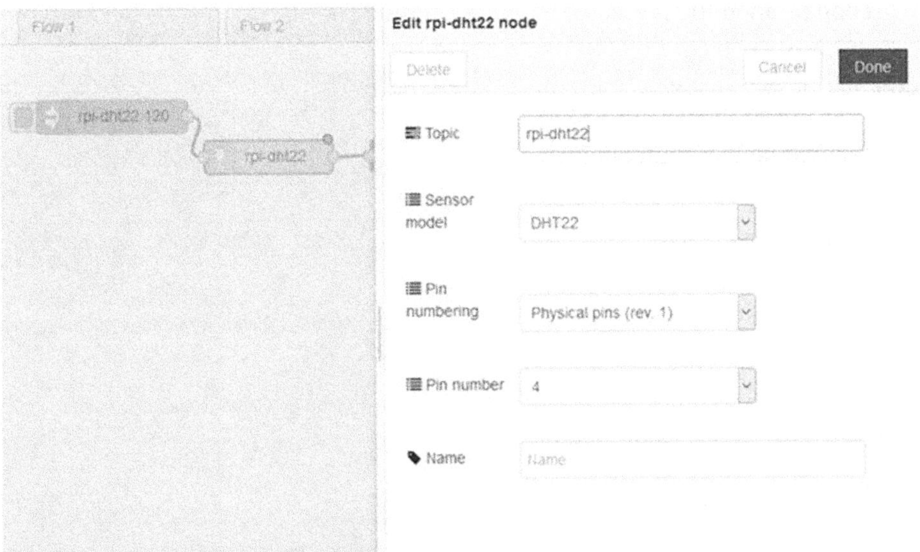

```
sudo wget http://repo.mosquitto.org/debian/mosquitto-repo.gpg.
key
sudo apt-key add mosquitto-repo.gpg.key
cd /etc/apt/sources.list.d/
sudo wget http://repo.mosquitto.org/debian/mosquitto-jessie.
list
sudo apt-get update
sudo apt-get install mosquito
```

- Install the three parts of the Mosquitto, properly:

```
mosquitto - the MQTT broker
mosquitto-clients - command line clients, very useful in
debugging
python-mosquitto - the Python language bindings
sudo apt-get install mosquitto mosquitto-clients python-
mosquitto
```

- As is the case with most packages from Debian, the broker is immediately started. Since we have to configure it first, stop it:

```
sudo /etc/init.d/mosquitto stop
```

- Before using Mosquitto, we need to set up the configuration file. The configuration file is located at /etc/mosquitto.

```
sudo nano /etc/mosquitto/mosquitto.conf
```

- Next add the next six lines:

```
 log_type error
log_type warning
log_type notice
log_type information
connection_messages true
log_timestamp true
```

- Now start the mosquitto server:

```
sudo /etc/init.d/mosquitto start
```

- Broker subscribe a specific topic

```
mosquitto_sub -d -t hello/world
```

- Broker publishes a message on a specific topic

```
mosquitto_pub -d -t hello/world -m "Hello"
```

For Clients

- Install mosquitto client:

```
sudo apt-get install mosquitto-client
```

- Client subscribes a specific topic

```
mosquitto_sub -h <broker ip> -p 1883 -v -t 'topic'
-u <user id> -P <password
```

- Client publishes a message on a specific topic

```
mosquitto_pub -h <broker ip> -p 1883 -t 'topic' -u
<user id> -P <password> -m "Message"
```

NODE-RED

Node-RED is a product tools created by IBM for implementing aggregated equipment gadgets, APIs and online administrations as a component of the Internet of Things. Node RED gives a program-based stream manager, which can be utilized to make JavaScript capacities. Components of applications can be spared or shared for re-utilization. The runtime is based on Node.js. The streams made in Node-RED are put away utilizing JSON.

Node-RED is a tool for implementing the Internet of Things in new and intriguing ways, supporting equipment gadgets, APIs, and online administrations. It is based on top of Node.js and exploits the colossal hub module environment to provide an instrument that is equipped for coordinating a wide range of frameworks. Furthermore, its lightweight nature makes it perfect to keep running at the edge of the system, for example, on the Raspberry Pi, and other hack-accommodating stages.

Node-RED contains the accompanying Watson IoT hub that helps users to unite devices, gateways and applications to Watson IoT Platform and make IoT arrangements, rapidly.

Node-Red Installation on Raspberry Pi

- First install its library:

```
bash <(curl -sL https://raw.githubusercontent.com/node-red/
raspbian-deb-package/master/resources/update-nodejs-and-
nodered)
```

- Update nodejs

```
update-nodejs-and-nodered
```

- Go to .node-red folder and rebuild npm.

```
cd ~/.node-red
npm rebuild
```

- Goto .node-red folder.

```
cd ~/.node-red
npm ls --depth=0
```

- Start node-red.

```
node-red-start
```

SENSORS

Sensors are devices that are used for detecting and reacting to electrical or optical signals. They are able to convert any type of physical quantity to be measured into a signal that can be read, displayed, stored or used to control some other quantity. It converts physical parameters like temperature, humidity, pressure, blood, speed, etc. into a signal that can be measured, electronically.

There are several features for a sensor:

- Usually used for environmental measurements.
- Calibration changes over time.
- Sensors detect smallest changes.
- Reading varies in repeated measurements.

DHT22

DHT is the temperature and humidity sensor. It has digital sensor and has a low cost. It measures the surrounding air and capacitive humidity by using a thermostat and spits out a digital signal. It is simple to use; however requires wary wanting to get data.

It is the costlier version, which obviously has better specifications.DHT22 measuring temperature is between -40 to +125℃ with +-0.5degree accuracy while DHT11 measuring temperature is between 0 to 50℃ with +-2degree accuracy. DHT11 has less measuring range of humidity than DHT22. DHT22 measuring range is from 0 to 100% with 2-5% accuracy while DHT11 have 20 to 80% with 5% accuracy (Govindan & Azad, 2015).There are two specifications where the DHT11 is better than the DHT22. Both sensors have 3 to 5 volts and their max used yielded when measuring is 2.5mA. The DHT22 sampling rate is 0.5Hz one reading every two seconds and the DHT11 is 1Hz or one reading every second. DHT11 has a small size (Govindan & Azad, 2015).

4.2 BMP085

Barometric pressure and temperature are measured by BMP085. It is a low-cost sensing tool. This sensor is with PCB that has a 4.3V regulator, I^2C level shifter, and pull-up resistors. It is the successor of the SMD500.

Figure 10. DHT22 sensors

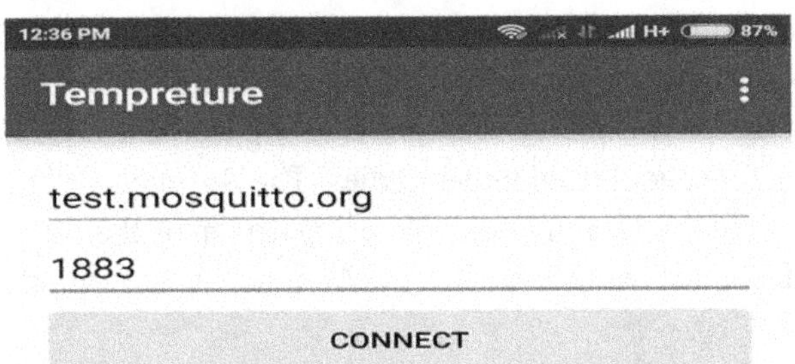

Figure 11. BMP085 sensors

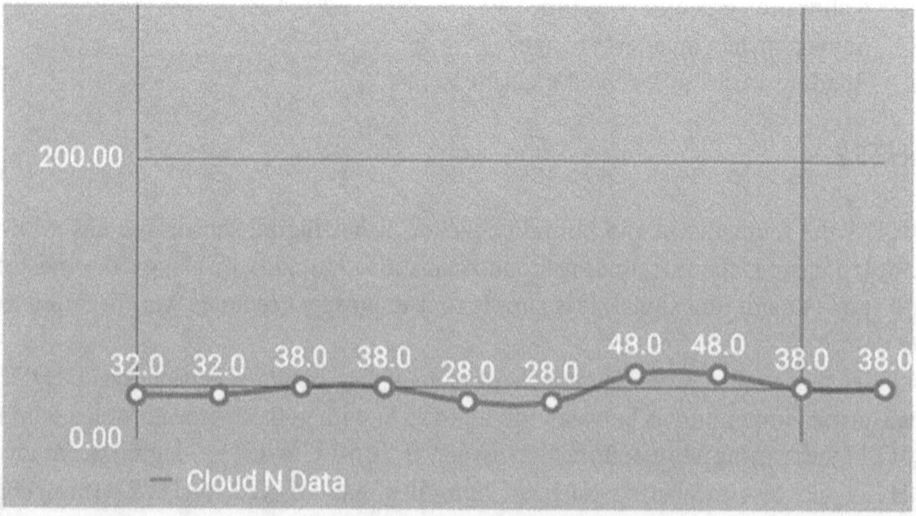

The BMP085 sensor depends on piece-resistive MEMS innovation for EMC vigor, high precision and linearity and additionally long term dependability. It arrives in an ultra-thin, yet powerful 8-pin fired lead-less chip carrier (LCC) package. The BMP085 is intended to be associated straightforwardly to a miniaturized scale controller of a cell phone by means of the I2C bus.

The BMP085 comes as completely aligned, prepared to utilize sensor module without the requirement for extra outer hardware. Weight and temperature information are given as 16 bit values by means of the I2C interface (Chen & Lin, 2014).

RASPBERRY PI 3

It was set up by the Raspberry Pi establishment in UK("RASPBERRY PI 3 MODEL B,"). It has been prepared for open utilization since 2012 with making a minimal effort instructive microcomputer for understudies and kids. The fundamental pure-posture of planning the Raspberry Pi board is to support learning, experimentation and advancement for school level understudies. The Raspberry Pi board is versatile and easy to use. A colossal fragment of this being driven by the versatile businesses. 98% of the cell phones were utilizing ARM innovation (Hunkeler, Truong, & Stanford-Clark, 2008).

The Raspberry Pi comes in two models; which are model A and B. The primary distinction between model A and B is the USB port. The model A board devours

Figure 12. Raspberry Pi 3 Mode B

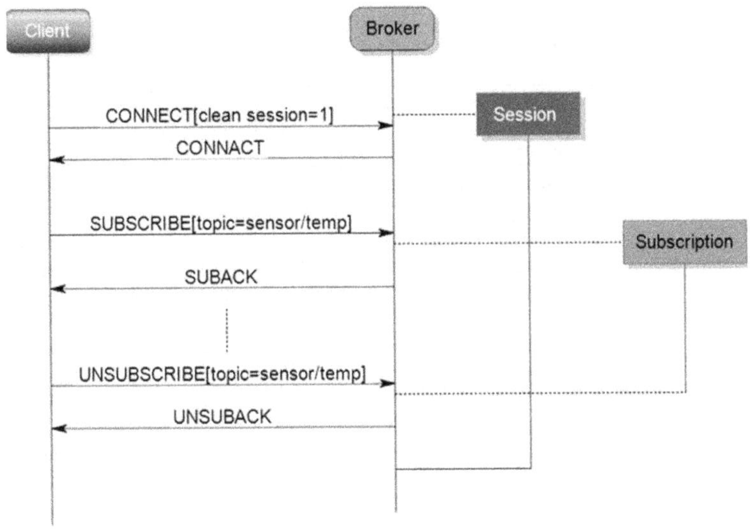

less power and that does exclude an Ethernet port. The model B board incorporates an Ethernet port and is outlined in china. The Raspberry Pi accompanies an arrangement of open source advancements, i.e. correspondence and sight and sound web technologies. In the year 2014, the establishment of the Raspberry Pi (shown in table 2) board propelled the PC module, that bundles a model B Raspberry Pi board into the module for use as a piece of inserted frameworks, to energize their utilization ("Meteoric growth: The Internet of Things is scaling exponentially,").

APPLICATION

Step-1: Create IBM Bluemix service

- ◦ Login to Bluemix using Bluemix account
- ◦ Click on Catalog in top
- ◦ Select Boilerplates section and click on Internet of things platform starter (Figure 13)

- Give the unique name of your app. I used "bluemixMobMqtt".
- Click on create and wait for the application to start.
  - ◦ For adding IoT services.
- Click on ADD A SERVICES
- Choose the Internet of things service in the Internet of things section.
- Click Create.

Table 2. Raspberry Pi 3 detail

Type	Model-B
Generation	3
Date of release	2016, February
Architecture	ARMv8-A (64/32-bit)
SoC	Boardcom BCM2837
CPU	1.2 GHz 64-bit quad-core ARM Cortex-A53
GPU	Boardcom VideoCore IV@250MHz,OpenGL ES 2.0, MPEG-2 and VC-1,1080p30 H.264/MPEG-4 AVC high-profile decoder and encoder
Memory	1 GB
USB 2.0 ports	4(on-board 5-port USB hub)
Video for input	Camera interface connector with 15-pin
Video for output	HDMI, composite video have 3.5mm TRRS jack, MIPI display interface-DSI for raw LCD panels
Audio input	I²S for 2 board
Audio output	Analog via 3.5mm phone jack, HDMI for digital
Storage(on-board)	USB Boot Mode and Micro SDHC slot
Network(on-board)	Ethernet 10/100 Mbit/s, wireless 802.11n, Bluetooth 4.1
Low-level peripherals	17xGPIO plus the same specific function and HAT ID bus
Power rating	800 mA
Power source	5V via Micro USB
Size	85.60mm x 56.5mm
Weight	45g
Console	Micro-USB cable or optional GPIO power connector for serial cable

Figure 13. IBM Bluemix catalog and select Boilerplate

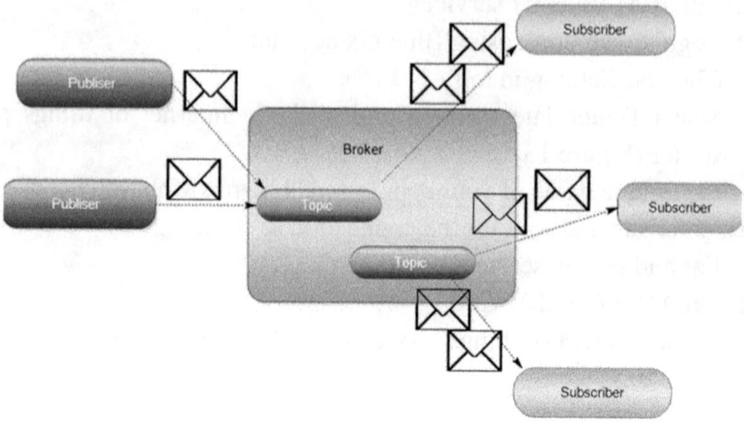

- Click Restage.
  - Launch the IoT services
- Navigate the application on overview and click Internet of things
- Click the Launch dashboard to open IoT console.
  - Register the devices
- Click Add Device on the Devices tab (Figure 14).
- Choose Create a Device type for the Device type option.
- Fill in the Device Type as "Android".
- Fill in the Device ID with a unique id like "123456789"
- Click Continue
- Copy the information (Figure 15).

Step-2: Start Node-red

- Add Watson IoT node
- Configure with their information and insert the information (Figure 16).

Figure 14. IBM Watson Add Device

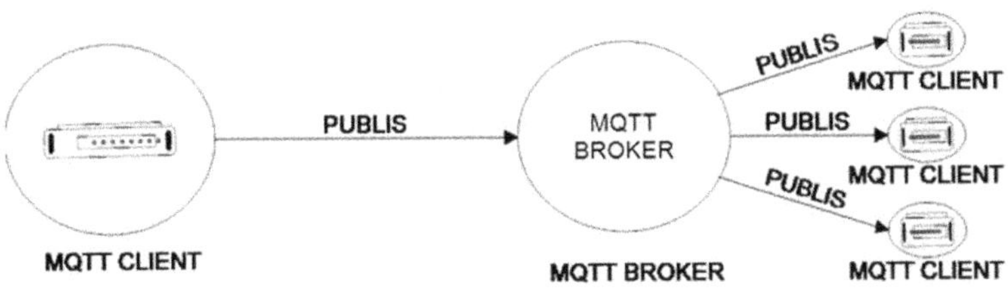

Figure 15. Copy information of the Device

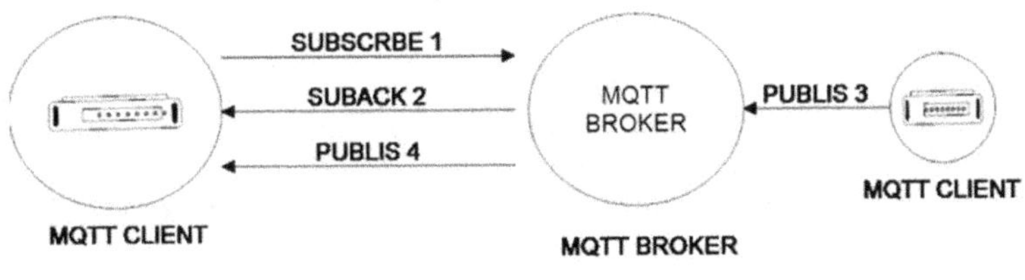

Figure 16. Configure Watson IoT node

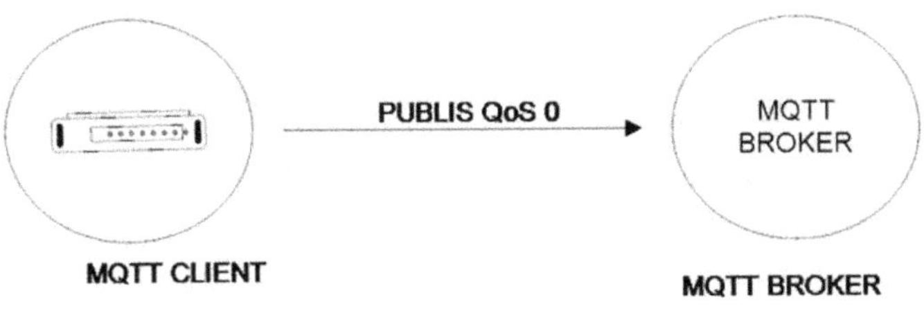

- Add DHT22 node
- Configure this node (Figure 17)

Step-3: Make Android app
  - This is configured with MQTT protocol.
  - Enter Broker id and port address (Figure 18).
- *Make a graph of temperature (Figure 19).*

Figure 17. Configure DHT22 node

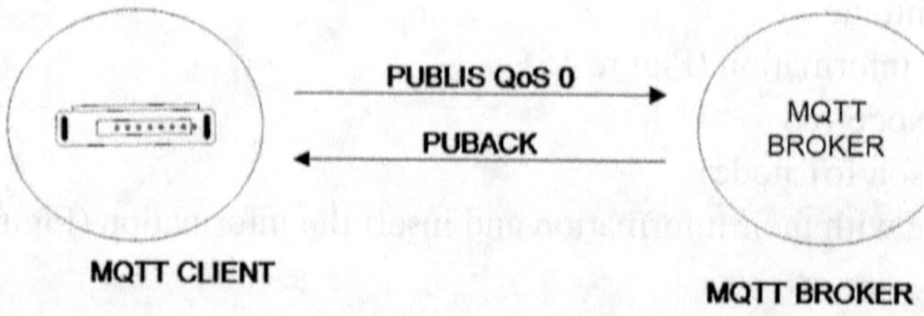

Figure 18. Connect with mosquito broker

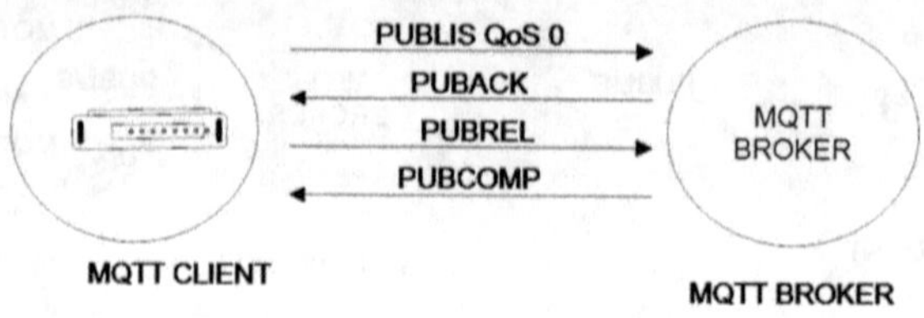

Figure 19. Graph of temperature

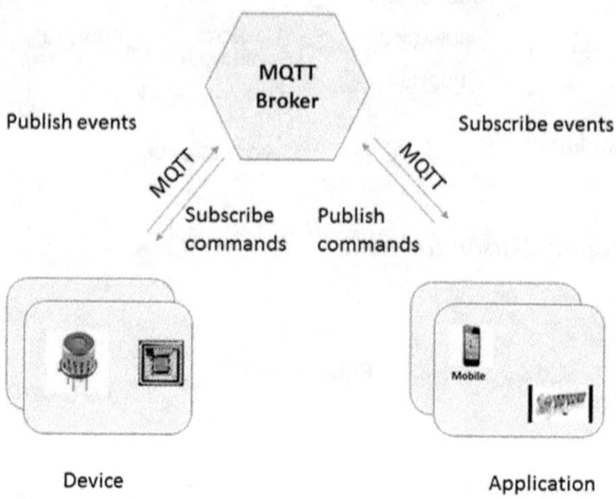

CONCLUSION

In this chapter, the designing and implementation of a Smart City based IoT applications have been described. With the help of sensors, DHT22 and BMP082, Wi-Fi Raspberry Pi 3 and MQTT, we can make systems that are used for transmitting environmental information such as humidity, temperature and pressure. The data is primarily sensed and sent by sensors to Raspberry Pi. Afterwards, with the help of Raspberry Pi and MQTT broker, we can monitor that data anywhere by the mobile device, computer system, and any embedded device that is subscribed.

REFERENCES

Andy Banks, D. L. (2012). *An introduction to the MQTT transport for Mobile Messaging & M2M*. Retrieved from https://developer.ibm.com/messaging/2012/12/05/introduction-mqtt-transport-mobile-messaging-m2m/

Atzori, L., Iera, A., & Morabito, G. (2010). The Internet of Things: A survey. *Computer Networks*, *54*(15), 2787–2805. doi:10.1016/j.comnet.2010.05.010

Bhatt, C., Dey, N., & Ashour, A. (2017). *Internet of Things and Big Data Technologies for Next Generation Healthcare*. Springer. doi:10.1007/978-3-319-49736-5

Bhayani, M., Patel, M., & Bhatt, C. (n.d.). *Proceedings of the International Congress on Information and Communication Technology*. Retrieved from https://link.springer.com/chapter/10.1007/978-981-10-0767-5_37 doi:https://doi.org/10.1007/978-981-10-0767-5_37

Chen, H. W., & Lin, F. J. (2014). *Converging MQTT resources in ETSI standards based M2M platform*. Paper presented at the Internet of Things (iThings), 2014 IEEE International Conference on, and Green Computing and Communications (GreenCom), IEEE and Cyber, Physical and Social Computing (CPSCom), IEEE. doi:10.1109/iThings.2014.52

Collina, M., Bartolucci, M., Vanelli-Coralli, A., & Corazza, G. E. (2014). *Internet of Things application layer protocol analysis over error and delay prone links*. Paper presented at the Advanced Satellite Multimedia Systems Conference and the 13th Signal Processing for Space Communications Workshop (ASMS/SPSC), 2014 7th. doi:10.1109/ASMS-SPSC.2014.6934573

GibbonsD. (2017). *MQTT*. Retrieved from https://github.com/mqtt/mqtt.github.io/wiki/server-support

González García, C., García-Bustelo, C. P., Espada, J. P., & Cueva-Fernandez, G. (2014). Midgar: Generation of heterogeneous objects interconnecting applications. A Domain Specific Language proposal for Internet of Things scenarios. *Computer Networks*, *64*, 143–158. doi:10.1016/j.comnet.2014.02.010

Govindan, K., & Azad, A. P. (2015). *End-to-end service assurance in IoT MQTT-SN.* Paper presented at the Consumer Communications and Networking Conference (CCNC), 2015 12th Annual IEEE. doi:10.1109/CCNC.2015.7157991

Hunkeler, U., Truong, H. L., & Stanford-Clark, A. (2008). *MQTT-S—A publish/subscribe protocol for Wireless Sensor Networks.* Paper presented at the Communication systems software and middleware and workshops, 2008. comsware 2008. 3rd international conference on.

Locke, D. (2010). *MQ Telemetry Transport (MQTT) V3.1 Protocol Specification*. Retrieved from http://www.ibm.com/developerworks/library/ws-mqtt/

Luzuriaga, J. E., Cano, J. C., Calafate, C., Manzoni, P., Perez, M., & Boronat, P. (2015). *Handling mobility in IoT applications using the MQTT protocol.* Paper presented at the Internet Technologies and Applications (ITA). doi:10.1109/ITechA.2015.7317403

Meteoric growth: The Internet of Things is scaling exponentially. (2017). Retrieved from https://www.internet-der-dinge.de/en.html

Raspberry Pi 3 Model B. (2017). Retrieved from https://www.raspberrypi.org/products/raspberry-pi-3-model-b/

Sensor, Types of Sensor. (2017). Retrieved from https://www.electrical4u.com/sensor-types-of-sensor/

Sensors: Different Types of Sensors. (2017). Retrieved from http://www.engineersgarage.com/articles/sensors

Shah, T., & Bhatt, C. M. (2014, April). The Internet of things: Technologies, Communications and Computing. *CSI Communications*, *38*(1), 7.

Singh, M., Rajan, M., Shivraj, V., & Balamuralidhar, P. (2015). *Secure MQTT for internet of things (IoT)*. Paper presented at the Communication Systems and Network Technologies (CSNT), 2015 Fifth International Conference on.

Tan, L. (2010). Future Internet: The Internet of Things. In *2010 3rd Int. Conf. Adv. Comput. Theory Eng*. IEEE. doi:10.1109/ICACTE.2010.5579543

Chapter 10
Preparation of Raspberry Pi for IoT-Enabled Applications

Manoj Devare
Amity University – Mumbai, India

ABSTRACT

This chapter shares the experiences in systematic, well-tested, and executed step-by-step procedure for the preparation of the Raspberry Pi single board computer (SBC) for the internet of things (IoT)-enabled applications. This chapter is useful for beginners and professionals working for automation of smart factories with the help of IoT and Cloud. Moreover, interesting data exchange techniques like low power wireless alternatives ZigBee, LORA, BLE, 6LowPAN, SigFox, and multi-queue telemetry transport (MQTT) are also stated. The related IoT preceding and succeeding technologies, like machine-to-machine(M2M), cyber-physical-systems (CPS), web of things (WoT), SCADA are also the part of insights. Various supporting technologies for the success of IoT like commercial and open source IoT cloud platforms, virtual agents(VA), and digital twins are also discussed.

INTRODUCTION

The first industrial revolution (IR 1.0) happened in 1984; the invention of the steam engine which has positively affected the human and animal hard work converted into the machinery efforts and also increased the import and export of the things. The second industrial revolution (IR 2.0) was happed around 1870, where the electricity was invented, and industrial products and the assembly lines were major contributions. The IR 2.0 resulted with the huge amount of increase in the capacity of the product manufacturing in less cost of the production. This resulted in the

DOI: 10.4018/978-1-5225-3805-9.ch010

side effect of the degradation in traditional employment, and the new field of the employments was increased. The IR 3.0 happened in 1969, where Electronics, Computer and Information Technology (IT) made the self- running automation. The positive results were caused a reduction in the product cost, marketing of the products and services. This also resulted into the computerization of the white-collar jobs. The IoT is the concept to allow the Internet-based communication to happen between physical objects including mobiles, smart watches, robots, drones, sensors, and controllers. (Wang et al., 2014; Garcia et al., 2014; Meana-Liorian et al., 2016)

To implement the IoT as fourth industrial revolution (IR 4.0), this is not new but evolved from the SCADA systems as industrial automation since the 1970s, leveraging the recent advancements in the information technology, to make available data in smart formats at the fingertips. The enabling technologies are mostly web-based portals, Android apps, alerts based mechanisms on the machine-learning techniques. The specially designed protocols like Multi-Queue Telemetry Transport (MQTT) for the Machine to Machine (M2M) and/or the IoT is also discussed.

The IoT characterizes the anytime, anywhere and anything. Anytime & any place means on the move, outdoors, indoors, night time, daytime, away from the PC, or at the PC. Anything means between PCs, Human to Human (H2H), i.e. not using PC, Human to Thing (H2T), using generic equipment, and Thing to Things (T2T).

ITU-T defines the IoT as: "A global infrastructure for the Information Society, enabling advanced services by interconnecting (physical and virtual) things based on, existing and evolving, interoperable information and the communication technologies".

The European Union (EU) and more specifically the EU Projects Research Cluster in the IoT (IERC) gives the following definition: "A dynamic global network infrastructure with self-configuring capabilities based on standard and interoperable communication protocols where physical and virtual 'things' have identities, physical attributes, and virtual personalities and use intelligent interfaces, and are seamlessly integrated into the information network."

The emergence of Mobile, the high-speed internet made everything available at the fingertips. The IR 4.0 is set up the standards for the IoT, and improving personal lives, our workplace, future industrial manufacturing efficiencies & capabilities, the field of the future internet, and next-generation networks. There are several applications found in healthcare domain. Very interesting examples to monitor the heart activities of the senior members of a family like grandparents and sending an SMS or email as an alert message to the responsible family member. The health monitoring devices are powered by human body's thermal energy, and frequently monitors heart rhythms and detects the small problems.

For example, for improving the boiler efficiency the business initiative perhaps involves some questions that what is different time intervals when the boiler outage happened? What are the different components are getting damaged? What are the different reasons for the failure of the boiler temperature/ pressure /fuel/ operator? What should particular actions be taken care on the occurrence of typical failure? What is the ignored scheduled maintenance? These are the IoT based project questionnaires includes descriptive, predictive or prescriptive options.

The beginner can use this research work as the helping document for the preparation of the Pi. Here the necessary steps are discussed for installation of the Raspbian OS, booting the Pi device and accessing it remotely using the different tools and methods. This work also discusses connecting the LORA shield with Raspberry Pi the automation engineers use SBC or microcontroller for connecting to the sensors and actuators. Before reading values from the sensors, it is necessary to prepare the Pi for developing any application. A generalized approach and steps are discussed here which can be useful for the developers of the IoT based applications. There are certain interfaces provided by the manufacturer of the Pi, and certain interfaces can be added as a custom requirement. For instance, there is need of certain low power wireless technology to work with Pi. One of the sections of this work describes the low-power options available for the Pi.

The Pi can be considered as one of the options for developing the successful IoT application. This work does not indicate the superiority of the Pi over other hardware(s) or platforms. Another interesting section describes the various Cloud services available for connecting the Pi to push the data store and compute for taking further actions. As the Cloud is pay-as-you-go model, pushing smaller messages to the Cloud charge certain billing amount, hence pushing the data after a certain interval, and in bulk can be a better option. This introduces the Edge Computing (Pelino & Hewitt, 2016).

The IoT is an idea of making devices and objects smarter by linking them to the Internet, and extended service of data processing and data analysis using machine learning techniques. Smart things are physical objects that can connect to the registration server or home gateway through a network interface. Here the things can be anything right from the computer, human being, animal, plant, home appliance, industrial instrument, device, automobile, things, people, robots, 3D Printers, drones, boilers and much more. The things get the unique identifier i.e. IP address due to the huge address space of 128 bit long the Internet Protocol version 6, and even from IPV4 having 32-bit address space, as both versions existing at the same time. There are several areas of the applications for the IoT e.g. automotive, home appliances, smart energy, smart city, wearable, industrial, power grid, healthcare devices, security, supply chain, and logistics. Several examples are available with various professional players including Texas Instrument. The emerging area of Internet of Vehicles (IoV) connecting the autonomous cars and vehicles. Not only the systems getting the new sensors, but also old sensor based systems are getting replaced with newer one.

Figure 1 shows search pattern by the Internet users, where, "Interest over time" is a number represent search interest relative to the highest point on the chart for the given region and time. A value of 100 is the peak popularity of the term. A value of 50 means that the term is half as popular. Likewise, a score of 0 means the term was less than 1% as popular as the peak. The graph shows the searching pattern of the users about Raspberry Pi and Arduino is nearly same, as an alternative to each other, for the IoT applications.

The search patterns show the decrease in the search pattern for Cloud, as it became more mature technology, while the hype of the IoT is still showing searching patterns, adding curiosity to new individuals. As diverse field specialists are required for the IoT including the process automation, computer scientist, electrical engineer, electronic engineer and so on. The IoT terminology is reached to its peak of the hype cycle. If the expected investments are found in the Industrial IoT (IIoT), then the point of disappointment to the industry will not be appearing, and it will reach the plateau of maturity. As per the Gartner's innovation hype cycle, it has lots of flying colors to show.

It is interesting to understand the technology hype cycle created by Wikipedia user Jeremy Kemp where the visibility over the time shows the technology trigger which actually starts with some exciting articles wrote by technology leaders for short time of visibility, however, once it reaches the peak of the hype-inflated expectations (like famous actors in the movies), it drops the trough of disillusionment (asking self- analyzing questions over imaginations done through the marketing), and again

Figure 1. Trends.google.com Searching Pattern of Cloud Computing and IoT since 2012 to May 2017

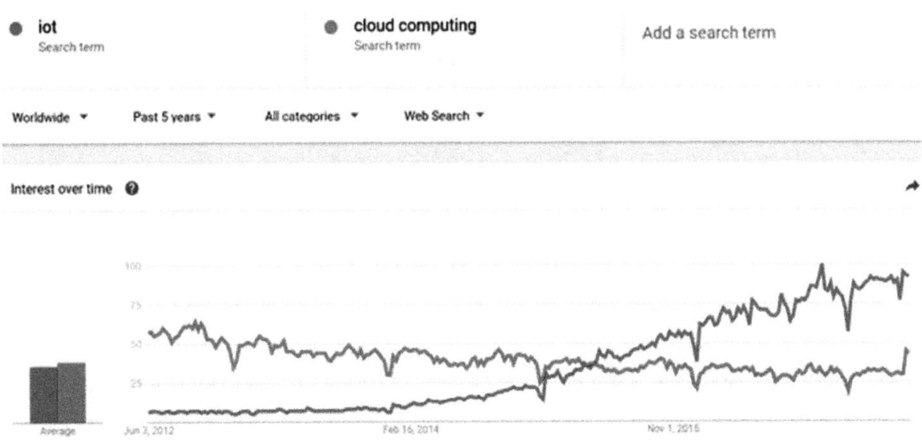

takes slow pickup to the slope of enlightenment (serious achievements) over the time and then maintains the plateau of productivity for technology maturity and productivity is visible. Similarly, Gartner hype cycle 2012 shows that the technology hypes vary from less than 2 years to more than 10 years. As per the Gartner report, it is observed that the IoT is for more than 10 years.

Figure 2 shows the statistics of the Internet users by world regions since the year 2011 to 2015. There is a huge amount of the internet users as per the data are shown by the "ourWorldinData", (which internally uses World Bank's data) and more the IoT users and devices are going to be added into it, in the near future due to the IoT hype (Murphy & Roser, 2017). As far as the use of the internet is considered, the social networking websites like YouTube has over a billion users–almost a third of all people on the Internet–and every day, people watch hundreds of millions of hours of YouTube videos and generate billions of views. 1.49 billion Monthly active users worldwide as of June 2015. For every one minute 11820 Reddit vote cast, 267320 tweets, 1966647 Google searches (onesecond.designly.com), 4890383 Facebook likes are happening. This is showing a huge amount of data production for the further business process enhancements.

The remaining chapter is divided into the sections including current technological trends, IoT related terminologies, Investments in IIoT, characteristics of IoT products and services, wireless technologies that enables IoT, phases in the IoT based projects, Cloud & other IoT platforms supporting to Pi, state-of-the-art use cases of Pi, the MQTT and message broker, preparing Raspberry Pi for IoT applications, access Pi

Figure 2. The Internet users by world region since 2011 to 2015

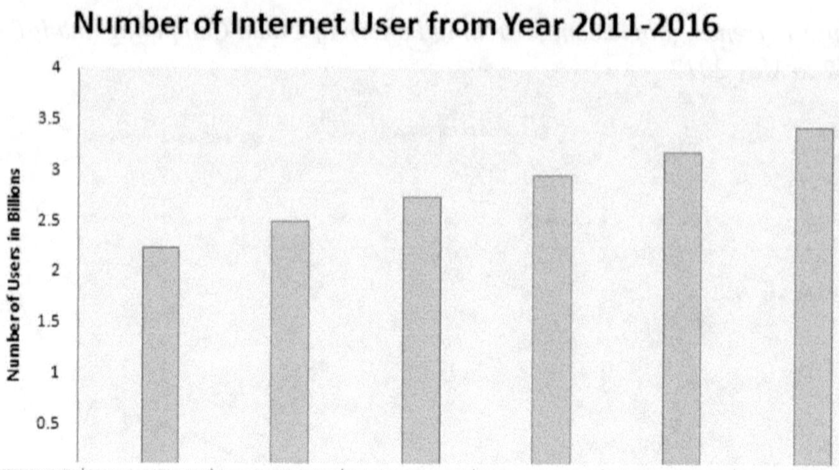

Year	2011	2012	2013	2014	2015	2016
Internet Users	2,231,957,359	2,494,736,248	2,728,428,107	2,956,385,569	3,185,996,155	3,424,971,237

from LAN in the internet, implementing security in Pi communications, developing fail-safe Pi, connecting LORA shield, reading analog values from Pi, accessing industrial buses.

CURRENT TECHNOLOGICAL TRENDS

The current status of technologies in the year 2017, that remain on the hype for more than ten years, like Human Augmentation, 3D Bioprinting, volumetric and holographic display, mobile robots, the IoT, Mesh Networks. Augmented content recognition, 3D scanners, autonomous vehicles, natural-language question and answer, Silicon anode batteries, speech-to-speech translation, crowdsourcing, gamification, HTML5, hybrid Cloud computing, 3D printing, complex event processing, application stories, augmented reality, Near Field Communication (NFC) payment, audio mining/speech analytics, M2M communication services, home health monitoring, virtual worlds, consumer telematics lived five to ten years. The hype duration of 2 to 5 years for the big data, wireless power, Bring Your Own Device (BYOD), social analytics, private Cloud computing, in-memory database management systems, NFC, Cloud computing, gesture control, in-memory analytics, text analytics, Mobile OTA payments, consumerization, biometric authentication methods, and speech recognition. Hosted virtual desktops, media tablets, idea management, predictive analytics lived for less than two years of the hype cycle.

Machine Learning, Deep Learning, Virtual Assistant (VA), augmented and virtual reality, everything on-demand, self-service analytics, Blockchain, Digital Twin, react JS, Smart Factory, Quantum Computing, artificial intelligence, are the technology buzzwords which cannot be avoided anyways with IIoT.

Digital Twin is combining the IoT and smart connected product capabilities connected back to the data and context provided by Computer Aided Design (CAD), Project Life Cycle Management (PLM), Application Life Cycle Management (ALCM), and Service Lifecycle Management (SLM) systems in a completely consistent way. It also requires the ability to pull data from other systems such as ERP, supply chain, and external systems. It seems more suitable for IoT applications, as Oracle has implemented virtual twin and predictive twin.

IoT RELATED TERMINOLOGIES

Figure 3 shows the Internet users interest in web-search for IoT related terminologies. There is some overlap between the different terminologies like M2M (Yamanoue et al., 2012) communications, Web-of-Things (WoT), the IoT (which is referred by

Figure 3. The Internet Users Interest in Web-Search for IoT and Related Terminologies in trends.google.com

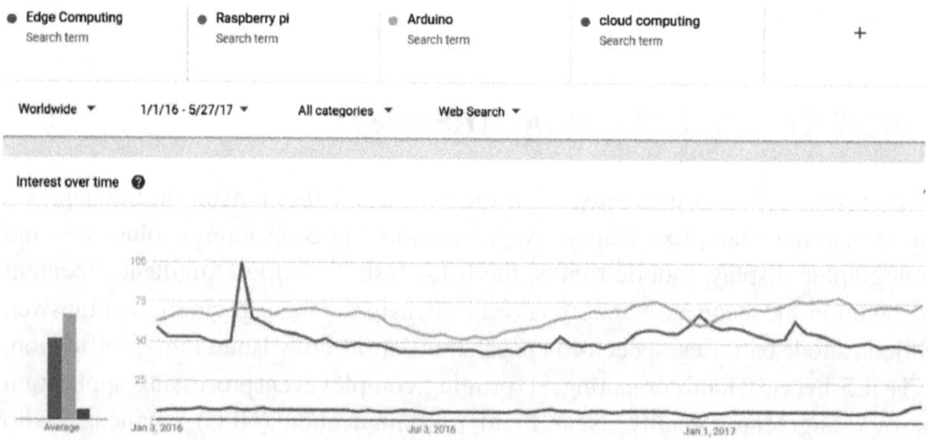

the telecommunications and networking communities), and Cyber-Physical-Systems (CPS) which is mostly referred by mechanical, aerospace, aeronautics engineers, computer scientist working on embedded systems testing and verification; are always discussed with the IoT. The IoT is broader terminology became more widely accepted in the consumer-friendly commercial environment.

The M2M is introduced by telecommunication service providers refer to the communication and interactions between machines, devices and collecting the sensor data without the assistance of a human. For example, device interactions and exchange of information is occurring through Cloud computing infrastructure. The M2M emphasis on machines interactions via one or more 3G, 4G, 5G, satellite, public networks. Hence, M2M is part of the IoT, while M2M standards (such as OneM2M) have a prominent place in the IoT standards landscape. It also enables the composition of workflows comprising all of the above interactions. The IoT includes the notion of the Internet connectivity (which is provided in the most of the networks outlined above) but is not necessarily focused on the use of telecommunication networks. The scope of the IoT applications is broader and includes systems that are not accessible through the web such as conventional Wireless Sensor Networks (WSN) and Radio Frequency Identification (RFID) systems (Wang, 2014).

Most of the CPS systems and applications, IoT are networked systems involve physical sensing and embedded devices i.e. both combine aspects of the physical and digital world. The CPS is a term that refers the systems or problems that involve large-scale organizational and physical processes, real-time control, and time critical problems.

The WoT tries to integrate IoT to the Web, with the option on the application layer added over the IoT's network layer. The WoT enables access and control over IoT resources and applications using mainstream web technologies such as HTML 5.0, JavaScript, Ajax, PHP, and Ruby on Rails etc. The approach of building the WoT is therefore based on REST APIs, which enable both developers and system engineer to benefit from the popularity and maturity of web technologies. (Biron & Follett, 2016).

An actuator is a component that manipulates the environment or the area around them. The actuator also converts the electrical signals into motion, light, heat, or cooling. The sensors sense the environment, the area around them, or through interactions. For example photodetectors, temperature sensor, thermostat, thermistor, thermocouple, RFID, metal sensor, potentiometer, push-button, and smoke detectors.

There are some platforms which enable the wireless sensor data processing such as Intel Edison, Parallel Board, Raspberry Pi, Arduino, ESP8266, and BeagleBone. Components are physical objects that connect to microcontroller (MCU-PT) or Single Board Computer (SBC-PT) and typically may or may not have a network interface. These are simple devices that only communicate through their analog or digital slots. The "things" are used to create self-contained physical objects like coffee makers or smoke alarms.

The Serial Peripheral Interface (SPI) is a synchronous serial data protocol used by microcontrollers for communicating with one or more peripheral devices quickly over short distances. With an SPI connection, there is always one master device (usually a microcontroller) which controls the peripheral devices. The SPI devices communicate in a full-duplex mode using a master-slave architecture with a single master. The interface was developed by Motorola and has become a de-facto standard. Typical applications include sensors, secure digital cards, and liquid crystal displays (LCD).

The Gemalto company designed eSim (eUICC) technology, which is secure embedded SIM is a remotely managing multiple mobile network operator subscriptions and be compliant with GSMA specifications. It is available in various form factors, either plugged-in or soldered; the eSIM is easy to integrate in any kind of device (Gelmalto, 2017).

An Arduino is a low-cost microcontroller motherboard for embedded projects. A microcontroller is a simple computer that can run one program at a time, over and over again. It is very easy to use. Arduino is best used for repetitive tasks like opening and closing a garage door, reading the outside temperature and reporting it to Twitter, or driving a simple robot. It is possible to connect the open platforms to store sensor data in the Cloud.

There are three different visions to develop the applications using IoT, namely "thing oriented", "the Internet-oriented" and "semantic-oriented". The RFID,

NFC, UID, sensors, actuators, spimes, everyday objects are considered as the part of thing oriented vision. The Internet 0, WoT, IP for smart objects is the Internet-oriented thinking. The semantic execution environment thinking about the IoT uses the semantics technologies, reasoning over data, and execution environment concepts. In this context, autonomous and proactive behavior, context awareness, collaborative communication, and elaboration are just some required capabilities. The IoT vision consisting of the RFID as one part, and there are many other communication technologies consisting within it. Another IoT philosophy which includes the connectivity at anytime, anyplace, anyone, and anything (Atzori, Iera, and Morabito, 2010). analyses the differences between the concept of smart objects, not-Smart objects, and things. The combination of the smart objects and the IoT are supporting to each other. The network of the interconnected objects provides the intelligent system. The level of intelligence can be considered as the information handling capacity, notification of the problems, and decision-making. The sensors and actuators are generally not smart objects, whereas the microcontrollers, smartphones, robots are considered as the smart objects. Some objects are intelligent through the network, intelligence in the object or a combined form of intelligence (García, Llorián, Bustelo & Lovelle, 1988).

The M2M also called as Machine Type Communication (MTC) and its application in the smart city, with the capillary and cellular techniques of access such as LTE. The challenge of efficiently accessing multiple devices in the random & multiple fashions and avoiding network congestion with the use of reinforcement approach is discussed (Hasan, Hossain, & Niyato, 2013) & (Poole, 2017).

INVESTMENTS IN IIoT

The McKinsey & Company, on June 2015, analysts project by 2025, data from connected devices will yield insights driving the potential economic value of as much as USD 11 trillion. It's a $737 billion market, reaching $1.3 trillion by 2020. The total global economic value of the IoT technology could be as much as $6.2 trillion by 2025. The IoT market expenditures are growing by 27% annually through 2018. The EU is investing €192 million in the IoT research and innovation from 2014 to 2017.

According to Capgemini's predictions and the concept of Smart Factories (SF) framework called as a digital industrial revolution to add $500 billion to the global economy in next 5 years. Audi's €1 billion SF in San José Chiapa, Mexico. Faurecia's $64 million SF in Columbus, Indiana. Adidas' high-tech Speed-factory in Ansbach, Germany. Siemens' smart plant in Amberg, Germany. General Electric's (GE)

"Brilliant Factory" in Pune, India. ABB's smart plant in Beijing, China. These are the state-of-the-art examples for IIoT.

As per the SparkLabs Top, 10 IoT start-ups include View, Proteus Digital Health, Jawbone, Sonos, SigFox, Trilliant, Alarm.com, Anki, and Inrix. These companies work in energy efficiency (Home & Office), healthcare, wearable, home automation, IoT Platform, home security, home entertainment, and transportation. The major giants including Apple having Homekit platform, Google Brillo Platform and Nest Labs (acquired by Google), and Amazon echo (hub). The major players in wearable are Fitbit (smart fitness band & smartwatches), Pebble (smartwatches), Oculus VR (Virtual Reality Glasses), GO Pro (Smart Camera), Xiaomi, Garmin, Samsung, Google. iRobotics is leading in consumer robotics.

Consumer Robotics market required robot in domestic tasks personal, healthcare, educational, and entertainment. Intel has invested $67M into 8 Chinese robotics start-ups. Google acquired 10 companies for its new robotics division. Asustek and Xiaomi are looking to move into robotics potentially for elderly and children, Samsung has launched a new $100M Robotics lab, and Canon has spent $3.2B to focus on robotics. Service robotics refers to robotics that can be used for service purposes, such as assistance, human autonomous chores, and entertainment. As per the research by MarketsandMarkets predicted $18 billion connected robotics sector. There are startups Jibo, Aldebaran Softbank, Savioke (Relay hotel service Bot), Neato (Smart Vacuum Bot), Somabar (Smart Robotic Bartender), KnightScope (Smart Security Bot). The well-established robot service players iRobot (Smart Cleaning bots), LG (added augmented reality feature into the cleaning Bot), Amazon Echo (can read Kindle books loudly).

The IIoT players are Cisco, GE, Capgemini, and Siemens. Huawei working in Telecommunication, and acquisition of Neul. The RetailNext enables retailers and manufacturers to collect, analyze and visualize data about in-store customer engagement. DeepMind (acquired by Google) working in artificial intelligence models eschew pre-scripted forms of AI and instead rely on experiential learning based on rudimentary capabilities using deep learning. The Airware works for the aerospace or drones for aerial information platform for rapid development and safe operation of commercial drones, providing hardware, software and Cloud services. Matterport works in 3D Printing, which enables a realistic 3D model.

CHARACTERISTICS OF IoT PRODUCTS AND SERVICES

The IoT combines aspects and technologies from ubiquitous computing, pervasive computing, the internet protocol, sensing technologies, communication technologies, information network, embedded devices, systems and hardware with or without human interventions. The smart object is the basic block in the IoT applications, and it impacts society, environment, economy and individual citizens.

The IoT based software applications possesses characteristics features including intelligence i.e. smartness, connectivity for accessibility, reliability, autonomous, compatibility to send data, sensing for awareness of the physical world & people, ability of expressing using visualizing user interfaces to a screen, energy harvesting, power efficiency, safety for moving data and physical things in the environment. The flexibility of scaling of the IoT application can be static or dynamic dependent on the financial, functional or non-functional software requirement specifications of the customer.

IoT 1.0 has focused on systems dashboards, device management, simple sensor connectivity and monitoring. The IoT 2.0 focus on platforms with big data infrastructure, predictive models, startups, mobile, streaming, the IoT Middleware, M2M enablement. The IoT 3.0 includes systems of insight, ecosystems & alliances, service platforms, physical models, industry services and Clouds (Dertien, 2015).

The electronics industry looks the IoT as "ubiquitous sensing", however, it is not just sensors sensing ability, data collection and carrying data to other location but intelligent decision-making included. The IoT enabled products or services are mostly based on the software technologies. The variety of end-users including engineers, site manager, top-level management perhaps use the Android-based applications, Web-enabled portals or desktop systems. As smartphones are available, BYOD works fine and suitable for IoT functionalities. These applications mostly need notification services such as SMS, automated video or voice calls, email services, alerts, graphical images, or plots with good graphics capabilities. Without the Internet connectivity, most of the mentioned services may not work fine.

WIRELESS TECHNOLOGIES THAT ENABLES IOT

Gateway is a point on a network that receives and sends information from many other points on the network and transmits information to another network, maintaining sessions and subscriptions for all connected devices in the IoT solution. The router used at the home, on the internet is one type of gateway. For this MQTT, WebSockets, & HTTP are the options.

As the "Smart factories" having the sensor data or smart objects are sending the data, the wireless technologies play a significant role in the data transfer. The wireless technologies provide the hassle-free data communication. There are many IoT applications, where the conventional electricity sources are not available for the established microcontrollers or similar devices; hence low power consumption is highly appreciated for several operations in the IoT devices. Hence, much of the efforts have been observed for fulfilling the low-power requirements of the IoT applications.

The recent data from businessinsider.com shows that network and communication technologies employed by the IoT services or products are 80% Wi-Fi, 60% Cellular, 59% Bluetooth, 46% Ethernet, 31% LPWAN, 21% ZigBee, 11% Z-Wave, and 8% use some other technologies. Bluetooth, Zigbee, Z-wave, are PAN-based protocol are some of the other useful protocols.

The ZigBee is a wireless, PAN-based, open, low-cost, low data transfer rate, low-power, energy efficient, secure, IEEE 802.15.4, physical radio specification and operates in unlicensed bands including 2.4 GHz, 900 MHz, 868 MHz in Europe, 915 MHz in the USA and Australia, 784 MHz in China. It operates in the Industrial, Scientific, and Medical (ISM) radio bands. It operates with data rates vary from 20 Kbit/s (868 MHz band) to 250 Kbit/s (2.4 GHz band). It allows devices to last for years on a single battery. With the Green Power Feature, don't even need any batteries. It harnesses the power of the mesh to connect every product to every other product. So if one of the products fails, the others will continue to communicate without interruption. ZigBee nodes can stay in sleep mode most of the time, drastically extending battery life.

So unlike Wi-Fi, if a user having two devices with ZigBee chips, it's possible that they won't be able to operate with each other. This technology also has a low-channel bandwidth of 1MHz. It's restricted to wireless personal area networks (WPAN) and reaches an average 10 to 30 meters for usual applications.

Bluetooth is based on standard 802.15.1 and ZigBee is for low rate devices (LR-WPAN). They can automatically form ad hoc networks as devices within range are detected. They only address devices in their own networks and do not currently connect to the internet.

XBee is not the same as ZigBee instead, XBee is a brand of radio communication modules (made by Digi) that can support a number of protocols, including ZigBee, 802.15.4, WiFi, etc. Its range is 10 to 30 meters. ZigBee is often used in-home automation products, though it is not the only option.

To interface of Zigbee with Raspberry Pi-2 for a proper wireless communication, through four USB ports, so it is better to use a Zigbee Dongle for this interface. The XBee 1mW Wire Antenna Series 1 (2 numbers), XBee Explorer Dongle (2 numbers).

The LoRa, LoRaWAN is a Low Power Wide Area Network (LPWAN) specification intended for wireless battery operated Things in regional, national or global network. The LoRaWAN target key requirements of the IoT such as secure bi-directional communication, mobility and localization services, data rates range from 0.3 kbps to 50 kbps. It is having a star-of-star topology in which gateways are transparent bridge relaying messages between end-devices and central network server in the back-end. The communication between end-devices and gateways is spread out on different

Table 1. Wireless technologies characteristics for IoT applications

	Power Source	Range	Throughput	Typical Topology
ZigBee	No Battery	100m	Up to 20 kbps	Mesh, Star
6LowPAN	No Battery	100m	Up to 20 kbps	Mesh, Star
BLE	Coin Cell	10m	Up to 20 kbps	Peer-to-Peer, Star
Bluetooth	AAA	10-50m	2 Mbps	Peer-to-Peer, Star
Wi-Fi	AA	100m	20 Mbps	Peer-to-Peer, Star
SigFox	--	3 and 10km	100 - 600 bps	Star
Sub-1 GHz	Coin Cell	10 km	Up to 20 kbps	Mesh, Star, Peer-to-Peer

frequency channels and data rates. The LoRaWAN network server is managing the data rate and RF output for each end-device individually by means of an adaptive data rate (ADR) scheme. Table 1 shows the summary of the wireless technologies for IoT applications having a power source, coverage range, throughput, and typical topology applicable for each of the technology.

The LoRaWAN has several different classes of end-point devices to address the different needs reflected in the wide range of applications. Bi-directional end-devices (Class A) have end-devices of Class A allow for bi-directional communications. Bi-directional end-devices with scheduled receive slots (Class B): In addition to the Class A random receive windows, Class B devices open extra receive windows at scheduled times. Bi-directional end-devices with maximal receive slots (Class C), end-devices of Class C have nearly continuously open receive windows, only closed when transmitting.

The 6LoWPAN combines the IPv6 and Low-power Wireless Personal Area Networks (LoWPAN). IP version 6 is solving the shortage of the IP addresses with huge address space of 128 bits. 6LoWPAN, therefore, allows for the smallest devices with limited processing ability to transmit information wirelessly using the IP. The ZigBee is the competitor of 6LoWPAN.

Sigfox LPWA is made for the IoT applications compatible with Bluetooth, GPS 2G/3G/4G and Wi-Fi, 12-bytes payload, low-energy consumption, follow star network topology, Ultra Narrow Band radio modulation. The Sigfox can connect with Raspberry Pi by enabling the SigFox service.

The basic Bluetooth was designed for the file and data exchange in the small range by creating the Piconet among the small gadgets like mobile phones, laptops, single board computers, laptops, microcontrollers etc. In Piconet, usually, there are many slave stations and one master station. Few stations may appear in the parked state. The parked state can go into the active mode if one of the devices goes in the parked mode. Frequency 2400-2483.5 MHz range within the ISM 2.4 GHz frequency band. Bluetooth Low Energy (BLE) i.e. Bluetooth 4.0, this is a wireless, personal-area network with short-range and low-power consumption that allows for objects to transmit data. This is the "next-generation" of Bluetooth that solves many of the pairing and performance headaches from earlier Bluetooth.

General Packet Radio Service (GPRS) is a wireless communication standard for 2G and 3G cellular networks which support a number of bandwidths and provides data rates of 56-114 kbps. As cellular companies move to more advanced networks, GPRS networks may be more cost-effective for the IoT networks. The Industrial, Scientific, and Medical (ISM) band is an unlicensed part of the RF spectrum used for general-purpose data communication. In the US, the ISM bands are 915MHz, 2.4 GHz, and 5.5 GHz, whereas 2.4 GHz is the global unlicensed frequency, and has increasing amounts of interference.

As the IoT has diversified areas for potential projects, it is necessary to understand how the devices work, and they can publish topics and gateways should receive the telemetry messages. There are standard and custom communication protocols like Zigbee, BACnet (Bacnet, 2017), LLRP, Modbus, ZPL, & Simple Network Management Protocol (SNMP). There is data ingestion and transformation protocols TCP/IP socket communication, message queues like MQTT, AMQP, COAP (RFC7252, 2017), DDS, Kafka and HTTP/HTTPS over REST API. This section also explains the short description of each of the protocols.

The BACnet is a data communication protocol for Building Automation and Control Networks. BACnet is developed under American Society of Heating, Refrigerating and Air-Conditioning Engineers (ASHRAE). Low-Level Reader Protocol (LLRP) standard is a specification for the network interface between the RFID reader and its controlling software or hardware. Nowadays, NFC is alternative technology to RFID. The Modbus is a serial communication protocol developed by Modicon in 1979 to use with its programmable logic controllers (Programmable Logic Controllers-PLCs). The Modbus is a method used for transmitting information over serial lines between electronic devices. ZPL is Zebra Programming Language for the Printers, for page labeling.

Advanced Message Queuing Protocol (AMQP) is an open standard application layer protocol for message-oriented middleware. The defining features of AMQP are message orientation, queuing, routing (including point-to-point and publish-and-subscribe), reliability and security. The Constrained Application Protocol (CoAP) is a web transfer protocol for use with constrained nodes and networks in the IoT. The protocol helpful in smart energy and building automation. The DDS is a protocol for the IoT which enables network interoperability for connected machines, enterprise systems, and mobile devices. The Apache Kafka is distributed streaming platform for a real-time publish-subscribe platform for data pipelines between system and applications. Kafka runs on one or more servers, stores records in the form of topics.

The WebRTC is an open framework for the web to real-time communication in the browser. It includes the fundamental building blocks for high-quality communication on the web, such as network, audio and video components used in voice and video chat applications, can be accessed through a JavaScript API, enabling developers to easily implement their own RTC web app. The WebRTC effort is being standardized on an API level at the W3C and at the protocol level at the IETF (Bharathi & Mubeen, 2016; Webrtc, 2017).

Long Term Evolution (LTE) is a cellular system for carrying M2M and the IoT based data transfer having long battery life, enhanced coverage, large volume-low data rates.

The RFID, WSN and RSN are interesting technologies useful for IoT. The RFID is very small in size, with ISO 18000 standard, provides asymmetric communication with 10-meter range, do not have to process, and no sense. The RFID having an indefinite life, time uses the harvested power. WSN having sensing and processing capabilities, and peer-to-peer communication in 100 m of range, utilizes battery power, and a maximum of 3 years of lifetime. WSN occupies small size and follows IEEE 802.15.4 standard. Robotic Sensor Network (RSN) provides the sending, processing capabilities, asymmetric communication, with a limited range of 3 meters. RSN having an indefinite lifetime, use the harvested power, with small size. The Service-Oriented Architecture (SOA) based middleware development for the IoT platforms is an interesting activity. There are several applications of IoT have been discussed in the domain of transportation and logistics, assisted driving, mobile ticketing, environment monitoring, and augmented maps, healthcare, tracking, smart environments, comfortable homes and offices, industrial plants, smart museum, and gym. There are personal and social problems like social networking, historical queries, losses, thefts, robot taxi, and gaming applications. The open research issues are also discussed like standards, mobility support, naming, transport protocol, traffic characterization and QoS support, authentication, data integrity, privacy, and digital forgetting (Atzori, Iera, & Morabito, 2010).

(Wang, Xu, Bi, & Xu, 2014) discusses many applications of the RFIDs in factory automation, distributed and process control, supply chain management, real-time monitoring of health, kids tracking etc. The RFID uses the RF signals, tag, and reader for automatic recognition and management of the targeted objects. A tag is consisting of a chip and an antenna, a tag communicates with a reader by the principle of inductance coupling or electromagnetic reflection. A reader is to read the identity label of a targeted object; it can also write the information on reading cards. An antenna can be attached to a tag, a reader, or to an interface to the reader via a coaxial cable. The WSN and RFID combination provides best possible characteristics for the different industrial applications. The RFID is not reliable, hence WSN checks for the data more frequently. However, it produces the redundant data, which intern waste the energy, delay in the services, and wastage in the network resources. The improved data cleaning algorithm for enterprise information system based on the WSN, RFID is represented. The low-power Zigbee protocol is used for the integration of WSN with RFID. The five-layer architecture proposed consisting of a physical layer, data link layer, network layer, transport layer, and application layer.

PHASES IN THE IoT BASED PROJECTS

The IoT based project phases are substantially different and the possibility of the inclusion and expansions are broader, as compared to normal software development process. These phases can be categorized as Process Monitoring, Data Collection, Processing, Optimization, Finding Opportunities and finally developing more mature technique. The planning, deployment and managing the IoT project are important (Turner, 2016).

The IoT is considered as the convergence of the Information Technology (IT) and Operational Technology (OT). For the IoT based processes and products; the "monitoring" phase includes the use of display or user interface (mostly graphical user interface) to show the performance and status of the machinery and/or the user of the machinery. Data collection and processing involves more insights to machine learning or similar techniques were more supportive external state-of-the-art data is used as a benchmark. The recommendations, modifications, inclusion of processes find more opportunities in the business. For any business, the profit improvement includes "opportunities discovery" i.e. development of new products, services, the discovery of markets, channels, audience, and partners. The "metamorphosis" phase converts the immature techniques into more mature technology.

The analytics includes data science to apply on the IoT datasets. The variety of data sources, data capturing intervals, and involvement of human are some of the important factors during the design and implementation of the IoT process automation. Different data science models can be an option for applying. Such as making choice of neural network to train with the sample training data with the specified number of the input layer, hidden layer, and an output layer. The first model may include the five input layer neurons, one hidden layer with 10 neuron units and one output layer includes 3 neurons. The performance of the first model can be compared with the second model where a number of neurons in the hidden layer can be increased as say 15 neurons. Likewise, the comparison of many models is possible to find an optimal solution before going into the production phase.

Analytics model such as logistic regression, predictions, symbolic aggregate approximation, support vector machine, a Bayesian network, correlation analysis, decision tree, linear regression, random forest, fuzzy logic and so on can be the choice for the IoT data analytics.

As per the Forrester Wave report for quarter 4 of 2016, the Leaders in predictive analytics are SAS, IBM, SAP, FICO, RapidMiner, KNIME, Angoss. Strong Performers are Statistics, Alpine Data, H2O.ai, Microsoft, Dataiky, Domino Data Labs. The Challengers is Salford systems.

CONNECTING IoT PLATFORMS WITH VIRTUAL AGENTS

As per the definition is given by chatbots.org, a Virtual Agent (VA) or Chatbot is a computer generated, animated, AI virtual character (usually with anthropomorphic appearance) that serves as an online customer service representative. It leads an intelligent conversation with users, responds to their questions and performs the adequate non-verbal behavior. It is interesting to attach the IoT applications with VAs. This section discusses the review on VAs.

Siri is a VA which takes the user at a specific location without visiting the website or app of Uber, OLA or Lyft. Other examples are Alexa, Google Now, or Cortana. It is interesting to connect the IoT applications with various VAs for solving the problems in Industrial Automation.

RooBot is a Personal Shopping Assistant helps to find the products the user want, at the best price from the shopping universe. ShopiiBot is a simple shopping ChatBot tool. Send a picture to ShopiiBot and it will find a similar product in less than a second. Alternatively just ask ShopiiBot what product user is looking for and for what price and ShopiiBot will search thousands of retailers to find the best products. Italian language speaking chatbot Marina helps to purchase gift within 10 minutes for the person based on the information that user (e.g. wife, girlfriend, or mother), and budget.

Colombina is a framework for the development of electronic assistant's personalities for aggregation and processing various types of data. It sends a command to connected devices and produces human-friendly responses. The Singapore Weather Bot developed using live weather API by National Environment Agency in Singapore tells the current weather, forecast and pollutant standards index level in different locations in Singapore.

"BO.T" talks about Bolivia, its culture, geography, society and more. "Travel by chat" is travel industry supporting chatbot at Hong Kong www.imimr.biz. The women health related answer related "Eva" provides reward points calculations.

Walnut discovers and learns useful skills that are useful as per person's daily work and job role, after observing a large set of data points; it shows 2-4 minutes video every day. Erwin provides various riddles and clues to solve them. "Goschoolwise" provides an EdTech chat-bot to help high school counselors. The website is a proof of concept and a B2C implementation. The chatbot is for high schools is SchoolWise to harnesses the power of IBM Watson for college admissions. Learn about the schools beyond just numbers. Get to know the SchoolDNA and if the school is a good fit for you. IBM Watson is a technology platform that uses natural language processing and machine learning to reveal insights from large amounts of unstructured data.

CLOUD AND OTHER IoT PLATFORMS SUPPORTING RASPBERRY PI

The IoT applications are different from the traditional web-based applications, or the normal mobile applications. Here, the sensor based data (or some other data) perhaps pushed to Cloud or web server. The reactions to the event happened perhaps immediate or deferred. This is absolutely dependent on the choice of the seriousness priority by the product or service users.

As shown in Figure 4, the architecture of the IoT application shows layered approach where platform, data acquisition, data storage, software service, service composition, application service, & clients are used for any type of the IoT based projects. The platform such as Pi provides the entry or starting point to receive the sensor data. It is possible that more than one platform can be chosen by the implementer. The data acquisition is possible through the multiple platforms and in different formats such as MQTT message, XML document, JSON data, raw data, images, voice, video, a combination of structured or unstructured data, or data in the flat file etc. This layer raises the issue of the interoperability and compatibility if multiple platforms are involved with different protocols in the communication. The data storage can be any DBMS or data storage facility provided by the big data storage implementers. Nowadays, most often Cloud is the choice for data storage. The software service and service composition layer needs for the further decision-making and analytics. The ending interface can be any Graphical User Interface made using any web-technologies or Mobile app.

For example, the physical entrance of the undesirable person to the restricted and sensitive area can cause an immediate reaction to the user of the system, or it is possible that the entry can be recorded. If in case, the Cloud service or the web server is used, the processing can be done at the same time or data analytics can be performed at a slower rate. The real-time applications do not afford the delay caused in the processing. Such as crunching the data received from the application, solving the problem with the use of big data available in the database, using some intelligent method for solving the desired result takes time.

Figure 4. General Architecture for the IoT Based Projects

To avoid further delay, in the applications, the data must be processed near to its source of production. For example, if the infrared waves are generated by the motion sensor or the temperature readings noted from the temperature sensor can be noted by programming logic used wrote in such a fashion that, the timer can push the data to the database after every 5 seconds. Consider the industrial application where some chemical liquid composition is heated on a constant increase in the temperature. Due to some unavoidable circumstances, the heater suddenly raises the temperature. It is expected that the IoT application should react if; the rise in the temperature in the consecutive 20 readings is more than 3 degree Celsius. In such as case, if the data is pushed on the Cloud, and trigger to stop an actuator (here heater) is delayed due to some processing, it will cause some perils.

Hence, it is recommended that the data should be processed at the boundary instead of the centralized computing and storage. The "edge computing" unlike Cloud computing, pushes more data processing out to the edge of the network, close to the source of the data. As the IoT applications are distributed in nature, the reaction time matters a lot. The Edge computing is not going to replace the Cloud computing but it will be supporting technology for real-time and sensitive data requirements. The edge computing will move the computing to the edge would result in the distributed, unsecured and hard to manage data processing. Edge computing will push the computing to the sensors, embedded PCs, hubs, gateways, routers, and on-premises servers to address key itself. Due to edge computing, the huge amount of traffic get reduced and saves the cost of server and Cloud platform. There are many programmable logic controllers (PLCs) are available those work faster with the processors to capture the data from the sensors, however, due to lack of memories, the data should be pushed to the PC or Cloud in specific intervals. There are standard stand-alone systems Dell, Mitsubishi, Marvel, Samsung, Intwine, Harman, and Adlink.

EdgeX Foundry is vendor-neutral open source project supporting IIoT edge computing. It supports the interoperability and compatibility. It provides the IP and non-IP based connectivity. It supports to the distributed IoT fog architecture.

This section will discuss the various cloud platforms which support the IoT services and products. Most of these platforms support the Raspberry Pi. For example, Amazon IoT, Reliance Unlimit collaboration with Cumulocity, Google core IoT, CISCO Jaspar, IBM Watson IoT, Android Things, Kaa, & Cass IoT.

The Kaa IoT Platform is open-source middleware to build for connecting devices used for applications to smart cars and smart cities. Uber industry IoT, the manufacturing industry using sensors to measure temperature, humidity, energy consumption, power on and off, security alerts for potential physical breach, and actual productions. The Kaa is suitable for the industrial automation projects of any scale, because of its ability to integrate with low-power MCUs and process telemetry data using an entire variety of popular protocols. The Kaa platform provides hardware layer for sensors, Programmable Logic Controllers (PLCs), loaders, gateways, industrial machinery, and handheld devices. On the application layer the operator's dashboard, real-time alerts on the mobile and email, data analytics and storage, field service application, customer web-portals work fine. To work with Kaa, the Kaa server instance should be up and running. The suggested is the local Kaa Sandbox either with Oracle VirtualBox or to launch Kaa Sandbox on Amazon Web Services (AWS). If AWS is running with Kaa, the user can register with debit card number on the website of AWS, to use Elastic Cloud 2 (EC2) service.

(García, Bustelo, Espada, & Fernandez, 2014) and (García, Espada, Valdez, & García-Díaz, 2014), The Midgar is an SOA and platform for interaction of the Smart Objects & IoT for expanding intelligence through the interconnection of ubiquitous, heterogeneous objects and the generation of applications. Midgar provides a Domain-Specific Language (DSL) capable of abstracting the application generation problem and encapsulating the domain level data handling. Midgar allows registering objects, use a graphic editor to generate a model defined by the DSL. There are several objects interacting with each other, coming from a different background such as manufacturer company. Hence they produce the different types of messages, and not easy to comprehend in automation and programming. Midgar platform addresses this problem of heterogeneity in the messages produced by the objects and uses the model-driven engineering.

(García, Bustelo, Espada,& Fernandez, 2014) and (García, Meana-Llorián, G-Bustelo, Lovelle, & Garcia-Fernandez, 2017) The service providers IoT platforms Xively, Exosite, SensorCloud, Carriots, Azure IoT Suit, AWS, IBM IoT, and Etherios are discussed. The investigation related platforms like QuadraSpace, Paraimpu, QuadraSpace, and SIoT. There are some beta version IoT platforms like ThingSpeak, Sensorpedia, SenseWeb, Evrythng, Open.Sen.se. Other IoT Platforms are Nimbits and Kaa.

(Yamanoue, Oda, & Shimozono, 2012) used people-to-machine collaboration by using the proposed M2M system consisting of Arduino, Android with the mobile terminal, and PukiWiki software. The system collects human motion data at a remote place and uploaded the data to a wiki page by using the M2M system. They have also successfully controlled a device at a remote place that writes a command on a wiki page by using the M2M system. Here the mobile terminal consists of Arduino board, sensors, and actuators. The mobile terminal also reads commands on the wiki page and controls the actuators of the Arduino board. This system realizes an open communication forum for not only people but also for machines. The other development API libraries are also discussed as Pachube as real-time open data web service, twitter APIs, twitter4J, ArduinoTweetLib, TinySCADA, and ProtoZOA.

STATE-OF-THE-ART USE CASES OF RASPBERRY PI

(Garima, Agarwal & Reddy, 2015) discussed the daughter board to exchange the data text, PDF, image and audio formats. Most of the time, the wireless communication such as Bluetooth, Wi-Fi, ZigBee etc. may not provide the secure and reliable communication. For the IoT applications, the inexpensive solutions are required to work with the hardware platforms like Raspberry Pi. Usually, the embedded hardware is equipped with UART and I2C ports. The daughter board is developed to support the Bluetooth communication using UART. This model shows that time requirements for the transmission of the equal sized, different file formats are approximately same. A Similar type of the protocols can be developed for Wi-Fi and ZigBee.

(Ramya & Rajan, 2016) used Raspberry Pi for controlling the industrial devices, managing the power utilities and monitor the employee works. The Wi-Fi and password protected Server PC is used. The system sends an alert in a critical situation, by observing gas leakage and boiler temperature, and makes the use of the solar panel. The embedded Linux based system uses the motion based sensor for the live streaming of video camera for remote sensing and surveillance.

(Naik & Harode, 2016) developed the manufacturing plant monitoring system using the embedded Web Server, Raspberry Pi 3, temperature sensor-LM35, humidity sensor-HIH4000 / HSY220, light Sensor -IR module, camera-RPI, Liquid Crystal Display, Relay-SPDT, switch, buzzer, and Python-based coding is done to find the suspicious moment found near the plant.

(Nivedha, Shambavi, Abhirami, Jyothi, & Darwin, 2016) have designed the hazardous environment monitoring system for industry using Raspberry Pi, micro chip LPC2148, Zigbee, RS232, gas sensor, fire sensor, and current measurement.

(Bharathi & Mubeen, 2016) developed an alert based system by tracking current, voltage, temperature & light intensity. Using Raspberry Pi, LM35 & LDR Sensors, water level sensor (IC CD4066) ZIGBEE and Wi-Fi. From slave board, the data is sent to the master and from master, the data is sent to the personal computer.

(Ajith, Shetty, Ketan, & Shanmugasundaram, 2015) developed the DS1820 a system using Raspberry Pi, digital thermometer, embedded web server-based, for avoiding the critical situation in the industrial environment.

(Szabó & Gontean, 2016) developed an industrial robotic arm SCORBOT-ER III using Raspberry PI, Microprocessor, imaging TP-LINK TLSC3230 IP cameras, D-Link H4 USB HUB, D-Link DGS-1024D switch to execute numerous task in a factory. A simple microchip is used to control the complex autonomous robot system.

(Dharmapurikar & Waghmare, 2015) uses Raspberry Pi B, PIR sensor, LDR Sensor, Flex Sensor, MEMS Sensor, ARM7 LPC2103 to minimize the rate of failures, the overall cost of the system, & increases the productivity, efficiency of overall industrial operations.

(Mahindrakar & Biradar, 2015) developed the smart home automation system using Raspberry Pi B, LDR Sensor for Lights on / off, PIR Sensor, LM sensor for the fan on/off, fire detection sensor, water level sensor for the heater on/ off.

(Prasad & Kumar, 2016) have designed and implemented wireless industrial automation system for low power consumption using sensor and & Raspberry Pi using Python programming. The sensors used for plant monitoring are a temperature sensor, gas sensor, ultrasonic sensor, Raspberry PI, DC Motors, USB Camera, Wi-Fi Dongle, buzzer, and cooling fan.

(K. Mehta, S. Mehta & Raviya, 2014) developed the real-time IoT based system, to record and monitor temperature sensor DS8B20, humidity sensor DHT22 & pressure BMP-085 web-based anytime and anywhere. It turns off the devices after the particular values from the sensor. It also provides the alerts on email and mobile.

(Abinath, Sudhakar, Indhumathi, Sathish & Rajeshwari, 2015) the website is developed for monitoring Raspberry Pi fixed in the industry to have a network. The microcontroller helps in ADC/DAC conversion and to generate pulse signals. The relay acts as a switch in turning OFF and ON other appliances. The Driver circuit is used to control the input to the Motor. The voltage divider is used for the purpose of measuring the voltage. Proximity sensor along with a timer IC is used to measure the speed of the motor.

(Patel, Wadekar, Wabale & Datkhore, 2015) developed home appliances controlling system using Raspberry Pi. The electrical switches are controlled through the web-based system.

(Daş & Tuna, 2015) developed M2M based smart home system by recording the temperature & humidity using sensor and adjusting the air conditioning system automatically, and used the COAP & Session Initiation Protocol (SIP).

(Hsiao, Lian & Sung, 2016) They developed the mobile app based IoT system using Raspberry Pi, ZigBee, Wi-Fi, Network Address Translation (NAT), Bluetooth, and NFC, which replaced the remote control.

(Crisnapati, Wardana, & Aryanto, 2016) developed "Rudas" as multi-purpose an energy-efficient system for IP-based network connected to the internet and embedded sensors. The maintenance of the sensor devices is important called device management (DM). It includes a Raspberry Pi, microcontroller, responsive web technology, database system, environmentally sensitive devices, tornado server software, cameras, Cloud Computing. It uses fuzzy logic to adjust the intensity of light and air condition.

(Comitz & Kersch, 2016) collected and analyzed real-time aviation data using the IoT devices and kept in a flat file. The collection is performed using a Raspberry Pi, an RTL-SDR radio, custom software was written, Open Source dump1090 software program, and R Programming is used.

(Gupta, Patchava, & Menezes, 2015) designed a secure authorization based web-based system to continuously monitoring and store the Electrocardiogram (ECG) and other vital parameters in MySQLDB database. The System used the GSM-based system to generate alert to the Doctors for any abnormal observations.

(Ibrahim, Elgamri, Babiker, & Mohamed, 2015) a developed environmental monitoring system using the Raspberry Pi, and Python Programming. It takes information about the surrounding, such as recording the temperature, humidity, light level, concentrations of the carbon monoxide, & harmful air pollutants. It's also designed to detect earthquakes through an assembled seismic sensor.

(Meana-Llorian, García, G-Bustelo, Lovelle, & Garcia-Fernandez, 2016), uses the fuzzy logic to and the IoT to control the indoor temperature. (García, Meana-Llorián, G-Bustelo, Cueva Lovelle, Garcia-Fernandez, 2017) testing the hypothesis of integrating the use of computer vision in the smart city with the help of the IoT applications.

THE MQTT AND MESSAGE BROKER

Message Queue Telemetry Transport (MQTT) is lightweight, M2M or the IoT protocol invented by Dr. Andy Stanford-Clark, and Arlen Nipper, in 1999. TCP/IP port 1883 and 8883 (over SSL) is reserved with Internet Assigned Numbers Authority (IANA) for use with MQTT. Telemetry is also called as the process of recording and transmitting the readings of an instrument. MQTT is also useful in Supervisory control and data acquisition (SCADA).

In 1970, SCADA became popular and so microprocessor, PLCs, and mainframes too. SCADA is used for controlling industrial processes real-time data through Human-Machine Interface (HMI) by monitoring, gathering, locally or at remote locations, and process real-time data, directly interact with devices such as sensors, valves, pumps, motors, software, and record events into a log file. Before SCADA, relays, and timers had been used to provide some level of supervisory control without having to send people to remote locations to interact with each device, with limited automation functionality. Relays and timers are having problems of reconfiguring, fault-find and the control panels occupy rack of space.

For the security, the user name and password with an MQTT packet in V3.1, and application encryption of the data is possible across the network can be handled with SSL, during send and receive. Additional security can be added by an encrypting application data that it sends and receives, but this is not something built-in to the protocol, in order to keep it simple and lightweight.

Figure 5 shows MQTT protocol with a publish-subscribe mechanism for subscribing the message from the humidity sensor DHT22 by the Computer and Mobile device. A messaging broker system is based on publish-subscribe protocol,

Figure 5. MQTT Publish-Subscribe Mechanism with Broker and Client

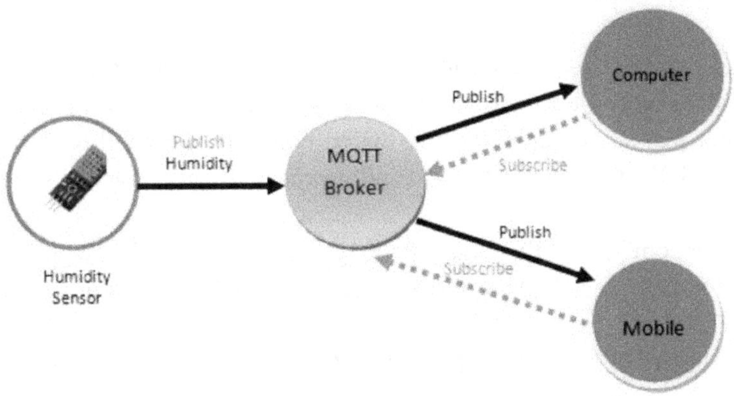

where broker work as a post office (also called as a server) accepts messages from clients and then delivers them to any interested clients. Messages belonging to a topic. The client is a "device" that either publishes a message to a topic, subscribes to a topic, or both. The topic is a namespace (or place) for messages on the broker. The process of publishing means, a client sending a message to the broker, using a topic name. Subscribing means, a client tells the broker which topics interest it. Once subscribed, the broker sends messages published to that topic. If configured properly, the broker sends "missed" messages. A client can subscribe to multiple topics. Telling to the broker to stop sending particular topic is called as unsubscribe. There are topics which can have subtopics. When devices connect, they can either publish information on those topics or subscribe to receive information.

MQTT is used with many companies like Toshiba Concert for smart grid solutions, Libelium Meshlium, uses natively to communicate from the field. Eurotech uses in SCADA, Monitoring, and controllers, Cell labs use in automated meter readings. Cirrus Link - Arlen Nipper's company (helped to produce ODB2 GSM / GPS / MQTT dongles for Mobile Devices). Shaspa user for home automation, Choral for GPS / GSM tracking module (check which models have MQTT). Elecsys for Industrial Communications Gateway and remote monitors. Flukso developed Fluksometer an electricity metering device with native MQTT support. ReMake uses electricity metering systems publish all readings to the on-device MQTT broker. Owasys developed owa11 model is an IP67 asset tracking and telemetry unit reporting location, events, and input output information using MQTT.

The MQTT can be used with the Raspberry Pi, by installing both MQTT client (Pub / Sub Client) and broker (Mosquitto) needs to be installed on Pi. If Amazon Web Service (AWS) IoT Cloud is used, then MQTT subscribe publish can be done through the interface provided online through the account.

PREPARING RASPBERRY PI FOR IoT APPLICATIONS

The "social compare" shows the comparison of the six different Raspberry Pi models including Raspberry Pi 3, Pi zero W, Pi Zero, Pi 2, Pi model B, Pi A+. It shows the different features comparison like wired connectivity, wireless connectivity, dimensions, SOC, price, release date, and power rating and power sources (Alba, 2016).

"Engineer.com" shows the industry strength raspberry pi called MyPi developed by Gavin Levfield and Andrew O'Connell, which is having audio out, dual HD Camera, HDMI, SD Card, SIM, mPCI-E (3G/4G modems and some even with GPS function), Battery Backed RTC, R-Pi HAT Connector, ASIO Connectors, DC In, USB2.0, RS232, ASIO Out, 10/100 Ethernet, & Status LEDs.

For IIoT Raspberry Pi is best suitable options, with the alternative of National Instruments LabView 2014, supported with LINX. Another combination is with visual studio 2015, with Raspberry Pi for those who like to program with C#, good with Windows 10 IoT Core. The Labview 2016 real-time module is suitable with myRIO. There is LabVIEW myRIO 2016 toolkit available.

A Raspberry Pi is a general-purpose computer, usually with a Linux operating system, and the ability to run multiple programs. Raspberry Pi is best used when there is need of full-fledged computer like driving a more complicated robot, performing multiple tasks, doing intense calculations, and monitoring plants and connecting with twitter.

Figure 6 shows the various components required for the Raspberry Pi. The sensors, actuator, connecting pins, multi-meter, and LAN Cable. There are Breadboard GI12, solderless PCB circuit test board, nickel plated 840 points, Raspberry Pi B model SBC, SD Card USB pin closet to hold the SD card, Digital Multimeter (LCD Display) with probe pair (KG172), LAN Cable, single channel relay board module (Controllable with 5V or 3.3V single), PIR infrared motion sensor detector module, Robodo Electronic SG 90 Tower pro micro servo motor, Noctronique DHT11 digital temperature humidity sensor module, 120 pieces point jumper wires male to male, male to female, female to female.

The Raspberry Pi 3 Model B is used in this case. All the connections of Raspberry Pi are done with the laptop having Windows 7 operating system. The micro USB cable which is generally used for recharging the mobile battery is used to provide power supply to Pi. The USB can be connected to a device like a laptop, or direct connection to electrical plug with necessary precaution. The direct power connection must be regulated. The Raspberry Pi is having a red light indicator for the successful power connection.

Figure 6. The IoT Enabled Kit and Raspberry Pi

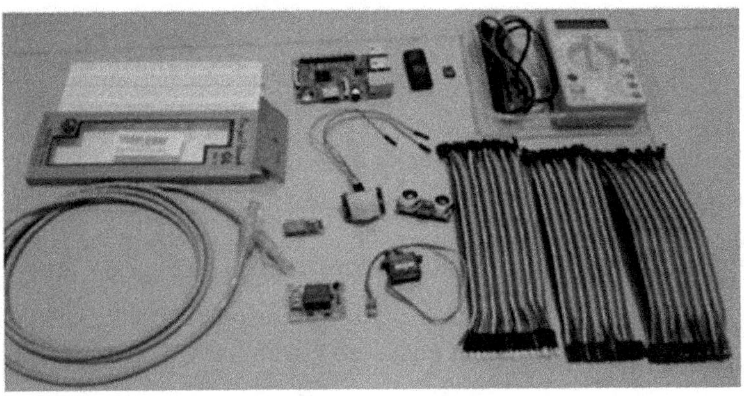

MicroSD card Class 4 is used with 16 GB storage capacity is used. The SDFormatter V4.0 is used to format the SD card in the laptop. The SD card can be connected to with USB pin holder to the laptop. The NOOBS (New out of box software) version 2 is downloaded and extracted the zip archive in the SD card. The archive file size is 1.08 GB. The extraction process of the NOOBS to the SD cards is not sufficient. The OS should be installed with the help of monitor display. The HDMI cable is mostly available in the home running from TV set top box to the TV screen. The same cable can be used for connecting the Pi to display screen or TV. One can connect the USB mouse and keyboard with Pi.

HOW TO PERFORM REMOTE CONFIGURATION

It is not always feasible to use the Pi with plugged in with input keyboard, mouse, and monitor. One can connect remotely with Pi taking help of Putty and SSH. In this case, Putty version 0.67 is used. Putty provides command-line or shell based operating interface after successful connection with remote Pi. Whereas, if the user wants to see the GUI of Pi, then VNC server and viewer can be useful. Figure 7 shows the PIR motion sensor connected to the Pi, female to female jumper wires connection of GND, VCC and OUT pins, LAN cable for the remote login.

To remotely connect to Pi, the IP address is necessary to be known. There are certain basic network troubleshooting commands used to connect to the Pi. One can run the Windows tool "cmd" as administrator. The networking commands are useful for remote connection to Pi.

```
arp -a,
getmac,
ipconfig -all,
ping,
ipconfig /release,
ipconfig /renew,
netstat
```

For the connection between the laptop to Pi, the LAN cable UTP CAT5e is used with an RJ45 connector on both sides. It is necessary to share the internet connection with Pi. The connection may be wired or wireless to the laptop. The Pi is having green colored light for the Wi-Fi access point connected to the internet i.e. 802.11.b/g/n and also has Bluetooth 4.1. The internet on a laptop can be shared with the Pi using the network and sharing center in Windows OS. There is an option in the properties window of the network adapter, i.e. sharing tab. Click on the "Allow other network users through this computer's Internet connection". Select the home network connection as "local area network". This will provide the IP address 192.168.137.1 to the local computer and also assign another IP address to Pi 192.168.137.x. It is necessary to know the exact IP address of Pi using NMAP tool.

In this case, the NMAP 7.30 tool installed on the laptop to know the IP address of the Pi. The command

```
"nmap -sn 192.168.137.1/24"
```

The Virtual Network Connector (VNC) viewer and server are used for the connection with the remote Pi. The following command should be executed within the Pi.

```
"sudo raspi-config"
```

You can first connect to Pi using Putty SSH and then execute the command. To enable the VNC server, navigation to the advanced options and then select "VNC option" as "Yes". Now start the VNC server from a remote laptop. Enter the IP address, which is observed using the NMAP tool. The DEFAULT username "pi" and password "raspberry" is useful o display the graphical screen. However, for security purpose, it is always suggested to change the default password. One can use the Sonic Pi Music composition language, Scratch teaching programming for young children and beginners, Java programming, Python, and Pixel.

HOW TO ACCESS RASPBERRY PI THINGS IN A LAN FROM THE INTERNET

There are some techniques to connect Pi from another computer or mobile device so that it will be available to access the Internet. There is an option to connect remotely using SSH or VNC. Although it is compromised with security, in the case of router port forwarding it is one such mechanism to remotely access the Pi. It will be tricky to configure the router in case of Pi behind the firewall or availability of multiple routers (Pi, 2017).

The alternatives are remot3.it (Remote3.it, 2017), by Weaved Inc, Dataplicity (Dataplicity, 2017), Yaler.net (Yaler GmbH,2017), Losant (Sidwar, 2017), Remote IoT (Remote-IoT, 2015). The commercial service providers like remot3.it provide service for remote access where no on-premises IT skills required, no dedicated

Figure 7. Raspberry Pi B model connection to PIR Motion Sensor

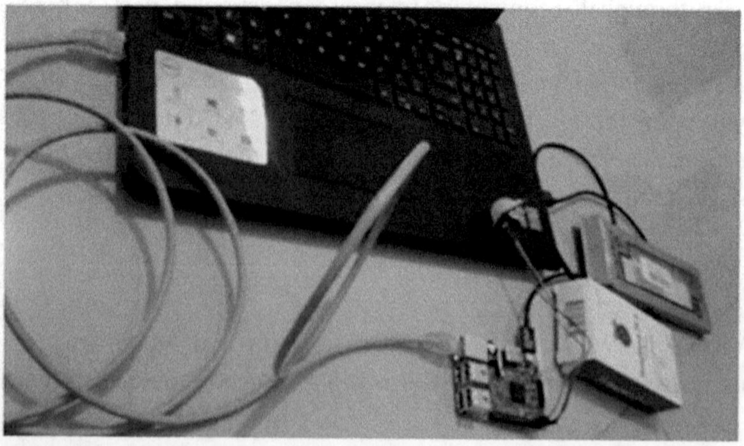

hardware like VPN & firewall or personnel required on-site. The cloud-based service is used to access the bulk of devices. On can install remot3.it device-side agent on any device with a TCP/IP stack. It is available APIs of the web-based access for Android, Linux, iOS, OS X, Windows, CE(Compact Embedded), Embedded Configurable Operating System (eCos), and more. Dataplicity is a secure web-sockets connection with HTTPs that works behind the Network Address Translation (NAT). It does not require root privileges, port forwarding, VPN, Static IPs, DynDNS (Branscombe, 2017), SSH, telnet or any other network services to operate. The client is self-contained and does not open any local or network ports on the device. To use the Dataplicity, it is necessary to install the agent on the Pi.

To access Raspberry Pi without connecting it to a monitor, there are few options. VNC for remote access to the Pi's graphical interface, viewed in a window on another computer, SSH to access the command line of the Pi from another computer, SFTP to copy files between your Pi and another computer using SFTP (Secure File Transfer Protocol), SCP to copy files between your Pi and another computer using SCP (Secure Copy Protocol), SSHFS to copy files between your Pi and another computer using SSHFS (Secure Shell File system), rsync to synchronize folders between the Pi and another computer using rsync over SSH. FTP to copy files between your Pi and another computer using File Transfer Protocol (FTP), Web Server to set up a website or a web page to display some information about the Pi, using a web browser on another machine, on the network or on the internet. Ngrok is a secure tunnel to the local host. (Ngrok, 2017) & (Remote-IoT, 2015).

CONNECTING SENSOR TO PI

This section discussed the procedure to connect the PIR motion sensor. The passive infrared (PIR) sensors useful in finding to sense motion and detects whether a human has moved in or out of the sensors range. It is made up of round metal with rectangular crystal in the center, which detects the infrared radiation. The sensor is actually split into two halves, to detect the swing high or low IR radiation. It takes power supply from 3.3v-5 v input voltage. The range is up to 20 feet (6 meters) 110 degrees x 70 degrees detection range. The PIR sensor itself has two slots in it; each slot is made of a special material that is sensitive to IR. The lens used here is not really doing much and there are two slots can ‘see’ out past some distance (basically the sensitivity of the sensor). When the sensor is idle, both slots detect the same amount of IR, the ambient amount radiated from the room or walls or outdoors. When a warm body like a human or animal passes by, it first intercepts one-half of the PIR sensor, which causes a positive differential change between the two halves. When the warm body leaves the sensing area, the reverse happens, whereby the sensor generates a negative differential change. These change pulses are what is detected.

Table 2 shows the typical GPIO pins layout for the Raspberry Pi. The female to female connection pin is used to connect PIR Motion sensor with Pi. Connect the pin labeled VCC on the PIR sensor to the 5V pin on the Raspberry Pi. This provides power to the PIR sensor; connect the sensor pin labeled GND to a ground pin on the Raspberry Pi. This completes the circuit. Connect the pin labeled OUT to GPIO pin 4.

Write following simple code in Python Integrated Development Environment (IDLE) of Raspberry Pi.

```
from pi zero import MotionSensor

pir = MotionSensor(4)
while True:
 if pir.motion_detected:
 print("Motion detected!")
```

HOW TO IMPLEMENT SECURITY IN RASPBERRY PI COMMUNICATIONS

The Pi is used in the real-world applications hence necessary to have higher security. It is suggested to replace the default passwords, and use strong username and passwords, unique to each device. The encrypted data and files systems should be

Table 2. GPIO pins layout of Raspberry Pi B model

Naming		Pins	
3V3	5V	O	O
GP2	5V	O	O
GP3	GND	O	O
GP4	GP14	O	O
GND	GP15	O	O
GP17	GP18	O	O
GP27	GND	O	O
GP22	GP23	O	O
3V3	GP24	O	O
GP10	GND	O	O
GP09	GP25	O	O
GP11	GP8	O	O
GND	GP7	O	O

used like LUKS, libgcrpt or some others. The communication should be encrypted and for this OpenSSL, SSH or some other options can be used. The robust device ID authentication is required. The secure storage of encryption keys and credentials are required. The critical details are stored on the removable SD card. The keys must by encrypt because the SD card can be easily removed and copied quickly. The case of remote access to the device, these encrypted keys need to convert. Attackers can use these keys for physical access. There are two key management problems; one is how to store keys security on Pi or similar device. How to communicate (symmetrical) keys securely between trusted parties. One more option is to use Transport Layer Security (TLS), and encrypted and authenticated socket connections. This can be combined with the HTTPS and MQTT.

Use Sudo as the Pi user to run commands as root. To become root for any length of time, use sudo -i, then exit (or Ctrl-D) to go back to the pi account. The following commands are useful.

The root password is disabled.

```
$ sudo passwd root
$ sudo init 1
$ passwd
$ sudo su
$ sudo whoami
$ passwd -l pi
```

The device behind the firewall is also an exposure. All the programs that listen to network sockets become part of the attack surface. Running following command as root shows which programs are listening to sockets. Update the packages with the commands. To reduce the attack surface, turn off and uninstall any software that doesn't need to listen to the network. This reduces your system's attack surface.

```
$netstat -ap
$sudo apt-get update && sudo apt-get upgrade
```

Hardware-rooted trust keys stored in tamper-resistant silicon having some options like Hardware Security Module (HSM) appliance installed inside a secure server room, removable USB Key, trusted platform module to authenticate PC, single chip integrated onto computer motherboard. Zymkey's primary mode of operation is to generate key pairs a private key, and a public key within the encryption engine. This key generation operation is performed inside the silicon, the private key never leaves the silicon and there are no operational or debug instructions available to read the private key. The Microchip ATECC508A integrates ECDH (Elliptic Curve Diffie Hellman) security protocol an ultra-secure method to provide a key agreement for encryption/decryption, along with Elliptic Curve Digital Signature Algorithm (ECDSA) sign-verify authentication for the IoT.

Advanced Encryption Standard (AES) is the specification for encryption of electronic data established in 2001. Operates on a public/private key system, and planning for key management is an important aspect when implementing AES encryption. For example, the AWS IoT uses the Transport Layer security with X.509 certificates. The IoT devices must have multi-factor authentication, and some of the IoT devices use the OpenSSL security. (Sáchez-Arias, García,& G-Bustelo, 2017) discusses after systematic analysis, recommends using AES, RSA, and SHA-3.

The BYOD strategy can bring the business data with the person, and this can be hacked during the patch updates for the operating systems. Imagine the hacker has taken control of the hospital system and doctor, nurse or patient is not able to access the historical data. Imagine that the hacker controlled the autonomous car. In September 2016, the Mirai malware attacked the networked devices running out of date versions of Linux especially IP cameras and home routers, which caused the distributed denial of service attack (DDoS). The IoT devices must be protected from worms and botnets.

HOW TO DEVELOP FAILSAFE THINGS WITH RASPBERRY PI

Fail-safe is the situation which caused a piece of machinery to revert to a safe condition in the event of a breakdown or malfunction. It is necessary that a system or plan that comes into operation in the event of something going wrong or that is in place to prevent such an occurrence, and making the devices safe dependent on the main system so that failure can be improbable. There is need of systematic analysis of the failure events and their consequences. Poka yoke which is Japanese terminology related with the manufacturing industry to avoid the mistakes done by the machine operators. Sometimes the foolproof or idiot-proof systems concept is used to design a machine that is made so simple and easy to understand that it is unable to go wrong or be used wrongly.

The damage of the SD card is possible due to power failure; it can be a costly and time-consuming operation to replace when installing in a remote location. The SD card mounting in reading the only mode can avoid corrupt files system. The Raspian OS or microprocessor of the Pi crashes then it will no longer send out Pulse Width Modulation (PWM) pulses. A GPIO pin may get stuck. PWM feature of the GPIO drivers to drive a relays with some additional hardware.

It is possible that the Pi is used to control the room temperature. If the program controlling the circuit crashes or the Pi hangs, GPIO pins will remain in the state they were set at. So if heating is on (GPIO pin high) the heating will stay on in the event of a crash. For fail-safe, the circuit to go low and the relay to deactivate if something goes wrong is required. Following command puts the CPU/GPU into a very low-power state making the system safe to power off. There is no way of waking up from this state without power cycling. There is a way to wake the board through GPIO. A falling edge on GPIO1 or GPIO3 will wake the board up, and it will continue to boot into Linux. Sometimes, the metallic pins are used to the short two pins, while booting the Pi. Following command is useful in such a situation.

```
$sudo halt
```

LORA SHIELD CONNECTION WITH RASPBERRY PI

The Table 3 shows the variables set for accessing LORA shield in the C++ program. This section provides the step by step procedure to connect Dragino LORA (Long Range) Shield v1.1 connecting to Raspberry Pi 3 models B. The Lora Shield allows the user to send data and reach extremely long ranges up to 22 km (in LOS link) and 2 km (NLOS) at low data-rates (Libelium, 2017) . Figure 8 shows the connection of the LORA shield Connectivity to Pi.

Table 3. Program variables setting for LORA Shield Connection

Variables	Set the Spreading Factor as	Location of Latitude and Longitude as

int ssPin =6;
int dio0 =7;
int RST =0;
	Sf_t sf=SF7;	float lat = 18.9345640;
		float lon= 73.1611440;
		int alt=5;

Figure 8. LORA Shield Connectivity to Pi

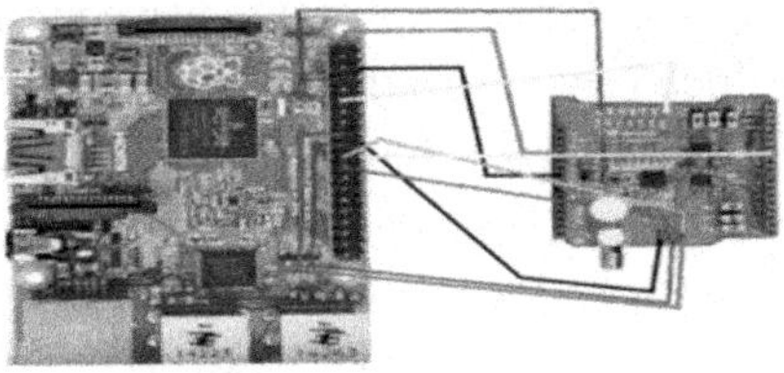

One can also build the LORA gateway using SX 1276 chip of 868.1 MHz.

In Raspbian, there are settings for the Raspberry Pi configurations, from Menu-Preferences- Interface-SPI-Enable – OK. Following steps to perform the step by step configurations.

```
pi@raspberrypi:~ $ mkdir gateway
pi@raspberrypi:~ $ cd gateway
```

Now download files from GIT-Hub.

```
pi@raspberrypi:~ /gateway $ git clone https://github.com/
tftelkamp/single_chan_pkt_fwd.git
pi@raspberrypi:~ /gateway $ cd single_chan_pkt_fwd
pi@raspberrypi:~ /gateway / single_chan_pkt_fwd
$ sudo leafpad main.cpp
```

Once the file is open set following variables.

Set platform, email, description, and server IP address variables.

```
pi@raspberrypi:~ /gateway / single_chan_pkt_fwd $ make
pi@raspberrypi:~ /gateway / single_chan_pkt_fwd $ sudo ./
single_chan_pkt_fwd
```

If in case the message is received as “unrecognized transceiver”. Actually, the V1.3 is 3.3 volts, and V.1.0 and V1.2 are of 5 volts. These pins should be connected properly. After running this command, you will be getting the gateway id (MAC).

READING ANALOG VALUES FROM RASPBERRY PI

In the case of the Pi, any signal between the 3.3v to 0v is considered as the analog signal, i.e. not just high or low. For example, sine wave signal going up and down. The digital signal is one which is having either high or low value such as high means 3.3v volt or low means 0v. The digital values used to ON or OFF the LED or button.

This is an example to read the values of the Potentiometer using PCF8591 Analog to digital converter (ADC). There are 16 pins to the ADC. The Potentiometer (e.g. volume controller) has three legs. For the ADC converter, there is I2C0 SDA (Data) converter at pin 3 and I2C0 SCL (Clock) converter at pin 5.

For connection, Raspberry Pi must be connected with either with Ethernet or Wi-Fi dongle. You need a breadboard, PCF8591 (ADC), four male to female jumper wires, few male to male jumper wires, and potentiometer. To twist the potentiometer use the screwdriver, having the 5v capacity. Now put PCF8592 at the center of the breadboard, and add the potentiometer in the same rows of the ADC. The pin +5v is located on the pin 2 of the Pi(top right). The pin 6 is on Pi is ground, connect it to the breadboard. The two male to male jumper wire is used to connect with the ground and power of the breadboard.

AIN0 go up, AIN1, AIN2, AIN3 will go ground, also hardware address A0, A1, A2 must go to ground. Vss (negative supply) also goes to the ground. VDD get the +5v. One analog output pin 15. Vref is going with +5v. AGND, EXT, OSC also goes to ground.

In pi start lxterminal, the i2c drivers must be installed. Use the following command to install.

```
pi@raspberrypi$ sudo nano /etc/modprobe.d/raspi-blacklist.conf
```

Add following lines to activate the i2c pins, and save.

```
#blacklist spi-bcm2708
#blacklist i2c-bcm2708
```

Now use the following command to install some packages from the internet.

Table 4. Connection of the Potentiometer and Raspberry Pi

Details	Pin	Pin	Details
3.3v	1	2	5v
I2C0 SDA	3	4	DNC
I2C0 SCL	5	6	GROUND
GPIO4	7	8	UART TXD
DNC	9	10	UART RXD
GPIO 17	11	12	GPIO 18
GPIO 21	13	14	DNC
GPIO 22	15	16	CPIO 23
DNC	17	18	GPIO 24
SP10 MOSI	19	20	DNC
SP10 MISO	21	22	GPIO 25
SP10 SCLK	23	24	SP10 CE0 N
DNC	25	26	SP10 CE1 N

```
$sudo nano /etc/modules
$sudo apt-get install python-smbus
$sudo apt-get install i2c-tools
```

Now close lxterminal. Now start Python 2.6.6. Write following code

```
from smbus import SMBus

bus=SMBus(0)

print("Read the A/D")
print("Ctrl C to stop")
bus.write_byte(0x48, 0)
last_reading =-1

while(0 == 0):
reading = bu.read_byte(0x48)
if(abs(last_reading - reading) > 2):
print(reading)
last_reading = reading
```

After saving this Python code using the following command to read values from ADC, you can use ctrl+c to stop the program. Use the screwdriver to twist the potentiometer and clockwise and anti-clockwise. The variations in the values from 0 to 255 can be easily observed, on the screen, as the output of the program.

```
$ sudo python potreead.py
```

HOW TO CONNECT THE BLUETOOTH

There are several devices like Bluetooth enabled like speakers or earphones. The Bluetooth controller on the Raspberry Pi has a dependency on bluez and bluez firmware packages. To install and configure Bluetooth login as root with the following command, and update all the packages.

```
pi@raspberrypi:~ $sudo su -
root@raspberrypi:~#apt-get update
root@raspberrypi:~#apt-get dist-upgrade
root@raspberrypi:~#init 6
pi@raspberrypi:~ $sudo su -
root@raspberrypi:~# apt-get install pi-bluetooth
root@raspberrypi:~#dpkg -l bluez
root@raspberrypi:~#dpkg -l bluez-firmware
root@raspberrypi:~#bluetoothctl
[bluetooth]#help
[bluetooth]#list
[bluetooth]#devices
```

To view the information about the Bluetooth controller use

```
[bluetooth]#show <mac-of-bluetooth>
```

put your device to be connected to Pi in discovery mode.

```
[bluetooth]#power on
[bluetooth]#agent on
[bluetooth]#scan on
```

Once the id of the Bluetooth is received then enable the device and use the following command.

```
[bluetooth]#connect <mac-of-device>
```

In Raspberry Pi open the terminal, log in as root, and install Blueman for X-Windows.

```
root@raspberrypi:~#apt-get install blueman
```

Go in the Bluetooth manager from the menu of the Pi, for further activities.

ACCESSING INDUSTRIAL BUSES

There are many peripherals that can be added to a microprocessor over the Inter-integrated Circuit (I2C) and Serial Peripheral Interface Bus (SPI) of the Pi. The I2C Protocol is invented by Philips intended to allow multiple "slave" digital integrated circuits to communicate with one or more "master" chips. Like the SPI, it is only intended for short distance communications within a single device.

The Pi is having one SPI bus which is a synchronous (four wire) serial communication interface in full duplex mode and master slave arrangement. The master device originates the frame for reading and writing. Multiple slave devices are supported through selection with individual slave select (SS) lines. The I2C and SPI master driver are disabled by default on Raspbian. To enable it, use "raspi-config", or ensure the line "dtparam=spi=on" in "/boot/config.txt", and reboot. To enable these peripheral the following steps are useful. Run sudo raspi-config, Use the down arrow to select 9 Advanced Options, Arrow down to A6 SPI, select yes when it asks you to enable SPI, also select yes when it asks about automatically loading the kernel module, use the right arrow to select the <Finish> button. Select yes when it asks to reboot.

A Universal Asynchronous Receiver/Transmitter (UART) performs asynchronous serial communication in which the data format and transmission speeds are configurable. UART which allows login session from a serial terminal application, such as PuTTY.

ZIGBEE SUPPORT FOR IoT

ZigBee is an open global standard for wireless technology-based on IEEE 802.15.4 specification designed to use low-power digital radio signals for PAN. ZigBee operates to create networks that require a low data transfer rate, energy efficiency, and secure networking. It has a fixed data-rate of 250 kbit/s and range of distances to 10–100 meters in the line-of-sight. A ZigBee has benefits that nodes can stay in sleep mode most of the time, drastically extending battery life. ZigBee is recent competitor of Low-power Wireless Personal Area Networks (LoWPAN). 6LoWPAN is wireless mesh for networks that operate over longer ranges.

ZigBee name is based on the wiggly dance that honey bees do. Similarly, data in a ZigBee network is "hopping" around a mesh of transceivers until a route to the host (usually the internet) is found. This speed, coupled with low-transmit power, hence to achieve the desired coverage the repeaters and a high density of nodes are often needed to obtain the desired coverage. It needs 128 bits symmetric encryption keys. The ZigBee devices are Zigbee Coordinator (ZC), Zigbee Router (ZR), Zigbee End Device (ZED). There are ZigBee's M2M and IoT Applications like Wireless Light Switches, Electrical Meter Smart Grid, demand response, Industrial Equipment Monitoring.

SIGFOX SUPPORT FOR IoT

Sigfox is lowest energy-consumption, a lightweight protocol to handle an infrequent small burst of messages. It sets up antennas on towers (like a cell phone company) and receives data transmissions from devices like parking sensors or water meters. Sigfox is compatible with Bluetooth, GPS 2G/3G/4G, and Wifi. Sigfox is Low Power Wide Area (LPWA) IoT network to provide high capacity and high service level while operating in the unlicensed ISM frequency bands. Sigfox is global IoT network to listen to several objects broadcasting data, without the need to establish and maintain network connections. Sigfox offers a software-based communications solution, where all the network and computing complexity is managed in the Cloud, rather than on the devices. An uplink message has up to 12-bytes payload and takes an average 2s over the air to reach the base stations. The payload allowance in downlink messages is 8 bytes. A device is not attached to a specific base station, unlike cellular protocols. The broadcasted message is received by any base station in the range, which is 3 in average (Sigfox, 2017).

The Sigfox Shield for Raspberry Pi - 868 MHz with XBee Socket is available, however, the user must contact Sigfox in order to acquire a license to connect the devices to the Sigfox Network. Things like basic alarm systems, location monitoring, and simple metering are all examples of one-way systems that might make sense for this network. There are some limitations, such as shorter battery life for battery-powered applications, and an inability to guarantee a message is actually received by the tower. (Ray, 2015)

CONCLUSION

The choice of the IoT platform is depending on the domain of the IoT project, the scope of the outcomes to be achieved, project implementation strategy, and skilled expertise availability. For example, the knowledge of programming language such as embedded C, Python, Java etc. and matching availability of libraries on the particular platform for connecting particular sensors can change the decision while making the choice of the platform (s) in heterogeneous nature of the IoT projects. The feasibility study of the project and duration required to complete the project is highly dependent on the choice of the platform. After the choice of Raspberry Pi, preparing it for the IoT applications is systematic step by step procedure, following the steps can avoid any damage to the hardware such as providing the wrong electrical power supply; choice of the poor components, such as low- quality SD cards may provide harm to the embedded hardware, which internally may affect adversely by the delay in the time required for completion of the IoT project.

REFERENCES

Abinath, T. R., Sudhakar, V., Indhumathi, G., Sathish, P., & Rajeshwari, S. (2015). Web-Based Control Of Industry Appliances Using Raspberry Pi. *International Journal of Computer Science and Mobile Computing*, *4*(4), 10–14.

Ajith, K. P., Shetty, K. K., & Shanmugasundaram, M. (2015). Embedded Web Server Application for Industrial Automation. *Indian Journal of Science and Technology*, *8*(S2), 272–277. doi:10.17485/ijst/2015/v8iS2/72374

Alba, M. (2016). *Industrial-Grade Raspberry Pi for the IoT*. Retrieved May 12, 2017, from http://www.engineering.com/IoT/ArticleID/12627/Industrial-Grade-Raspberry-Pi-for-the-IoT.aspx

Atzori, L., Iera, A., & Morabito, G. (2010). The Internet of Things: A survey. *Elsevier's Journal of Computer Networking*, 1-19.

Bacnet. (2017). *Bacnet - A Data Communication Protocol For Building Automation And Control Networks*. Retrieved May 15, 2017, from http://www.bacnet.org/

Bharathi, M., & Mubeen, S. (2016). Wireless Industrial Parameter Monitoring Using Raspberry PI 3. *International Journal of Innovative Technology and Research*, *4*(4), 3315–3318.

Biron, J., & Follett, J. (2016). *Foundational Elements of an IoT Solution, the Edge, The Cloud And Application Development*. O'Reilly Media, Inc.

Branscombe, M. (2017). *Influencer: 4 Questions You Need to Answer in Your Move to the Cloud.* Retrieved July 25, 2017, from https://dyn.com/

Comitz, P., & Kersch, A. (2016). *Aviation Analytics and the Internet of Things.* IEEE.

Crisnapati, P. N., Wardana, I. N. K., & Aryanto, I. K. (2016). Rudas: Energy and Sensor Devices Management System in Home Automation. *2016 IEEE Region 10 Symposium (TENSYMP),* 184-187.

Daş, R., & Tuna, G. (2015). Machine-to-Machine Communications for Smart Homes. *International Journal of Computer Networks and Applications*, *2*(4), 196–202.

Dataplicity. (2017). *Connect your Pi to the Internet.* Retrieved August 18, 2017, from https://docs.dataplicity.com/docs/get-pi-connected-to-the-internet

Dertien, S. (2015). *Defining The Infrastructure For The Big Data, Manufacturing Leadership: Product Lifecycle Report.* Retrieved May 15, 2017, from https://www.ptc.com/en/product-lifecycle-report/defining-the-infrastructure-for-big-data-analytics

Dharmapurikar, A. A., & Waghmare, R. B. (2015). An Effective Wireless Solution For Industrial Automation By Using Raspberry Pi. *International Journal of Engineering Educational Technology*, *3*(2), 1–8.

García, C. G., Bustelo, B. C. P., Espada, J. P., & Fernandez, G. C. (2014). Midgar: Generation of Heterogeneous Objects Interconnecting Applications. A Domain-Specific Language Proposal for Internet of Things Scenarios. *Journal of Computer Networks*, *64*, 143–158. doi:10.1016/j.comnet.2014.02.010

García, C. G., Espada, J. P., Valdez, E. R. N., & García-Díaz, V. (2014). Midgar: Domain-Specific Language to generate Smart Objects for an Internet of Things Platform. *Proceedings of IEEE 8th International Conference on Innovative Mobile and Internet Services in Ubiquitous Computing*, 352-357. doi:10.1109/IMIS.2014.48

García, C. G., Llorián, D. M., Bustelo, B. C., & Lovelle, J. M. C. (2017). A Review about Smart Objects, Sensors, and Actuators. *International Journal of Interactive Multimedia and Artificial Intelligence*, *4*, 7–10.

García, C.G., & Meana-Llorián, D., G-Bustelo, B.C. P., Cueva Lovelle, J.M., & Garcia-Fernandez, N. (2017). Midgar: Detection Of People Through Computer Vision In The Internet of Things Scenarios To Improve The Security In Smart Cities, Smart Towns, And Smart Homes. *Future Generation Computer Systems.*

Garima, A. N., & Reddy, S. R. N. (2015). Design & Development Of Daughter Board For Raspberry Pi to Support Bluetooth Communication Using UART. *Proceedings of the International Conference on Computing, Communication, and Automation (ICCCA2015)*, 949-954.

Gemalto. (2017). *Gemalto On-Demand Connectivity*. Retrieved May 28, 2017, from http://www.gemalto.com/iot/consumer-electronics/embedded-sim-uicc

Gupta, M. S., Patchava, V., & Menezes, V. (2015). Healthcare based on IoT Using Raspberry Pi. *International Conference on Green Computing and Internet of Things (ICGCloT)*, 796-799. doi:10.1109/ICGCIoT.2015.7380571

Hasan, M., Hossain, E., & Niyato, D. (2013). Random Access for Machine-to-Machine Communication in LTE-Advanced Networks: Issues and Approaches. *Smart Cities IEEE Communications Magazine*, 86-93.

Hsiao, S. J., Lian, K. Y., & Sung, W. T. (2016). Employing Cross-Platform Smart Home Control System with IoT Technology-Based IEEE Computer Society. *International Symposium on Computer, Consumer, and Control*, 264-267.

Ibrahim, M., Elgamri, A., Babiker, S., & Mohamed, A. (2015). Internet of Things based Smart Environmental Monitoring using the Raspberry-Pi Computer. IEEE.

Libelium. (2017). *Extreme Range Links: LoRa 868 / 900MHz SX1272 LoRa module for Arduino Waspmote and Raspberry Pi*. Retrieved 25 July, 2017, from https://www.cooking-hacks.com/documentation/tutorials/extreme-range-lora-sx1272-module-shield-arduino-raspberry-pi-intel-galileo/#step4_2

Mahindrakar, S., & Biradar, R.K. (2015). Internet of Things: Smart Home Automation System using Raspberry Pi. *International Journal of Science and Research,* 901-905.

Meana-Llorian, D., & García, C. G., G-Bustelo, B.C.P., Lovelle, J.M.C., & Garcia-Fernandez, N. (2016). IoFClime: The Fuzzy Logic and the Internet of Things to Control Indoor Temperature Regarding the Outdoor Ambient Conditions. *Future Generation Computer Systems.*

Mehta, K. D., Mehta, S. B., & Raviya, K. S. (2014). Analysis of TOI (Things of Internet) Industrial Monitoring System on Raspberry Pi Platform. *International Journal of Computer Science and Mobile Applications*, *2*(11), 33–40.

Murphy, J., & Roser, M. (2017). *'The Internet'.* Retrieved on June 5, 2017, from https://ourworldindata.org/internet/

Naik, P., & Harode, U. (2016). Raspberry Pi and IoT Based Industrial Automation. *International Journal of Industrial Electronics and Electrical Engineering*, *4*(10), 49–52.

Ngrock. (2017). *Secure tunnels to Localhost*. Retrieved July 25, 2017, from https://ngrok.com/docs

Nivedha, S., Shambavi, P., Abhirami, N., Jyothi, A.P., & Darwin, B.R. (2016). Raspberry Pi Based Hazardous Environment Monitoring Using Wireless Communication. *IEEE Transactions on Electrical and Electronics Engineering, 4*(3), 47-51.

Patel, T. K., Wadekar, U., Wabale, A., & Datkhore, S. S. (2015). Appliances Control Using Ethernet and Raspberry PI. *International Journal of Advanced Research in Computer Science and Software Engineering*, *5*(3), 494–497.

Pelino, M., & Hewitt, A. (2016). *The Forrester Wave: IoT Software Platforms, Q4 2016, The 11 Providers That Matter Most and How They Stack Up*. Academic Press.

Pi. (2017). *Access Your Raspberry Pi Over The Internet*. Retrieved July 19, 2017, from https://www.raspberrypi.org/documentation/remote-access/access-over-Internet/README.md

Poole, I. (2017). *LTE-M, LTE Machine to Machine, M2M*. Retrieved May 15, 2017, from http://www.radio-electronics.com/info/cellulartelecomms/lte-long-term-evolution/lte-m-m2m-machine-to-machine.php

Prasad, M. M., & Kumar, M. N. (2016). Wireless Industrial Automation System. *South Asian Journal of Engineering and Technology*, *2*(21), 140–146.

Ramya, V., & Rajan, G. T. (2016). Raspberry Pi Based Energy Efficient Industrial Automation System. *International Journal of Innovative Research in Computer Science and Engineering IJIRCSE*, *2*(1), 1–7.

Ray, B. (2015). *What Is SigFox?* Retrieved July 21, 2017, https://www.link-labs.com/blog/what-is-sigfox

Remote3.it. (2017). *Remote Manage Networked Devices Anywhere*. Retrieved August 19, 2017, from https://www.remot3.it/web/index.html

Remote-IoT. (2015). Remote IoT Device Management. Retrieved July 25, 2017, from https://remote-iot.com/web/index.htm

RFC 7252. (2017). Constrained Application Protocol. Retrieved May 15, 2017, from http://coap.technology

Sáchez-Arias, G., González García, C., & Pelayo, B. C. (2017). Midgar: Study of Communications Security among Smart Objects Using A Platform Of Heterogeneous Devices For the Internet of Things. *Future Generation Computer Systems, 74*, 444–466. doi:10.1016/j.future.2017.01.033

Sidwar, K. (2017). *Keep an Eye on Your Fridge with a Photon, Photocell, TMP36 and Buzzer*. Retrieved August 18, 2017, from https://www.losant.com/blog/keep-an-eye-on-your-fridge-with-a-photon-photocell-tmp36-and-buzzer

Sigfox. (2017). *Sigfox Technology Overview*. Retrieved July 21, 2017, from https://www.sigfox.com/en/sigfox-iot-technology-overview

Szabó, R., & Gontean, A. (2016). *Industrial Robotic Automation with Raspberry PI Using Image Processing*. University of West Bohemia. doi:10.1109/AE.2016.7577287

Turner, V. (2016). *Reducing The Time To Value For Internet Of Things Deployments*. Retrieved May 15, 2017, from https://blogs.oracle.com/iot/reducing-the-time-to-value-for-internet-of-things-deployments-idc

Wang, L., Xu, D. L., Bi, Z., & Xu, Y. (2014). Data Cleaning for RFID and WSN Integration. *IEEE Transactions on Industrial Informatics, 10*(1), 408–418. doi:10.1109/TII.2013.2250510

Webrtc. (2017). *Web browsers with Real-Time Communications*. Retrieved May 15, 2017, from https://webrtc.org/faq/#what-is-webrtc

Yaler, G. H. (2017). *Access devices from the Web*. Retrieved July 25, 2017, from https://yaler.net/

Yamanoue, T., Oda, K., & Shimozono, K. (2012). A M2M system using Arduino, Android, and Wiki Software. *IEEE International Conference on Advanced Applied Informatics*, 123-128. doi:10.1109/IIAI-AAI.2012.33

KEY TERMS AND DEFINITIONS

BLE: Bluetooth low energy is a wireless PAN technology designed for novel applications in the healthcare, fitness, beacons, security, and home entertainment industries.

Edge Computing: Refers to the computing infrastructure that exists close to the sources of data like industrial machines and industrial controllers such as SCADA systems.

Industry 4.0: Automation of manufacturing and operations that involve the modern digital technologies, such as the Cloud, big data and analytics, and cyber physical systems and the IoT.

Internet of Things: The internet of things (IoT) is the inter-networking of physical devices, vehicles (also referred to as "connected devices" and "smart devices"), buildings, and other items embedded with electronics, software, sensors, actuators, and network connectivity that enable these objects to collect and exchange data.

LoRaWAN: It is a low power wide area network (LPWAN) specification bi-directional communication, mobility, and localization services complement for the IoT and M2M connectivity.

MQTT: Lightweight messaging protocol based on the publish/subscribe mechanism called multi-queue telemetry transport protocol designed for constrained devices and low-bandwidth, unreliable networks suitable for M2M and IoT.

NFC: Near field communication uses tags and transmitter to allow data exchange among the compatible devices in the range of 4cm, using the radio wave transmission and electromagnetic field of induction.

Raspberry Pi: The credit card-sized single board computer having GPIO pins, industrial buses, wireless protocol connectivity useful for the development of the IoT-based process automation work.

WoT: Web of things is a process of connecting IoT-based objects with the use of HTML 5.0, JavaScript, Ajax, PHP, and Ruby on Rails, etc.

Chapter 11
IoT and Big Data in Public Health:
A Case Study in Colombia

Fernando Enrique Lopez Martinez
University of Oviedo, Spain

Maria Claudia Bonfante
Rafael Núñez University, Colombia

Ingrid Gonzalez Arteta
Rafael Núñez University, Colombia

Ruby Elena Muñoz Baldiris
Rafael Núñez University, Colombia

ABSTRACT

Technology can transform lives, and nowadays, the internet of things and big data are helping developing countries to improve healthcare outcomes and deliver better services. In Colombia, a lot of municipalities do not have reliable healthcare information systems, and still, a lot of the current processes that collect critical information related to public health are being made manually. Small groups of researchers are trying to include different stakeholders in active IoT and big data projects by using connected sensors and other IoT technologies that drive improvement in healthcare. According to the World Health Organization, hypertension is considered one of the most prevalent chronic diseases in Latin America today, and it has had an exponential growth in the last 10 years. This chapter utilizes data acquisition sensors, large medical datasets, and machine-learning methods to perform predictive analytics in a hypertensive population in Cartagena to assist public health organizations to create proactive care programs to prevent the increase of this disease in Cartagena.

DOI: 10.4018/978-1-5225-3805-9.ch011

INTRODUCTION

In Colombia, a lot of municipalities do not have reliable healthcare information systems, and still, a lot of the current processes that collect critical information related to public health and patient treatments have been made manually. In Cartagena, where this research has taken place, just a few healthcare organizations guarantee the correct collection and control of the information used by the government to generate epidemiological profiles, clinical studies, and reports that help to create checks and policies for population's social development and healthcare management.

The population in Cartagena has increased by 35 percent in the last ten years, and unfortunately, this increase happened in sub-developed areas, areas without health care facilities and poor access to health treatment. This population is moving from rural areas to Cartagena looking for better healthcare treatment. This increase in the population affects long-range planning of community health and medical facilities. By law, Colombian government should be able to provide opportunely and confidently primary care, dental, behavioral health, emergency and public health services to the entire population and the healthcare facilities are obligated to accept all patients and provide prevention of disease, detection, and treatment of any illness and quality of life.

In addition, and due to the low capacity of the health care centers to treat and retain patients, healthcare professionals are allowing patients to be moved home to continue with their recovery or treatments and the need for monitoring their statuses at home is evident. Cartagena's local government and other stakeholders are supporting small scale interconnected devices to allow monitoring and operations to facilitate a better engagement between healthcare facilities and population. In this scenario, distributed computing, cloud computing, big data analytics and Internet of Things provide efficient solutions and cost-effective results driven by IoT monitoring.

Healthcare providers and healthcare organizations may want these patients to have monitoring devices that can monitor blood pressure, blood sugar levels, oxygen levels and environmental temperature in everyday activities and, report it in real-time to secure cloud platforms.

Advances in sensor data collection and processing are allowing to perform data analytics in real-time (Aggarwal, 2013). Leading incredible advances in patient monitoring that can be used to improve how patient's health is being monitored in their homes and how public health is using technology to increase their capabilities to capture data and generate meaningful proactive treatments for the population.

Some researchers in Cartagena are experimenting with systems that interconnect sensors with low power Wi-Fi enable IoT chips to measure variables that support public health studies. Placing IoT as the primary source for data, the main goal for the researchers is to assist the government and healthcare organizations in making better public health and healthcare decision support systems. Many different stake holders are directly involved in active big data and IoT projects including Universities, Hospitals and Startups companies. All these institutions are driving improvements to population well-being in healthcare and socializing with the population about the use of the technology to reach their goals because the cultural context is essential to the success of this type of technical projects.

The chapter will provide a clear and a high-level overview and background of the necessities in health care management in Cartagena, the needs of controlling and monitoring the health of patients in different areas of the city and the essential process of collecting data to understand the impact on blood pressure for a population with Hypertension. Later, the chapter describes some considerations to configure a basic low-cost sensor implementation to collect the data and the platforms and frameworks will be used for this project. The chapter will also mention some concerns and recommendations related to people that need to be trained properly to use this type of technology, more participation from the government to support this type of research, and future research option for the creation of smart IoT environments to monitor and control patients in the city of Cartagena.

BACKGROUND

Disease outbreak is a real concern for Cartagena's government due to the increase in poor areas of the population (Alesma, 2015) and the low capacity of beds for patient treatment at the health care facilities. Home patient care population is increasing considerably in the recent years (OECD, 2015) making it necessary to find ways of controlling and monitoring the health of patients and the effects of any disease on the neighboring population. With IoT patient monitoring, healthcare providers can monitor patient's health and with governmental health entities to perform health patterns analysis on diseases that allow to control or confine diseases outbreaks to certain geographical areas while the source or cause of the outbreak is identified.

In Colombia, eight of the ten leading causes of mortality are chronic or non-communicable diseases (Webster, 2012). Cardiovascular disease was the main contributor, with age standardized mortality ratio of 239 per 100 000, followed by malignant neoplasms (116 per 100 000), chronic respiratory diseases (54 per 100 000) and diabetes (32 per 100 000) (Webster, 2012). Hypertension is a non-communicable disease that is affecting the population of Cartagena and healthcare organizations are creating strategic alliances with scientists and high-tech companies to find better ways of controlling and monitoring the affected population.

There is a recent increase in home care devices that can be used to collect and send data via wireless to analytic platforms that will allow predicting trends for disease control. Also, sensors to detect environmental variables like temperature that can affect blood pressure. Collecting temperature data to understand the impact on blood pressure, is vital for a population with Hypertension or other blood pressure related diseases.

The challenge in this scenario is how to use these type of devices in the population and what to do with all the data generated by the devices or connected sensors. Then, specialized IT infrastructure will be necessary for collection, aggregation, analysis, and presentation of the enormous amount of data created for IoT. Careful design and development are required for this type of implementation.

The local government is also seeing new improved learning opportunities to change the way of doing things, enhanced public health processes and improve decision-making in healthcare, emergency services, and epidemic control.

In U.S the company Amitech has been implemented several Population Health and IoT solution saving millions of dollars lowering health care costs and improving the quality of living (Amitech, 2016). Also, a recent study of diabetic patients that included the use of wireless blood pressure and blood glucose measurement devices, coupled with an internet-connected pillbox that transmitted data directly to participating primary care providers, showed the potential for home monitoring devices to support patients keep their chronic conditions under control (Jennifer, 2015). Another application of secure IoT in healthcare is proposed in (Kuo-Hui Yeh, 2016) with the implementation of a health care system with the Raspberry PI platform. And, multiple wearable sensor nodes with solar energy and Bluetooth energy project to measure body temperature and heartbeats as described in (Taiyang Wu, 2017) to show the importance of medical monitoring in population health management.

BIG DATA AND IoT SAMPLE

The Internet of Things (IoT) is a network of physical devices and other items, embedded with electronics, software, sensors, and network connectivity, which enables these objects to collect and exchange data (Zanella, 2014). "Big Data" refers to the tools, processes, and procedures allowing an organization to create, manipulate, and manage huge amounts of data. While many definitions have been proposed, the joint denominator seems to include the "three V's"—Volume (vast amounts of data), Variety (significant heterogeneity in the type of data available in the set), and Velocity (speed at which a data scientist or user can access and analyze the data) (Auffray, 2016). Defined as such, healthcare has become one of the key emerging users of big data (Dimitrov, 2016).

Information and communication technologies such as IoT and big data have been used with success in a lot of global development projects to improve healthcare outcomes. Therefore, to translate all this knowledge, experience and impact of IoT and big data development to improve public health in Cartagena, adds efficiency and effectiveness in the healthcare sector.

The main focus of this research is to show a basic architecture and a basic guideline for Cartagena's government and all the parties involved like Universities and start-up tech companies that allow them to visualize what needs to be done to create low-cost IoT solutions. This basic architecture will involve how to create inexpensive sensors, how to manage sensor's data generation and configuration of the data streams, data storage, and analysis.

Before talking about the basic architecture, there are five key capabilities to consider (Dimitrov, 2016) that every implementation should consider before starting any IoT project:

1. **Simple Connectivity:** It should be easy to connect devices to devices, devices to cloud –based services and platforms.
2. **Easy Device Management:** All sensors and devices used in the implementation should be easy to manage and to maintain. Basic maintenance operations need to be performed to ensure the correct functionality of the sensors.
3. **Information Ingestion:** Logically transform and store IoT data. Facilitate the exchange of data across multiple platforms and the cloud, making it easy to pull in the data that is needed.
4. **Informative Analysis:** To have the ability to gain insights from enormous volumes of IoT generated data to make better decisions and optimize operations. To have the ability to create dashboards to present analytics easy to understand and manipulate.
5. **Reduce Risk:** Generate alert notifications of points of failure and isolate incidents generated anywhere in the environment.

Any IoT system includes a set of functions and parameters that need to be considered as described in (Geneva, 2012). For healthcare monitoring, the following are the characteristics and their respective importance:

1. **Data Volume and Bandwidth Needs:** High
2. **Quality of Service:** High
3. **Amount of Signaling:** High
4. **Time Sensitive:** Very High
5. **Mobility:** Yes
6. **Server Initiated Communication:** Yes
7. **Complexity:** Intermediate
8. **Robustness:** High

9. **Cost:** Very Low
10. **Battery Life:** Very High
11. **Alert / Warning:** Yes
12. **Frequency of Visit / Replacement:** Yes

Connectivity will be developed on a small scale, and the model should be as simple and cost-effective as necessary for approval of the local government.

Based on the previous characteristics, the research group is suggesting a simple IoT – big data architecture to show to the local government in Cartagena a low-cost solution to monitor Home patients and an option to collect data for the epidemic department, specifically to detect areas with high rate of hypertensive patients. The actual population for this research has been defined and Approved by the DADIS (Health Distrital Administrative Department) organization in Cartagena. Figure 1. Shows the conceptual diagram of the low-cost implementation for this research.

IoT technologies will be used to assist Cartagena's health department administrative district (DADIS) via sensor technology, big data and analytics to monitor, predict and protect hypertensive patients. This will be a small scale project that will be presented to Cartagena's government and expanded to meet the needs of the Colombian government. The basic model is to collect data from the sensors, and this data is sent to a cloud based server platform to be monitored and analyzed and alert physicians and entities of abnormal changes in patient's health.

Sensors and Hardware Platforms

- Arduino Uno R3
- e-health sensor shield v2.0 (Arduino compatible)
- Radio signal supported (BT, ZigBee, 4G / 3G / GPRS)
- Oxygen in the blood (SPO2) sensor

Figure 1. IoT big data framework diagram

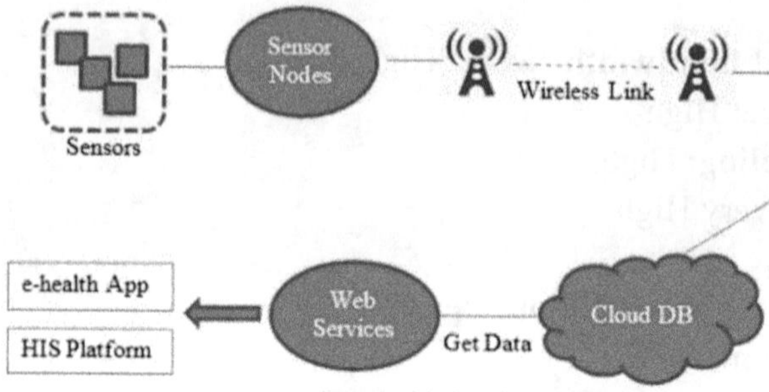

Figure 1. IoT Big Data Framework diagram

- The body temperature sensor
- Sphygmomanometer sensor
- DHT22 sensor (ambient humidity and temperature)
- XBee breakout board
- XBee 2mW Wire Antenna - Series 2
- Raspberry Pi 2
- Antenna Wireless Network Dongle

Cloud Platforms

- Microsoft Azure IoT Suite (Azure IoT Suite requires an Azure subscription)
- Amazon Web Services IoT Platform (Create an AWS Account)

Big Data Technology

- Azure HDInsight cloud Apache Hadoop and MapReduce Platform
- Amazon EMR (Hadoop & Spark)

Dashboards and Analytics Tools

- Amazon Kinesis Analytics
- Azure Data Lake Analytics

In order to get real time sensitive data the sensor used will be the e-health sensor shield v2.0 that allows Arduino and Raspberry Pi to perform biometric and medical monitoring. And, an inexpensive DHT22 sensor that captures ambient humidity and temperature. These sensors are considered Not-smart Objects as described by (González, 2017). They permit to measure physical parameters of the immediate environment. The e-health sensor shield v2.0 (e-class website) will capture data like pulse, oxygen in the blood, body temperature and blood pressure necessary for the prediction models. Arduino will be used as the sensor node and Raspberry Pi as the IoT gateway. The wireless link can be formed by using XBee series two wireless access point. The IoT gateway will use REST and MQTT protocols to communicate with the cloud platform depending on which platform will be used. For the cloud solution, there are two considerations, IoT Suite of Microsoft Azure and AWS IoT Platform.

Since IoT and big data so closely link, big data processing will be done using Hadoop File System (HDFS) and MapReduce. For data analysis, aggregation and presentation, Business intelligence and analytics tool provided by Microsoft Azure suite (Microsoft, 2014) or AWS platform (Amazon, 2013) will be used. Python will be the language used to perform the DEA (Data exploratory Analysis), visualizations, and the fitting model libraries.

The authors will not specify implementation details in this document. However, this is an end to end scenario and architecture can be used for any healthcare IoT and big data project involving the use of sensor nodes, gateways, data ingestion, data aggregation, and visualization. A step by step guide for prototyping a sensor node with Arduino and Raspberry Pi can be found in (Janakiram, 2014).

The object of the study for the data collected will be to Track and treat Hypertension population in Cartagena Colombia. And, the initial features used in the models (Data from sensors, surveys and EMR – Electronic Medical Record System) are:

- Age
- Race
- Height
- Weight
- Blood pressure
- Alcohol habits
- Tobacco habits
- Room Temperature
- Physical activities
- Family history of high blood pressure
- Cholesterol levels
- Diabetes symptoms
- Medications
- Diet habits.
- Electrolytes like Sodium, Potassium, and Chloride.
- Kidney related like Bun and Creatinine lab tests.
- Thyroxin (T4) or Thyroid stimulating hormone (TSH) abnormality.
- Abnormality of the adrenal gland - cortisol and aldosterone levels

BIG DATA AND IoT CONCERNS

Regardless of all the sensational of opportunities that IoT and big data bring to the city Cartagena in the public health sector, significant challenges exist in the healthcare field. The local government has a lot of concerns regarding data privacy and security, infrastructure, governmental laws, and costs. The local government is working closely with Universities and research groups to design local policies and regulatory frameworks to develop IoT and big data projects. In addition, local universities are creating learning opportunities to generate human and technological capabilities with sufficient skills that allow the implementation and use of sensors for public health monitoring in relation to the IoT and big data.

Issues related to how to represent, store, interconnect, search and organize information generated by IoT are very challenging (Atzori, 2010). The creation of interdisciplinary teams to model and reasoning over the data is necessary to work with the complexity of these enabling technologies.

RECOMMENDATIONS

In the short term, to guarantee success in this type of endeavors, people need to be trained properly to use the technology. The local government needs to be sure there are enough trained people to deploy this type of technology and develop a strategic plan to adopt new technology by the population. People sometimes are resistant to this type of changes or implementation. Another important area to consider is to create local data regulations and policies to data collected by sensors and data sent to cloud-based servers. The government should also create privacy, security and anonymity policies to guarantee confidentiality on the population information that will be collected and transmitted.

The government must invest in the telecommunications infrastructure because spectrum and bandwidth issues can obstruct the adoption and deployment of IoT devices and services.

Safety measures to protect private health information from malicious users and software should be implemented. Different possibilities to create a secure relationship between objects are reviewed on (G. Sánchez-Arias, 2017). It focuses on techniques and strategies that can be used in the communication between the objects to create secure IoT environments.

Healthcare institutions must create campaigns to generate trust and confidence in IoT projects that will include health population. Establish strategic relationships with universities and research groups to authorize and accelerate research in IoT and big data applied to public health.

FUTURE RESEARCH DIRECTIONS

The world is experiencing a rapid proliferation of chronic diseases and a huge healthcare expenditure to try to control it. Providing healthcare monitoring outside of clinical environments with monitoring devices has been recently in the focus of a lot of research groups and governments. Startup tech companies should take advantage of this situation and generate IoT and big data projects that use body sensors and actuators combined with analytic techniques to monitor and improve public health and population health management. The creation of smart IoT environments to monitor and control patients that use RFID tags and readers, video cameras, e-health sensors, motion detector sensors, image processing devices and location tracking sensors. Will allow creating healthcare applications to monitor and control chronic diseases, wellness management, activity monitor, and Machine learning solutions to improve health population and patient health.

There are several projects in the field of chronic disease and wellness management that can be implemented in Cartagena. Like an application to monitor remote mobile patients' ECG (electrocardiogram) (Agrawal, 2014) and Personal Care Connect project (Blount, 2007) that will help to improve the adoption of this type of IoT technology.

CONCLUSION

Internet of Things is allowing healthcare organizations to improve patient care and monitoring. Co-work relationships between sensors (Atzori, 2011) and security policies over patient data provides real-time information that can be used to improve population health. Big data is allowing collection, storage and manipulation of the data generated by the devices and governments are using this massive amount of data generated by IoT to gather, analyze and process information related to epidemic diseases and wellness management. Despite, there are still some challenges that need to be addressed and managed in the right way like Healthcare Privacy Data, IT Integration, Wireless infrastructure, cyber security and evolution of technologies for IoT medical devices. Research groups are using low-cost sensors and easy to use technology to provide solutions to support healthcare organizations in this large area of knowledge and technology.

The Colombian government is currently working on laws and policies to support this type of technologies, but in the meantime, it should encourage health care institutions to move from the fee for service model to value-based care model and support this type of IoT and big data initiatives.

On the other hand, a lot of money is being spent on healthcare innovation in Colombia, and there are a lot of researchers with increased interest in IoT that can make good things to happen in order to change the situation of public health and healthcare today in Colombia. The investment should be to bring the technology to the population and deploy sensors and devices that allow health monitoring where patients can be advised and monitored from everywhere, thus reducing healthcare cost and increasing wellness on the population. A health care dashboard will be created that will enable clinicians and healthcare executives to improve their decision support process for a hypertensive population.

ACKNOWLEDGMENT

This research was supported by Rafael Nuñez University in Cartagena Colombia; Sysnet S.A.S Company in Cartagena Colombia; Sysdevelopment LLC in the USA.

REFERENCES

Aggarwal, C., Ashish, N., & Sheth, A. (2013). The Internet of Things: A Survey from the Data-Centric Perspective. *Managing and Mining Sensor Data*, 383-428. 10.1007/978-1-4614-6309-2_12

Alsema, A. (2015). *Almost half of Colombia's countryside lives below poverty line.* Retrieved February 13, 2017, from Available at: http://colombiareports.com/almost-half-of-colombias-countryside-lives-under-poverty-line/

Amitech Population Health & IoT. (n.d.). Available at: http://cdn2.hubspot.net/hubfs/2528494/WHITE_PAPER_population_health_and_IoT.pdf?submissionGuid=79bec32c-269b-4c34-9f8d-50b874d80d65

Atzori, L., Iera, A., & Morabito, G. (2010). The Internet of Things: A survey. *Computer Networks*, *54*(15), 2787–2805. doi:10.1016/j.comnet.2010.05.010

Atzori, L., Iera, A., & Morabito, G. (2011). SIoT: Giving a Social Structure to the Internet of Things. *IEEE Communications Letters*, *15*(11), 1193–1195. doi:10.1109/LCOMM.2011.090911.111340

Auffray, C., Balling, R., Barroso, I., Bencze, L., Benson, M., Bergeron, J., ... Zanetti, G. (2016). Making sense of big data in health research: Towards an EU action plan. *Genome Medicine*, *8*(1), 71. doi:10.1186/s13073-016-0323-y PMID:27338147

AWS IoT Developer Guide. (n.d.). Amazon Web Services. Available at: http://docs.aws.amazon.com/iot/latest/developerguide/iot-dg.pdf

Blount, M., Batra, V. M., Capella, A. N., Ebling, M. R., Jerome, W. F., Martin, S. M., ... Wright, S. P. (2007). Remote health-care monitoring using Personal Care Connect. *IBM Systems Journal*, *46*(1), 95–113. doi:10.1147/sj.461.0095

Bresnick, J. (n.d.). *Smart Pillbox Produces 80% Diabetic Medication Adherence Rate*. Available at: https://healthitanalytics.com/news/smart-pillbox-produces-80-diabetic-medication-adherence-rate

Chen, C.-M., Agrawal, H., Cochinwala, M., & Rosenblut, D. (2004). Stream Query Processing for Healthcare Bio-Sensor Applications. *20th International Conference on Data Engineering*, 791-794.

Dimitrov, D.V. (2016). Medical Internet of Things and Big Data in Healthcare. *Health Inform Res., 22*(3), 156-163. 10.4258/hir.2016.22.3.156

e-Health Sensor Platform V2.0 for Arduino and Raspberry Pi. (n.d.). Available at: https://e-class.teilar.gr/modules/document/file.php/CS103/IOT%20-%20SENSORS%20-%20ACTUATORS/e-Health%20Sensor%20Platform%20V2.pdf

González García, C., Meana-Llorián, D., Pelayo G-Bustelo, C., & Cueva-Lovelle, J. M. (2017). B.C.P. G-Bustelo, J.M.C. Lovelle, A review about Smart Objects, Sensors, and Actuators. *Int. J. Interact. Multimed. Artif. Intell., 4*(3), 7–10. doi:10.9781/ijimai.2017.431

ITU. (2012). *Impacts of M2M Communications & Non-M2M Mobile Data Applications on Mobile Networks*. Available at: www.itu.int/md/T09-SG11-120611-TD-GEN-0844/en

Janakiram, M. S. V. (2014). *Prototyping a Sensor Node and IoT Gateway with Arduino and Raspberry Pi*. Available at: https://thenewstack.io/author/janakiram/

Microsoft. (n.d.). *Azure Solutions for Internet of Things (IoT)*. Available at: https://opbuildstorageprod.blob.core.windows.net/output-pdf-files/en-us/Azure.azure-documents/live/iot-suite.pdf

OECD. (2015). *OECD Reviews of Health Systems: Colombia 2016*. Paris: OECD Reviews of Health Systems.

Webster, P. C. (2012, April 3). Health in Colombia: The chronic disease burden. *Canadian Medical Association Journal, 184*(6), E293–E294. doi:10.1503/cmaj.109-4126 PMID:22392946

Wu, Wu, Redoute, & Yuce. (2017). An Autonomous Wireless Body Area Network Implementation towards IoT Connected Healthcare Applications. *IEEE Access*. DOI: 10.1109/ACCESS.2017.2716344

Yeh. (2016). A Secure IoT-Based Healthcare System with Body Sensor Networks. *IEEE Access*. DOI: 10.1109/ACCESS.2016.2638038

Zanella, A., Bui, N., Castellani, A., Vangelista, L., & Zorzi, M. (2014). Internet of things for smart cities. *IEEE Internet Things, 1*(1), 22-32.

KEY TERMS AND DEFINITIONS

Arduino: Is an open source electronic platform to build interactive projects receiving inputs from sensors and controlling actions by using the development environment.

AWS: Is Amazon Web Services, a platform that offers on-demand cloud computing.

Big Data: Extremely large data sets generated by humans, applications, or machines. The data sets may be analyzed computationally to reveal patterns, trends, and associations.

Cloud Computing: Is the practice of using remote servers and services hosted on the internet to store, manage, and process data.

Disease: Is a disorder of a function in a human or a particular abnormal condition.

Hypertension: Is an abnormally high blood pressure.

IoT: Internet of things is the interconnection of physical devices that enable these devices to collect and exchange data.

Microsoft Azure: Microsoft platform of integrated cloud services.

Raspberry Pi: Is a small single-board computer.

Sensor: Is a device that detects or measures a physical property.

Compilation of References

ABB. (2017, March). *System 800xA Extended Automation*. Retrieved from http://new.abb.com/control-systems/system-800xa/800xa-dcs

Abinath, T. R., Sudhakar, V., Indhumathi, G., Sathish, P., & Rajeshwari, S. (2015). Web-Based Control Of Industry Appliances Using Raspberry Pi. *International Journal of Computer Science and Mobile Computing*, *4*(4), 10–14.

Acceleo. (2017). *Obeo. Acceleo Generator*. Retrieved April 25, 2017 from http://www.eclipse.org/Acceleo/

Acerbis, R., Bongio, A., Brambilla, M., & Butti, S. (2015). *Engineering the Web in the Big Data Era*. In Lecture Notes in Computer Science: Vol. 9114. *Model-Driven Development Based on OMG's IFML with WebRatio Web and Mobile Platform* (pp. 605–608). Berlin: Springer-Verlag.

ADM. (2017). *Architecture-driven modernization task force*. Retrieved April 25 from http://www.adm.org

Aggarwal, C., Ashish, N., & Sheth, A. (2013). The Internet of Things: A Survey from the Data-Centric Perspective. *Managing and Mining Sensor Data*, 383-428. 10.1007/978-1-4614-6309-2_12

Aislelabs. (2015). *The Hitchhikers Guide to iBeacon Hardware: A Comprehensive Report*. Retrieved from www.aislelabs.com/ reports/beacon-guide

Ajith, K. P., Shetty, K. K., & Shanmugasundaram, M. (2015). Embedded Web Server Application for Industrial Automation. *Indian Journal of Science and Technology*, *8*(S2), 272–277. doi:10.17485/ijst/2015/v8iS2/72374

Ala, A. F., Abdallah, K., Mohsen, G., Ammar, R., & Mehdi, M. (2015). Toward Better Horizontal Integration Among IoT Services. *IEEE Communications Magazine Communications Standards*, (Supplement), 72–79.

Ala, A. F., Mohsen, G., Mehdi, M., Mohammed, A., & Moussa, A. (2015). Internet of Things: A Survey on Enabling Technologies, Protocols, and Applications. *IEEE Communications Surveys and Tutorials*, *17*(4), 2347–2376. doi:10.1109/COMST.2015.2444095

Alba, M. (2016). *Industrial-Grade Raspberry Pi for the IoT*. Retrieved May 12, 2017, from http://www.engineering.com/IoT/ArticleID/12627/Industrial-Grade-Raspberry-Pi-for-the-IoT.aspx

Alsema, A. (2015). *Almost half of Colombia's countryside lives below poverty line*. Retrieved February 13, 2017, from Available at: http://colombiareports.com/almost-half-of-colombias-countryside-lives-under-poverty-line/

Améndola, F., & Favre, L. (2013). Adapting CRM Systems for Mobile Platforms: An MDA Perspective. *International Journal of Computer & Information Science*, *14*(1), 31–40.

Amitech Population Health & IoT. (n.d.). Available at: http://cdn2.hubspot.net/hubfs/2528494/WHITE_PAPER_population_health_and_IoT.pdf?submissionGuid=79bec32c-269b-4c34-9f8d-50b874d80d65

Andy Banks, D. L. (2012). *An introduction to the MQTT transport for Mobile Messaging & M2M*. Retrieved from https://developer.ibm.com/messaging/2012/12/05/introduction-mqtt-transport-mobile-messaging-m2m/

Anilkumar, B. G., Bhagyalakshmi, K. C., Lavanya, K., & Gowranga, K. H. (2016). A Bluetooth Low Energy Based Beacon System for Smart Short Range Surveillance. *IEEE International Conference on Recent Trends in Electronics Information Communication Technology*, 1181-1184.

Antonio, J. J., Miguel, A. Z., & Antonio, F. G. S. (2010). An Architecture Based on Internet of Things to Support Mobility and Security in Medical Environments. *IEEE CCNC Proceedings*, 1-5.

Ashton. (2009). Internet of Things. *RFiD Journal*.

ASM. (2017, March). Retrieved from http://www.asmconsortium.net

Aspinall, M. J. (1979). Use of a decision tree to improve accuracy of diagnosis. *Nurs Res.*, *28*(3), 182–185. PMID:254902

ASTM. (2011). *Abstract Syntax Tree Metamodel, version 1.0, OMG Document Number: formal/2011-01-05*. Retrieved April, 25, 2017 from http://www.omg.org/spec/ASTM

ATL. (2017). *Atlas Transformation Language Documentation*. Retrieved April 25, 2017 from http://www.eclipse.org/atl/documentation/

Atzori, L., Iera, A., & Morabito, G. (2010). The Internet of Things: A survey. *Elsevier's Journal of Computer Networking*, 1-19.

Atzori, L., Iera, A., & Morabito, G. (2010). The Internet of Things: A survey. *Computer Networks*, *54*(15), 2787–2805. doi:10.1016/j.comnet.2010.05.010

Atzori, L., Iera, A., & Morabito, G. (2011). SIoT: Giving a Social Structure to the Internet of Things. *IEEE Communications Letters*, *15*(11), 1193–1195. doi:10.1109/LCOMM.2011.090911.111340

Auffray, C., Balling, R., Barroso, I., Bencze, L., Benson, M., Bergeron, J., ... Zanetti, G. (2016). Making sense of big data in health research: Towards an EU action plan. *Genome Medicine*, *8*(1), 71. doi:10.1186/s13073-016-0323-y PMID:27338147

Ault, A., Zhong, X., & Coyle, E. J. (2005). K-nearest-neighbor analysis of received signal strength distance estimation across environments. *Proceedings of the First Workshop on Wireless Network Measurements*.

AWS IoT Developer Guide. (n.d.). Amazon Web Services. Available at: http://docs.aws.amazon.com/iot/latest/developerguide/iot-dg.pdf

Azizyan, M., Constandache, I., & Choudhury, R. R. (2009). Surround-sense: mobile phone localization via ambiance fingerprinting. *Proceedings of the 15th Annual International Conference on Mobile Computing and Networking, MOBICOM 2009*.

Bacnet. (2017). *Bacnet - A Data Communication Protocol For Building Automation And Control Networks*. Retrieved May 15, 2017, from http://www.bacnet.org/

Bahl, P., & Padmanabhan, V. N. (2000). RADAR: an in-building rf-based user location and tracking system. *Proceedings of the INFOCOM*, 775–784. doi:10.1109/INFCOM.2000.832252

Bender, M., Michel, S., Parkitny, S., & Weikum, G. (2007). A Comparative Study of Pub/Sub Methods in Structured P2P Networks. *Lecture Notes in Computer Science*, *4125*, 385–396. doi:10.1007/978-3-540-71661-7_37

Bharathi, M., & Mubeen, S. (2016). Wireless Industrial Parameter Monitoring Using Raspberry PI 3. *International Journal of Innovative Technology and Research*, *4*(4), 3315–3318.

Bhatt, C., Dey, N., & Ashour, A. (2017). *Internet of Things and Big Data Technologies for Next Generation Healthcare*. Springer. doi:10.1007/978-3-319-49736-5

Bhayani, M., Patel, M., & Bhatt, C. (n.d.). *Proceedings of the International Congress on Information and Communication Technology*. Retrieved from https://link.springer.com/chapter/10.1007/978-981-10-0767-5_37 doi:https://doi.org/10.1007/978-981-10-0767-5_37

Biron, J., & Follett, J. (2016). *Foundational Elements of an IoT Solution, the Edge, The Cloud And Application Development*. O'Reilly Media, Inc.

Blount, M., Batra, V. M., Capella, A. N., Ebling, M. R., Jerome, W. F., Martin, S. M., ... Wright, S. P. (2007). Remote health-care monitoring using Personal Care Connect. *IBM Systems Journal*, *46*(1), 95–113. doi:10.1147/sj.461.0095

Bluetooth SIG. (2015). *Bluetooth Technology Basics*. Retrieved from www. bluetooth.com/what-is-bluetooth-technology/bluetooth-technology-basics/low-energy

Bonomi, F., Milito, R., Zhu, J., & Addepalli, S. (2012). Fog Computing and its Role in the Internet of Things. In *Proceedings 1st MCC workshop on Mobile Cloud Computing* (pp. 13–16). ACM. doi:10.1145/2342509.2342513

Bowen, J., & Hinze, A. (2011). Supporting mobile application development with model-driven emulation. *Journal of the ECEASST*, *45*, 1–5.

Brambilla, M., Cabot, J., & Wimmer, M. (2012). *Model-Driven Software Enginneering in Practice, Synthesis Lectures on Software Engineering*. Morgan & Claypool Publishers.

Branscombe, M. (2017). *Influencer: 4 Questions You Need to Answer in Your Move to the Cloud*. Retrieved July 25, 2017, from https://dyn.com/

Braun, P., & Eckhaus, R. (2008). Experiences on model-driven software development for mobile applications. In *Proceedings of Engineering of Computer-Based Systems, IEEE International Conference and Workshop on the Engineering of computer Base Systems* (pp. 490-493), Washington, DC: IEEE Computer Society. doi:10.1109/ECBS.2008.50

Breibvold, H. P., & Olausson, M. (2010, October). El Operario Eficaz. *Revista ABB, 4*(10), 6–11.

Bresnick, J. (n.d.). *Smart Pillbox Produces 80% Diabetic Medication Adherence Rate*. Available at: https://healthitanalytics.com/news/smart-pillbox-produces-80-diabetic-medication-adherence-rate

Bruneliere, N., Cabot, J., Dupé, G., & Madiot, F. (2014). MoDisco: A Model Driven Reverse Engineering Framework. *Information and Software Technology, 56*(8), 1012–1032. doi:10.1016/j.infsof.2014.04.007

Bruno & Delmastro. (2003). Design and analysis of a Bluetooth-based indoor localization system. In *Lecture Notes in Computer Science: Vol. 2775. Personal Wireless Communications* (pp. 711–725). Springer.

Cámara de Ópticos. (2013, March). *Salud y tendencias visuales de los españoles*. Retrieved from http://camaraopticos.com/salud-visual-y-tendencias-de-los-espanoles/

Canfora, G., Dipenta, M., & Ceruelo, L. (2011). Achievements and Challenges in Software Reverse Engineering. *Communications of the ACM, 54*(4), 142–151. doi:10.1145/1924421.1924451

Cannasse, N. (2014). Haxe. Too good to be True? *GameDuell Tech Talk*. Retrieved April 25, 2017 from http://www.techtalk-berlin.de/news/read/nicolas-cannasse-introducing-Haxe/

Castellani, A. P., Bui, N., Casari, P., Rossi, M., Shelby, Z., & Zorzi, M. (2010). Architecture and protocols for the Internet of Things: A case study. In *2010 8th IEEE Int. Conf. Pervasive Comput. Commun. Work*. IEEE. doi:10.1109/PERCOMW.2010.5470520

CEPM. (2017). *Case Study – CEPM*. White Paper by Ingenu,1-2.

Cetinkaya, O., & Akan, O. (2015). A dash7-based power metering system. *12th Annual IEEE Consumer Communications and Networking Conference (CCNC)*, 406-411.

Chang, W. G., & Lin, F. J. (2016). Challenges of Incorporating OMA LWM2M Gateway in M2M Standard Architecture. *IEEE Conference on Standards for Communications and Networking (CSCN)*, 1-6.

Chen, C.-M., Agrawal, H., Cochinwala, M., & Rosenblut, D. (2004). Stream Query Processing for Healthcare Bio-Sensor Applications. *20th International Conference on Data Engineering*, 791-794.

Chen, H. W., & Lin, F. J. (2014). *Converging MQTT resources in ETSI standards based M2M platform.* Paper presented at the Internet of Things (iThings), 2014 IEEE International Conference on, and Green Computing and Communications (GreenCom), IEEE and Cyber, Physical and Social Computing (CPSCom), IEEE. doi:10.1109/iThings.2014.52

Chen, Ch., & Helal, S. (2008, October-December). Sifting Through the Jungle of Sensor Standards. *IEEE Pervasive Computing*, *7*(4), 84–88. doi:10.1109/MPRV.2008.81

Chen, Z., Zhu, Q., Jiang, H., & Soh, Y. C. (2015). Indoor localization using smartphone sensors and ibeacons. *Proceedings of the IEEE 10th Conference on Industrial Electronics and Applications (ICIEA '15)*, 1723–1728. doi:10.1109/ICIEA.2015.7334389

Chitta, S. (2016). MoveIt! An Introduction. In A. Koubaa (Ed.), *Robot Operating System (ROS): The Complete Reference* (Vol. 1, pp. 3–27). Springer. doi:10.1007/978-3-319-26054-9_1

Colitti, W., Steenhaut, K., DeCaro, N., & Buta, B., Dobrota, V. (2011). Evaluation of constrained application protocol for wireless sensor networks. In *Proceedings of the 18th IEEE Workshop onLocal and Metropolitan Area Networks (LANMAN '11)* (pp. 1–6) IEEE. doi:10.1109/LANMAN.2011.6076934

Collina, M., Bartolucci, M., Vanelli-Coralli, A., & Corazza, G. E. (2014). *Internet of Things application layer protocol analysis over error and delay prone links.* Paper presented at the Advanced Satellite Multimedia Systems Conference and the 13th Signal Processing for Space Communications Workshop (ASMS/SPSC), 2014 7th. doi:10.1109/ASMS-SPSC.2014.6934573

Comitz, P., & Kersch, A. (2016). *Aviation Analytics and the Internet of Things.* IEEE.

Cota, M. P., & Castro, M. R. G. (2013). *DCS 3D Operators in Industrial Environments: New HCI Paradigm for the Industry. In Virtual, augmented and mixed reality. Systems and applications* (pp. 271–280). Heidelberg, Germany: Springer.

Cota, M. P., & Castro, M. R. G. (2013). *Usability in a new DCS interface, in universal access. In Human computer interaction. Design methods, tools, and interaction techniques for einclusion* (pp. 87–96). Heidelberg, Germany: Springer.

Crisnapati, P. N., Wardana, I. N. K., & Aryanto, I. K. (2016). Rudas: Energy and Sensor Devices Management System in Home Automation. *2016 IEEE Region 10 Symposium (TENSYMP)*, 184-187.

Daqri. (2017, March). *Smart Helmet.* Retrieved from https://daqri.com/products/smart-helmet/

Dasnois, B. (2011). *Haxe 2 Beginner's Guide.* Packt Publishing.

Daş, R., & Tuna, G. (2015). Machine-to-Machine Communications for Smart Homes. *International Journal of Computer Networks and Applications*, 2(4), 196–202.

Dataplicity. (2017). *Connect your Pi to the Internet.* Retrieved August 18, 2017, from https://docs.dataplicity.com/docs/get-pi-connected-to-the-internet

Dehlinger, J., & Dixon, J. (2011). Mobile application software engineering: Challenges and research directions. In *Proceedings of the Workshop on Mobile Software Engineering* (pp. 29-32). Berlin: Springer-Verlag.

Dertien, S. (2015). *Defining The Infrastructure For The Big Data, Manufacturing Leadership: Product Lifecycle Report.* Retrieved May 15, 2017, from https://www.ptc.com/en/product-lifecycle-report/defining-the-infrastructure-for-big-data-analytics

Dharmapurikar, A. A., & Waghmare, R. B. (2015). An Effective Wireless Solution For Industrial Automation By Using Raspberry Pi. *International Journal of Engineering Educational Technology, 3*(2), 1–8.

Diaz Bilotto, P. (2015). *Software development for mobile applications through an integration of MDA and Haxe* (Undergraduate thesis). Computer Science Department, Universidad Nacional del Centro de la Provincia de Buenos Aires, Argentina.

Diaz Bilotto, P., & Favre, L. (2016). Migrating JAVA to Mobile Platforms through HAXE: An MDD Approach. In A. M. Cruz & S. Paiva (Eds.), *Modern Software Engineering Methodologies for Mobile and Cloud Environments* (pp. 240–268). Hershey, PA: IGI Global. doi:10.4018/978-1-4666-9916-8.ch013

Dickey, M. R. (2015, March). *How Google Glass Will Revolutionize 9 Industries.* Retrieved from http://www.businessinsider.com/google-glass-will-totally-disrupt-these-tktk-industries-2013-3?op=1

Dillmann, R., & Friedrich, H. (2005). Programming by Demonstration: A Machine Learning Approach to Support Skill Acquisition for Robots. Artificial Intelligence and Symbolic Mathematical Computation, 87–108.

Dimitrov, D.V. (2016). Medical Internet of Things and Big Data in Healthcare. *Health Inform Res., 22*(3), 156-163. 10.4258/hir.2016.22.3.156

Dreiseitl, S., & Ohno-Machado, L. (2002). Logistic regression and artificial neural network classification models: A methodology review. *Journal of Biomedical Informatics, 35*(5-6), 352–359. doi:10.1016/S1532-0464(03)00034-0 PMID:12968784

Dunkels, Gronvall, & Voigt. (2004). Contiki - A lightweight and flexible operatingsystem for tiny networked sensors. *29th Annual IEEE International Conference on Local Computer Networks,* 455 – 462.

Duthey, M., & Spina, C. (2016). *Migrating C/C++ to mobile platforms through MDD* (Undergraduate Thesis). Computer Science Department, Universidad Nacional del Centro de la Provincia de Buenos Aires, Argentina.

Eclipse. (2017). *Eclipse-The Eclipse Foundation open source community.* Retrieved from http://eclipse.org/

e-Health Sensor Platform V2.0 for Arduino and Raspberry Pi. (n.d.). Available at: https://e-class.teilar.gr/modules/document/file.php/CS103/IOT%20-%20SENSORS%20-%20ACTUATORS/e-Health%20Sensor%20Platform%20V2.pdf

e-Health Sensor Platform V2.0 for Arduino and Raspberry Pi. (n.d.). Retrieved from https://e-class.teilar.gr/modules/document/file.php/CS103/IOT%20-%20SENSORS%20-%20ACTUATORS/e-Health%20Sensor%20Platform%20V2.pdf

EISA. (2007). *Energy Independence and Security Act of 2007 (H.R. 6)*. EISA.

Ejarque, J., Micsik, A., & Badia, R. (2015). Towards Automatic Application Migration to Clouds. In *Proceedings IEEE 8th Int. Conf. on Cloud Computing (CLOUD)* (pp. 25-32). New York: IEEE.

Emerson. (2017, March). *Delta V*. Retrieved from http:// http://www.emerson.com/en-us/automation/deltav

EMF. (2017). *Eclipse Modeling Framework (EMF)*. Retrieved April 25, 2017 from http://www.eclipse.org/modeling/emf/

EnOcean. (2015). *The True Cost of Batteries, Why Energy Harvesting Is The Best Power Solution For Wireless Sensors*. White Paper, EnOcean, 1-6.

EnOcean. (2016). *BACnet and EnOcean enable Energy Efficient Buildings*. White Paper of EnOcean Alliance, 1-16.

Ensor, P. (1988). The Functional Silo Syndrome. *Association for Manufacturer Excellence (AME) Target, 16*, 1988.

Epson. (2017, March). *Epson Moverio BT-300*. Retrieved from https://epson.com/moverio-augmented-reality-smart-glasses?pg=3#sn

Errington, J. (2005). *Establishing Human Performance Improvements an Economic Benefit for a Human-Centered Operator Interface*. Human Factors and Ergonomic Society.

Favre, L., & Duarte, D. (2016). Formal MOF Metamodeling and Tool Support. In *Proceedings of the 4th International Conference on Model-Driven Engineering and Software Development. MODELSWARD 2016* (pp. 99-110). Roma, Italy: SCITEPRESS (Science and Technology Publications).

Favre, L. (2009) A Formal Foundation for Metamodeling. In *Proceedings of 14th Ada-Europe International Conference. Lecture Notes in Computer Science* (Vol 5570, pp.177-191). Berlin: Springer-Verlag. doi:10.1007/978-3-642-01924-1_13

Favre, L. (2010). *Model Driven Architecture for Reverse Engineering Technologies: Strategic Directions and System Evolution*. IGI Global. doi:10.4018/978-1-61520-649-0

Feng, X., Shen, J., & Fan, Y. (2009). REST: An alternative to RPC for Web services architecture. *2009 First International Conference on Future Information Networks*, 7-10. doi:10.1109/ICFIN.2009.5339611

Franz, O., & Barth, B. (2013). Results from PV GRID Research for Germany. *PV GRID EU Project Deliverables*. Available: http://www.pvgrid.eu/fileadmin/6.Germany_131022_PVGRID_RWE_BSW.pdf

Galeev. (n.d.). *Bluetooth 4.0: An Introduction to Bluetooth Low Energy-part II*. Z-Focus Consulting.

Galitiello, E., & Rolandi, B. (2015). *Reverse engineering of Object-Oriented Code* (Thesis). Computer Science Department, Universidad Nacional del Centro de la Provincia de Buenos Aires, Argentina.

García, C. G., Llorián, D. M., Bustelo, B. C., & Lovelle, J. M. C. (2017). A Review about Smart Objects, Sensors, and Actuators. *International Journal of Interactive Multimedia and Artificial Intelligence*, *4*, 7–10.

García, C.G., & Meana-Llorián, D., G-Bustelo, B.C. P., Cueva Lovelle, J.M., & Garcia-Fernandez, N. (2017). Midgar: Detection Of People Through Computer Vision In The Internet of Things Scenarios To Improve The Security In Smart Cities, Smart Towns, And Smart Homes. *Future Generation Computer Systems*.

Garima, A. N., & Reddy, S. R. N. (2015). Design & Development Of Daughter Board For Raspberry Pi to Support Bluetooth Communication Using UART. *Proceedings of the International Conference on Computing, Communication, and Automation (ICCCA2015)*, 949-954.

Gemalto. (2017). *Gemalto On-Demand Connectivity*. Retrieved May 28, 2017, from http://www.gemalto.com/iot/consumer-electronics/embedded-sim-uicc

Germany Trade & Invest. (2014). *Industrie 4.0: Smart Manufacturing for the Future*. Germany Trade & Invest.

Gevorgian, V., & Booth, S. (2013). Review of PREPA Technical Requirements for Interconnecting Wind and Solar Generation. National Renewable Energy Laboratory Technical Reports. NREL/TP-5D00-57089, pp. 12-13 (Nov 2013).

Ghamari, M., Janko, B., Sherratt, R. S., Harwin, W., Piechockic, R., & Soltanpur, C. (2016). A Survey on Wireless Body Area Networks for eHealthcare Systems in Residential Environments. *Sensors (Basel)*, *16*(6), 831. doi:10.3390/s16060831 PMID:27338377

GibbonsD. (2017). *MQTT*. Retrieved from https://github.com/mqtt/mqtt.github.io/wiki/server-support

Gomez, J. O., & Paradells, J. (2012). Overview and evaluation of Bluetooth low energy: An emerging low-power wireless technology. *Sensors (Basel)*, *12*(9), 11734–11753. doi:10.3390/s120911734

González García, C., & Espada, J. (2015). MUSPEL: Generation of Applications to Interconnect Heterogeneous Objects Using Model-Driven Engineering. In V. G. Díaz, J. M. C. Lovelle, & B. C. P. García-Bustelo (Eds.), *Handbook of Research on Innovations in Systems and Software Engineering* (pp. 365–385). Hershey, PA: IGI Global. doi:10.4018/978-1-4666-6359-6.ch015

González García, C., Espada, J. P., Valdez, E. R. N., & García-Díaz, V. (2014). Midgar: Domain-Specific Language to Generate Smart Objects for an Internet of Things Platform. *2014 Eighth Int. Conf. Innov. Mob. Internet Serv. Ubiquitous Comput.*, 352–357. doi:10.1109/IMIS.2014.48

González García, C., García-Bustelo, C. P., Espada, J. P., & Cueva-Fernandez, G. (2014). Midgar: Generation of heterogeneous objects interconnecting applications. A Domain Specific Language proposal for Internet of Things scenarios. *Computer Networks*, *64*, 143–158. doi:10.1016/j.comnet.2014.02.010

González García, C., Meana-Llorián, D., Pelayo G-Bustelo, C., & Cueva-Lovelle, J. M. (2017). A review about Smart Objects, Sensors, and Actuators. *Int. J. Interact. Multimed. Artif. Intell.*, *4*(3), 7–10. doi:10.9781/ijimai.2017.431

Google. (2017, March). *Google Glass*. Retrieved from https://developers.google.com/glass/

Govindan, K., & Azad, A. P. (2015). *End-to-end service assurance in IoT MQTT-SN*. Paper presented at the Consumer Communications and Networking Conference (CCNC), 2015 12th Annual IEEE. doi:10.1109/CCNC.2015.7157991

Granjal, J., Monteiro, E., & Silva, J. S. (2015). Security for the Internet of Things: A Survey of Existing Protocols and Open Research issues. *IEEE Commun. Surv. Tutorials. PP*, *25*. doi:10.1109/COMST.2015.2388550

Granjal, J., Monteiro, E., & Silva, J. S. (2015). *Security for the Internet of Things: A Survey of Existing Protocols and Open Research issues*. IEEE Communication Survey Tutorials.

Grefen, P. (2013). Networked Business Process Management. *International Journal of IT/Business Alignment and Governance*, *4*(2), 54–82.

Grefen, P. (2016, Fall). *Business information system architecture*. Eindhoven University of Technology.

Grefen, P., Vanderfeesten, I., & Boultadakis, G. (2016a). *Architecture Design of the HORSE Hybrid Manufacturing Process Control System* (Beta Working Paper Series No. 518). Eindhoven University of Technology.

Grefen, P., Eshuis, R., Mehandjiev, N., Kouvas, G., & Weichhart, G. (2009). Internet-Based Support for Process-Oriented Instant Virtual Enterprises. *IEEE Internet Computing*, *13*(6), 65–73. doi:10.1109/MIC.2009.96

Grefen, P., Eshuis, R., Mehandjiev, N., Kouvas, G., & Weichhart, G. (2016). *Business Information System Architecture, Fall 2016 Edition*. Eindhoven University of Technology.

Grefen, P., Mehandjiev, N., Kouvas, G., Weichhart, G., & Eshuis, R. (2009). Dynamic Business Network Process Management in Instant Virtual Enterprises. *Computers in Industry*, *60*(2), 86–103. doi:10.1016/j.compind.2008.06.006

Grefen, P., Vanderfeesten, I., & Boultadakis, G. (2016b). Supporting Hybrid Manufacturing: Bringing Process and Human/Robot Control to the Cloud. In *Proceedings 5th IEEE International Conference on Cloud Networking* (pp. 200–203). IEEE. doi:10.1109/CloudNet.2016.39

Guenter, K., Friedhelm, R., Zach, S., Sandeep, A., & Jan, H. (2014). *Lightweight M2M: Enabling Device Management and Applications for the Internet of Things*. White Paper, Open Mobile Alliance.

Guinard, D., & Trifa, V. (2009). Towards the Web of Things: Web Mashups for Embedded Devices. Workshop on Mashups, Enterprise Mashups and Lightweight Composition on the Web (MEM 2009). *Proceedings of WWW (International World Wide Web Conferences).*

Guinard, D., Fischer, M., & Trifa, V. (2010). Sharing using social networks in a composable Web of Things. *2010 8th IEEE International Conference on Pervasive Computing and Communications Workshops (PERCOM Workshops)*, 702-707. doi:10.1109/PERCOMW.2010.5470524

Guinard, D., Trifa, V., Mattern, F., & Wilde, E. (2011). From The Internet of Things to the Web of Things: Resource Oriented Architecture and Best Practices. In D. Uckelmann, M. Harrison, & F. Michahelles (Eds.), *Architecting The Internet of Things* (pp. 97–129). Berlin, Germany: Springer. doi:10.1007/978-3-642-19157-2_5

Gupta, M. S., Patchava, V., & Menezes, V. (2015). Healthcare based on IoT Using Raspberry Pi. *International Conference on Green Computing and Internet of Things (ICGCIoT)*, 796-799. doi:10.1109/ICGCIoT.2015.7380571

Gyrard, A., Patel, P., Datta, S., & Ali, M. (2016, October). Semantic web meets internet of things (The IoT) and web of things (wot). *The 15th International Conference on Semantic Web (ISWC).*

Hall, R. (2016). *Raspberry Pi Talks EnOcean-How to combine your Raspberry Pi board with the EnOcean Developer Kit*. Dolphin White Paper.

Hall, R., Pauls, K., McCulloch, S., & Savage, D. (2011). *OSGi in Action: Creating Modular Applications in Java*. Manning Publications.

Hans, R., Abels, S., Zöller, S., Miede, A., & Steinmetz, R. (2013). Enabling collaboration in virtual manufacturing enterprises with cloud computing. *Proceedings 19th Americas Conference on Information Systems, AMCIS 2013 - Hyperconnected World: Anything, Anywhere, Anytime*, 2, 1341–1350.

Hasan, M., Hossain, E., & Niyato, D. (2013). Random access for machine-to-machine communication in LTE-advanced networks: Issues and approaches. IEEE Communications Magazine, 51(6), 86-93.

Hasan, M., Hossain, E., & Niyato, D. (2013). Random Access for Machine-to-Machine Communication in LTE-Advanced Networks: Issues and Approaches. *Smart Cities IEEE Communications Magazine*, 86-93.

Hastie, T., Tibshirani, R., & Friedman, J. (2009). *Elements of Statistical Learning: Data Mining, Inference and Prediction* (2nd ed.). New York: Springer-Verlag. doi:10.1007/978-0-387-84858-7

Haxe. (2017). *The Haxe Language.* Retrieved April 25, 2017 from https://haxe.org/

Hekland, Petersen, & Doyle. (2008). When HART goes wireless: Understanding and implementing the WirelessHART standard. *IEEE International Conference on Emerging Technologies and Factory Automation (ETFA 2008)*, 899-907. doi:10.1109/ETFA.2008.4638503

Heller, W. (2015). *Daylight Harvesting based on EnOcean Finished Products.* White Paper, 1-3.

Helm-Murtagh, S. C. (2014). Use of Big Data by Blue Cross and Blue Shield of North Carolina. *NCMJ*, *75*, 195–197. PMID:24830494

Hermann, A., Drews, F., Bauer, J., Klemm, S., Roennau, A., & Dillmann, R. (2014). Unified GPU voxel collision detection for mobile manipulation planning. *IEEE International Conference on Intelligent Robots and Systems*, 4154-4160. doi:10.1109/IROS.2014.6943148

Hilliard, R. (2007). *All About IEEE Std 1471.* Retrieved from http://www.iso-architecture.org/ieee-1471/docs/all-about-ieee-1471.pdf

Hisakazu, H., & Jin, M. (2011). EPC based Internet of Things Architecture. *IEEE International Conference on RFID-Technologies and Applications*, 527-532.

HomePlug Alliance. (2012). *HomePlug GreenPHY v1.1.* Retrieved from http://www.homeplug.org/tech-resources/resources/ http://www.contiki-os.org/ http://mqtt.org

Honeywell. (2006, October). *TotalPlant Alcont and Printa. Configuration Manual & Application planning guide.* Author.

Hopcroft, Plotkin, Schwartz, Scott, & Vuillemin. (n.d.). *Art Gallery Theorems and Algorithms.* The International Series of Monographs on Computer Science Editor.

HORSE Architecture Team. (2016). *Complete System Design; HORSE Deliverable D2.2 (complete version, confidential).* Author.

Hsiao, S. J., Lian, K. Y., & Sung, W. T. (2016). Employing Cross-Platform Smart Home Control System with IoT Technology-Based IEEE Computer Society. *International Symposium on Computer, Consumer, and Control*, 264-267.

Hunkeler, U., Truong, H. L., & Stanford-Clark, A. (2008). *MQTT-S—A publish/subscribe protocol for Wireless Sensor Networks.* Paper presented at the Communication systems software and middleware and workshops, 2008. comsware 2008. 3rd international conference on.

H, Z., A, H., & M, M. (2015). Internet of Things (IoT): Definitions, Challenges and Recent Research Directions. *International Journal of Computers and Applications*, *128*(1), 37–47. doi:10.5120/ijca2015906430

Ibrahim, M., Elgamri, A., Babiker, S., & Mohamed, A. (2015). Internet of Things based Smart Environmental Monitoring using the Raspberry-Pi Computer. IEEE.

IDC. (2014). *IDC Reveals Worldwide Manufacturing Predictions for 2015, IDC Manufacturing Press Release.* IDC.

IEA. (2016). *Energy Efficiency of the Internet of Things.* Technology and Energy Assessment Report, IEA 4E EDNA.

IEC. (2013). Enterprise-Control System Integration - Part 1: Models and Terminology (2nd ed.). Geneva, Switzerland: IEC.

IEEE 802.15.4. (2011). IEEE Standard for Local and metropolitan area networks--Part 15.4: Low-Rate Wireless Personal Area Networks (LR-WPANs). Retrieved from http://standards.ieee.org/getieee802/download/802.15.4-2011.pdf

Ingenu. (2017). *The Six Secrets of Extremely Long Battery Life.* A White Paper By Ingénue, 1-3.

Islam, N., & Want, R. (2014). Smarthphones: Past, present and future. *Pervasive Computing, 13*(4), 82–92. doi:10.1109/MPRV.2014.74

ISO. (2017, March). Retrieved from http://www.iso.org

Itamir de Morais, B. F., & Gibeon, S. A. J. (2017). IoT-Based Healthcare Applications: A Review. Lecture Notes in Computer Science. Doi:10.1007/978-3-319-62407-5_4

ITU. (2012). *Impacts of M2M Communications & Non-M2M Mobile Data Applications on Mobile Networks.* Available at: www.itu.int/md/T09-SG11-120611-TD-GEN-0844/en

ITU-T. (2012). Series Y: Global Information Infrastructure, Internet Protocol Aspects and Next-Generation Networks, Overview of the Internet of things. ITU-T Y.2060.

Iulia, F., Razvan, R., Laura, R., & Dan, D. (2017). Survey of Standardized Protocols for the Internet of Things. *21st International Conference on Control Systems and Computer Science*, 190-197.

Janakiram, M. S. V. (2014). *Prototyping a Sensor Node and IoT Gateway with Arduino and Raspberry Pi.* Available at: https://thenewstack.io/author/janakiram/

Jara, A. J., Ladid, L., & Skarmeta, A. (2013). The Internet of Everything through IPv6: An Analysis of Challenges, Solutions, and Opportunities. *Journal of Wireless Mobile Networks, Ubiquitous Computing, and Dependable Applications, 4*(3), 97–118.

Ji, Z., & Qi, A. (2010). The application of internet of things(IOT) in emergency management system in China. *2010 IEEE Int. Conf. Technol. Homel. Secur.*, 139–142. doi:10.1109/THS.2010.5655073

Joshi, P., Nivangune, A., Kumar, R., Kumar, S., Ramesh, R., Pani, S., & Chesum, A. (2015). Understanding the Challenges in Mobile Computation Offloading to Cloud through Experimentation. In *2nd ACM Int. Conf. on Mobile Software Engineering and Systems* (pp.158-159). Florence, Italy: ACM. doi:10.1109/MobileSoft.2015.43

Karagiannis, V., & Chatzimisios, P. (2015). A survey on application layer protocols for the internet of things. *Transaction on IoT and Cloud Computing, 3*(1), 11–17.

Karbing, Rees, & Jaffe. (2017). *Journal of Clinical Monitoring and Computing 2016 end of year summary.* DOI: 10.1007/s10877-017-0008-0

KDM. (2016). *Knowledge Discovery Meta-Model (KDM), OMG Document Number: formal/2016-09-01*. Retrieved April, 25, 2017 from http://www.omg.org/spec/KDM/1.4

Kenji, A., Nizar, L., Fred, F., & Chakrabartty, S. (2016). Infrastructural Health Monitoring Using Self-powered Internet-of-Things. IEEE.

Kerem, O., Vedat, C., Mehmet, N., & Aydin, B. O. (2010). Current Benefits and Future Directions of NFC Services. *International Conference on Education and Management Technology*.

Khattak, H. A., Ruta, M., & Eugenio, D. S. (2014). CoAP-based Healthcare Sensor Networks: a survey. *IEEE Proceedings of 11th International Bhurban Conference on Applied Sciences & Technology (IBCAST)*, 499-503. doi:10.1109/IBCAST.2014.6778196

Kim, H. (2008). Frameworks of process improvement for mobile applications. *Engineering Letters*, *16*(4), 550-555. Retrieved April 25, 2017 from http://www.engineeringletters.com/issues_v16/issue_4/EL_16_4_13.pdf

Kim, Kim, Choi, & Jin. (2015). Accurate Indoor Proximity Zone Detection Based on Time Window and Frequency with Bluetooth Low Energy. *The 12th International Conference on Mobile Systems and Pervasive Computing (MobiSPC)*.

Kim, D.-Y., Kim, S.-H., Choi, D., & Jin, S.-H. (2015). Accurate Indoor Proximity Zone Detection Based on Time Window and Frequency with Bluetooth Low Energy. *Procedia Computer Science*, *56*, 88–95. doi:10.1016/j.procs.2015.07.199

Kindig, D., & Stoddart, G. (2003). *What Is Population Health*. American Journal of Public Health, *93*(3), 380–383.

Kononenko, I. (2001). Machine learning for medical diagnosis: History, state of the art and perspective. *Artif Intell Med.*, *23*(1), 89-109.

Kononenko, I. (2007). Inductive and Bayesian Learning. In *Medical Diagnosis* (pp. 317–337). Journal Applied Artificial Intelligence.

Kramer, D., Clark, T., & Oussena, S. (2010). MobDSL: A domain specific language for multiple mobile platform deployment. In *Proceedings of IEEE Int. Conf. on Networked Embedded Systems for Enterprise Applications* (pp. 1-7). Perth, Australia: IEEE. doi:10.1109/NESEA.2010.5678062

Kriz, Maly, & Kozel. (2016). *Research Article Improving Indoor Localization Using Bluetooth Low Energy Beacons*. Hindawi Publishing Corporation. doi:10.1155/2016/2083094

Kruchten, P. (1995). Architectural Blueprints—The "4+1" View Model of Software Architecture. *IEEE Software*, *12*(6), 42–50. doi:10.1109/52.469759

Kula, Ozyer, Tavliba, Cankaya, & S˙og˘uf˙oz¨u. (2014). IEEE 802.11 WLAN Based Real Time Indoor Positioning: Literature Survey and Experimental Investigations. *9th International Conference on Future Networks and Communications*.

Kuo, H. T., Chin, L. H., & Yun, F. L. (2015). A solution of a Newly Built Monitoring Automation System In Parallel to the Original Automation Management System. IEEE.

Lanthaler, M., & Gütl, Ch. (2012). On Using JSON-LD to Create Evolvable RESTful Services. *Proceedings of the 3th International Workshop on RESTful Design (WS-REST) at the of the 21st International World Wide Web Conference (2012)*, 25-32. doi:10.1145/2307819.2307827

Libelium. (2017). *Extreme Range Links: LoRa 868 / 900MHz SX1272 LoRa module for Arduino Waspmote and Raspberry Pi.* Retrieved 25 July, 2017, from https://www.cooking-hacks.com/documentation/tutorials/extreme-range-lora-sx1272-module-shield-arduino-raspberry-pi-intel-galileo/#step4_2

Linklabs. (2016). *A Comprehensive Look at Low Power, Wide Area Networks, For 'Internet of Things' Engineers and Decision Makers*. LinkLabs.

Linklabs. (2017). *LoW Power wide area network technology, Symphony Link Vs. LoRaWAN, A Guide for Engineers and Decision Makers*. Linklabs.

Liu, H., Darabi, H., Banerjee, P., & Liu, J. (2007). Survey of wireless indoor positioning techniques and systems. *IEEE Transactions on Systems, Man and Cybernetics Part C, 37*(6), 1067–1080. doi:10.1109/TSMCC.2007.905750

Locke, D. (2010). *MQ Telemetry Transport (MQTT) V3.1 Protocol Specification*. Retrieved from http://www.ibm.com/developerworks/library/ws-mqtt/

Long, W. J., Griffith, J. L., Selker, H. P., & D'Agostino, R. B. (1993). A comparison of logistic regression to decision-tree induction in a medical domain. *Computers and Biomedical Research, an International Journal, 26*(1), 74–97. doi:10.1006/cbmr.1993.1005 PMID:8444029

LoRa Alliance. (2015). *LoRaWAN specification.* Retrieved from https://www.lora-alliance.org/portals/0/specs/LoRaWAN%20Specification%201R0.pdf

LPWA. (2017). *What Is LPWA? An IoT Connectivity Guide*. A White Paper By Ingenu, 1-3.

Luzuriaga, J. E., Cano, J. C., Calafate, C., Manzoni, P., Perez, M., & Boronat, P. (2015). *Handling mobility in IoT applications using the MQTT protocol.* Paper presented at the Internet Technologies and Applications (ITA). doi:10.1109/ITechA.2015.7317403

Mads, L., Istvan, Z. K., Preben, M., Mads, S., & Steffen, H. (2016). Coverage and Capacity Analysis of LTE-M and NB-IoT in a Rural Area. IEEE.

Magtel, S. A. (2017). *Photovoltaic Solar with Tracker*. Retrieved from http://www.magtel.es/en/projects/photovoltaic-solar-with-tracker/

Mahindrakar, S., & Biradar, R.K. (2015). Internet of Things: Smart Home Automation System using Raspberry Pi. *International Journal of Science and Research,* 901-905.

Malý, I. (2016, July). Augmented reality experiments with industrial robot in industry 4.0 environment. *IEEE 14th International Conference on Industrial Informatics (INDIN)*, 19-21.

Marcos, J., Storkël, O., Marroyo, L., García, M., & Lorenzo, R. (2014). Storage requirements for PV power ramp-rate control. *Solar Energy*, *99*, 28–35. doi:10.1016/j.solener.2013.10.037

Martinez, L., Pereira, C., & Favre, L. (2017). Migrating C/C++ Software to Mobile Platforms in the ADM Context. *International Journal of Interactive Multimedia and Artificial Intelligence*, *4*(3), 34–44. doi:10.9781/ijimai.2017.436

McEwen, A., & Cassimally, H. (2013). *Designing the Internet of Things*. Wiley.

McMahon. (2015, March). *Three decades of DCS technology*. Retrieved from http://www.controlglobal.com/articles/2005/227.html

MDA. (2017). *The Model-Driven Architecture*. Retrieved April 25, 2017 from www.omg.org/mda/

Meana-Llorian, D., & García, C. G., G-Bustelo, B.C.P., Lovelle, J.M.C., & Garcia-Fernandez, N. (2016). IoFClime: The Fuzzy Logic and the Internet of Things to Control Indoor Temperature Regarding the Outdoor Ambient Conditions. *Future Generation Computer Systems*.

Mehta, K. D., Mehta, S. B., & Raviya, K. S. (2014). Analysis of TOI (Things of Internet) Industrial Monitoring System on Raspberry Pi Platform. *International Journal of Computer Science and Mobile Applications*, *2*(11), 33–40.

Menz, F., & Vachon, S. (2006, September). The Effectiveness of Different Policy Regimes for Promoting Wind Power: Experiences from the States. *Energy Policy*, *34*(14), 1786–1796. doi:10.1016/j.enpol.2004.12.018

Metavision. (2017, March). *Meta 2*. Retrieved from https://www.metavision.com

Meteoric growth: The Internet of Things is scaling exponentially. (2017). Retrieved from https://www.internet-der-dinge.de/en.html

Microsoft. (2017, March). *Hololens*. Retrieved from https://www.microsoft.com/microsoft-hololens/en-us

Microsoft. (n.d.). *Azure Solutions for Internet of Things (IoT)*. Available at: https://opbuildstorageprod.blob.core.windows.net/output-pdf-files/en-us/Azure.azure-documents/live/iot-suite.pdf

Miranda, J., Makitalo, N., Garcia-Alonso, J., Berrocal, J., Mikkonen, T., Canal, C., & Murillo, J. (2015). From the Internet of Things to the Internet of People. *IEEE Internet Computing*, *19*(2), 40–47. doi:10.1109/MIC.2015.24

Mitchell, T. M., Carbonell, J. G., & Michalski, R. S. (1986). *Machine Learning: A Guide to Current Research* (1st ed.). The Springer International Series in Engineering and Computer Science. Original. doi:10.1007/978-1-4613-2279-5

MoDisco. (2017). *Model Discovery*. Retrieved April 25, 2017 from https://eclipse.org/MoDisco/

MOF. (2016). *Meta Object Facility (MOF) Core Specification, Version 2.5, OMG Document Number:formal/2016-11-01*. Retrieved April 25, 2017 from http://www.omg.org/spec/MOF/2.5.1/

Mukhopadhyay, D., Saha, S., Rao, R., & Paranjpe, A. (2017). A Web-of-Things-Based System to Remotely Configure Automated Systems Using a Conditional Programming Approach. In *Proceedings of the 5th International Conference on Frontiers in Intelligent Computing: Theory and Applications* (pp. 303-311). Springer. doi:10.1007/978-981-10-3153-3_30

Muller. (2000). *Bluetooth Demystified.* McGraw-Hill Professional Publishing.

Muneer, B. Y., Mohammed, Q. S., & Dua, A. Z. (2016). Application Layer Protocols for the Internet of Things: A survey. IEEE.

Muñoz-Organero, M., Muñoz-Merino, P. J., & Delgado Kloos, C. (2012). Using Bluetooth to implement a pervasive indoor positioning system with minimal requirements at the application level. *Mobile Information Systems*, *8*(1), 73–82. doi:10.1155/2012/386161

Murphy, J., & Roser, M. (2017). *'The Internet'.* Retrieved on June 5, 2017, from https://ourworldindata.org/internet/

Naik, P., & Harode, U. (2016). Raspberry Pi and IoT Based Industrial Automation. *International Journal of Industrial Electronics and Electrical Engineering*, *4*(10), 49–52.

Neumann, M., Bach, Ch., Miclaus, A., Riedel, T., & Beigl, M. (2016). Always-On Web of Things Infrastructure using Dynamic Software Updating. In *Proceedings of the Seventh International Workshop on the Web of Things*. ACM. doi:10.1145/3017995.3017997

Ngrock. (2017). *Secure tunnels to Localhost.* Retrieved July 25, 2017, from https://ngrok.com/docs

Ngufor, C., & Wojtusiak, J. (2013). *Learning from Large-Scale Distributed Health Data: An Approximate Logistic Regression Approach.* Academic Press.

Nguyen, K. T., Laurent, M., & Oualha, N. (2015). Survey on secure communication protocols for the Internet of Things. *Ad Hoc Networks*, *32*, 17–31. doi:10.1016/j.adhoc.2015.01.006

Nivedha, S., Shambavi, P., Abhirami, N., Jyothi, A.P., & Darwin, B.R. (2016). Raspberry Pi Based Hazardous Environment Monitoring Using Wireless Communication. *IEEE Transactions on Electrical and Electronics Engineering, 4*(3), 47-51.

O'Kane, J. (2013). *A Gentle Introduction to ROS.* CreateSpace Independent Publishing Platform.

OASIS. (2012). *OASIS Advanced Message Queuing Protocol (AMQP) Version 1.0.* Retrieved from http://docs.oasis-open.org/amqp/core/v1.0/os/amqp-core-complete-v1.0-os.pdf

OCL. (2014). *OMG Object constraint language (OCL), version 2.4. OMG Document Number: formal/2014-02-03.* Retrieved April, 25, 2017 from http://www.omg.org/spec/OCL/2.4

OECD. (2015). *OECD Reviews of Health Systems: Colombia 2016.* Paris: OECD Reviews of Health Systems.

Olausson, M., Larsson, M., & Alfredsson, F. (2012). Colaborando en un nueva dimensión. *Revista ABB*, *2/12*, 6–11.

Omerth. (2017, March). *C-Thru*. Retrieved from http://www.omerh.com/c-thru#0

OPEN FL. (2017). *OPEN FL 4.7*. Retrieved April 25, 2017 from http://www.openfl.org/

Open Source Robotics Foundation. (2017a). *ROS FlexBE*. Retrieved April 27, 2017, from http://wiki.ros.org/flexbe

Open Source Robotics Foundation. (2017b). *ROS Introduction*. Retrieved April 27, 2017, from http://wiki.ros.org/ROS/Introduction

Park, M. (2015). IEEE 802.11ah: Sub-1-GHz license-exempt operation for the internet of things. *IEEE Communications Magazine*, *53*(9), 145–151. doi:10.1109/MCOM.2015.7263359

Pascal, U. (2015). RACS: Remote APDU Call Secure Creating Trust for the Internet. IEEE.

Pascal, U., & Xavier, A. (2016). Secure Mobile Payments Based on Cloud Services Concepts And Experiments. *IEEE 2nd International Conference on Big Data Security on Cloud, IEEE International Conference on High Performance and Smart Computing*, 333-338.

Patel, P., Gyrard, A., Thakker, D., Sheth, A., & Serrano, M. (2016). SWoTSuite: A Toolkit for Prototyping Cross-domain Semantic Web of Things Applications. *Proceedings of the 15th International Semantic Web Conference (ISWC)*.

Patel, T. K., Wadekar, U., Wabale, A., & Datkhore, S. S. (2015). Appliances Control Using Ethernet and Raspberry PI. *International Journal of Advanced Research in Computer Science and Software Engineering*, *5*(3), 494–497.

Patidar, P., Praneeta, S., Kataria, R., & Vidhyasagar, B. S. (2017). Analysis of Multi-Disease & Prediction of Suitable Drug for Healthcare Application using Big data. *International Journal of Research in Applied Science & Engineering Technology, 5*(4).

Payam, H. (2016). Integrated Millimeter-Wave/Terahertz Sensor Systems for Near-Field IoT. ACM.

Pelino, M., & Hewitt, A. (2016). *The Forrester Wave: IoT Software Platforms, Q4 2016, The 11 Providers That Matter Most and How They Stack Up*. Academic Press.

Peng, R., & Sichitiu, M. L. (2006). Angle of arrival localization for wireless sensor networks. *Proceedings of the 3rd Annual IEEE Communications Society on Sensor and Ad Hoc Communications and Networks (Secon '06)*, 1, 374–382.

Pérez Castillo, R., García Rodriguez, I., Gómez Cornejo, R., Fernández Ropero, M., & Piattini, M. (2013). ANDRIU. A Technique for Migrating Graphical User Interfaces to Android. In *Proceedings of The 25th International Conference on Software Engineering and Knowledge Engineering* (pp. 516-519). Academic Press.

Pérez Cota M., González Castro M.R. (2011, June). Interfaz Avanzada de Oprador de DCS. *6ª CISTI*, 37-41.

Pfisterer, D., Romer, K., Bimschas, D., Kleine, O., Mietz, R., Truong, C., ... Richardson, R. (2011, November). SPITFIRE: Toward a semantic web of things. *IEEE Communications Magazine*, *49*(11), 40–48. doi:10.1109/MCOM.2011.6069708

Pi. (2017). *Access Your Raspberry Pi Over The Internet*. Retrieved July 19, 2017, from https://www.raspberrypi.org/documentation/remote-access/access-over-Internet/README.md

Poole, I. (2017). *LTE-M, LTE Machine to Machine, M2M*. Retrieved May 15, 2017, from http://www.radio-electronics.com/info/cellulartelecomms/lte-long-term-evolution/lte-m-m2m-machine-to-machine.php

Porter, M. (1985). *Competitive Advantage: Creating and Sustaining Superior Performance*. Free Press.

Postel. (1980). *User Datagram Protocol*. Internet Engineering Task Force RFC 768.

Prasad, M. M., & Kumar, M. N. (2016). Wireless Industrial Automation System. *South Asian Journal of Engineering and Technology*, *2*(21), 140–146.

Priyanka, K., & Kulennavar, N. (2014). A survey on big data analytics in health care. *Int. J. Comput. Sci.Inform. Technologies*, *5*, 5865–5868.

Priyanka, T., & Yoohwan, K. (2016). Implementation and Comparison of M2M Protocols for Internet of Things. *Proceedings of 4th International Conference on Applied Computing and Information Technology*, 43-48.

QVT. (2012). *QVT: MOF 2.0 query, view, transformation: Version 1.1*. OMG Document Number: formal/2011-01-01. Retrieved from http://www.omg.org/spec/QVT/1.1/SMM

Ramya, V., & Rajan, G. T. (2016). Raspberry Pi Based Energy Efficient Industrial Automation System. *International Journal of Innovative Research in Computer Science and Engineering IJIRCSE*, *2*(1), 1–7.

Rao, S., Chendanda, D., Deshpande, C., & Lakkundi, V. (2015). Implementing LWM2M in Constrained IoT Devices. *IEEE Conference on Wireless Sensors*, 52-56.

Raspberry Pi 3 Model B. (2017). Retrieved from https://www.raspberrypi.org/products/raspberry-pi-3-model-b/

Ray, B. (2015). *What Is SigFox?* Retrieved July 21, 2017, https://www.link-labs.com/blog/what-is-sigfox

Raza, S., & Voigt, T. (2010). Interconnecting WirelessHART and legacy HART networks. *6th IEEE International Conference on Distributed Computing in Sensor Systems Workshops (DCOSSW)*, 1-8. Retrieved from http://ieeexplore.ieee.org/xpl/articleDetails.jsp?arnumber=5593285

Reising, D. V., Laberge, J., & Bullemer, P. (2010). *Supporting Operator Sitation Awareness With Overview Displays: A Series of Studies on Information vs. Vitualization Requeriments*. ICOCO.

Remote3.it. (2017). *Remote Manage Networked Devices Anywhere*. Retrieved August 19, 2017, from https://www.remot3.it/web/index.html

Remote-IoT. (2015). Remote IoT Device Management. Retrieved July 25, 2017, from https://remote-iot.com/web/index.htm

Remus & Kennedy. (2012). Special Focus on Nursing Informatics. *Innovation in Transformative Nursing Leadership: Nursing Informatics Competencies and Roles*, 14-26. doi:10.12927/cjnl.2012.23260

Review on Internet of Things (IoT) in Healthcare. (n.d.). Available from: https://www.researchgate.net/publication/309718253_A_Review_on_Internet_of_Things_IoT_in_Healthcare

RFC 7252. (2017). Constrained Application Protocol. Retrieved May 15, 2017, from http://coap.technology

Rinaldi, J. (2016). *OPC UA - Unified Architecture: The Everyman's Guide to the Most Important Information Technology in Industrial Automation*. CreateSpace Independent Publishing Platform.

Rosenblatt, F. (1958). The Perceptron: A Theory of Statistical Separability in Cognitive Systems (Project Para). Buffalo, NY: Cornell Aeronautical Laboratory.

RPMA. (2017). *An Educational Guide How RPMA Works*. A White Paper By Ingenu, 1-4.

Saahithyan, R., Samir, K. M., & Debabrata, D. (2016). Efficient Algorithm for Less Power Consumption in Extended-Coverage-GSM for Low Data-Rate IoT Devices. IEEE.

Sáchez-Arias, G., González García, C., & Pelayo, B. C. (2017). Midgar: Study of Communications Security among Smart Objects Using A Platform Of Heterogeneous Devices For the Internet of Things. *Future Generation Computer Systems*, *74*, 444–466. doi:10.1016/j.future.2017.01.033

Saint-Andre, P. (2011). *Extensible messaging and presence protocol (XMPP): Core*. IETF RFC 6120, 2011. Retrieved from https://tools.ietf.org/html/rfc6120

Samsung. (2017, March). *Gear VR*. Retrieved from http://www.samsung.com/global/galaxy/gear-vr/

Sánchez Cuadrado, J., Cánovas, J., & García Molina, J. (2014). Applying model driven engineering in small software enterprises. *Science of Computer Programming*, *89*, 176–198. doi:10.1016/j.scico.2013.04.007

Sánchez-Arias, G., & González García, C. (2017). Midgar: Study of communications security among Smart Objects using a platform of heterogeneous devices for the Internet of Things. Future Generation Computer Systems, 74, 444–466.

Sánchez-Arias, G., González García, C., & Pelayo G-Bustelo, B. C. (2017). B.C. Pelayo G-Bustelo, Midgar: Study of communications security among Smart Objects using a platform of heterogeneous devices for the Internet of Things. *Future Generation Computer Systems*, *74*, 444–466. doi:10.1016/j.future.2017.01.033

Schulte, S., Hoenisch, P., Hochreiner, C., Dustdar, S., Klusch, M., & Schuller, D. (2014). Towards Process Support for Cloud Manufacturing. *Proceedings IEEE 18th international Enterprise Distributed object computing conference*, 142–149.

Sean, B., David, I., & Prashant, S. (2016). Pervasive Energy Monitoring and Control through Low-Bandwidth Power Line Communication. *IEEE Internet of Things Journal*, 1-10.

Sensor, Types of Sensor. (2017). Retrieved from https://www.electrical4u.com/sensor-types-of-sensor/

Sensors: Different Types of Sensors. (2017). Retrieved from http://www.engineersgarage.com/articles/sensors

Shah, T., & Bhatt, C. M. (2014, April). The Internet of things: Technologies, Communications and Computing. *CSI Communications*, *38*(1), 7.

Shawish, A., & Salama, M. (2014). Cloud Computing: Paradigms and Technologies. *Inter-Cooperative Collective Intelligence: Techniques and Applications*, 39–67.

Shelby, Z., & Bormann, C. (2010). *6LoWPAN: The Wireless Embedded Internet*. Wiley.

Shelby, Z., Hartke, K., & Bormann, C. (2014). *The constrained application protocol (CoAP)*. Tech. Rep. *IETF RFC*, *7252*, 2014.

Sheng, Z., Yang, S., Yu, Y., Vasilakos, A., Mccann, J., & Leung, K. (2013). A survey on the IETF protocol suite for the internet of things: Standards, challenges, and opportunities. *IEEE Wireless Communications*, *20*(6), 91–98. doi:10.1109/MWC.2013.6704479

Shubair & Kiourti. (2017). *In-Body Devices for Wireless Biotelemetry: Implants and ingestibles*. Special Session organized at the 2017 IEEE AP-S Symposium on Antennas and Propagation and USNC-URSI Radio Science Meeting (AP-S/URSI 2017), San Diego, CA.

Sidwar, K. (2017). *Keep an Eye on Your Fridge with a Photon, Photocell, TMP36 and Buzzer*. Retrieved August 18, 2017, from https://www.losant.com/blog/keep-an-eye-on-your-fridge-with-a-photon-photocell-tmp36-and-buzzer

Siemens. (2017a, March). *Siemens Comos-Walkinside*. Retrieved from http://www.siemens.com/comos

Siemens. (2017b, March). *Simatic PCS7*. Retrieved from http://w3.siemens.com/mcms/process-control-systems/en/distributed-control-system-simatic-pcs-7/Pages/distributed-control-system-simatic-pcs-7.aspx

Sigfox. (2017). *Sigfox Technology Overview*. Retrieved July 21, 2017, from https://www.sigfox.com/en/sigfox-iot-technology-overview

Silva, M., & Freitas, D. (2014). Glassist: Using Augmented Reality on Google Glass as an Aid to Classroom Management. *XVI Symposium on Virtual and Augmented Reality (SVR)*, 37 – 44. doi:10.1109/SVR.2014.41

Singh, M., Rajan, M., Shivraj, V., & Balamuralidhar, P. (2015). *Secure MQTT for internet of things (IoT).* Paper presented at the Communication Systems and Network Technologies (CSNT), 2015 Fifth International Conference on.

Stankovic, J. (2014). Research Directions for the Internet of Things. *IEEE Internet of Things Journal, 1*(1), 3–9.

Steinberg, D., Budinsky, F., Paternostro, M., & Merks, E. (2009). *EMF: Eclipse Modeling Framework* (2nd ed.). Addison-Wesley.

Steinmetz, R., Schuller, D., Schulte, S., & Abels, S. (2012). Plug and play virtual factories. *IEEE Internet Computing, 16*(5), 78–82. doi:10.1109/MIC.2012.114

Stirbu, V. (2008). Towards a RESTful Plug and Play Experience in the Web of Things. *2008 IEEE International Conference on Semantic Computing*, 512-517. doi:10.1109/ICSC.2008.51

Storti, D., & Yurtoglu, M. (2015). *CUDA for Engineers: An Introduction to High-Performance Parallel Computing*. Addison-Wesley Professional.

Szabó, R., & Gontean, A. (2016). *Industrial Robotic Automation with Raspberry PI Using Image Processing*. University of West Bohemia. doi:10.1109/AE.2016.7577287

Tan, L. (2010). Future Internet: The Internet of Things. In *2010 3rd Int. Conf. Adv. Comput. Theory Eng*. IEEE. doi:10.1109/ICACTE.2010.5579543

Tata, S., Jain, R., Ludwig, H., & Gopisetty, S. (2017). Living in the Cloud or on the Edge: Opportunities and Challenges of IoT Application Architecture. *IEEE 14th International Conference on Services Computing*, 221-225.

Tech America Foundation. (2012). *Demystifying Big Data: TechAmerica Foundation paper.* Retrieved from http://www1.unece.org/stat/platform/pages/viewpage.action?pageId=80053387

Technica, P. (2005). *Easy X10 Projects for Creating a Smart Home.* Indy-Tech Publishing.

Teixeira, J. M., & Ferreira, R. (2014). Teleoperation Using Google Glass and AR, Drone for Structural Inspection. *XVI Symposium on Virtual and Augmented Reality (SVR)*, 28 – 36. doi:10.1109/SVR.2014.42

Thompson, C., Schmidt, D., Turner, H., & White, J. (2014). *Analyzing Mobile Application Software Power Consumption via Model-Driven Engineering. In Advances and Applications in Model-Driven Engineering* (pp. 342–366). Hershey, PA: IGI GLOBAL.

Thread, G. (2015). *Thread Stack Fundamentals*. Thread Group.

Thubert. (2011). *Compression Format for IPv6 Datagramsover IEEE 802.15.4-Based Networks.* Internet Engineering Task Force, RFC 6282.

Tonella, P., & Potrich, A. (2005). *Reverse engineering of Object-Oriented Code. Monographs in Computer Science.* Springer-Verlag.

Townsend, Cufi, Akiba, & Davidson. (2014). *Getting Started with Bluetooth Low Energy*. O'Reilly.

Truijens, J., Oosterhaven, A., Maes, R., Jägers, H., & van Iersel, F. (1990). *Informatie-Infrastructuur: een Instrument voor het Management*. Kluwer Bedrijfswetenschappen. (in Dutch)

Turner, V. (2016). *Reducing The Time To Value For Internet Of Things Deployments*. Retrieved May 15, 2017, from https://blogs.oracle.com/iot/reducing-the-time-to-value-for-internet-of-things-deployments-idc

Umamaheswari, S. (2017). Internet of Things and RPL Routing Protocol: A Study And Evaluation. *IEEE International Conference on Computer Communication and Informatics (ICCCI -2017)*.

Umamaheswari, S., & Vanitha, K. (2016). *Interaction Model of Service Discovery Using Visa Processing Algorithm and Constrained Application Protocol (CoAP)*. Springer.

Vanderfeesten, I., & Grefen, P. (2015). *Business Process Management Technology for Discrete Manufacturing* (Beta Working Papers No. 486). Eindhoven University of Technology.

Venkatesh. (n.d.). *Ultra Low Power 802.11n Wi-Fi – Wireless Connectivity for The Internet of Things*. Academic Press.

Vuzix. (2017, March). *Smart Glasses*. Retrieved from https://www.vuzix.com/Products/Series-3000-Smart-Glasses

Wang, L., Xu, D. L., Bi, Z., & Xu, Y. (2014). Data Cleaning for RFID and WSN Integration. *IEEE Transactions on Industrial Informatics*, *10*(1), 408–418. doi:10.1109/TII.2013.2250510

Want, R. (2011, July). Near Field Communication Smartphones. *Pervasive Computing*, 1-4.

Web of Things (WoT) Scripting API. (2017). W3C Editor's Draft 16 May 2017. Retrieved from https://w3c.github.io/wot-scripting-api

Web of Things (WoT). (2017). *Use Cases and Requirements for the Web of Things*. W3C Editor's Draft May 2017. Retrieved from https://w3c.github.io/wot/wot-ucr.html

Webrtc. (2017). *Web browsers with Real-Time Communications*. Retrieved May 15, 2017, from https://webrtc.org/faq/#what-is-webrtc

Webster, P. C. (2012, April 3). Health in Colombia: The chronic disease burden. *Canadian Medical Association Journal*, *184*(6), E293–E294. doi:10.1503/cmaj.109-4126 PMID:22392946

Winter & Thubert. (2011). *RPL, Internet-Draft, RPL: IPv6 Routing Protocol for Low power and Lossy Networks*. draft-ietf-roll-rpl-19.

Winter. (2012). *IPv6 routing protocol for low power and lossy networks*. Internet Engineering Task Force, RFC 6550.

Wu, Wu, Redoute, & Yuce. (2017). An Autonomous Wireless Body Area Network Implementation towards IoT Connected Healthcare Applications. *IEEE Access*. DOI: 10.1109/ACCESS.2017.2716344

XMI. (2015). *XML Metadata Interchange (XMI) Specification*. OMG Document Number: formal/2015-06-07. Retrieved April 25, 2017 from http://www.omg.org/spec/XMI/2.5.1

Yaler, G. H. (2017). *Access devices from the Web*. Retrieved July 25, 2017, from https://yaler.net/

Yamanoue, T., Oda, K., & Shimozono, K. (2012). A M2M system using Arduino, Android, and Wiki Software. *IEEE International Conference on Advanced Applied Informatics*, 123-128. doi:10.1109/IIAI-AAI.2012.33

Yang, S., Njoku, M., & Mackenzie, C. F. (2014). 'Big data' approaches to trauma outcome prediction and autonomous resuscitation. *British Journal of Hospital Medicine*, *75*(11), 637–641. doi:10.12968/hmed.2014.75.11.637 PMID:25383434

Yan, Y. L., Xiaoqiang, L. Z., & Wu, H. (2017). Research on Water Meter Reading System Based on LoRa Communication. *IEEE International Conference on Smart Grid and Smart Cities*, 248-251.

Yeh. (2016). A Secure IoT-Based Healthcare System with Body Sensor Networks. *IEEE Access*. DOI: 10.1109/ACCESS.2016.2638038

Younghwan, C., Yunchul, C., Dongmyoung, K., & Jungsoo, P. (2017). Scheme to Guarantee IP Continuity for NFC-based IoT Networking. *ICACT2017*, 695-698.

Yu, B. (2009). *Wireless Body Area Networks for Healthcare: A Feasibility Study*. Available from: https://www.ieee.org/documents/Yu_Final_Published_Paper_March2009.pdf

Zahid, F., Rosdiadee, N., & Mahamod, I. (2013). Recent advances in wireless indoor localization techniques and system. *J. Comput. Netw. Commun.*, *2013*. doi:10.1155/2013/185138

Zanella, A., Bui, N., Castellani, A., Vangelista, L., & Zorzi, M. (2014). Internet of things for smart cities. *IEEE Internet Things*, *1*(1), 22-32.

Zanella, A., Bui, N., Castellani, A., Vangelista, L., & Zorzi, M. (2014). Internet of Things for Smart Cities. *IEEE Internet of Things Journal*, *1*(1), 22–32. doi:10.1109/JIOT.2014.2306328

Zhao, K., Li, B., Andrew, D., & Chen, L. (2013). A Comparison of algorithms adopted in fingerprinting indoor positioning systems. *Proceedings of the International Global Navigation SatelliteSystems Society IGNSS Symposium.*

Zhong, N., Ma, J., Huang, R., Lui, J., Yao, Y., Zhang, Y., & Chen, J. (2016). *Research Challenges and Perspectives on Wisdom Web of Things (W2T). In Web Information Systems Engineering and Internet Technologies Book Series* (pp. 3–26). Springer.

Zhong, N., Yau, S. S., Ma, J., Shimojo, S., Just, M., Hu, B., & Anzai, Y. (2016). Brain Big Data in Wisdom Web of Things. In *Wisdom Web of Things* (pp. 339–349). Springer International Publishing. doi:10.1007/978-3-319-44198-6_15

Zigbee. (2004). *Zigbee Document*. Retrieved from http://www3.nd.edu/~mhaenggi/ee67011/zigbee.pdf

Zoran, B. B., Jelica, P., & Veljko, M. (2016). Web Performance Evaluation for Internet of Things Applications. *IEEE Translations and Content Mining*, *4*, 6974–6992.

Z-Wave. (2007). *Z-Wave Protocol Overview, v. 4*. Retrieved from https://wiki.ase.tut.fi/courseWiki/images/9/94/SDS10243_2_Z_Wave_Protocol_Overview.pdf

About the Contributors

Cristian González García is a Technical Engineer in Computer Systems, M.Sc. in Web Engineering, and a Ph.D. in Computers Science graduated from School of Computer Engineering of Oviedo in 2011, 2013, and 2017 (University of Oviedo, Spain). He has been a visiting Ph.D. candidate in the University of Manchester, United Kingdom. Besides, he has been working in different national and regional projects, in projects with private companies, and in the University of Oviedo as a professor. His research interests are in the field of the Internet of Things, Web Engineering, Mobile Devices, and Modelling Software with DSL and MDE.

Vicente García-Díaz is an associate professor in the Computer Science Department of the University of Oviedo. He has a PhD from the University of Oviedo in computer engineering. His research interests include model-driven engineering, domain specific languages, technology for learning and entertainment, project risk management, software development processes and practices. He has graduated in Prevention of Occupational Risks and is a Certified Associate in Project Management through the Project Management Institute.

Begoña Cristina Pelayo García-Bustelo is a lecturer in the Computer Science Department of the University of Oviedo. She has a PhD from the University of Oviedo in computer engineering. Her research interests include object-oriented technology, Web engineering, eGovernment, modeling software with BPM, DSL and MDA.

Juan Manuel Cueva Lovelle became a mining engineer from Oviedo Mining Engineers Technical School in 1983 (Oviedo University, Spain). He has a PhD from Madrid Polytechnic University, Spain (1990). From 1985 he has been a professor at the languages and computers systems area in Oviedo University (Spain), and is an ACM and IEEE voting member. His research interests include object-oriented technology, language processors, human-computer interface, Web engineering, modeling software with BPM, DSL and MDA.

* * *

Rakhi Dattatraya Akhare holds the degree of Master of Engineering in computer Engineering. She started her carrier from industry as a software developer and then joined as a Professor from 2010,she presented number of papers in national and international conferences. She guided UG level student projects. She is the Member of Professional body.

Irene Alonso holds an MSc in Computer Engineering from the Engineering Polytechnic School of the Oviedo University (Spain). She has been working abroad for nine years and a half. The first year was employed in France in the Institute of Research INRIA (Nancy) She was employed for five years at CERN participating in different projects about research, services, and innovation, being the manager of one of them and the main responsible in other two. Many of the projects were very important due to the relation with the cryogenics of that allows the superconductivity in the accelerator of particles. Also, she worked for the Swiss Government being part of the finance and taxes team. When she returned to Spain (Madrid), she was working in a French company being the manager for the social French safety team, later she was Woking for the German Deutsche Bank being the Business Analyst lead Currently, she is working in CTIC being Business Analyst Lead at IoT Team @ CTIC Web of Things team and the main responsible for the transfer of technologies.

Smita Sanjay Ambarkar currently Pursuing PhD in computer science from Mumbai University. She holds the degree of Master of Technology in computer science.She started her carrier as a Processor from 2003,she presented papers in national and international conferences also guided number of UG level student projects .She received the “Minor Research Grant’ from University of Mumbai for her project in 2013.

Chintan Bhatt (Ph.D.) is currently working as an Assistant Professor in Computer Engineering department, Chandubhai S. Patel Institute of Technology, CHARUSAT. He is a member of IEEE, EAI, ACM, CSI, AIRCC and IAENG (International Association of Engineers). His areas of interest include Internet of Things, Data Mining, Web Mining, Networking, Security Mobile Computing, Big Data and Software Engineering. He has more than 5 years of teaching experience and research experience, having good teaching and research interests. He has chaired a track in CSNT 2015 and ICTCS 2014. He has been working as Reviewer in Wireless Communications, IEEE (Impact Factor-6.524) and Internet of Things Journal, IEEE, Knowledge-Based Systems, Elsevier (Impact Factor-2.9) Applied Computing and Informatics, Elsevier and Mobile Networks and Applications, Springer. He has delivered an expert talk on Internet of Things at Broadcast Engineering Society Doordarshan, Ahmedabad on 30/09/2015. He has been awarded Faculty with Maximum Publication in CSIC Award and Paper Presenter Award at International Conference in CSI-2015, held at New Delhi.

Maria Claudia Bonfante has a Ph.D. from the University Pontificia of Salamanca in software engineering. Specialist in Information systems audit, and Systems Engineer from Politécnico Gran Colombiano. Colombian researcher recognized by Colciencias as part of the Neuro-diffuses research group. Participated in different research projects with the Colombian department of education and the Colombian administration of information technology. Director of the program in computer science University Rafael Núñez in Cartagena, Colombia and a lot of experience in designing and implementing IT strategic plans for digital academic projects and platforms.

Georgios Boultadakis holds a PhD in Radar Imaging and Signal Processing from the National Technical University of Athens (NTUA), and a Dipl-Ing degree from the Hellenic Air Force Academy - Engineering Department. He conducted his doctoral research in the Division of Information Transmission Systems and Material Technology of NTUA. His research concentrated on transmission technologies across the frequency spectrum including radio and microwave technologies and their applications, including theoretical and modeling work on applied electromagnetics, and was implemented within the NATO Research and Technology Organization/ Sensors and Electronics Technology panel works. Since 2001, he has acted as Research Associate of "Radar Systems & Remote Sensing Laboratory", focusing on valuable research in the areas of radar systems, remote sensing and generally in the area of radio and satellite communications, in the fields of ISAR/InSAR studies, 2D and 3D radio-coverage modeling in cellular wireless systems studies, high-frequency electromagnetic techniques studies, etc. For 15 years he worked as engineering manager for the Hellenic Air Force, in areas of ordinary/intermediate/depot level maintenance of avionics systems, as well as quality control/assurance engineer. He joined European Dynamics in 2014 as a Senior R&D consultant, where he has participated in/ coordinated proposals for European Commission HORIZON 2020 funded Research programme. His research interests include novel/ future ICT technologies, signal processing and pattern recognition techniques and electromagnetism, has published a number of scientific papers/book chapters and has presented work in international scientific conferences and workshops. He is Member of Institution of Engineering and Technology as well as reviewer for various scientific journals.

Manoj Devare received BSc & MSc degree from North Maharashtra University and PhD in Computer Science from Bharati Vidyapeeth University, India. He is currently holding position of Associate Professor at Amity Institute of Information Technology, Amity University Mumbai. He has 14 years of teaching and research experience with Post Graduate Courses in Computer Science. He worked as head of the department with Institutes affiliated to Pune University, India. His PhD thesis was based on the Congestion Controlling in Homogeneous and Heterogeneous Computer Networks. Dr. Manoj obtained the "Best Paper Award", in international conference ICSCI 2008, Hyderabad, India. Dr. Manoj has served as Post Doctorate Fellow at Centre of Excellence on HPC, University of Calabria, Italy under young researcher scheme. He has been developed Desktop Cloud system using full virtualization approach. His research deals with Internet of Things, Virtualization, Clouds, Machine Learning and innovative applications of those technologies to scientific problems. He has 02 Patents pending; he edited 02 book chapters in international books, 09 papers published in international journals. He published the 15 International and national conference Papers. He has delivered 08 national and international keynote speeches. He is continuously involved in the review process of the international journal papers, edited chapters from the reputed journals like Elsevier's Future Generation Computer Systems (FGCS), Springer's review system, Symbiosis International Journal. He is also worked in different roles as session chair, organizing committee member, Chairman of Board of Studies, Student Research Committee, University Research Committee of Amity University Mumbai. He is also engaged in the organizing national conferences in India to encourage research skills in post graduate students. He is also engaged with guiding to PhD candidates and evaluating the PhD thesis from various national and international universities.

María Díaz Rodríguez graduated as Computer Science Engineer (Universidade de Vigo). She is working in her PhD in Computer Science, Universidade de Vigo (Spain). She is working in an IT company. She is the member of the international research group SI1-GEAC (http://si1-geac.webs.uvigo.es/).

Liliana Favre is a full professor of Computer Science at Universidad Nacional del Centro de la Provincia de Buenos Aires in Argentina. She is also a researcher of CIC (Comisión de Investigaciones Científicas de la Provincia de Buenos Aires). Her current research interests are focused on model driven development, model driven architecture and formal approaches, mainly on the integration of algebraic techniques with MDA-based processes. She has been involved in several national research projects about formal methods and software engineering methodologies. Currently she is research leader of the Software Technology Group at Universidad Nacional del Centro de la Provincia de Buenos Aires. She has published several book chapters, journal articles and conference papers. She has acted as editor of the book UML and the Unified Process. She is the author of the book Model Driven Architecture for Reverse Engineering Technologies: Strategic Directions and System Evolution.

Ivan Gallego has a Bachelor's degree in Computer Science in Universidad de Oviedo (2009-2013). His main competencies include Big Data technologies, Internet of Things and W3C standardization. Professional career focused on the adaptation of new digital technologies to industrial environments. Experience as an R&D engineer in ArcelorMittal Global R&D Asturias in the development and research of Big Data technologies. Since 2016, member of a research line in CTIC Technology Centre focused in the development of Web of Things standards for the management of IoT devices. Additionally, he has academic experience in the field of logistics optimization.

Ingrid Gonzalez Arteta is a professional odontologist with a specialization in business management and healthcare services audit. Epidemiologist and student of a master in public health. A lot of experience in designing and developing healthcare businesses. Eighteen years of experience as a university professor in the areas of oral health, public health and social security with ten research publications in these areas.

Miguel Ramón González Castro graduated as Computer Science Engineer (UNED) and also as Telecommunications Engineer (Universidade de Vigo), a PhD with Cum Laude in Computer Science, Universidade de Vigo (Spain). He is the IT Industrial Manager at ENCE (Spain). He is the member of the international research group SI1-GEAC (http://si1-geac.webs.uvigo.es/). He has published quite extensively and has many publications (including books, book chapters, Scientific Citation Index journal articles, and international journal articles, as well as publications in refereed conference proceedings).

Paul Grefen is a full professor in the School of Industrial Engineering at Eindhoven University of Technology since 2003. He chaired the Information Systems subdepartment from 2006 to 2014. Currently, he is the Research Director of the School. He received his Ph.D. in 1992 from the University of Twente and held assistant and associate professor positions in the Computer Science Department. He was a visiting researcher at Stanford University in 1994. As a researcher and a manager, he has been involved in various European research projects as well as various projects within the Netherlands. He is an associate editor of the International Journal of Cooperative Information Systems and a member of the editorial board of the International Journal of Production Management and Engineering. He is an editor and author of the books on the WIDE and CrossWork projects, and has authored books on workflow management, electronic business and service-dominant business engineering. He is a member of the Executive Board of the European Supply Chain Forum. His current research covers architectural design of business information systems, inter-organizational business process management, and service-oriented business design and support. He teaches at the BSc, MSc, PDEng and PhD levels at TU/e and at the executive level for TIAS business school.

Fernando Lopez is currently a PhD student at University of Oviedo and CEO of SYSDEVELOPMENT LLC a Software development company in United States. Prior to this, he had worked in the Healthcare filed for more than 5 years doing research on Artificial Intelligence, Health Informatics and Data Mining. His Master of Computer Science from Technological of Monterrey University (Mexico) and University of Bucaramanga (Colombia), and his Bachelor of Engineering in Computer Science. He worked as a Faculty professor in Computer Science for 6 years teaching Programming Languages, Analysis and verification of algorithms and Data structure. He worked as a Senior Clinical Analyst at Englewood Hospital and Medical Center in New Jersey in the areas of Clinical Labs and Pathology for 4 years.

Andres G. Mangas is a Software Engineer with an interest in Big Data, WoT and full-stack Web development. He's currently working at Fundacion CTIC as the tech lead of the WoT team and is actively involved in pushing towards the adoption of W3C WoT standards in the industry landscape.

Edward Núñez-Valdéz has a Ph.D. from the University of Oviedo in Computer Engineering. Master in Software Engineering from the Pontifical University of Salamanca and B.S. in Computer Science from Autonomous University of Santo Domingo. He has participated in several research projects, He has taught computer science at various schools and universities and has worked in software development companies and IT Consulting for many years. He has published several articles in international journals and conferences. Currently working as Assistant Professor at the University of Oviedo in Spain. His research interests include Software Engineering, Object-Oriented technology, Web Engineering, Recommendation Systems, Modeling Software with DSL and MDA.

Hardik Patel has expertise in designing Embedded Electronics Systems as per customer specifications and guide team for achieving better quality, technically qualified product. He has done hands-on practice for various upcoming innovative tools and technology for product development. He is mentoring Entrepreneurship, Electronics Design & Development at engineering and polytechnical institutes to create awareness about electronics Innovation to emerging engineers and inspire them for innovations. He is advising new businesses on formation of corporations and business structures, drafting privacy policies and structuring commercial transactions.

Monika Patel completed her post graduation in computer engineering from Chandubhai S Patel Institute of Technology (CSPIT). She did her dissertation on Smart City based on MQTT using Wireless Sensors under the guidance of Asst. Prof. Chintan Bhatt and Mr. Hardik Patel. She has developed a data monitoring system for a particular location like home, cities, industries, hospitals, etc., where environmental information of various factors such as temperature, air pressure, humidity, and altitude need to be monitoring and get an update with a specific time interval. She also develops a mobile application for display environment data.

Manuel Pérez Cota is Professor and Researcher at the University of Vigo (UVIGO) in Vigo, Spain. He has a degree in Electrical Engineering (Universidad La Salle) and Electronics and Communications Engineering (Universidad Nacional Autónoma de México – UNAM, 1980), a PhD in Industrial Engineering (Universidad de Santiago de Compostela, 1990). He is the director of the international research group SI1-GEAC (http://si1-geac.webs.uvigo.es/). He was the first director and developer of the Computer Department (Computer Science School of the University of Vigo). He collaborates in different Master and PhD programs in Spain, Portugal, Germany, Argentina and Bolivia, and has been supervisor of several PhDs. He has been involved in different European and International projects. He has published quite extensively and has many publications (including books, book chapters, Scientific Citation Index journal articles, and international journal articles, as well as publications in refereed conference proceedings). He is a member of different international committees and associations (ACM, IEEE, AISTI, AIPO, ANALCT).

Ángel Retamar is Internet of Things Unit Manager at CTIC Technology Centre. He holds a BSc in Computer Science (2000) and an MSc in Computer Software Engineering (2003) by the University of Oviedo. He has a wide experience in systems architecture, interoperability, integration of heterogeneous systems and data analytics. From 2006 to 2009 he holds the position of CTO at Accenture Analytics R&D Centre. As a member of Web of Things Work Group at W3C Consortium where is collaborating in the definition of the new standard for Internet of Things. He joined CTIC in 2015.

S. Umamaheswari received her MCA degree from Bharathidasan University, Trichy, India, M.Phil degree and Ph.D. degree from Bharathiar University, Coimbatore, India. She had an experience as a Network Administrator. She is currently working as Associate Professor, Department of Computer Science, Dr. G. R. Damodaran

College of Science, Coimbatore, India. Her current research interests include web programming, cloud computing, mobile databases, Internet of Things, Data Analytics and mobile ad hoc networks. She has publications in peer reviewed journals and International Conferences. She is a Member of IEEE. She has served as Reviewer for scientific journals and a few International Conferences.

Hamed Vahdat-Nejad is currently an assistant professor at the computer engineering department of the University of Birjand. He was a visiting professor at the Daffodil International University in Dhaka in Summer of 2017. He received his PhD from computer engineering department of University of Isfahan in 2012, his master degree from Ferdowsi University of Mashhad in 2007, and his bachelor's degree from Sharif University of Technology in 2004. He was a research scholar at the Middleware laboratory of Sapienza University of Rome in 2011-2012 period. Currently, his research is focused on pervasive computing, cloud computing, and context-awareness. He has (co)published about 30 papers in conferences and journals, and leads the Pervasive & Cloud computing Lab at the University of Birjand. He has served as the chairman of the 1st & 2nd International Workshop on Context-aware Middleware for Ubiquitous Computing Environments, as well as the "3rd, 4th, and 5th International workshop on Pervasive and Context-aware middleware". He has served as TPC member for many conferences. Previously, he has served as associate and guest editor for Elsevier Computers and electrical engineering and Journal of Computing and Security, among others.

Irene Vanderfeesten is an assistant professor in Business Process Management and Information Systems at the School of Industrial Engineering at Eindhoven University of Technology (TU/e). She received her MSc degree in Computer Science (2004) and her PhD degree in Industrial Engineering (2009) from TU/e. Before joining the Information Systems group at TU/e in 2010 as an assistant professor, she worked as an IT consultant in the banking and insurance sector. She led the Business Process Management research cluster from 2012 to 2016 and was a visiting scholar at Penn State University, Smeal College of Business in 2016. She published scientific papers in various international journals (e.g. Information Systems, Business Information Systems Engineering, Decision Support Systems, and Computers in Industry) and conferences (e.g. BPM and CAiSE). She also served as PC member and reviewer for various scientific conferences and journals, and was involved in the organization of two scientific workshops in the field of business information systems engineering. Her current research interests include human aspects of business process management and information systems engineering; business modeling; business process redesign and improvement; and workflow management.

Index

R

S

T

U

V

W

X

Z

www.ingramcontent.com/pod-product-compliance
Lightning Source LLC
LaVergne TN
LVHW081348300926
849161LV00008B/2101
* 9 7 8 1 5 2 2 5 3 8 0 5 9 *